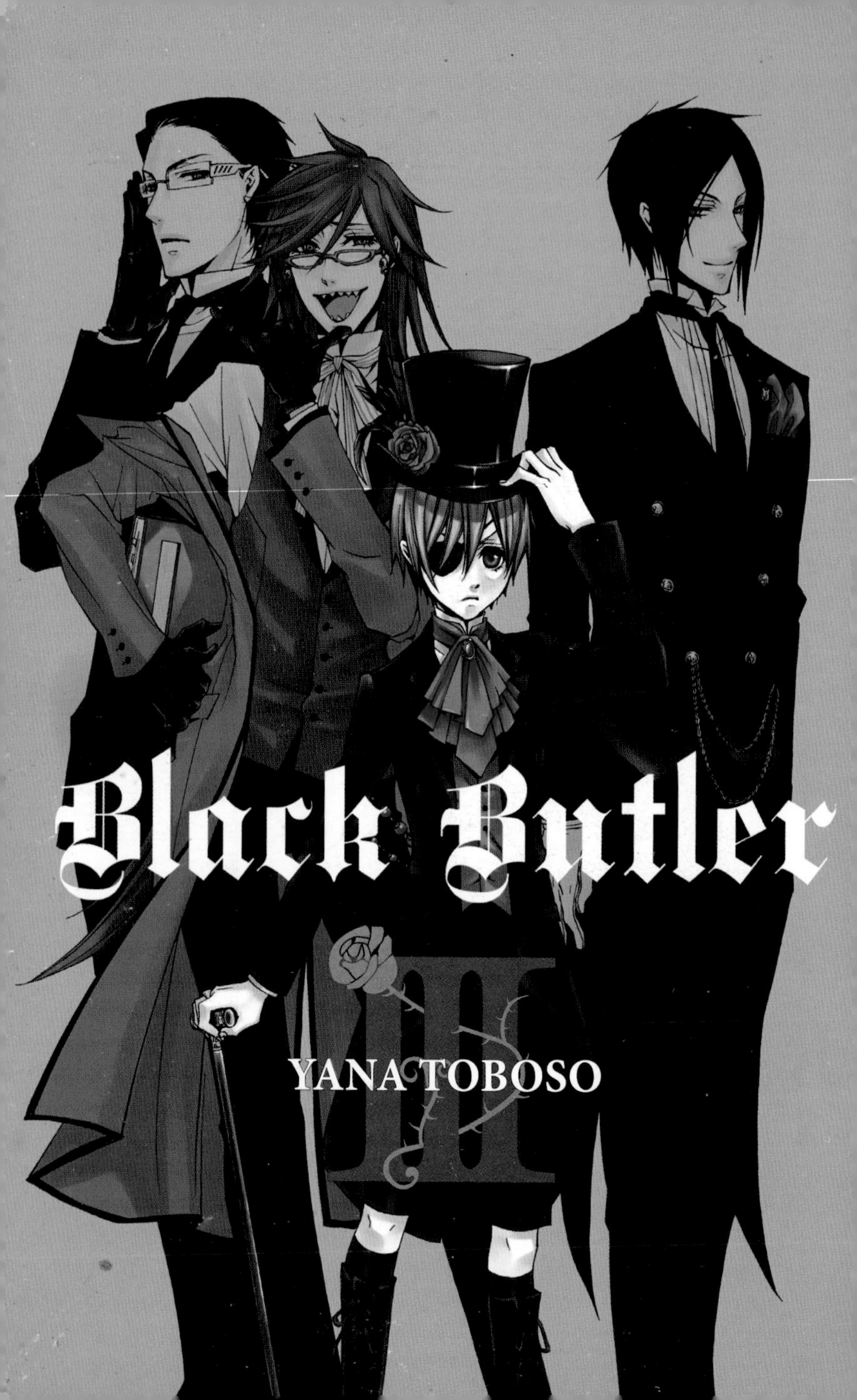
Black Butler
II
YANA TOBOSO

Contents

CHAPTER 10
In the morning ·····3
The Butler, Reflective

CHAPTER 11
At noon ············41
The Butler, Retrospective

CHAPTER 12
In the afternoon ····77
The Butler, Retaliatory

CHAPTER 13
At night ···········111
The Butler, Mourning

CHAPTER 14
At midnight ·······149
The Butler, On the Hunt

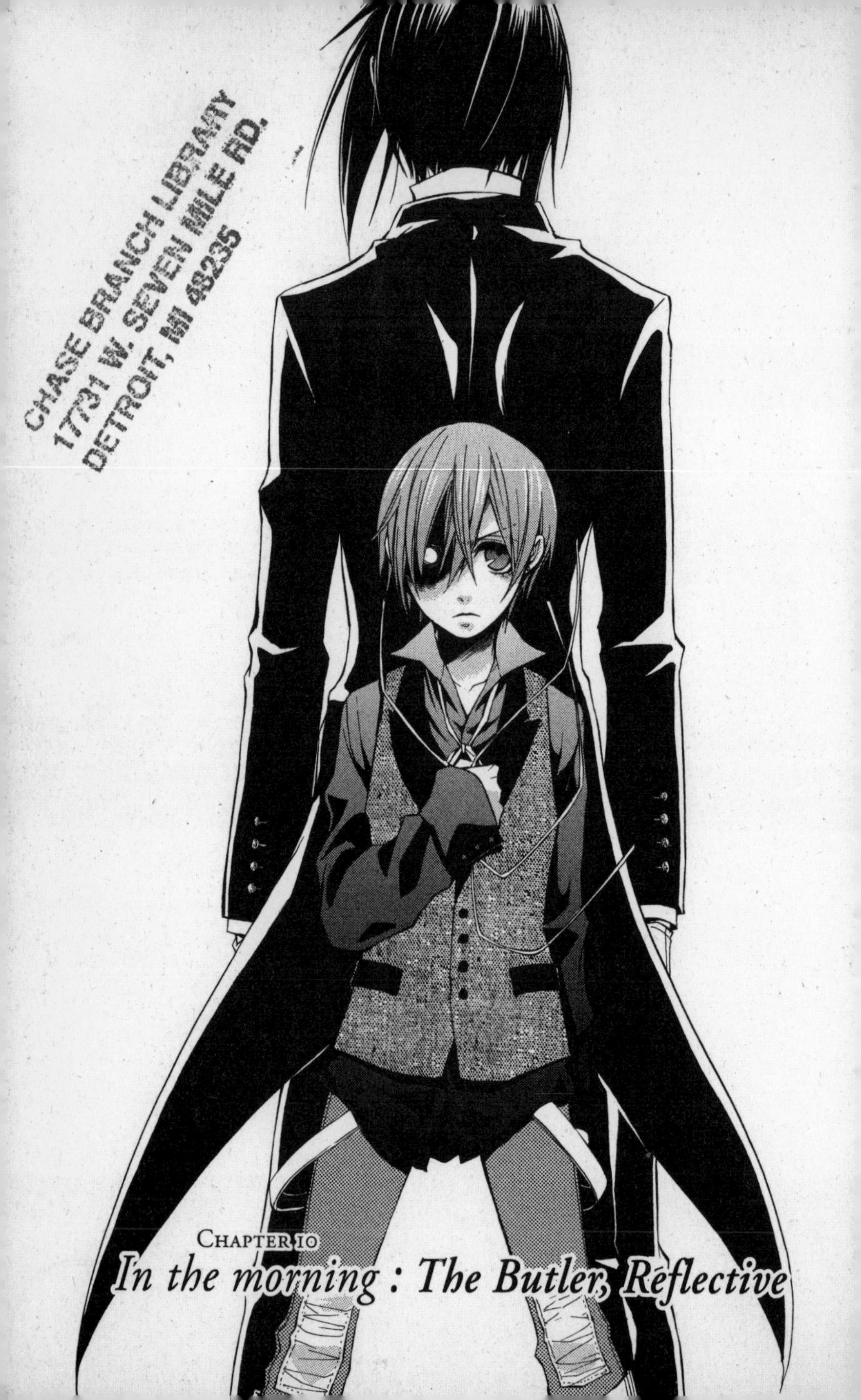

Chapter 10

In the morning : The Butler, Reflective

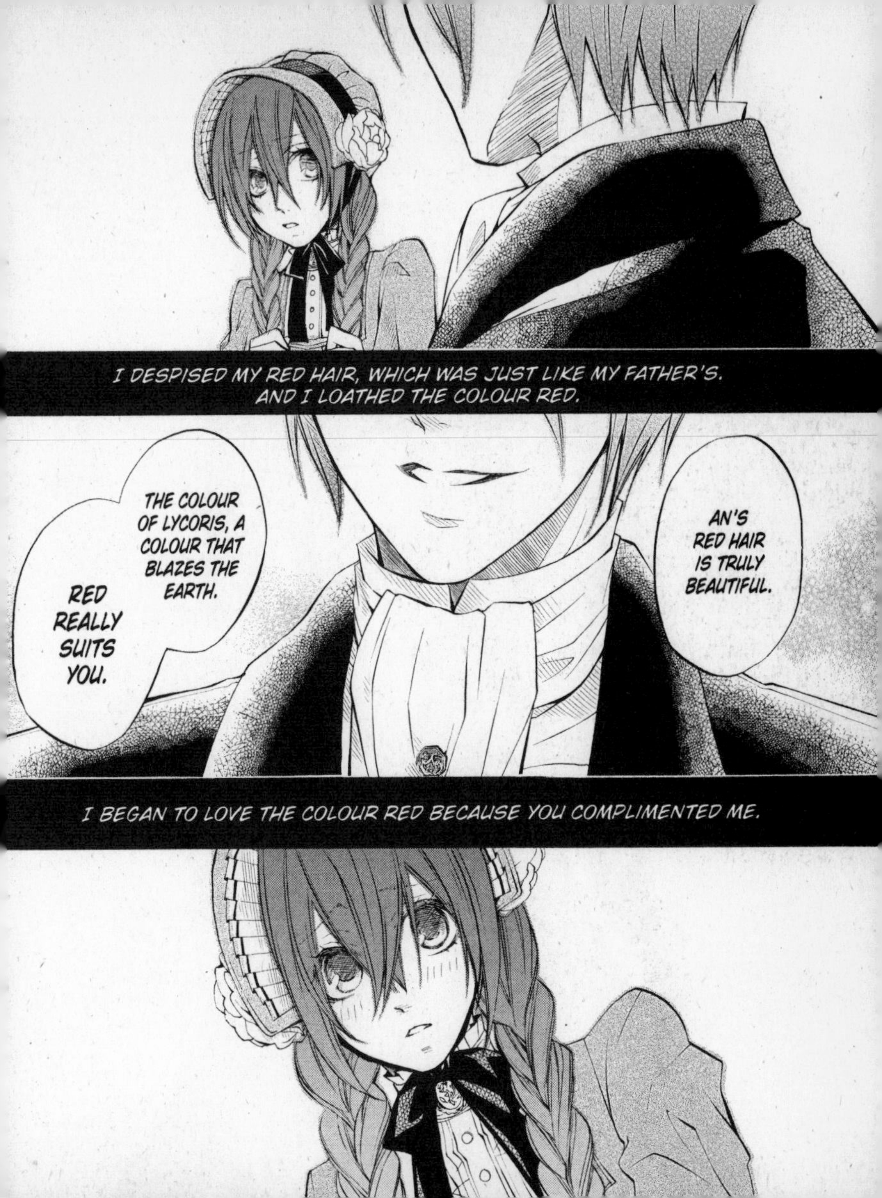
I DESPISED MY RED HAIR, WHICH WAS JUST LIKE MY FATHER'S.
AND I LOATHED THE COLOUR RED.
AN'S RED HAIR IS TRULY BEAUTIFUL.
THE COLOUR OF LYCORIS, A COLOUR THAT BLAZES THE EARTH.
RED REALLY SUITS YOU.
I BEGAN TO LOVE THE COLOUR RED BECAUSE YOU COMPLIMENTED ME.

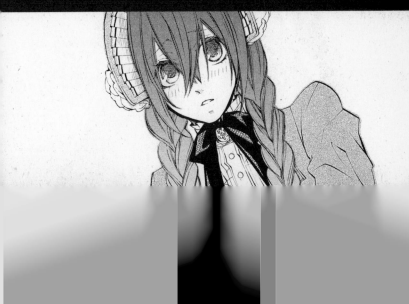

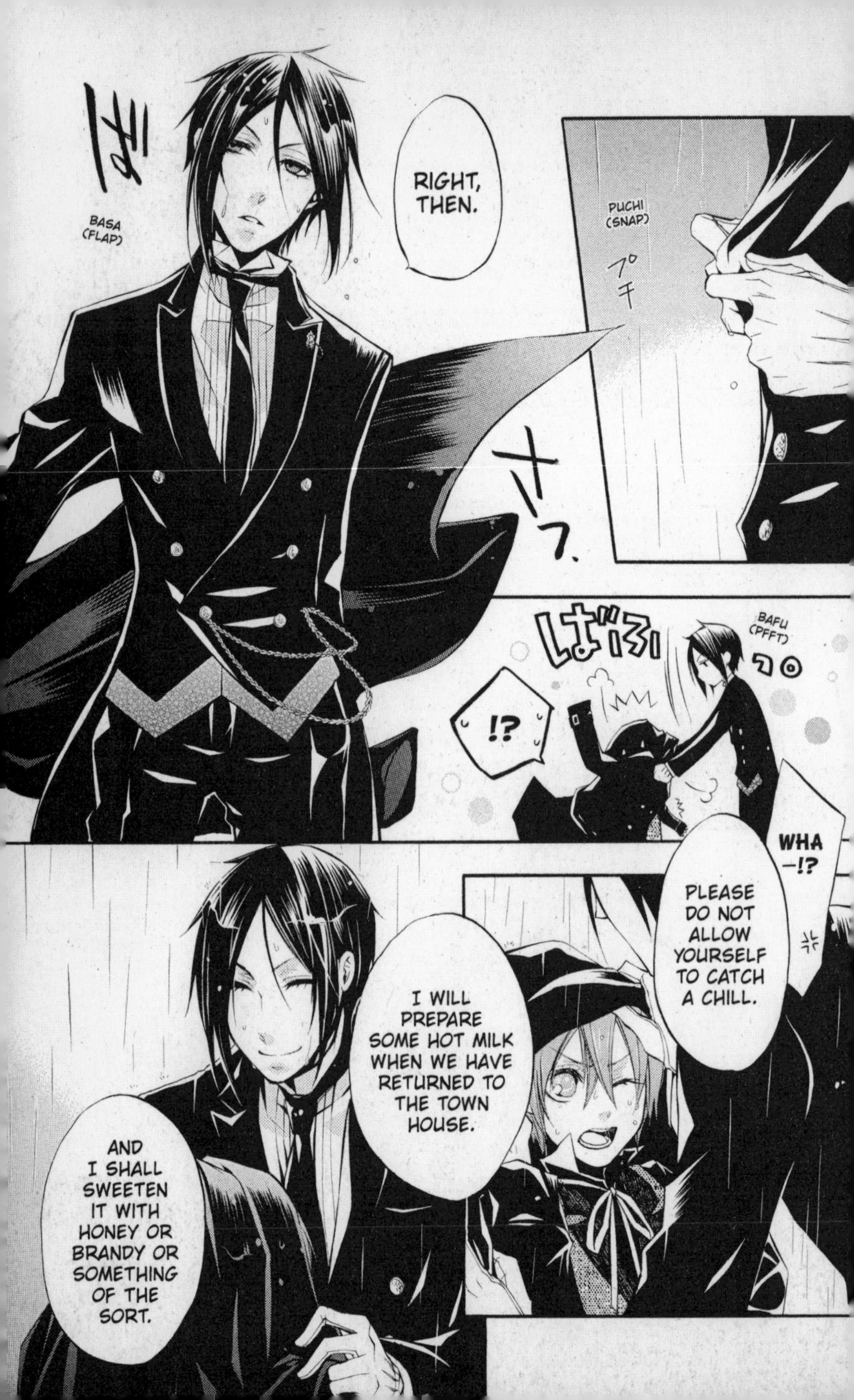
PUCHI (SNAP)
プチ
BAFU (PFFT)
!?
BASA (FLAP)
RIGHT, THEN.
WHA—!?
PLEASE DO NOT ALLOW YOURSELF TO CATCH A CHILL.
I WILL PREPARE SOME HOT MILK WHEN WE HAVE RETURNED TO THE TOWN HOUSE.
AND I SHALL SWEETEN IT WITH HONEY OR BRANDY OR SOMETHING OF THE SORT.

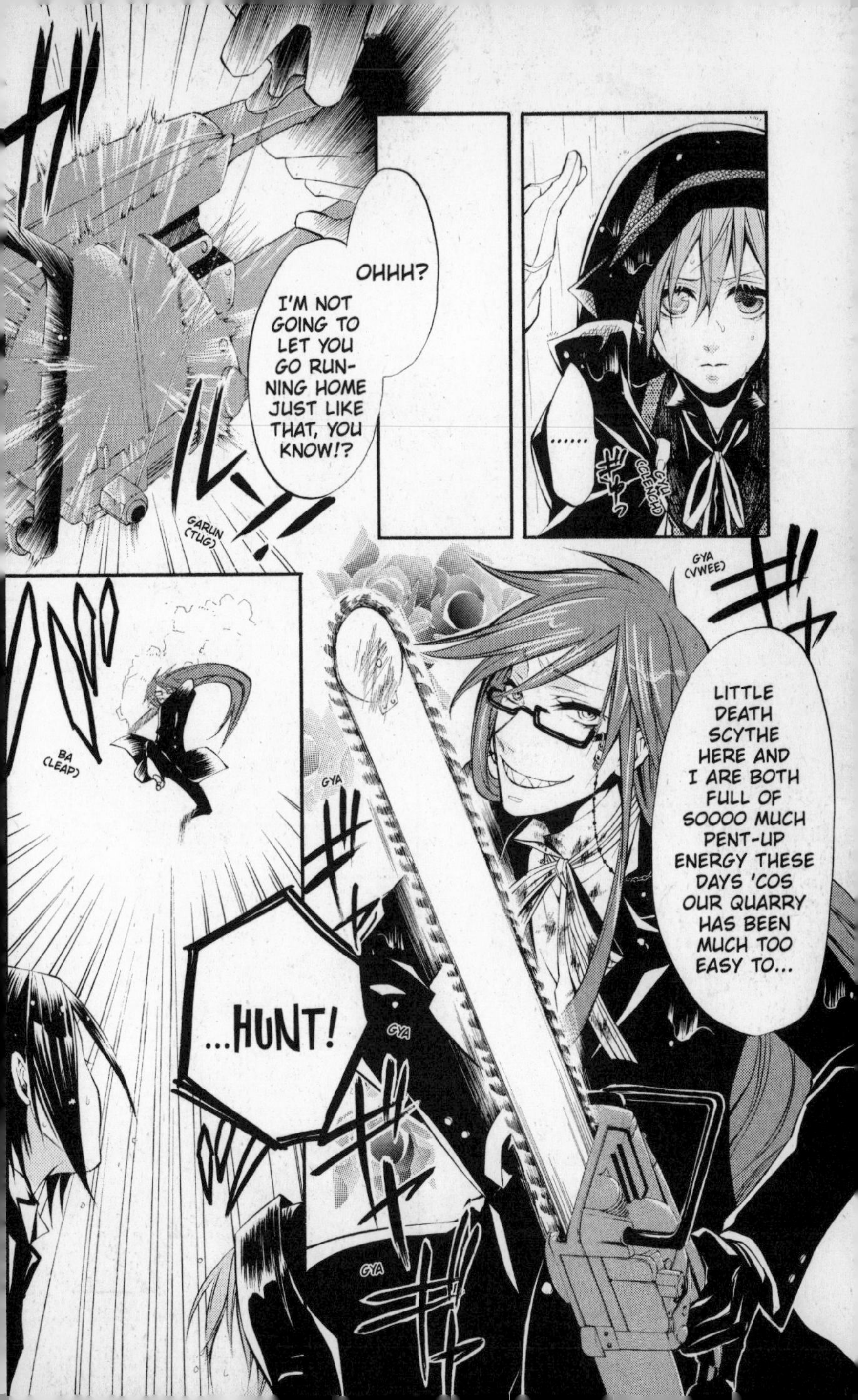
......
GYU (CLENCH)
OHHH?
I'M NOT GOING TO LET YOU GO RUN-NING HOME JUST LIKE THAT, YOU KNOW!?
GARUN (TUG)
GYA (VWEE)
LITTLE DEATH SCYTHE HERE AND I ARE BOTH FULL OF SOOOO MUCH PENT-UP ENERGY THESE DAYS 'COS OUR QUARRY HAS BEEN MUCH TOO EASY TO...
GYA
...HUNT!
GYA
GYA
BA (LEAP)

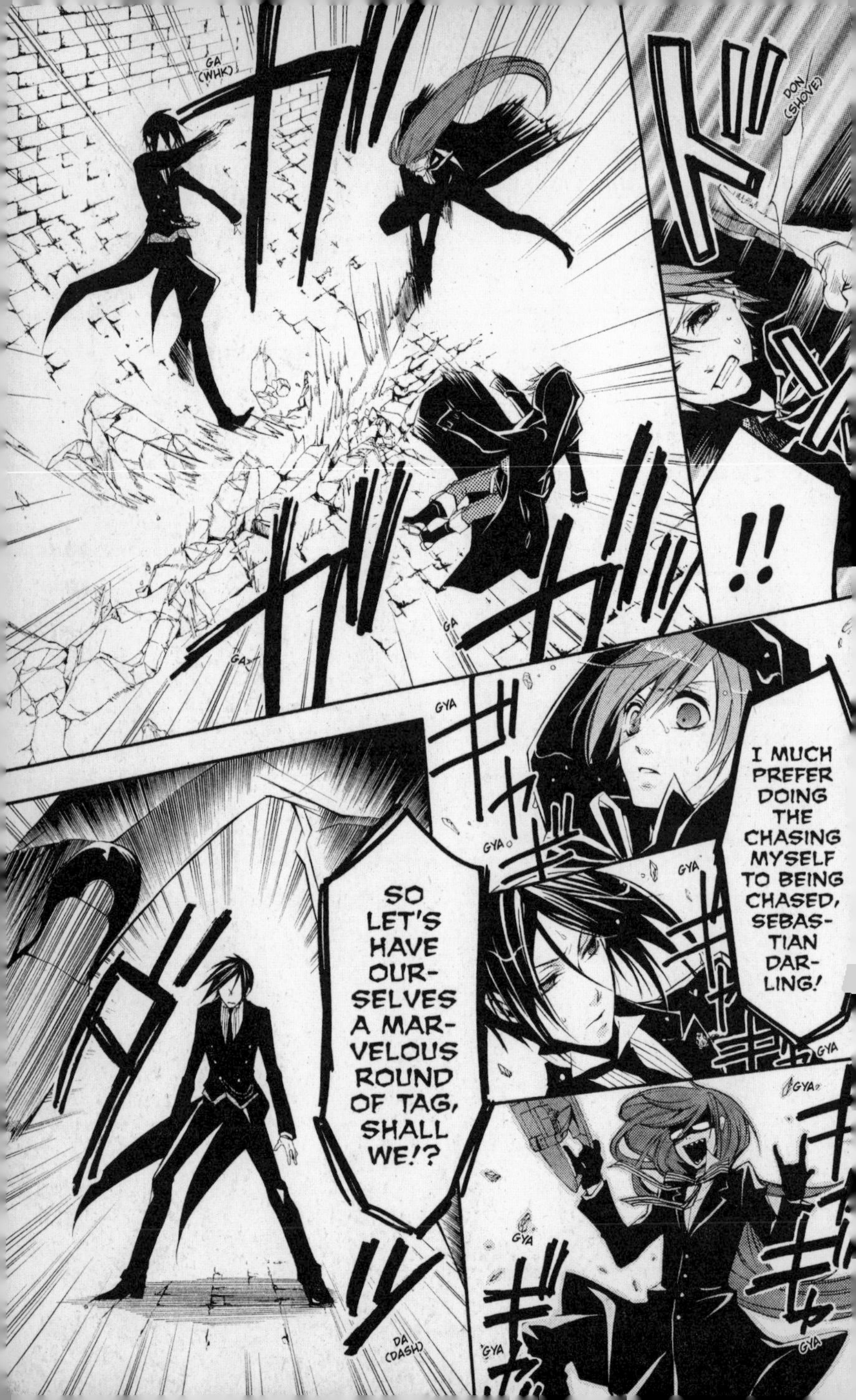
DON (SHOVE)
!!
GA (WHK)
GA
GA
GYA
GYA
I MUCH PREFER DOING THE CHASING MYSELF TO BEING CHASED, SEBASTIAN DARLING!
GYA
GYA
SO LET'S HAVE OURSELVES A MARVELOUS ROUND OF TAG, SHALL WE!?
GYA
GYA
GYA
GYA
DA (DASH)

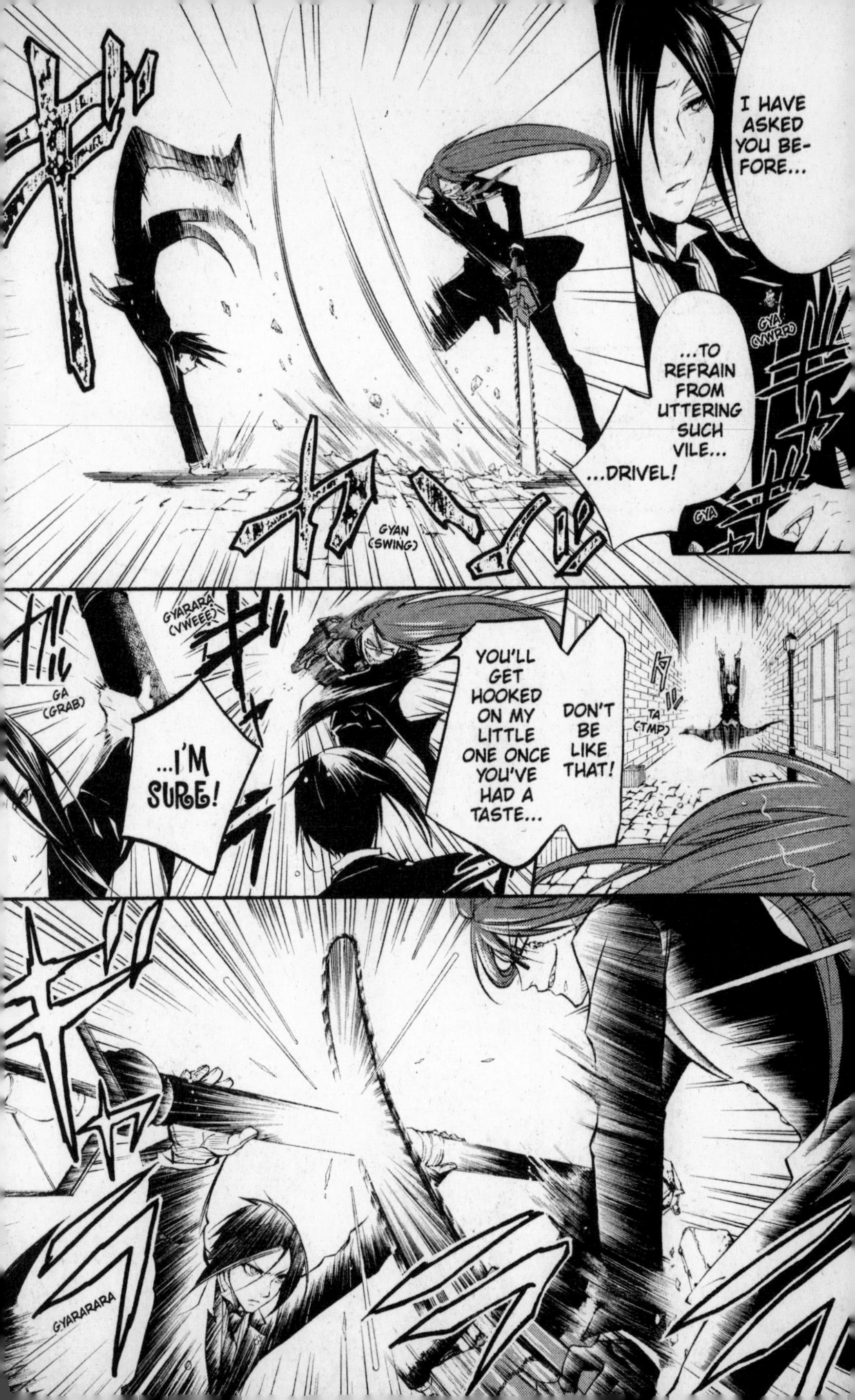
I HAVE ASKED YOU BEFORE...
GYA (VWRR)
GYA
...TO REFRAIN FROM UTTERING SUCH VILE...
...DRIVEL!
GYAN (SWING)
TA (TMP)
DON'T BE LIKE THAT!
YOU'LL GET HOOKED ON MY LITTLE ONE ONCE YOU'VE HAD A TASTE...
GYARARA (VWEEE)
GA (GRAB)
...I'M SURE!
GYARARARA

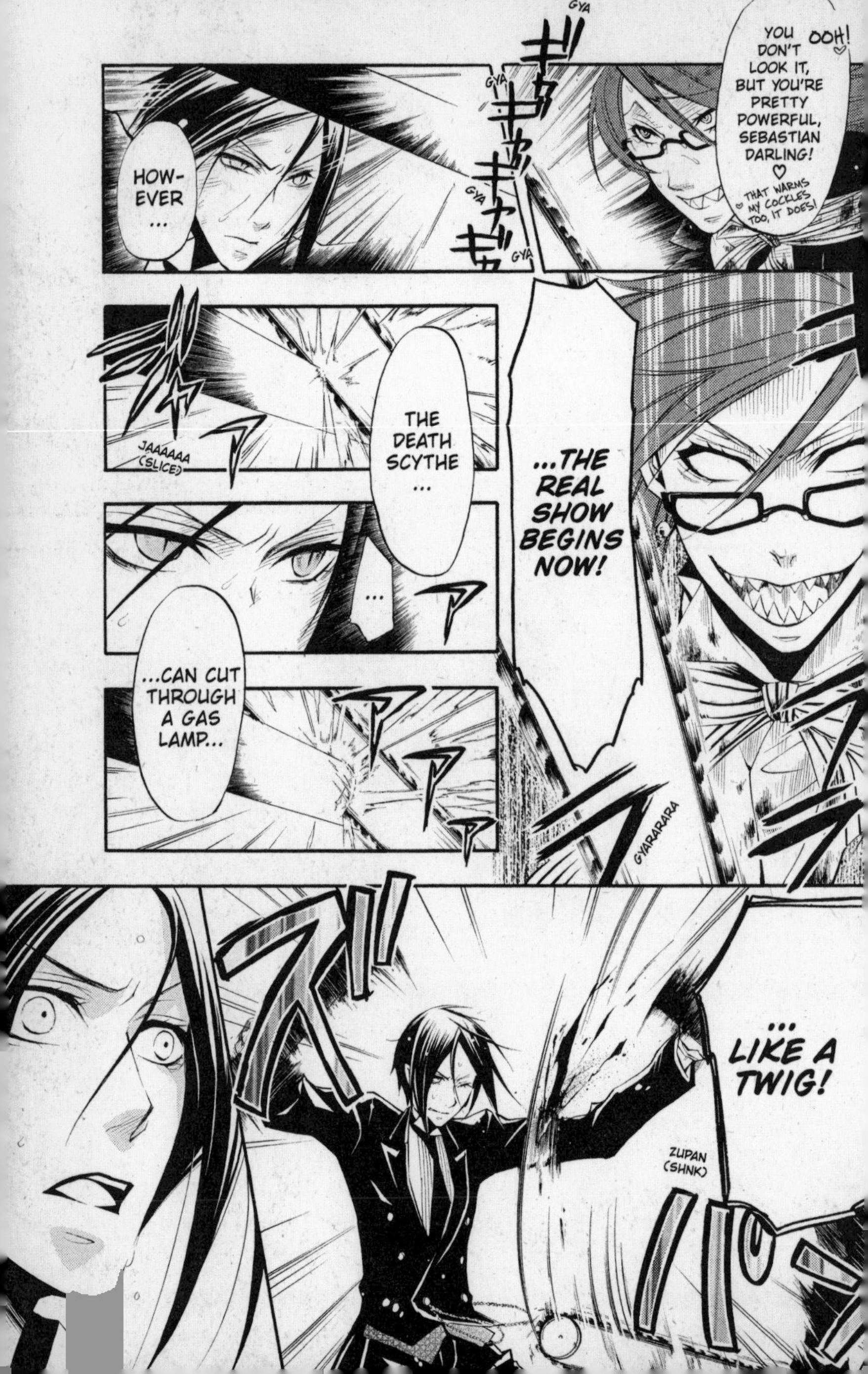
OOH! ♡
YOU DON'T LOOK IT, BUT YOU'RE PRETTY POWERFUL, SEBASTIAN DARLING! ♡
♡ THAT WARMS MY COCKLES TOO, IT DOES!
GYA
GYA
GYA
GYA
HOW-EVER ...
...THE REAL SHOW BEGINS NOW!
GYARARARA
THE DEATH SCYTHE ...
JAAAAAA (SLICE)
...
...CAN CUT THROUGH A GAS LAMP...
... LIKE A TWIG!
ZUPAN (SHNK)

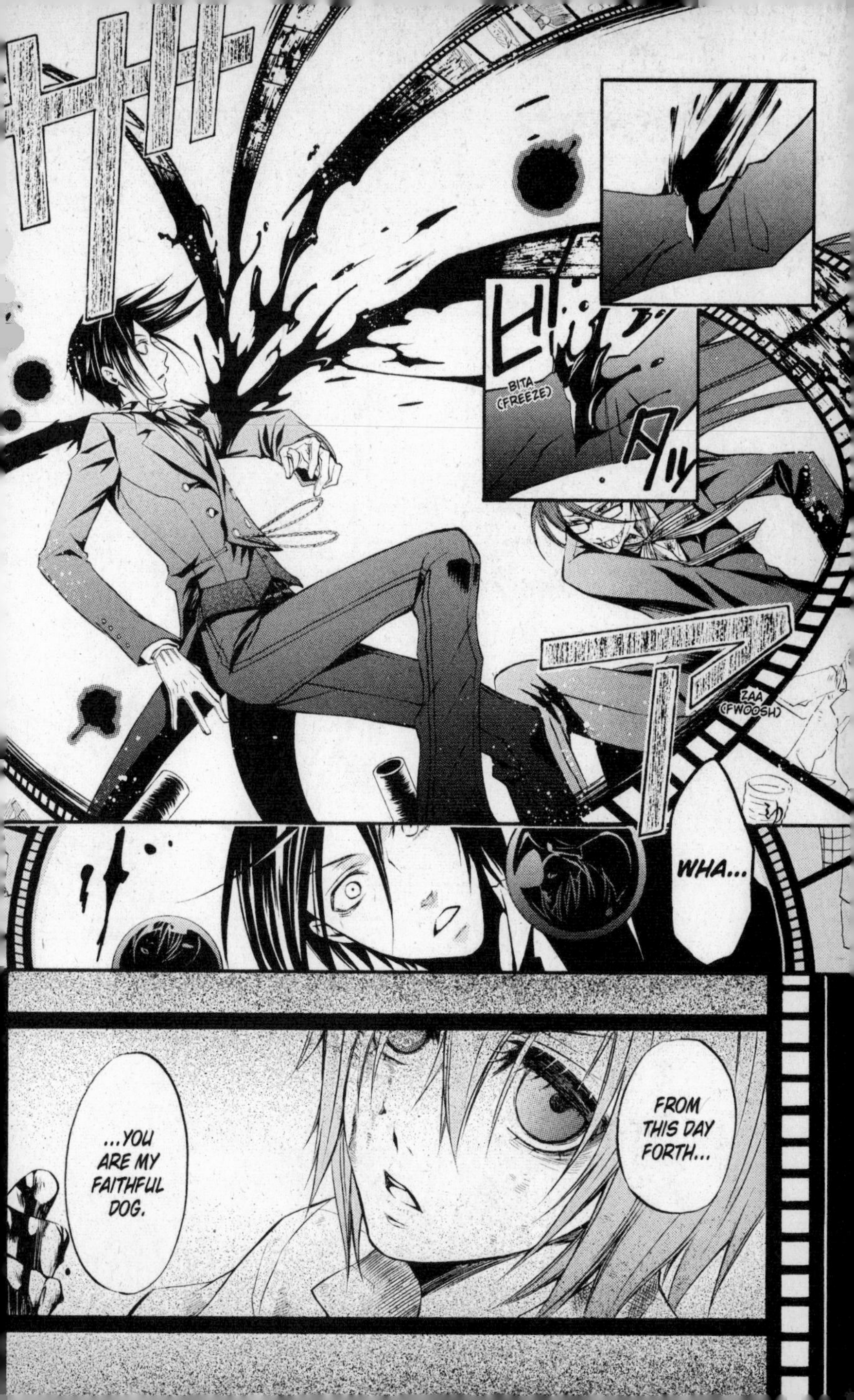
BITA (FREEZE)
ZAA (FWOOSH)
WHA...
FROM THIS DAY FORTH...
...YOU ARE MY FAITHFUL DOG.

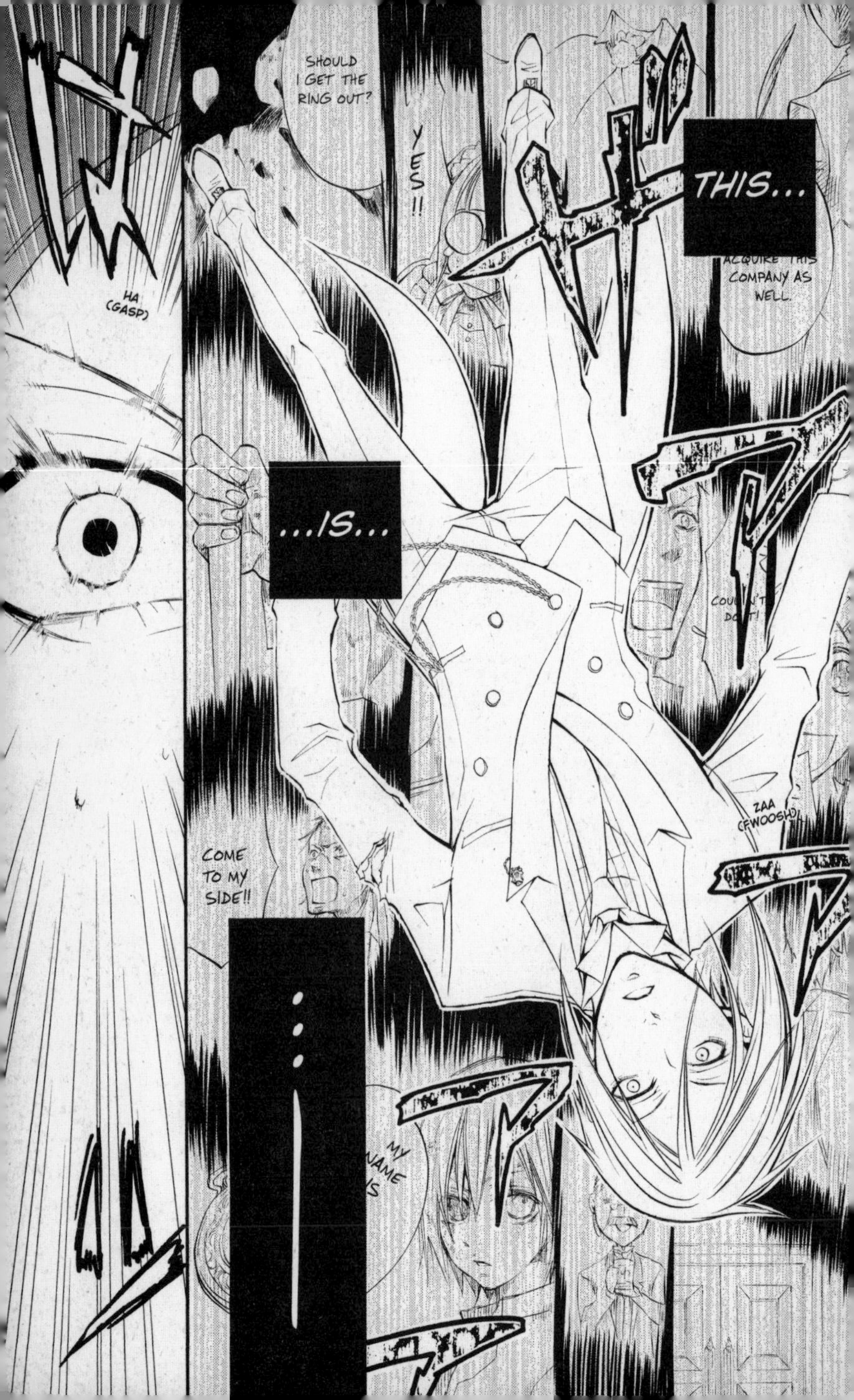
THIS...
ACQUIRE THIS COMPANY AS WELL.
COULDN'T DO IT!
ZAA (FWOOSH)
SHOULD I GET THE RING OUT?
YES!!
...IS...
COME TO MY SIDE!!
MY NAME IS
...!
HA (GASP)

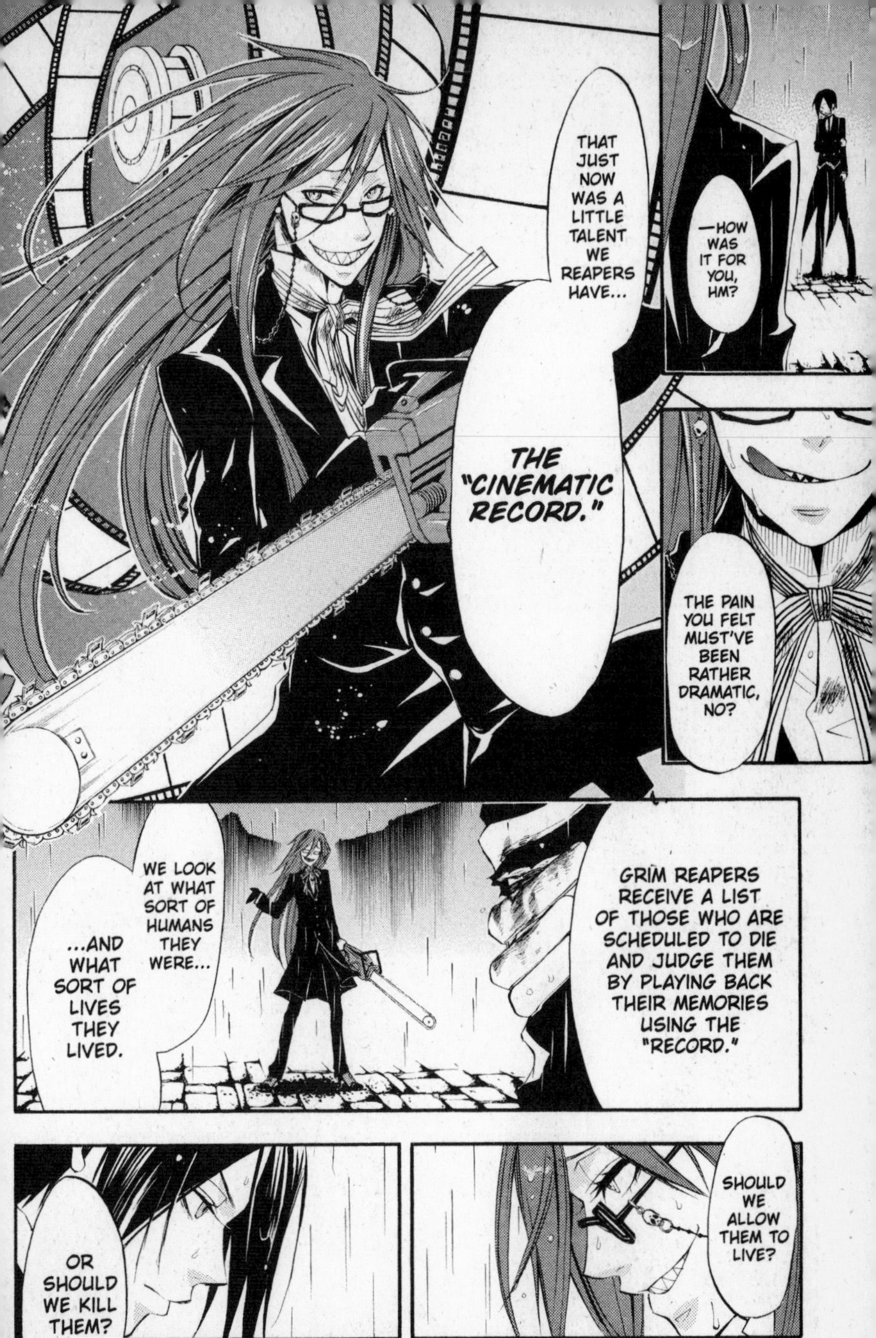
—HOW WAS IT FOR YOU, HM?
THE PAIN YOU FELT MUST'VE BEEN RATHER DRAMATIC, NO?
THAT JUST NOW WAS A LITTLE TALENT WE REAPERS HAVE...
THE "CINEMATIC RECORD."
GRIM REAPERS RECEIVE A LIST OF THOSE WHO ARE SCHEDULED TO DIE AND JUDGE THEM BY PLAYING BACK THEIR MEMORIES USING THE "RECORD."
WE LOOK AT WHAT SORT OF HUMANS THEY WERE...
...AND WHAT SORT OF LIVES THEY LIVED.
SHOULD WE ALLOW THEM TO LIVE?
OR SHOULD WE KILL THEM?

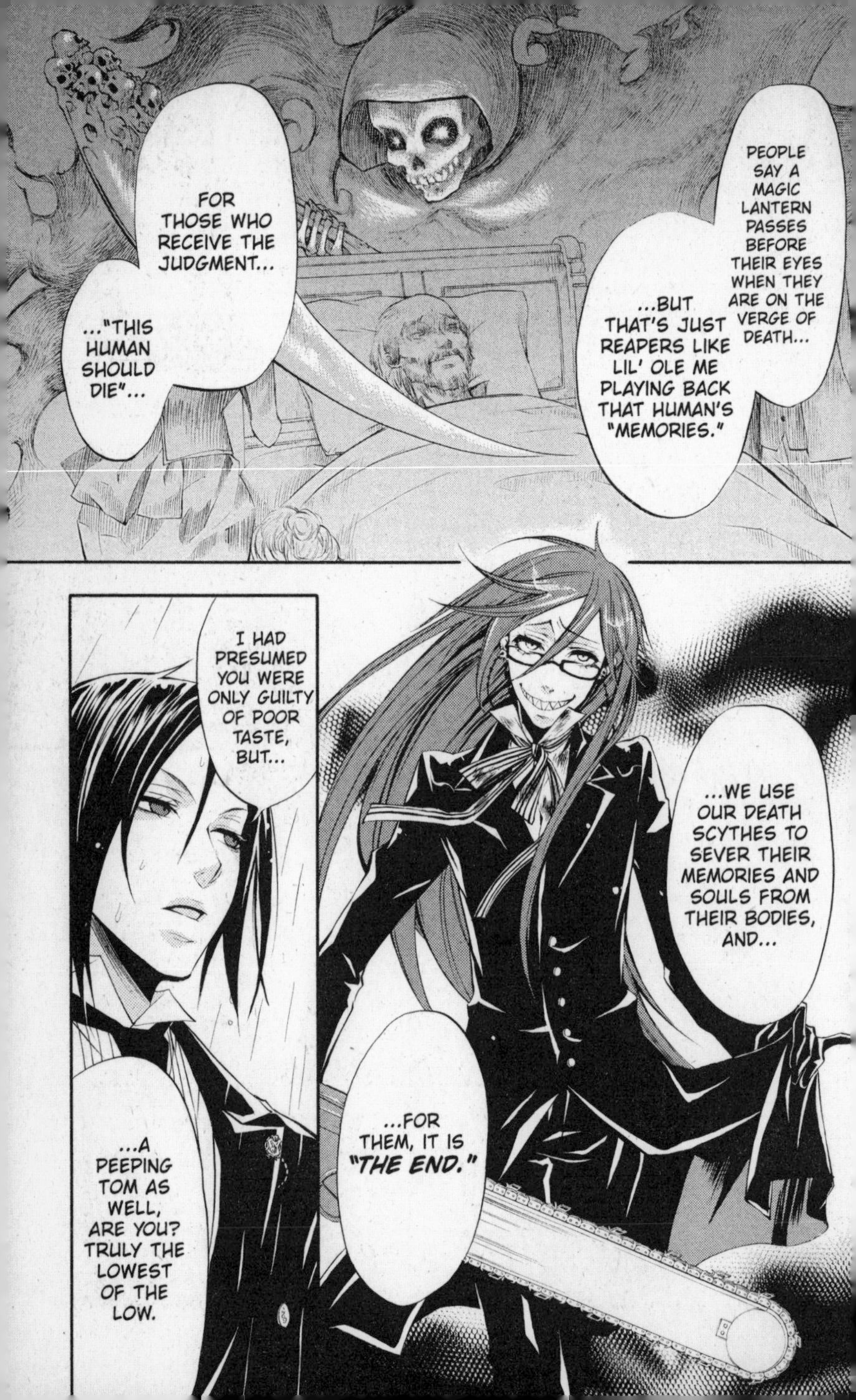
PEOPLE SAY A MAGIC LANTERN PASSES BEFORE THEIR EYES WHEN THEY ARE ON THE VERGE OF DEATH...
...BUT THAT'S JUST REAPERS LIKE LIL' OLE ME PLAYING BACK THAT HUMAN'S "MEMORIES."
FOR THOSE WHO RECEIVE THE JUDGMENT...
..."THIS HUMAN SHOULD DIE"...
...WE USE OUR DEATH SCYTHES TO SEVER THEIR MEMORIES AND SOULS FROM THEIR BODIES, AND...
...FOR THEM, IT IS *"THE END."*
I HAD PRESUMED YOU WERE ONLY GUILTY OF POOR TASTE, BUT...
...A PEEPING TOM AS WELL, ARE YOU? TRULY THE LOWEST OF THE LOW.

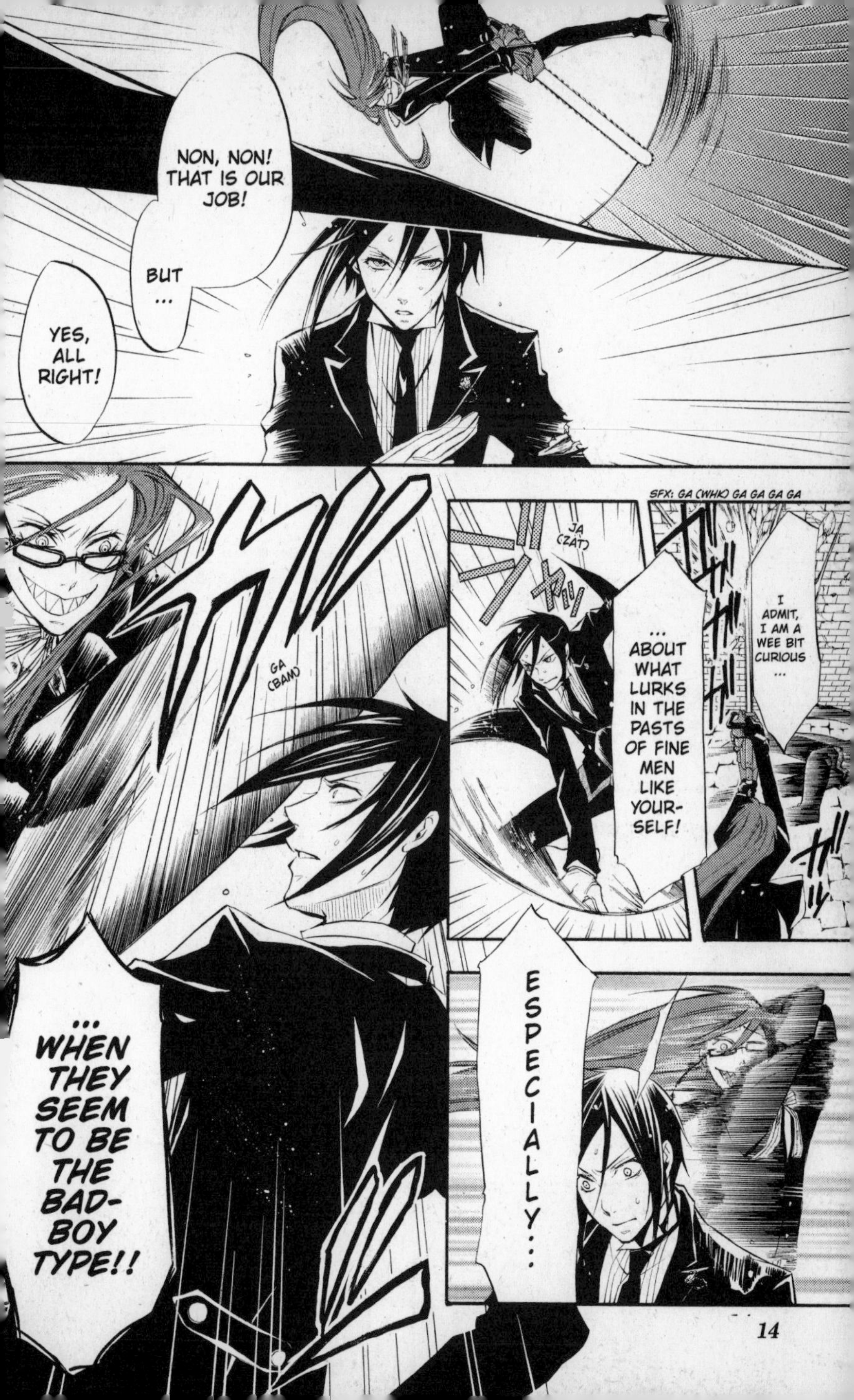
NON, NON! THAT IS OUR JOB!
BUT ...
YES, ALL RIGHT!
SFX: GA (WHK) GA GA GA GA
I ADMIT, I AM A WEE BIT CURIOUS ...
... ABOUT WHAT LURKS IN THE PASTS OF FINE MEN LIKE YOUR-SELF!
JA (ZAT)
ESPECIALLY...
GA (BAM)
... WHEN THEY SEEM TO BE THE BAD-BOY TYPE!!

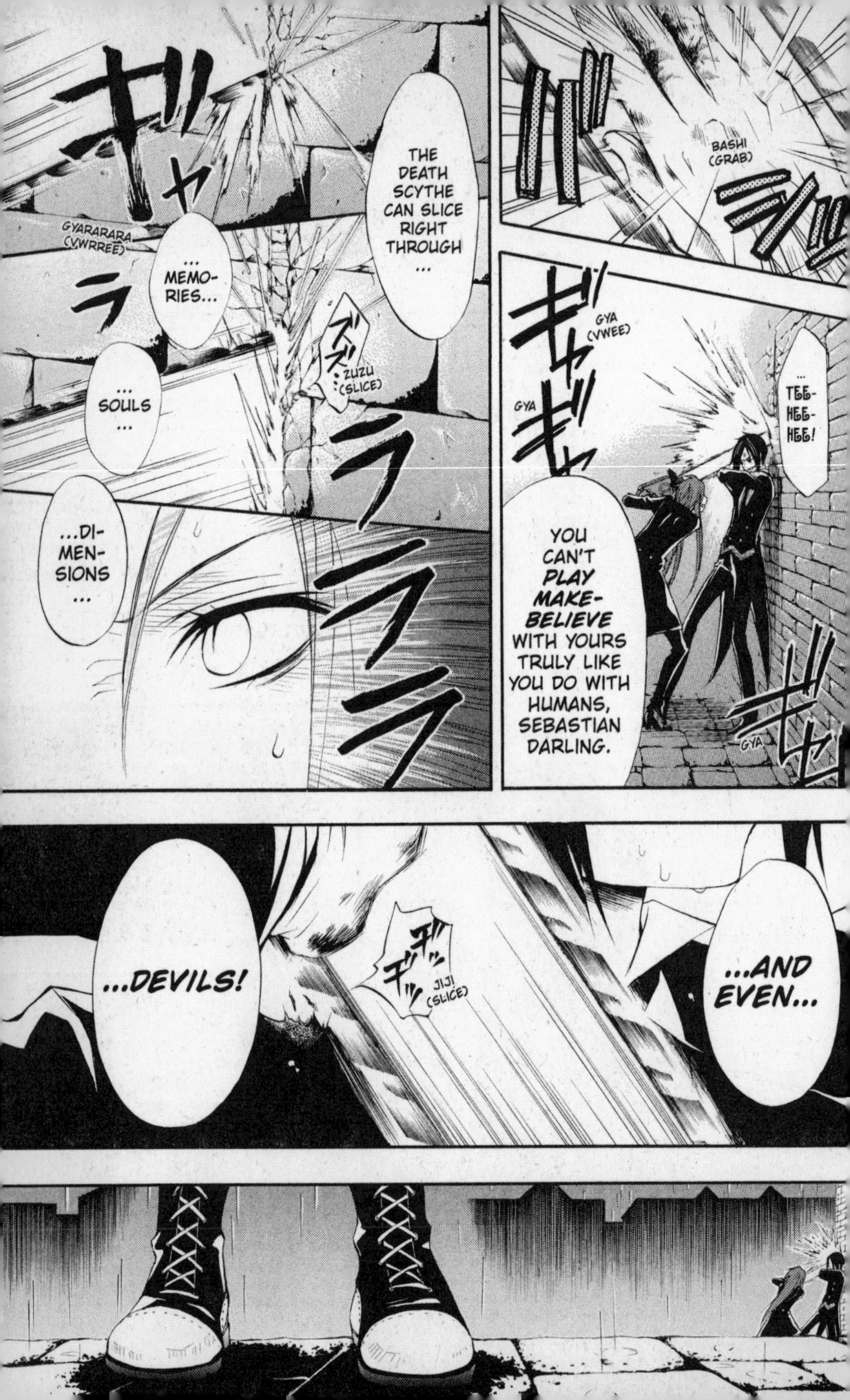
BASHI (GRAB)
GYA (VWEE)
GYA
... TEE-HEE-HEE!
YOU CAN'T PLAY MAKE-BELIEVE WITH YOURS TRULY LIKE YOU DO WITH HUMANS, SEBASTIAN DARLING.
GYA
THE DEATH SCYTHE CAN SLICE RIGHT THROUGH ...
GYARARARA (VWRREE)
... MEMORIES...
ZUZU (SLICE)
... SOULS ...
...DIMENSIONS ...
...AND EVEN...
JIJI (SLICE)
...DEVILS!

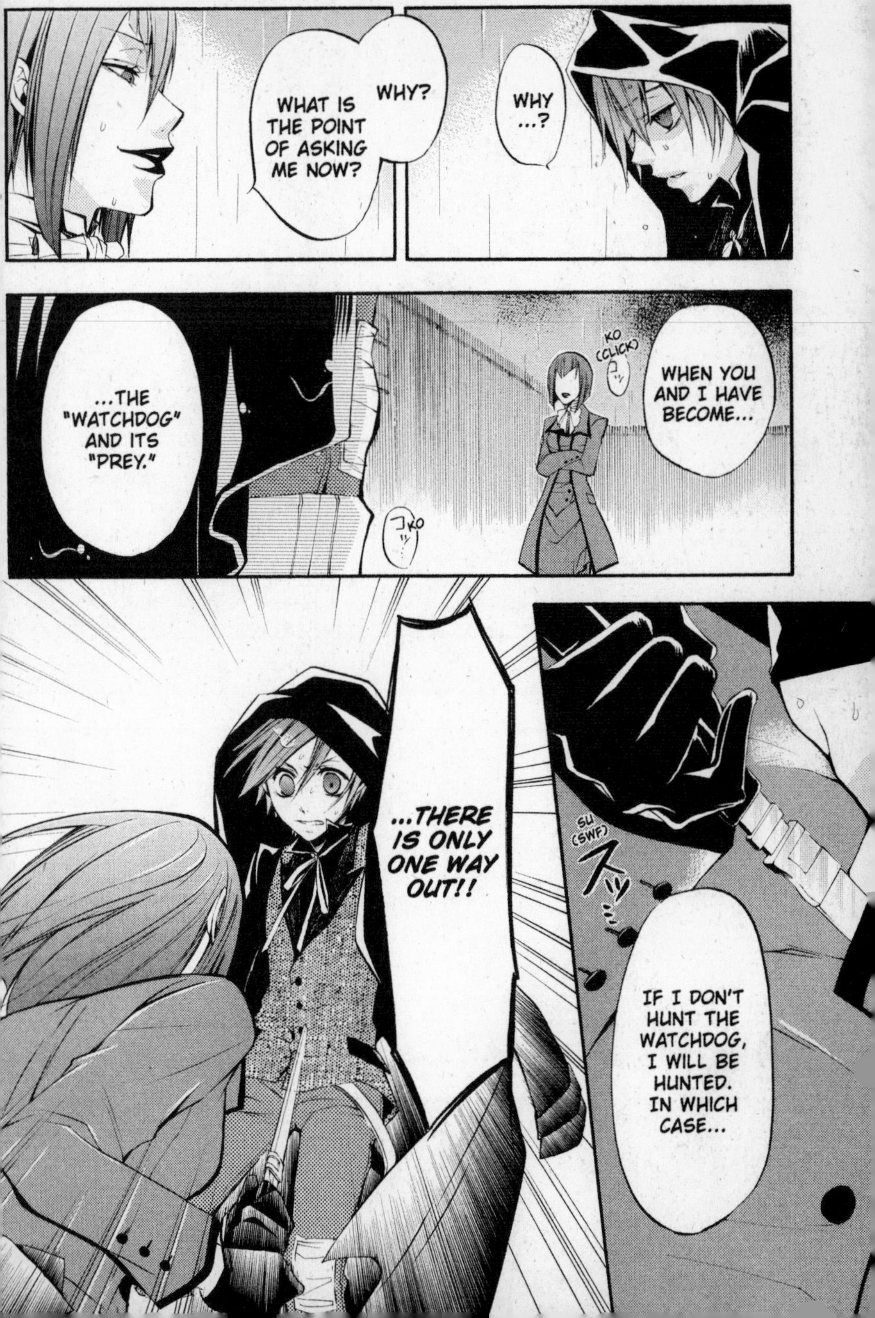
WHY ...?
WHY?
WHAT IS THE POINT OF ASKING ME NOW?
WHEN YOU AND I HAVE BECOME...
KO (CLICK)
コッ
コッ KO
...THE "WATCHDOG" AND ITS "PREY."
SU (SWF)
スッ
IF I DON'T HUNT THE WATCHDOG, I WILL BE HUNTED. IN WHICH CASE...
...THERE IS ONLY ONE WAY OUT!!

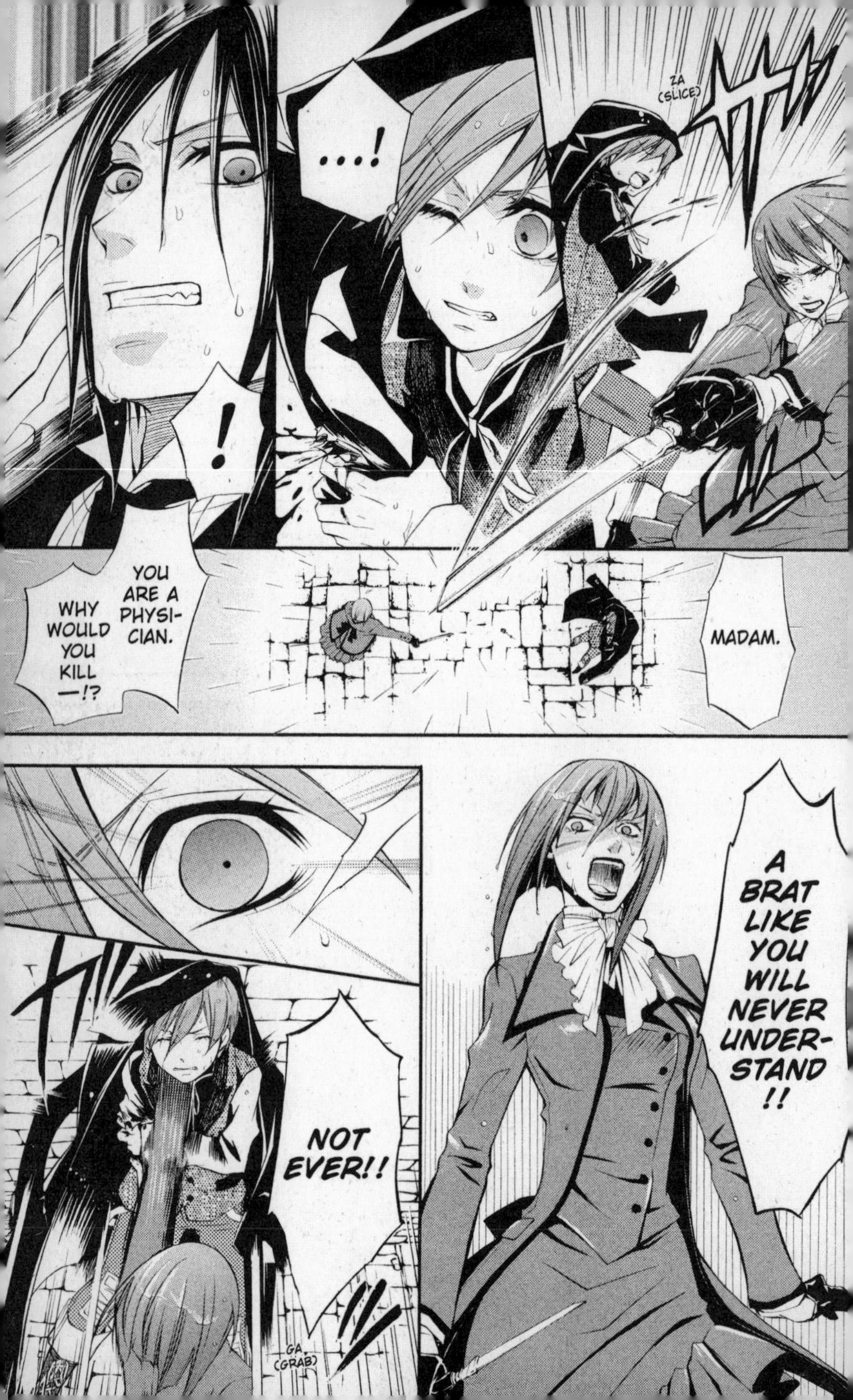

ZA (SLICE)
...!
!
MADAM.
YOU ARE A PHYSICIAN.
WHY WOULD YOU KILL—!?
A BRAT LIKE YOU WILL NEVER UNDERSTAND!!
NOT EVER!!
GA (GRAB)

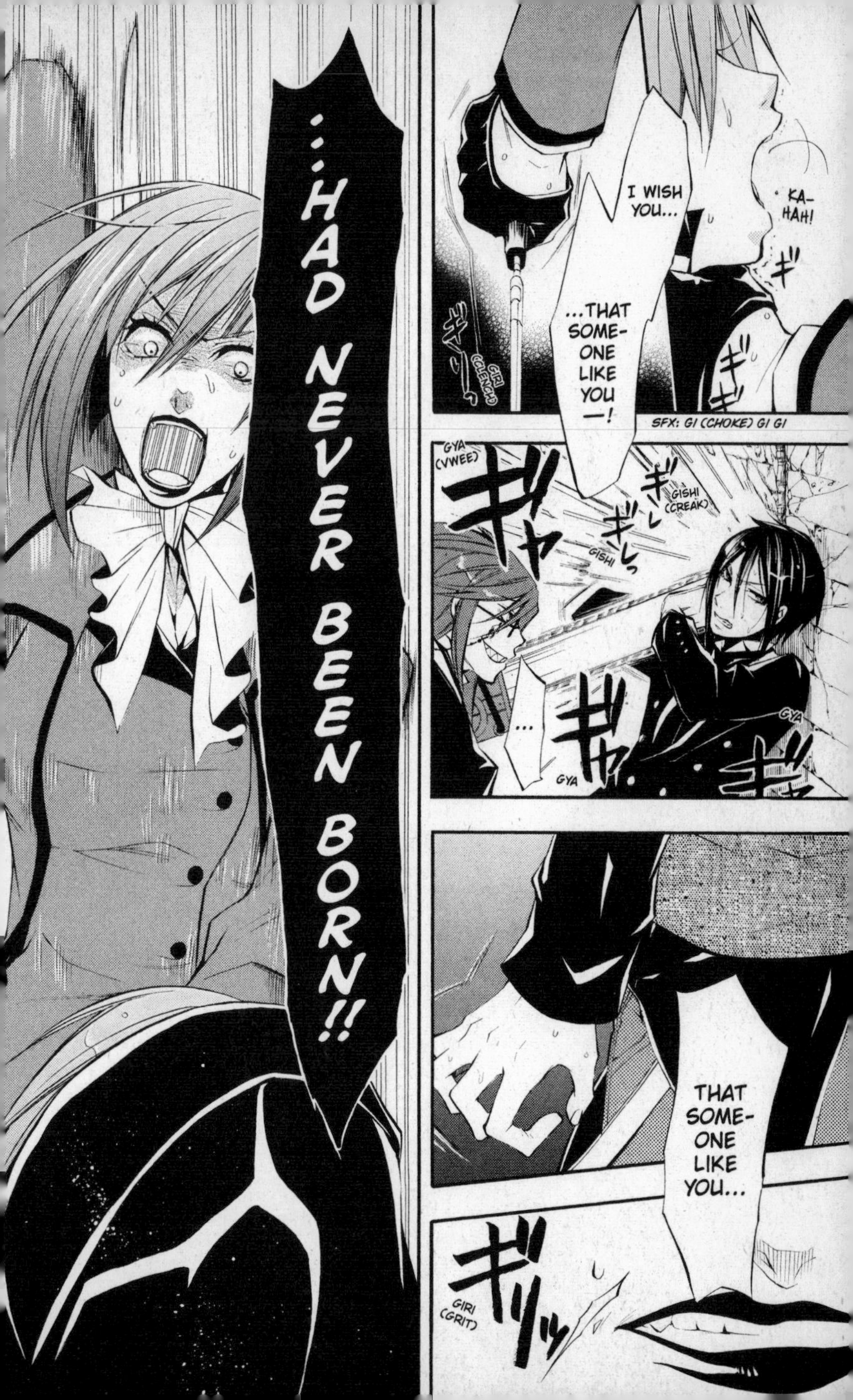
KA-HAH!
I WISH YOU...
...THAT SOME-ONE LIKE YOU—!
GIRI (CLENCH)
SFX: GI (CHOKE) GI GI
GYA (VWEE)
GISHI (CREAK)
GISHI
...
GYA
GYA
THAT SOME-ONE LIKE YOU...
GIRI (GRIT)
...HAD NEVER BEEN BORN!!

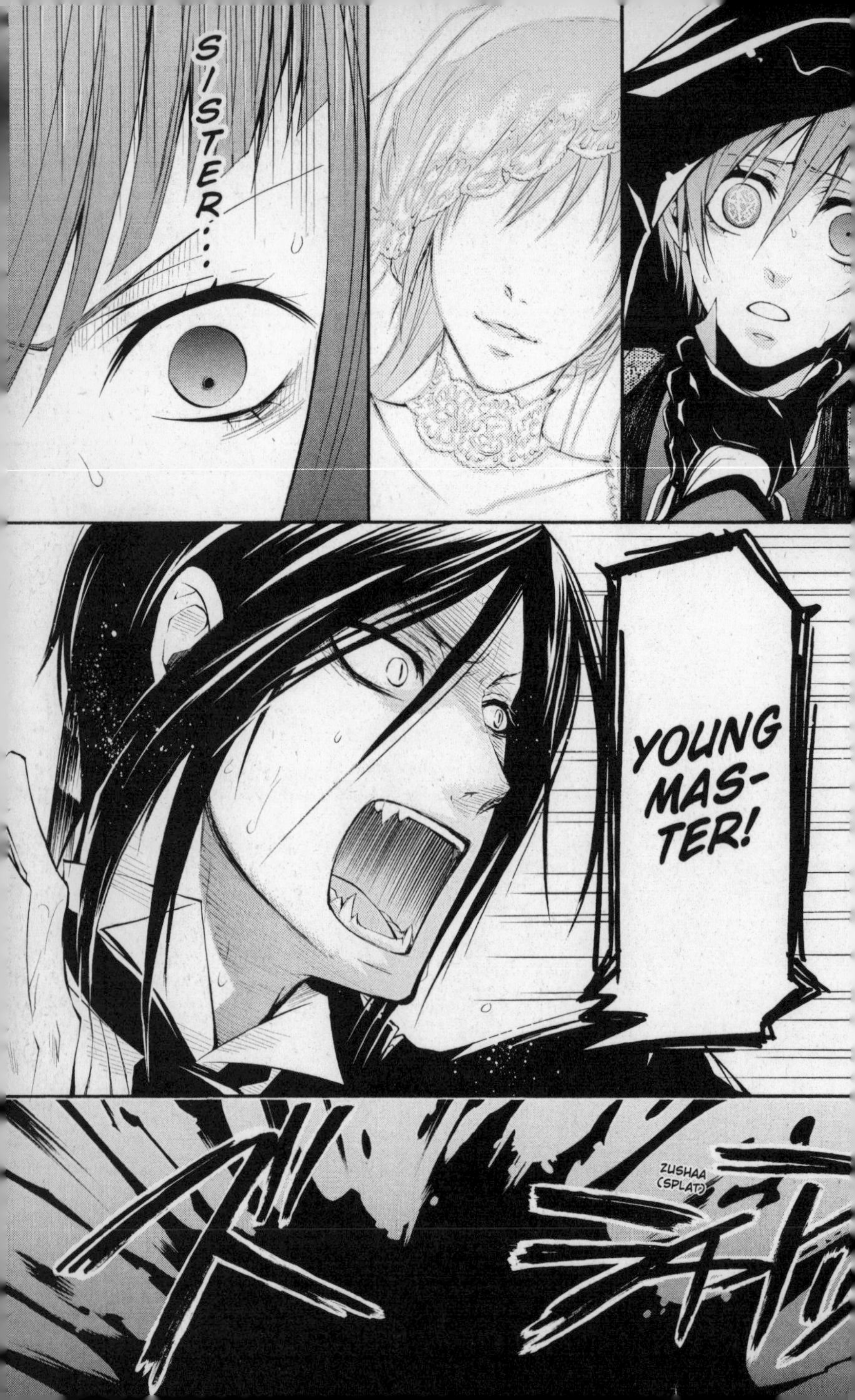
SISTER...
YOUNG MASTER!
ZUSHAA (SPLAT)

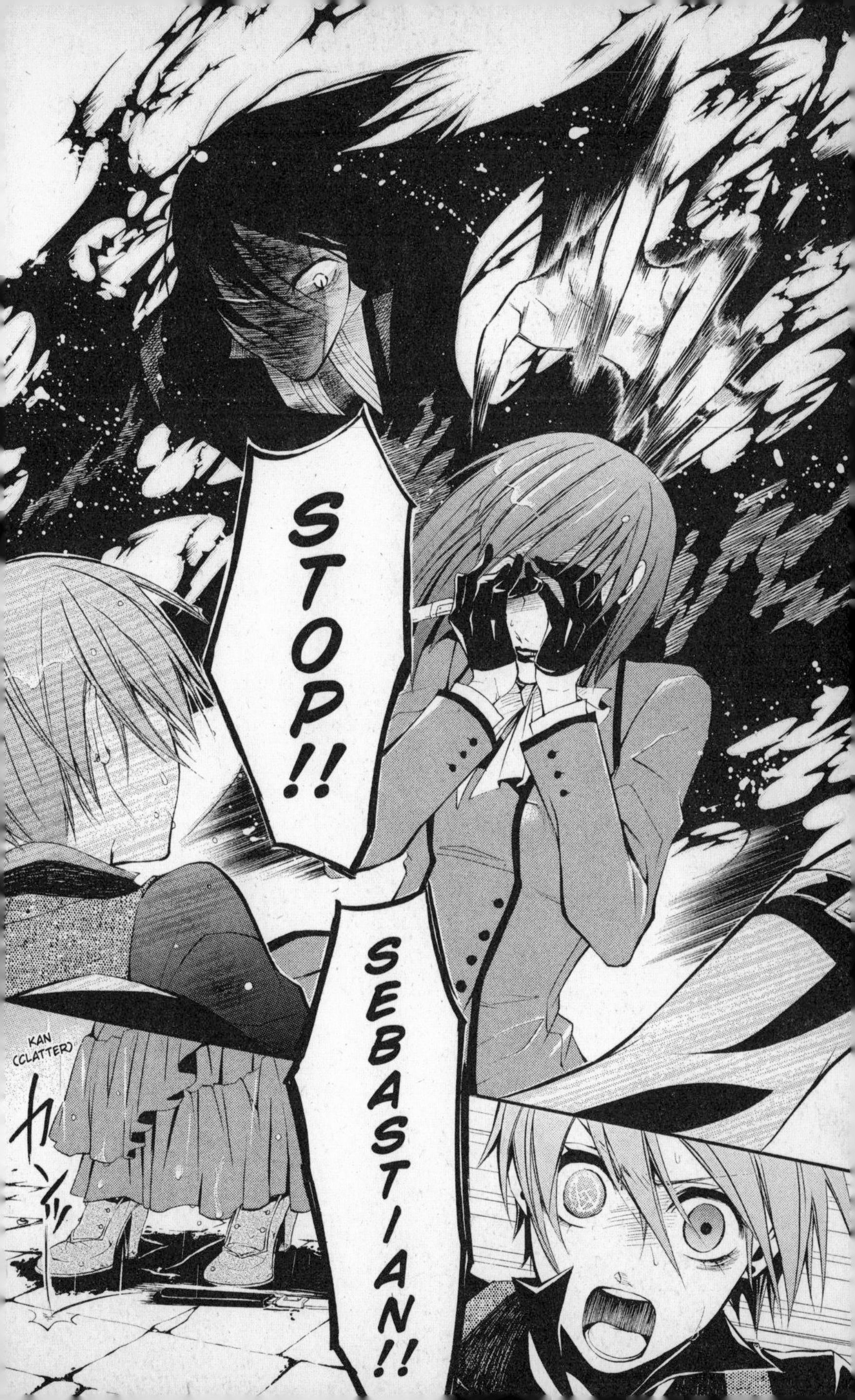
STOP!!
SEBASTIAN!!
KAN (CLATTER)

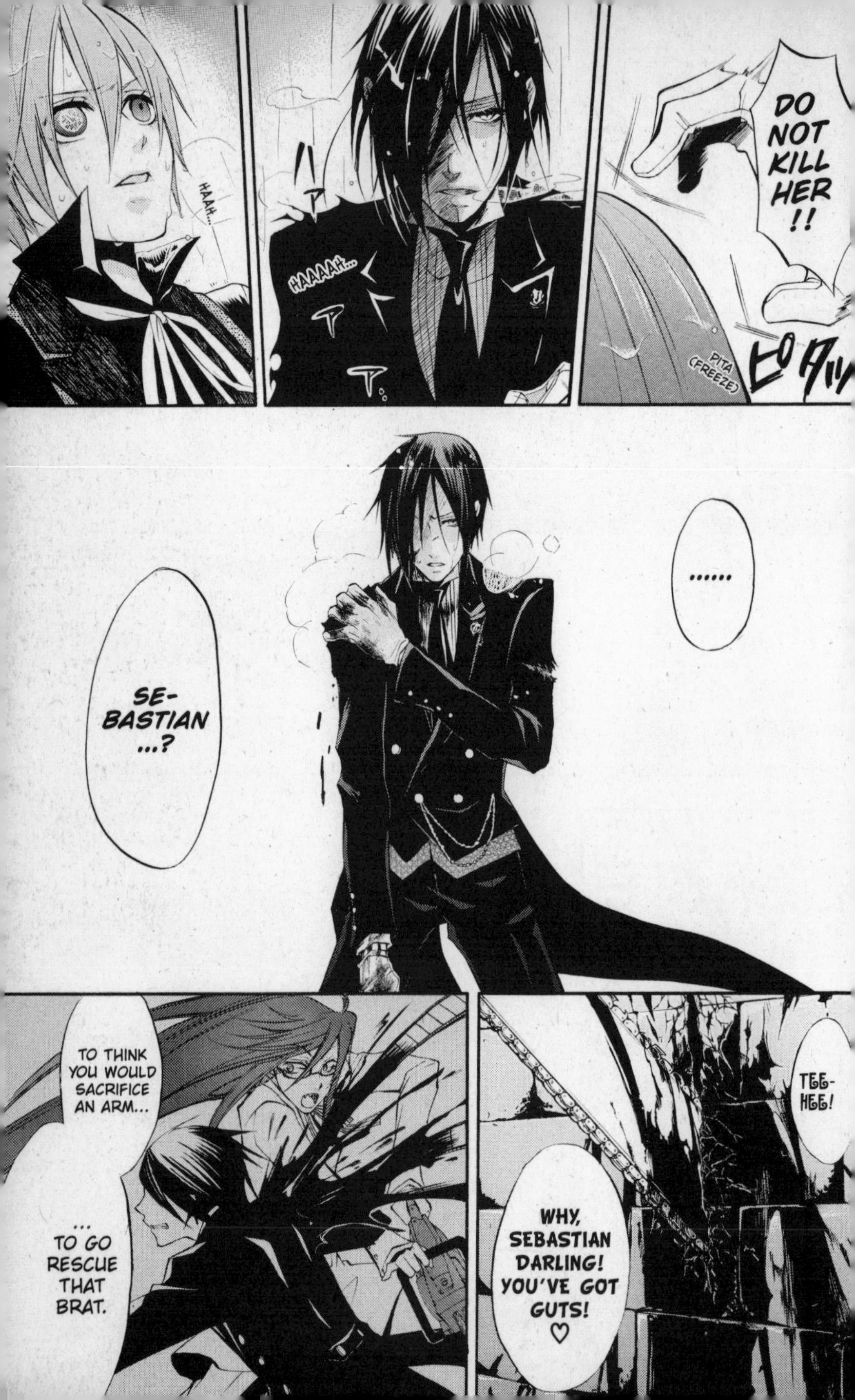
DO NOT KILL HER!!
PITA (FREEZE)
ピタッ
HAAAAH...
HAAH...
......
SE-BASTIAN ...?
TEE-HEE!
WHY, SEBASTIAN DARLING! YOU'VE GOT GUTS! ♡
TO THINK YOU WOULD SACRIFICE AN ARM...
...TO GO RESCUE THAT BRAT.

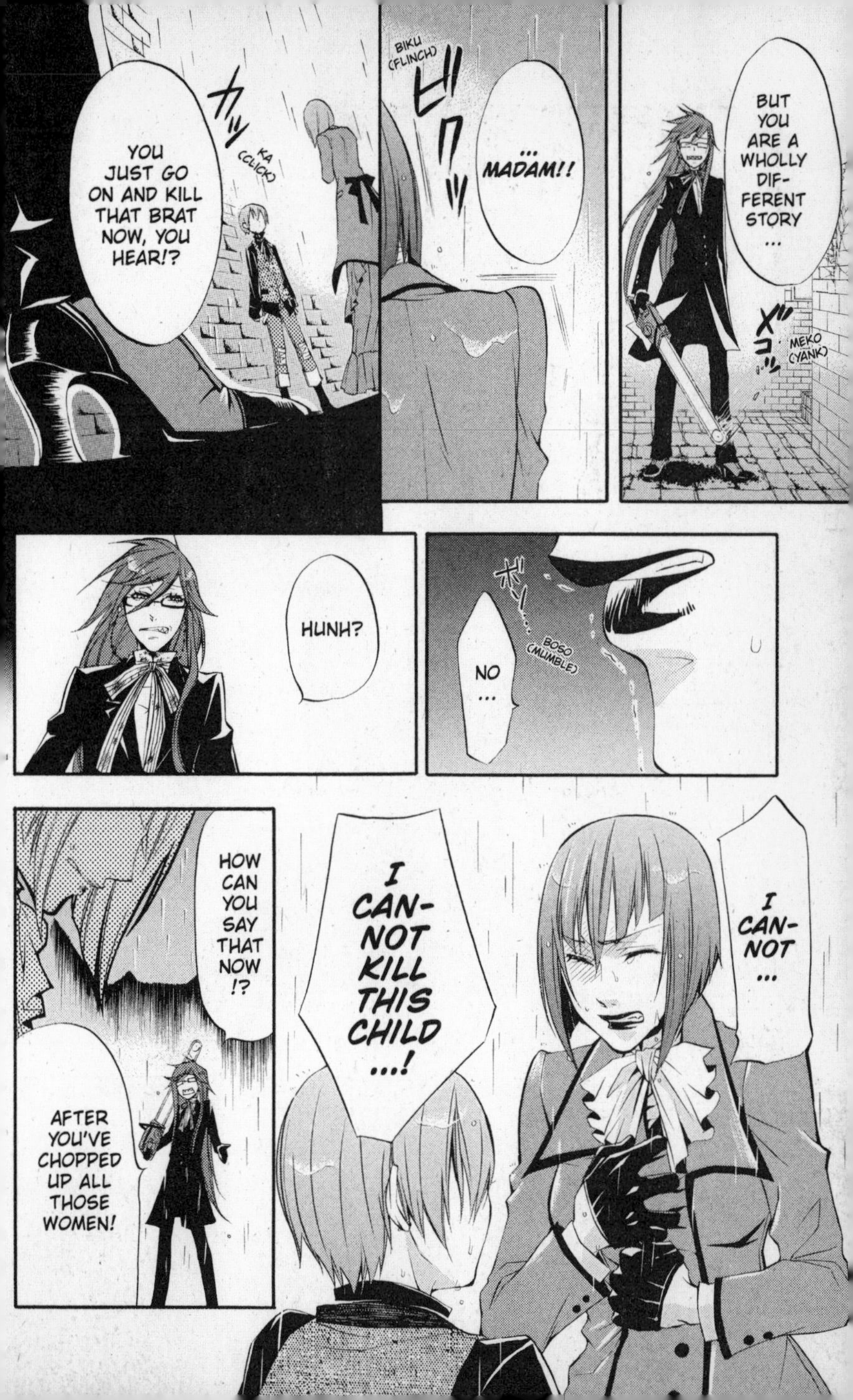
BUT YOU ARE A WHOLLY DIF-FERENT STORY ...
MEKO (YANK)
BIKU (FLINCH)
... MADAM!!
YOU JUST GO ON AND KILL THAT BRAT NOW, YOU HEAR!?
KA (CLICK)
NO ...
BOSO (MUMBLE)
HUNH?
I CAN-NOT ...
I CAN-NOT KILL THIS CHILD ...!
HOW CAN YOU SAY THAT NOW !?
AFTER YOU'VE CHOPPED UP ALL THOSE WOMEN!

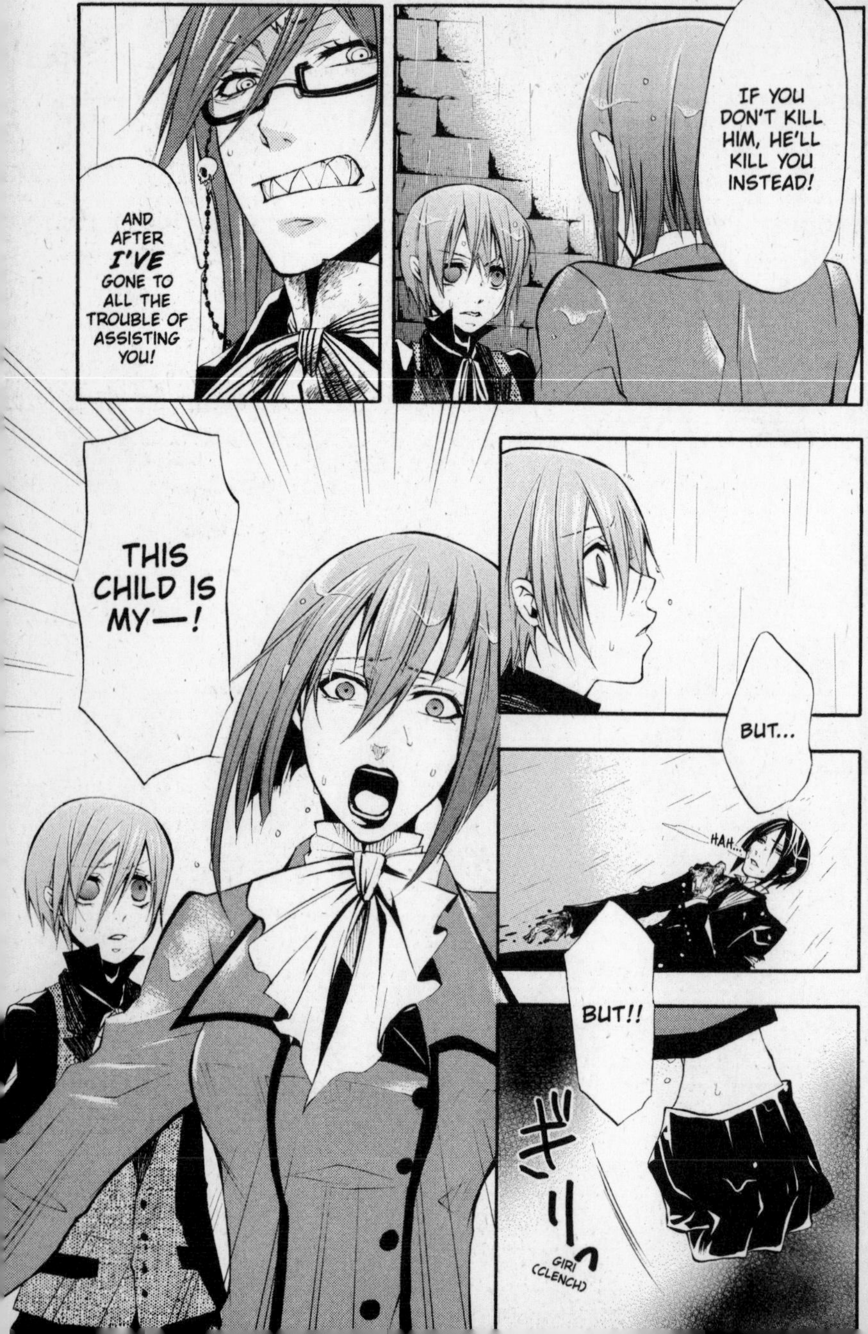
IF YOU DON'T KILL HIM, HE'LL KILL YOU INSTEAD!
AND AFTER *I'VE* GONE TO ALL THE TROUBLE OF ASSISTING YOU!
THIS CHILD IS MY—!
BUT...
HAH...
BUT!!
ギリ
GIRI (CLENCH)

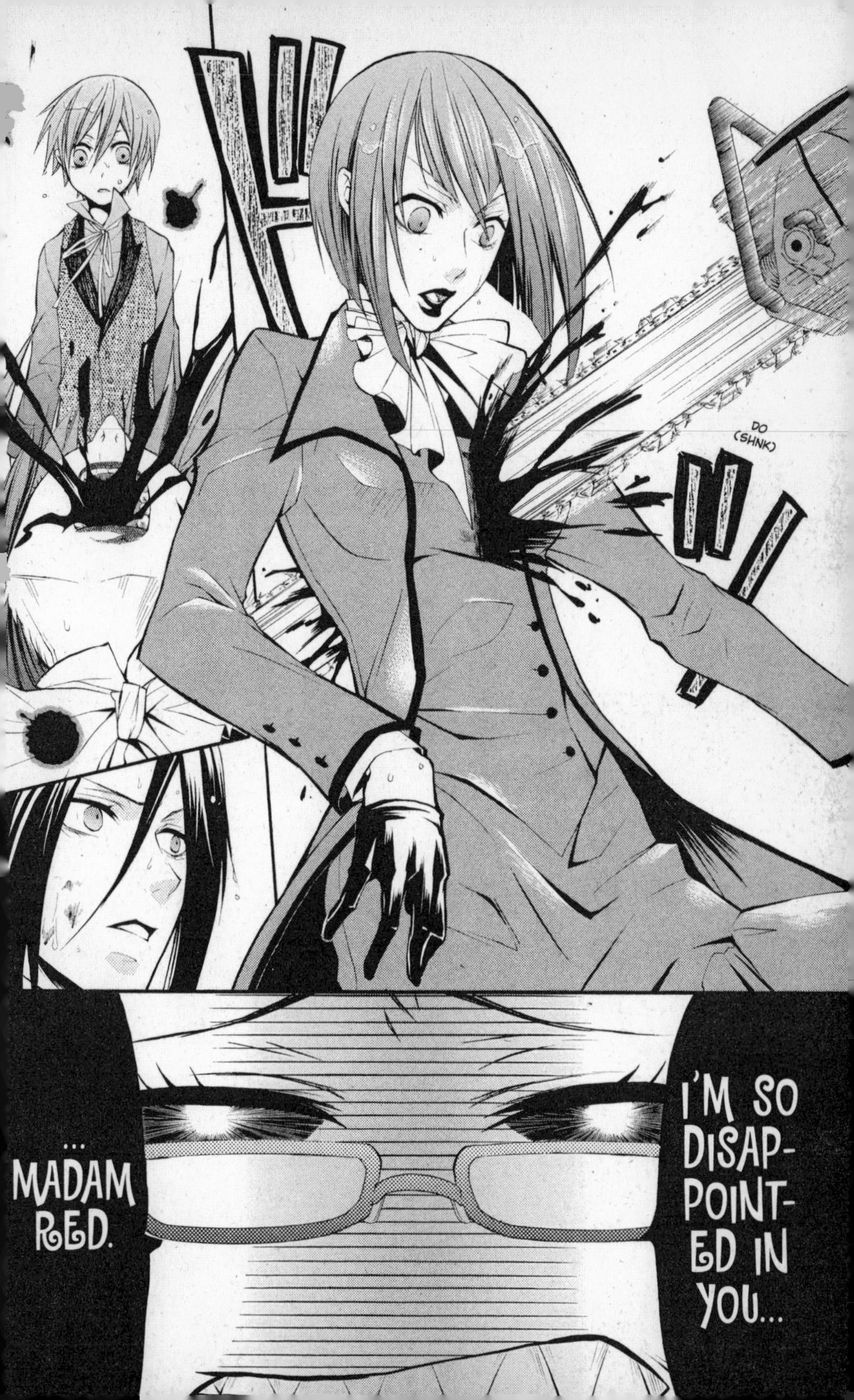
DO (SHNK)
I'M SO DISAP-POINT-ED IN YOU...
... MADAM RED.

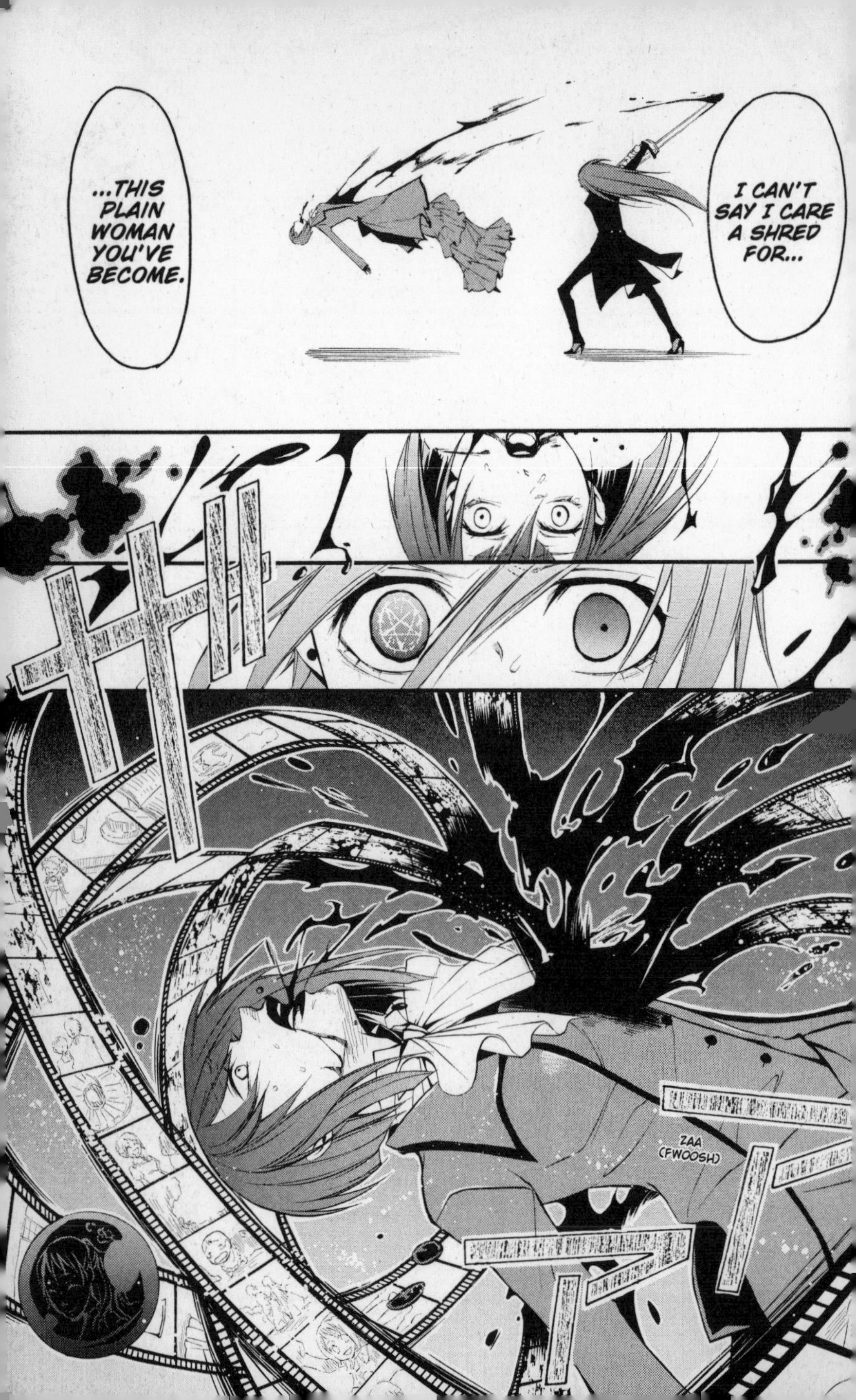
I CAN'T SAY I CARE A SHRED FOR...
...THIS PLAIN WOMAN YOU'VE BECOME.
ZAA (FWOOSH)

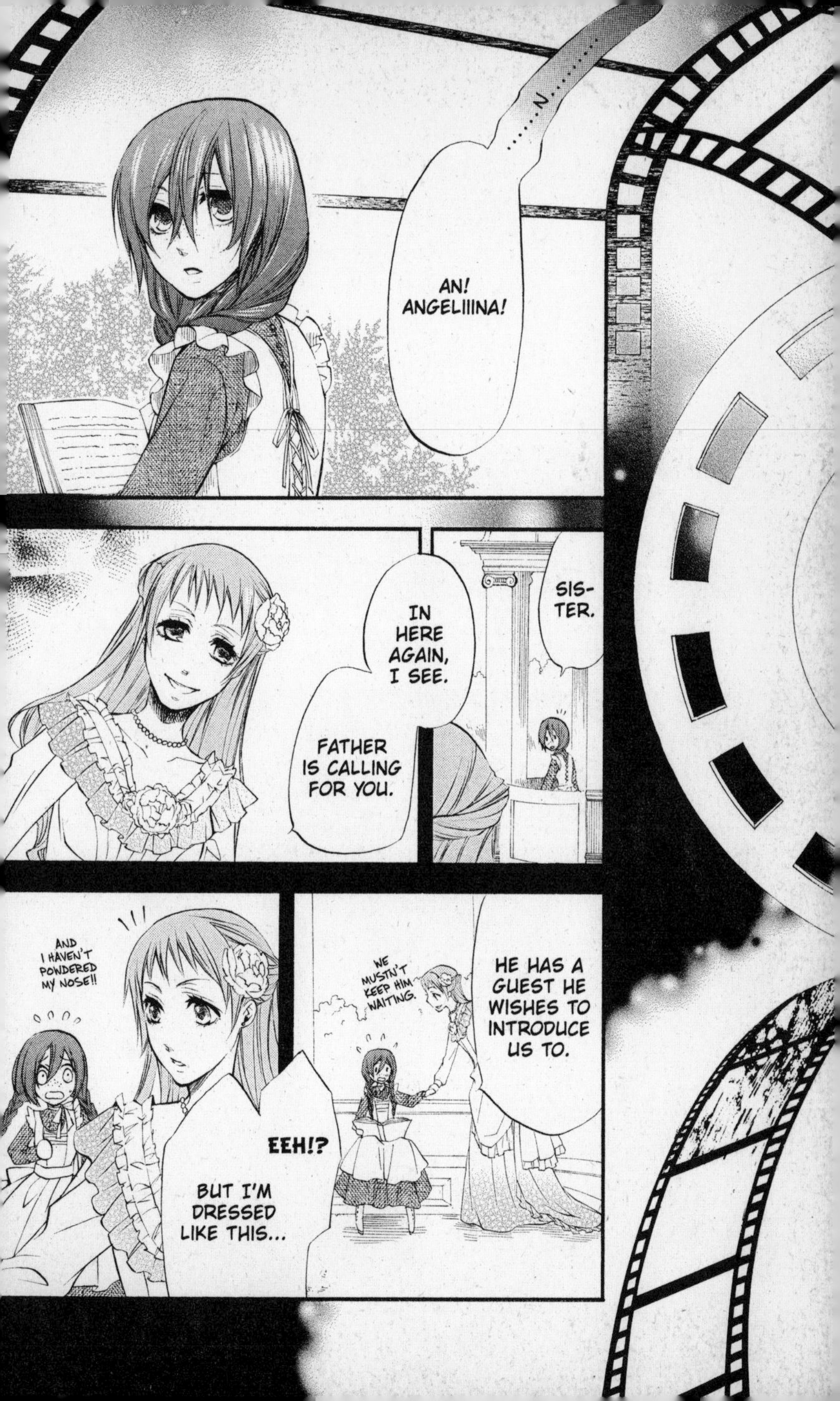

......N......
AN! ANGELIIINA!
SIS-TER.
IN HERE AGAIN, I SEE.
FATHER IS CALLING FOR YOU.
HE HAS A GUEST HE WISHES TO INTRODUCE US TO.
WE MUSTN'T KEEP HIM WAITING.
EEH!?
BUT I'M DRESSED LIKE THIS...
AND I HAVEN'T POWDERED MY NOSE!!

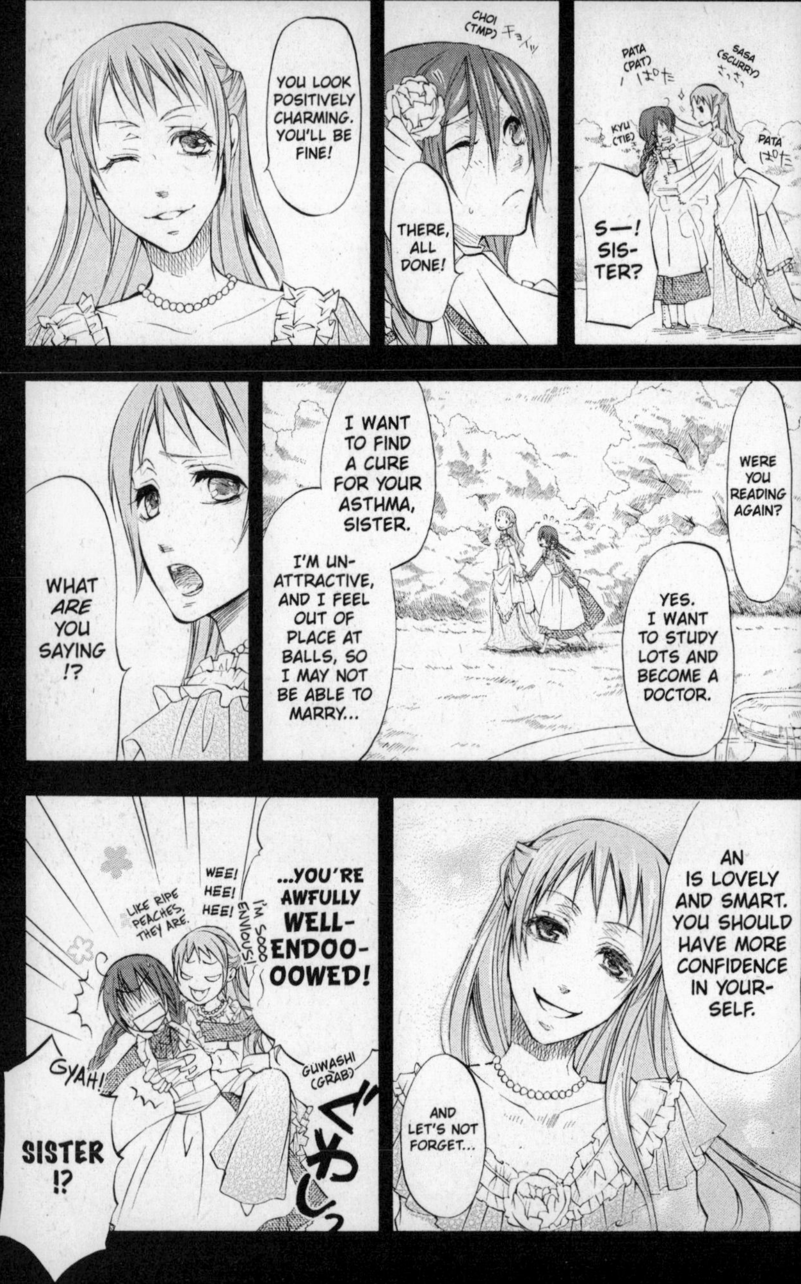
SASA (SCURRY)
PATA
PATA (PAT)
KYU (TIE)
S—! SIS-TER?
CHOI (TMP)
THERE, ALL DONE!
YOU LOOK POSITIVELY CHARMING. YOU'LL BE FINE!
WERE YOU READING AGAIN?
YES. I WANT TO STUDY LOTS AND BECOME A DOCTOR.
I WANT TO FIND A CURE FOR YOUR ASTHMA, SISTER.
I'M UN-ATTRACTIVE, AND I FEEL OUT OF PLACE AT BALLS, SO I MAY NOT BE ABLE TO MARRY...
WHAT ARE YOU SAYING!?
AN IS LOVELY AND SMART. YOU SHOULD HAVE MORE CONFIDENCE IN YOUR-SELF.
AND LET'S NOT FORGET...
...YOU'RE AWFULLY WELL-ENDOOO-OOWED!
I'M SOOO ENVIOUS!
WEE! HEE! HEE!
LIKE RIPE PEACHES, THEY ARE.
GUWASHI (GRAB)
GYAH!
SISTER!?

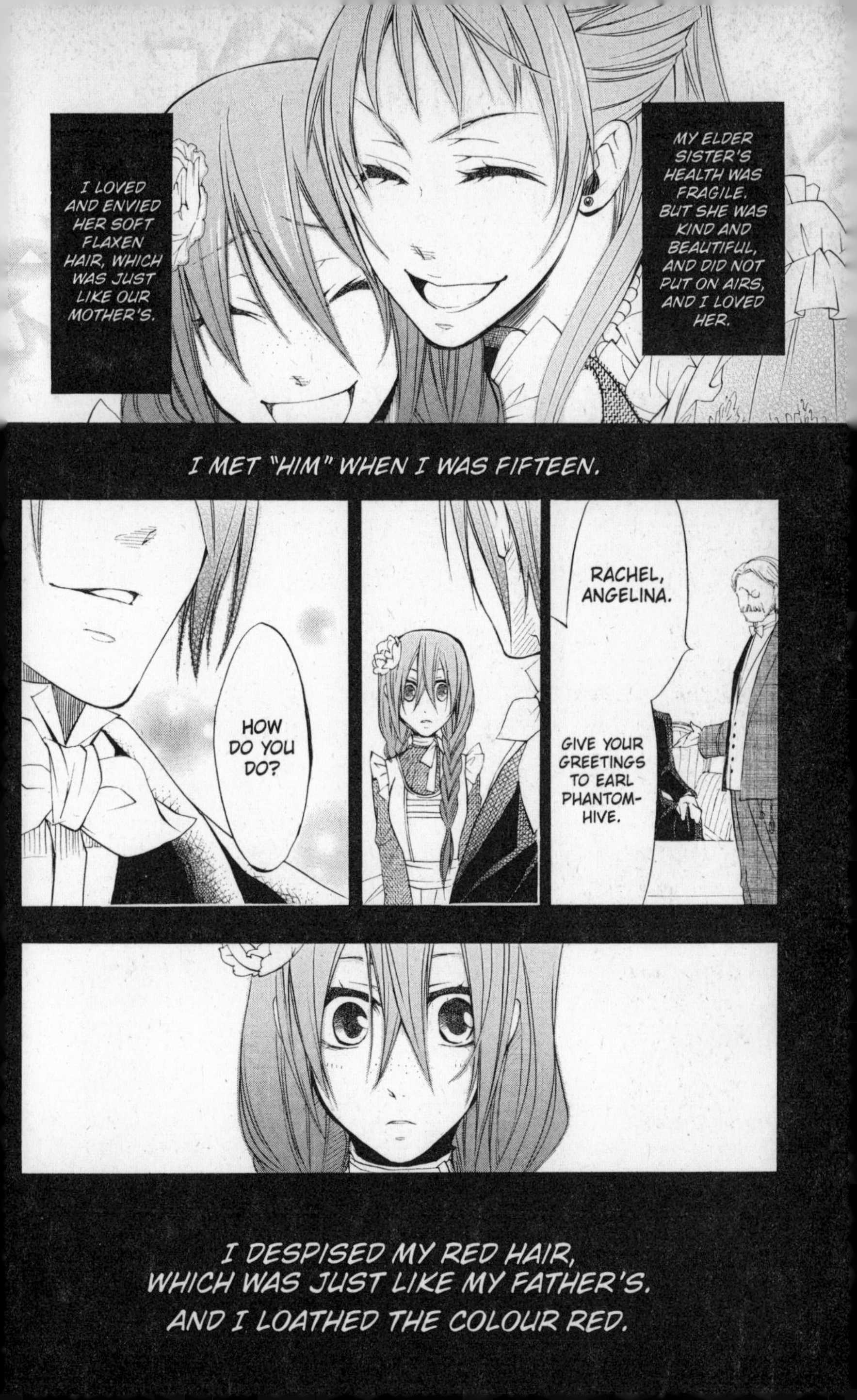
MY ELDER SISTER'S HEALTH WAS FRAGILE. BUT SHE WAS KIND AND BEAUTIFUL, AND DID NOT PUT ON AIRS, AND I LOVED HER.
I LOVED AND ENVIED HER SOFT FLAXEN HAIR, WHICH WAS JUST LIKE OUR MOTHER'S.
I MET "HIM" WHEN I WAS FIFTEEN.
RACHEL, ANGELINA.
GIVE YOUR GREETINGS TO EARL PHANTOM-HIVE.
HOW DO YOU DO?
I DESPISED MY RED HAIR, WHICH WAS JUST LIKE MY FATHER'S.
AND I LOATHED THE COLOUR RED.

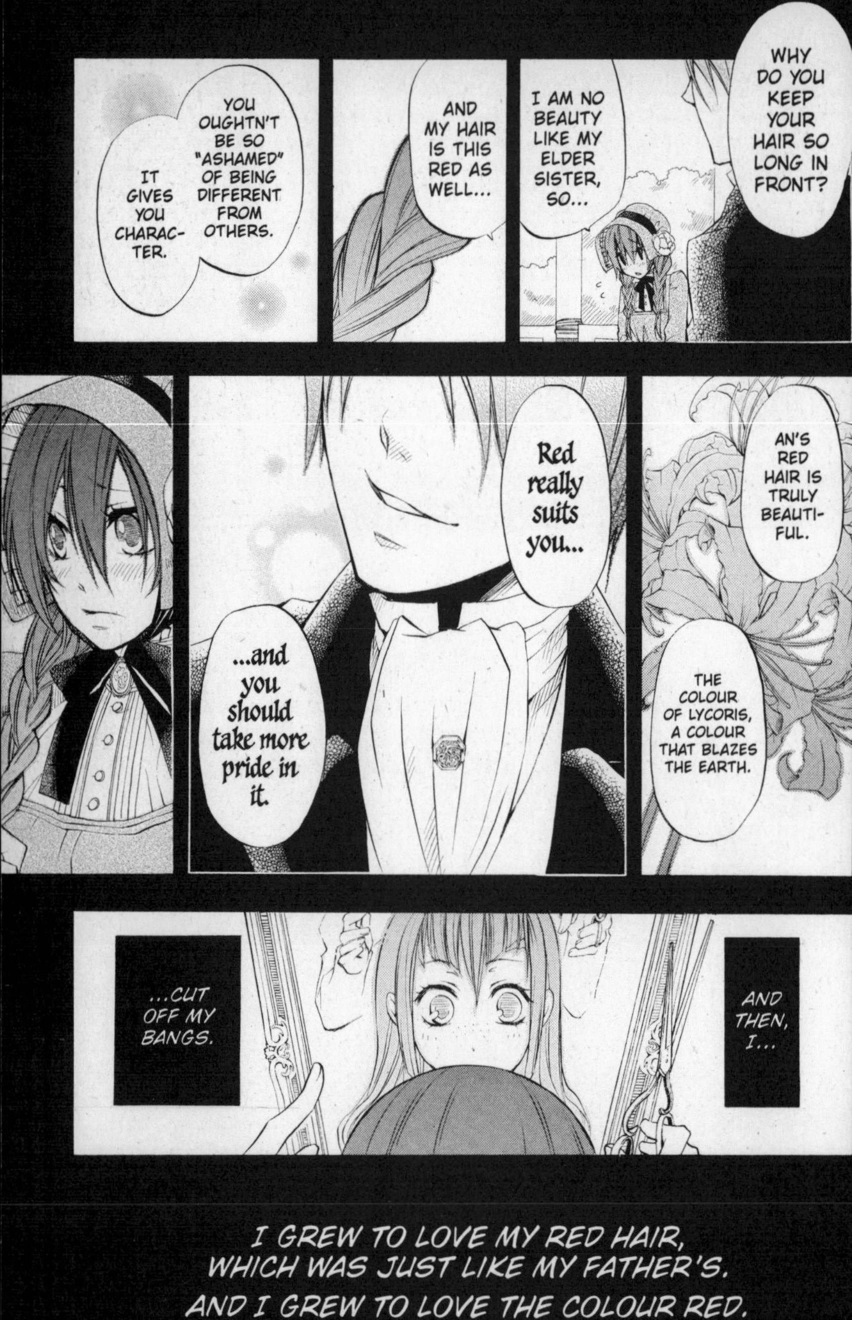
WHY DO YOU KEEP YOUR HAIR SO LONG IN FRONT?
I AM NO BEAUTY LIKE MY ELDER SISTER, SO...
AND MY HAIR IS THIS RED AS WELL...
YOU OUGHTN'T BE SO "ASHAMED" OF BEING DIFFERENT FROM OTHERS.
IT GIVES YOU CHARAC-TER.
AN'S RED HAIR IS TRULY BEAUTI-FUL.
THE COLOUR OF LYCORIS, A COLOUR THAT BLAZES THE EARTH.
Red really suits you...
...and you should take more pride in it.
AND THEN, I...
...CUT OFF MY BANGS.
I GREW TO LOVE MY RED HAIR, WHICH WAS JUST LIKE MY FATHER'S.
AND I GREW TO LOVE THE COLOUR RED.

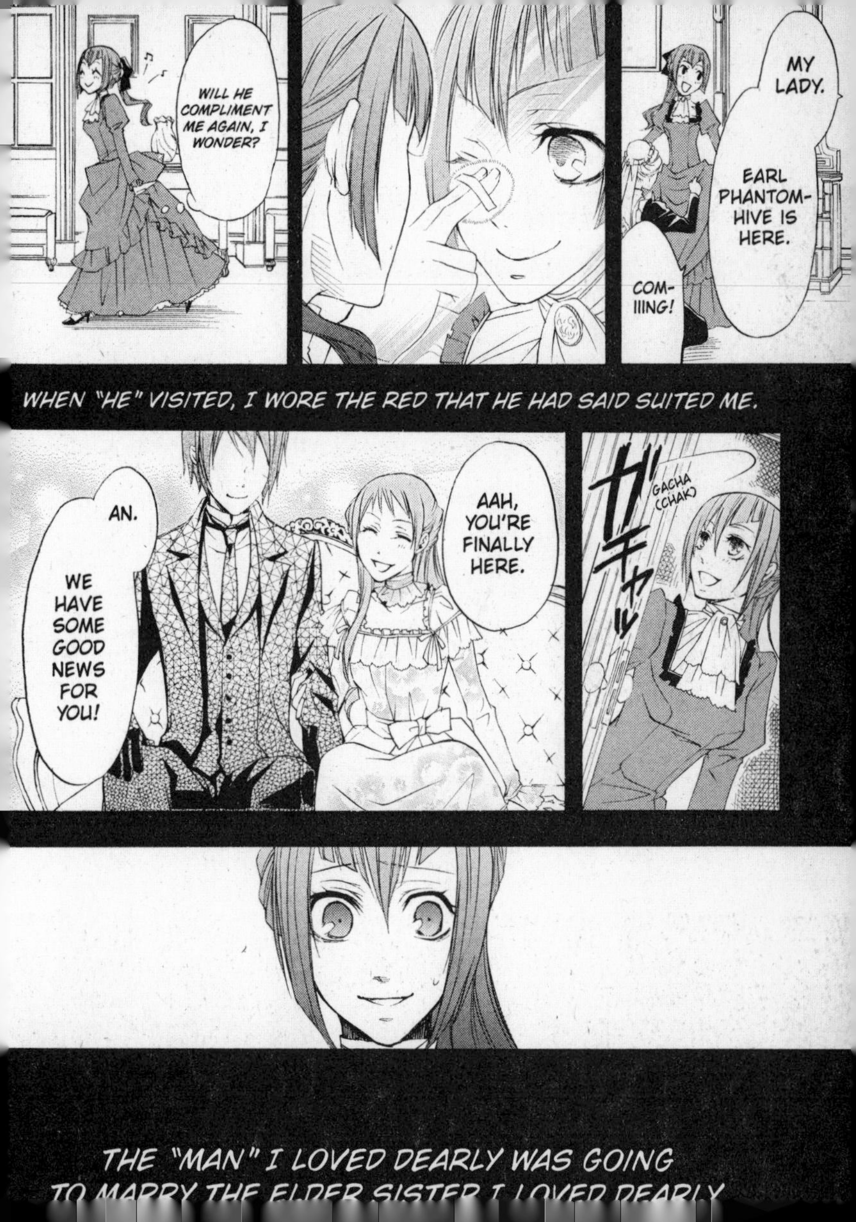
MY LADY.
EARL PHANTOM-HIVE IS HERE.
COM-IIING!
WILL HE COMPLIMENT ME AGAIN, I WONDER?
WHEN "HE" VISITED, I WORE THE RED THAT HE HAD SAID SUITED ME.
ガチャ
GACHA (CHAK)
AAH, YOU'RE FINALLY HERE.
AN.
WE HAVE SOME GOOD NEWS FOR YOU!
THE "MAN" I LOVED DEARLY WAS GOING TO MARRY THE ELDER SISTER I LOVED DEARLY.

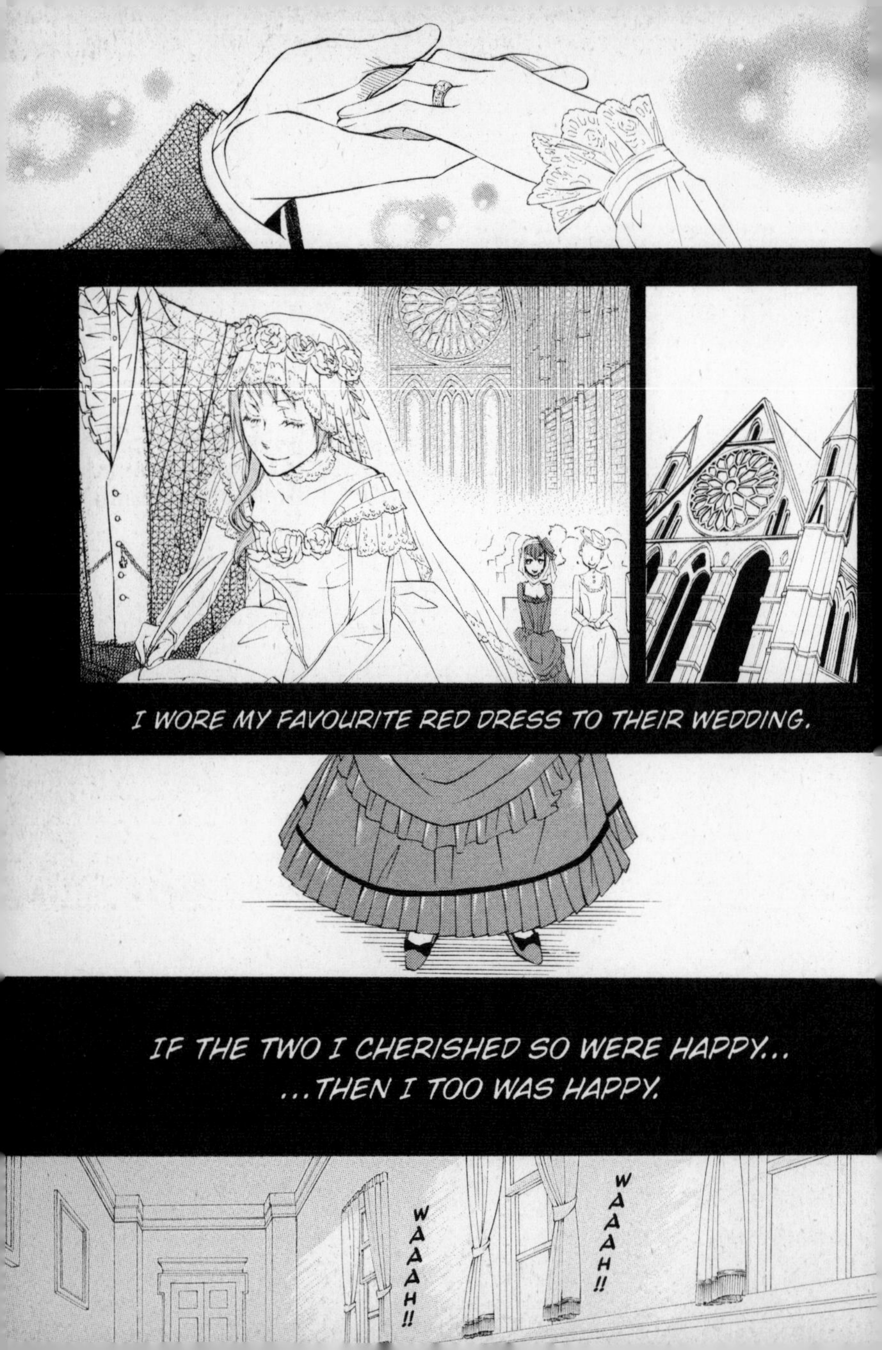

I WORE MY FAVOURITE RED DRESS TO THEIR WEDDING.
IF THE TWO I CHERISHED SO WERE HAPPY...
...THEN I TOO WAS HAPPY.
WAAAAH!!
WAAAAH!!

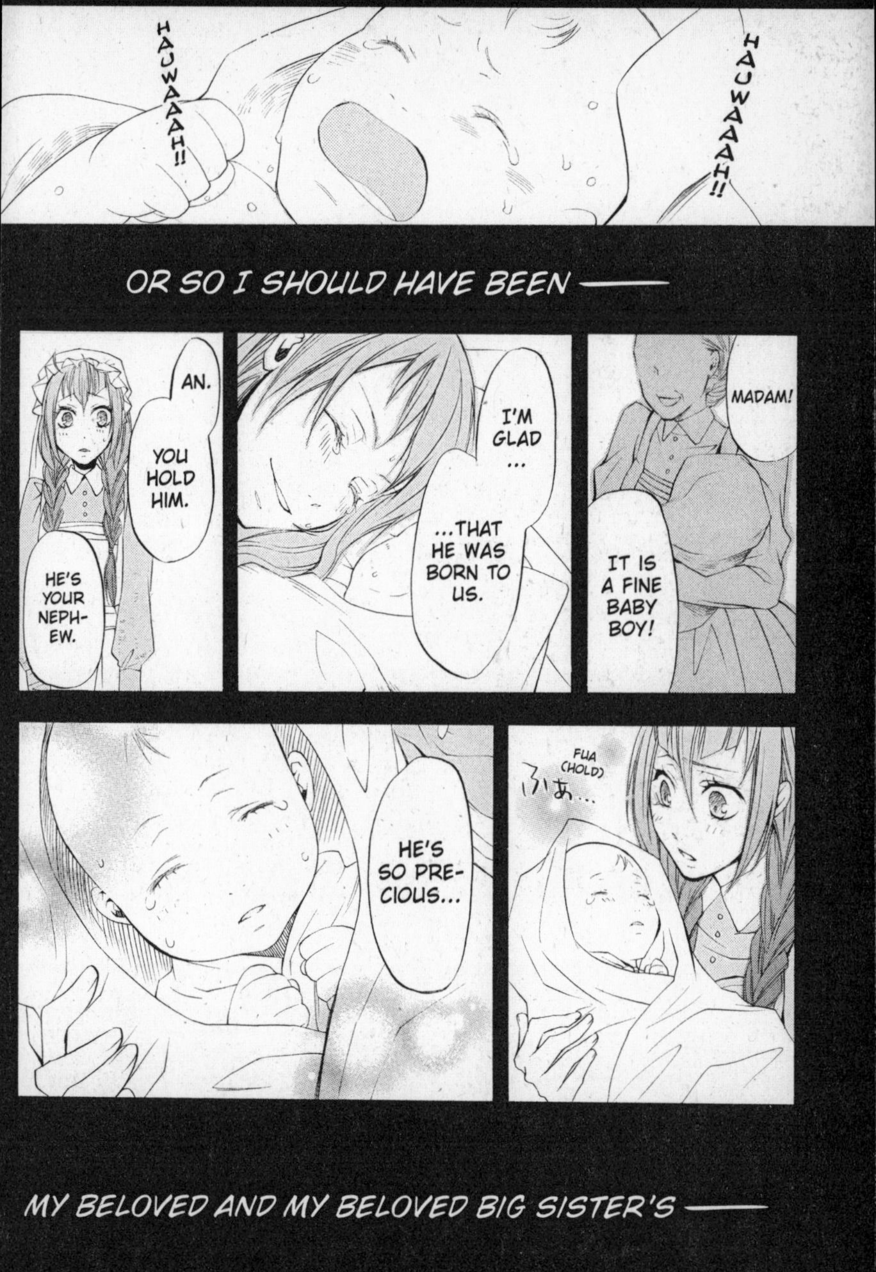
HAUWAAAAH!!
HAUWAAAH!!
OR SO I SHOULD HAVE BEEN ——
MADAM!
IT IS A FINE BABY BOY!
I'M GLAD...
...THAT HE WAS BORN TO US.
AN.
YOU HOLD HIM.
HE'S YOUR NEPH-EW.
ふあ…
FUA (HOLD)
HE'S SO PRE-CIOUS...
MY BELOVED AND MY BELOVED BIG SISTER'S ——

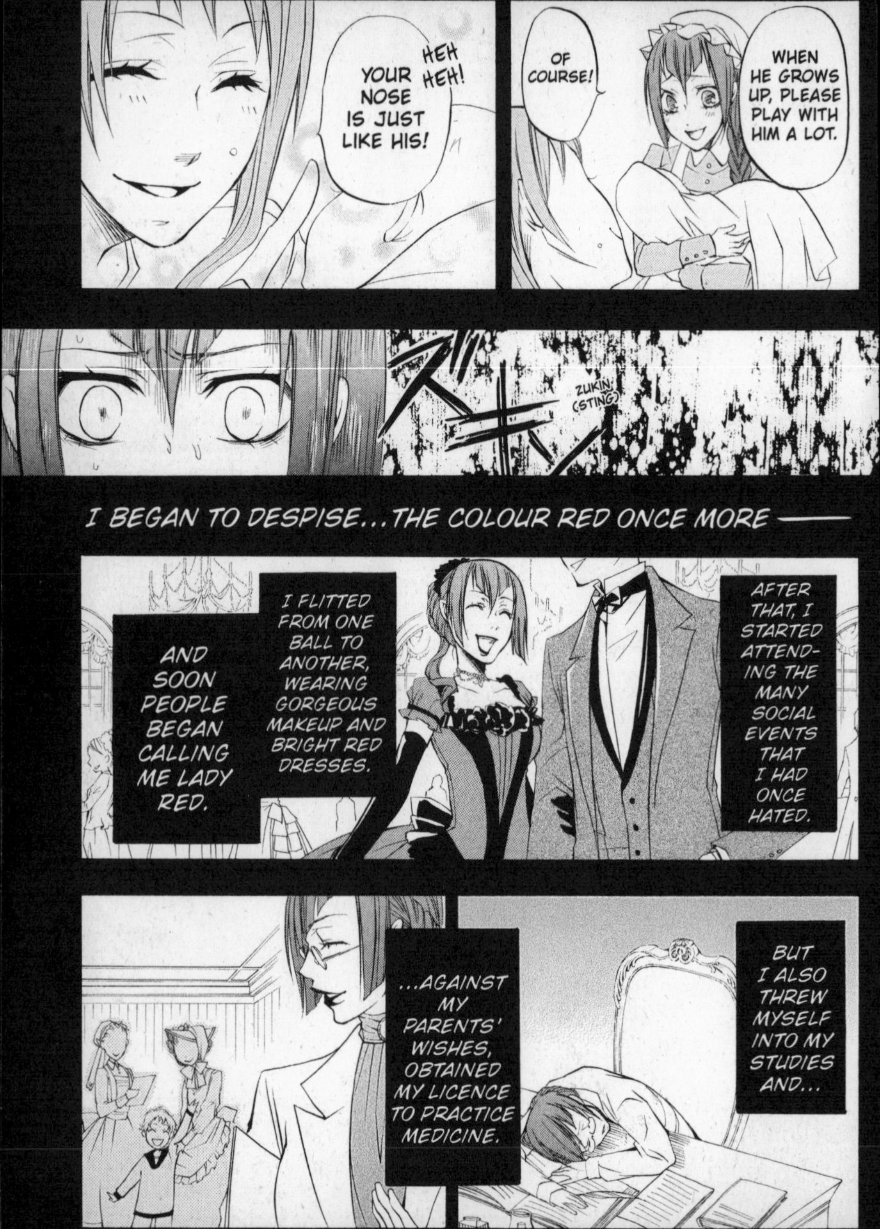
WHEN HE GROWS UP, PLEASE PLAY WITH HIM A LOT.
OF COURSE!
HEH HEH!
YOUR NOSE IS JUST LIKE HIS!
ZUKIN (STING)
I BEGAN TO DESPISE...THE COLOUR RED ONCE MORE ——
AFTER THAT, I STARTED ATTENDING THE MANY SOCIAL EVENTS THAT I HAD ONCE HATED.
I FLITTED FROM ONE BALL TO ANOTHER, WEARING GORGEOUS MAKEUP AND BRIGHT RED DRESSES.
AND SOON PEOPLE BEGAN CALLING ME LADY RED.
BUT I ALSO THREW MYSELF INTO MY STUDIES AND...
...AGAINST MY PARENTS' WISHES, OBTAINED MY LICENCE TO PRACTICE MEDICINE.

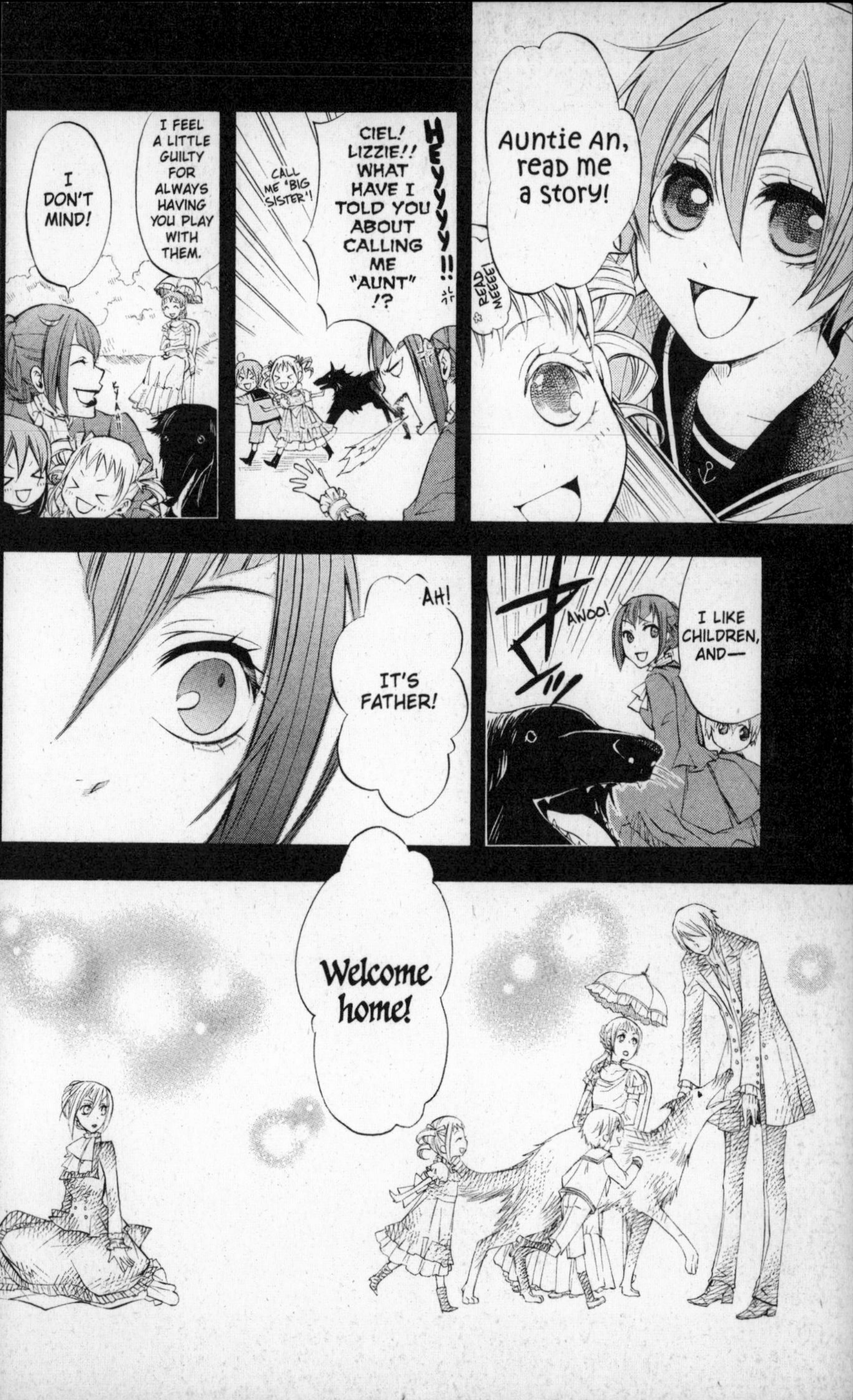

Auntie An, read me a story!
READ MEEEE!
HEYYYY!!
CIEL! LIZZIE!! WHAT HAVE I TOLD YOU ABOUT CALLING ME "AUNT" !?
CALL ME 'BIG SISTER'!
I FEEL A LITTLE GUILTY FOR ALWAYS HAVING YOU PLAY WITH THEM.
I DON'T MIND!
I LIKE CHILDREN, AND—
AWOO!
AH!
IT'S FATHER!
Welcome home!

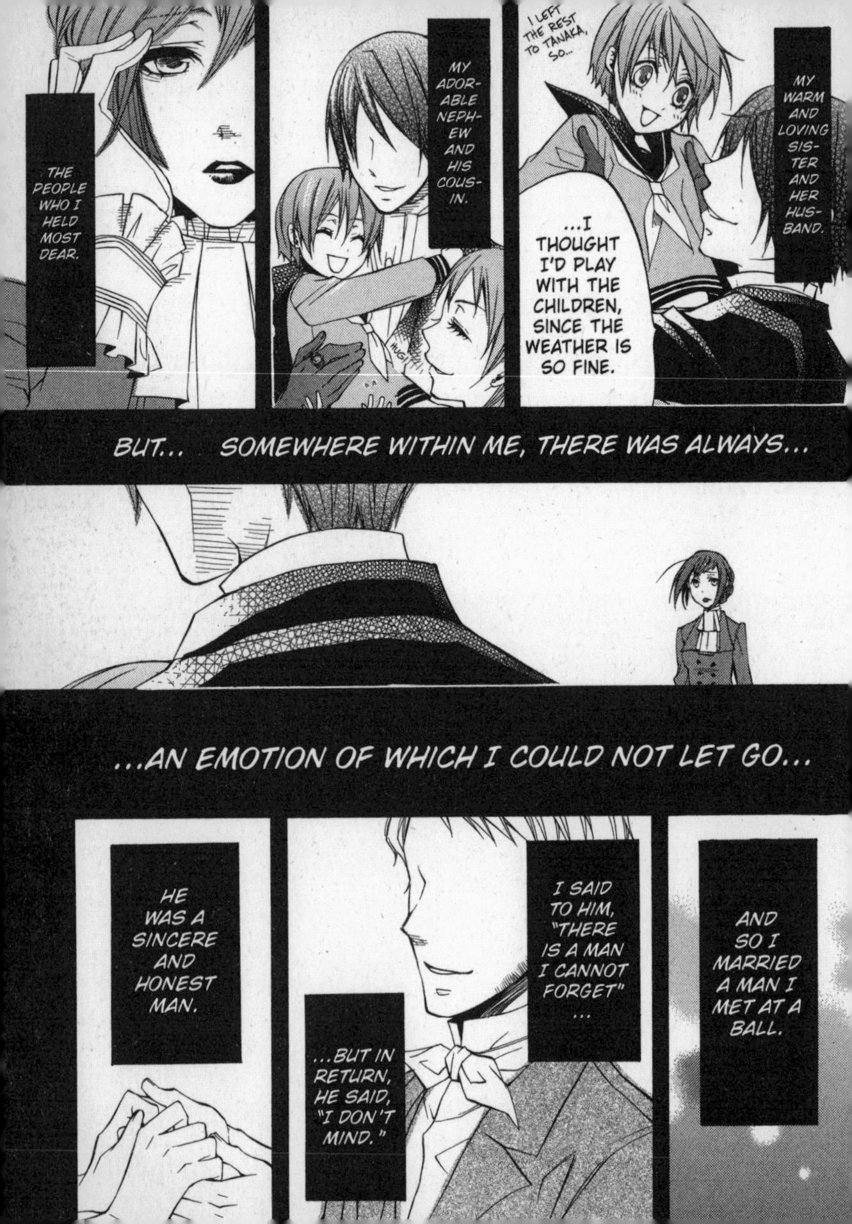
MY WARM AND LOVING SISTER AND HER HUSBAND.
I LEFT THE REST TO TANAKA, SO...
...I THOUGHT I'D PLAY WITH THE CHILDREN, SINCE THE WEATHER IS SO FINE.
MY ADORABLE NEPHEW AND HIS COUSIN.
HUG!
THE PEOPLE WHO I HELD MOST DEAR.
BUT... SOMEWHERE WITHIN ME, THERE WAS ALWAYS...
...AN EMOTION OF WHICH I COULD NOT LET GO...
AND SO I MARRIED A MAN I MET AT A BALL.
I SAID TO HIM, "THERE IS A MAN I CANNOT FORGET"...
...BUT IN RETURN, HE SAID, "I DON'T MIND."
HE WAS A SINCERE AND HONEST MAN.

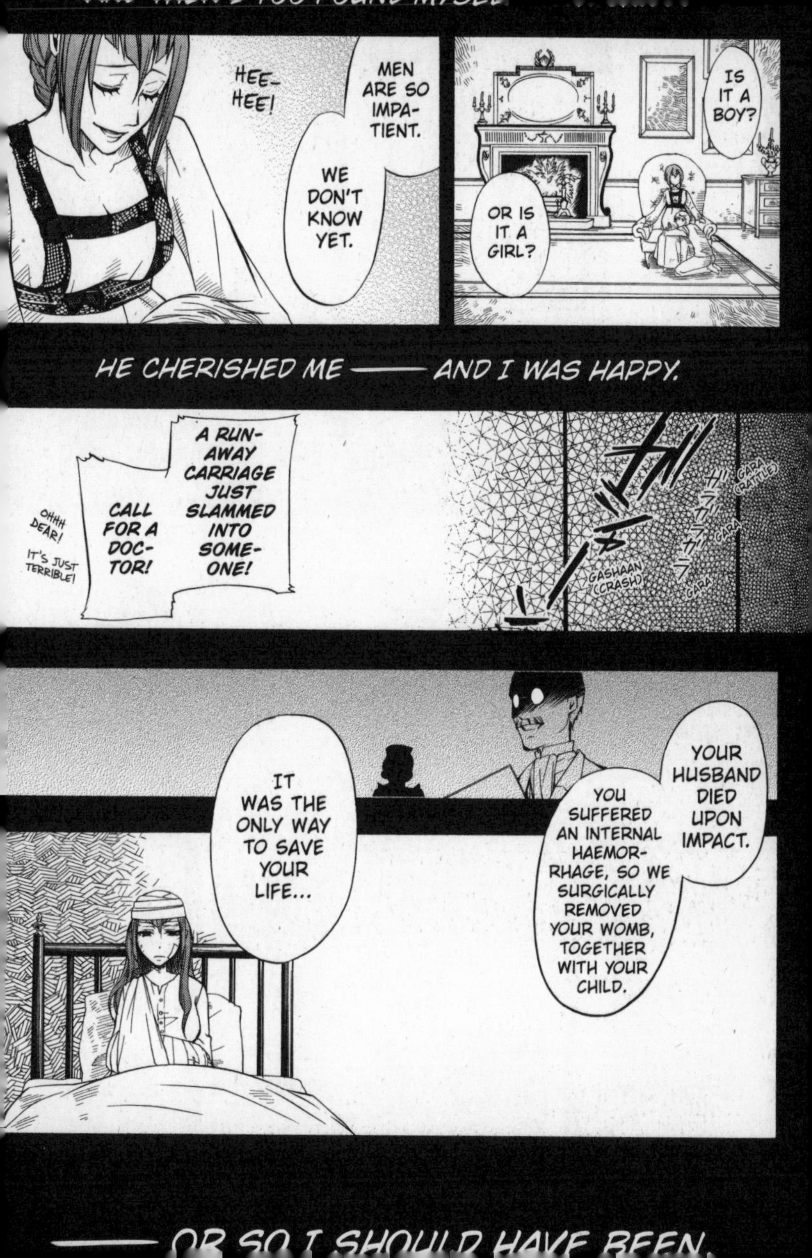
IS IT A BOY?
OR IS IT A GIRL?
MEN ARE SO IMPATIENT.
WE DON'T KNOW YET.
HEE-HEE!
HE CHERISHED ME —— AND I WAS HAPPY.
GARA (RATTLE)
GARA
GARA
GASHAAN (CRASH)
A RUNAWAY CARRIAGE JUST SLAMMED INTO SOMEONE!
CALL FOR A DOCTOR!
OHHH DEAR!
IT'S JUST TERRIBLE!
YOUR HUSBAND DIED UPON IMPACT.
YOU SUFFERED AN INTERNAL HAEMORRHAGE, SO WE SURGICALLY REMOVED YOUR WOMB, TOGETHER WITH YOUR CHILD.
IT WAS THE ONLY WAY TO SAVE YOUR LIFE...
—— OR SO I SHOULD HAVE BEEN.

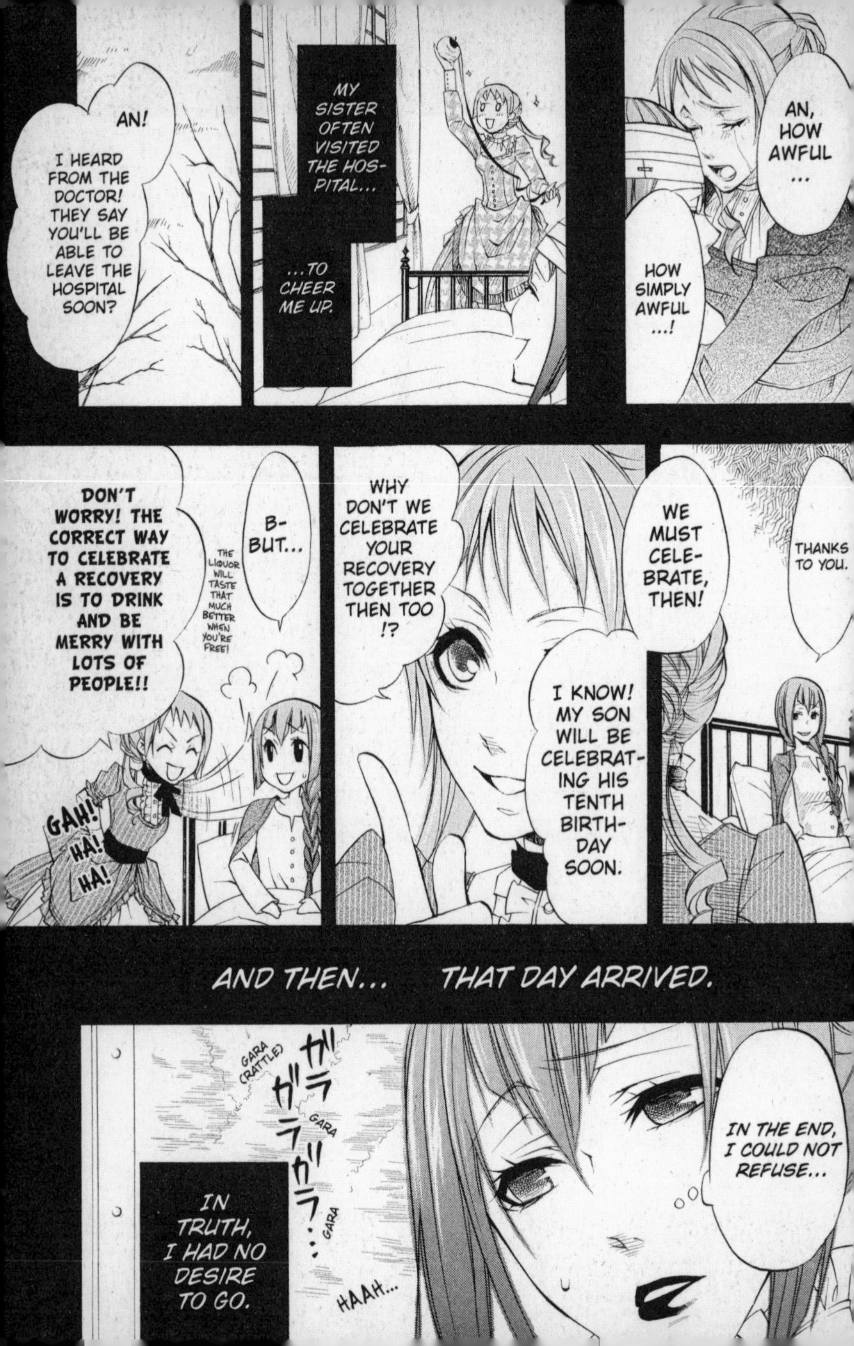
AN, HOW AWFUL ...
HOW SIMPLY AWFUL ...!
MY SISTER OFTEN VISITED THE HOSPITAL...
...TO CHEER ME UP.
AN!
I HEARD FROM THE DOCTOR! THEY SAY YOU'LL BE ABLE TO LEAVE THE HOSPITAL SOON?
THANKS TO YOU.
WE MUST CELEBRATE, THEN!
I KNOW! MY SON WILL BE CELEBRATING HIS TENTH BIRTHDAY SOON.
WHY DON'T WE CELEBRATE YOUR RECOVERY TOGETHER THEN TOO !?
B-BUT...
DON'T WORRY! THE CORRECT WAY TO CELEBRATE A RECOVERY IS TO DRINK AND BE MERRY WITH LOTS OF PEOPLE!!
THE LIQUOR WILL TASTE THAT MUCH BETTER WHEN YOU'RE FREE!
GAH! HA! HA!
AND THEN... THAT DAY ARRIVED.
IN THE END, I COULD NOT REFUSE...
ガラ ガラ ガラ ガラ...
GARA (RATTLE)
GARA
GARA
HAAH...
IN TRUTH, I HAD NO DESIRE TO GO.

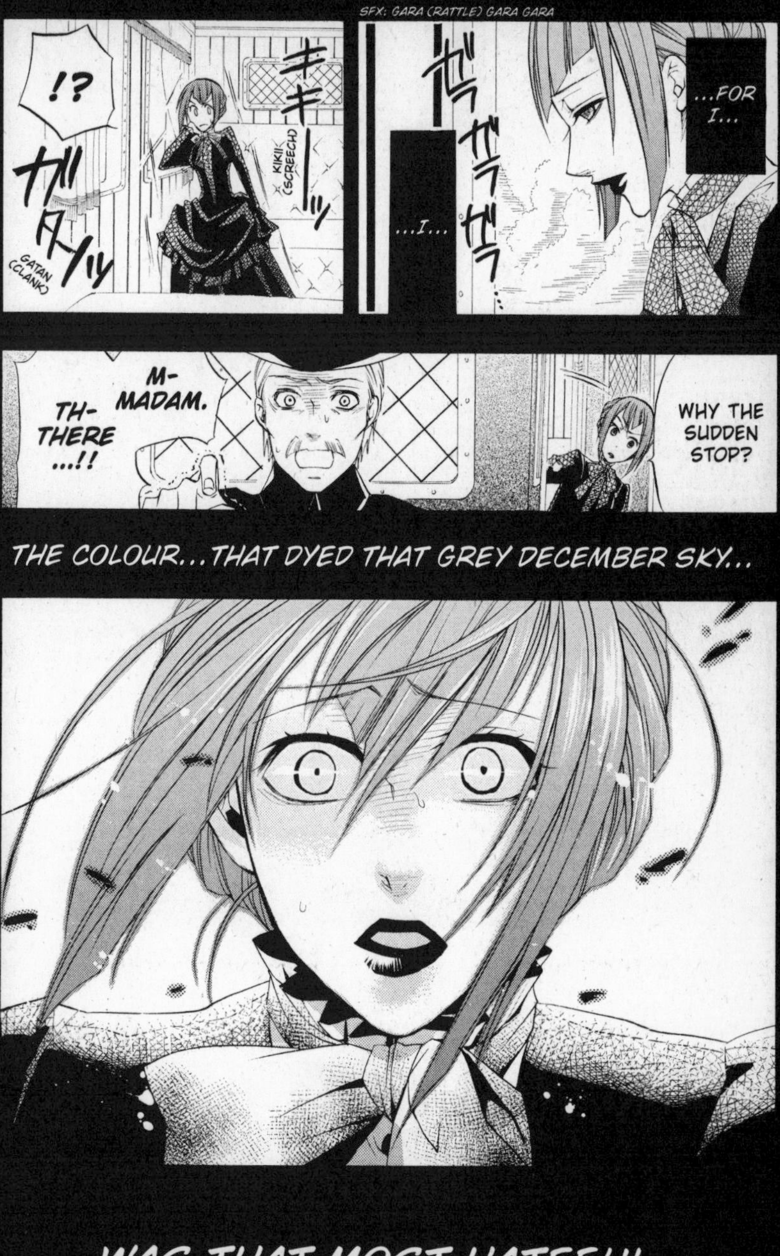
SFX: GARA (RATTLE) GARA GARA
...FOR I...
...I...
!?
KIKII (SCREECH)
GATAN (CLANK)
WHY THE SUDDEN STOP?
M-MADAM.
TH-THERE ...!!
THE COLOUR...THAT DYED THAT GREY DECEMBER SKY...
...WAS THAT MOST HATEFUL....

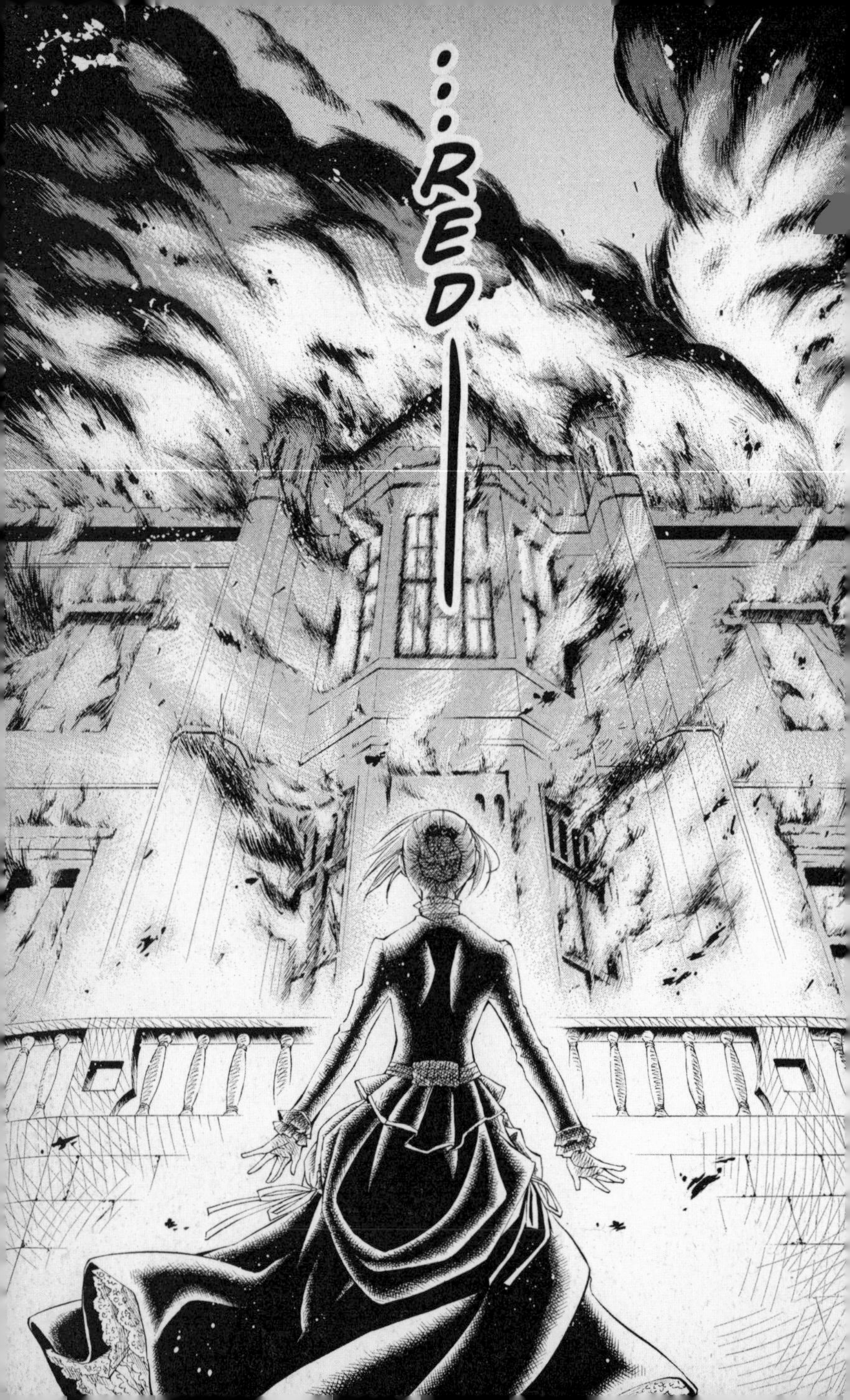
...RED—

Black Butler

Chapter 11

At noon : The Butler, Retrospective

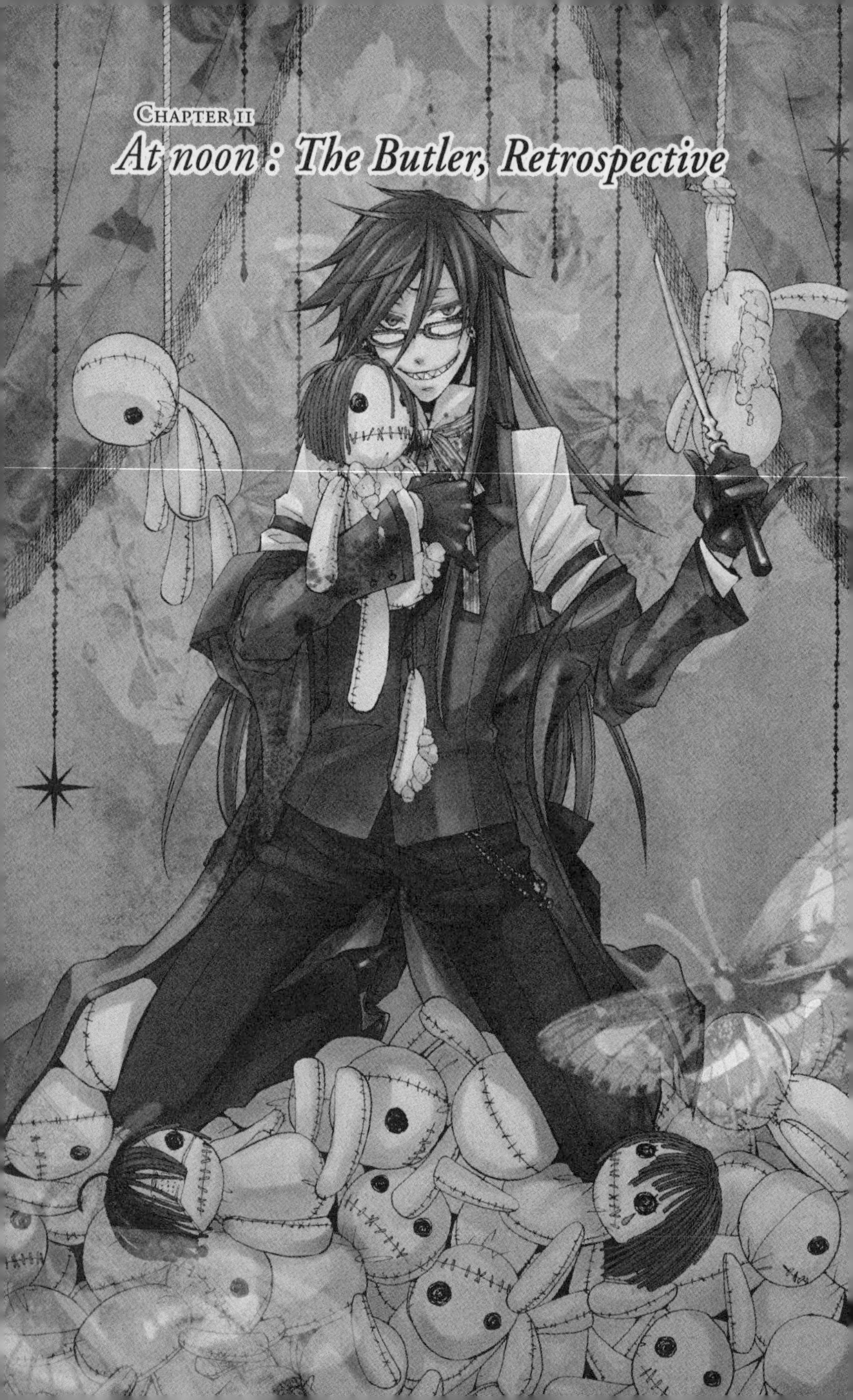

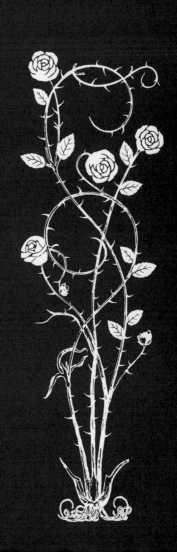

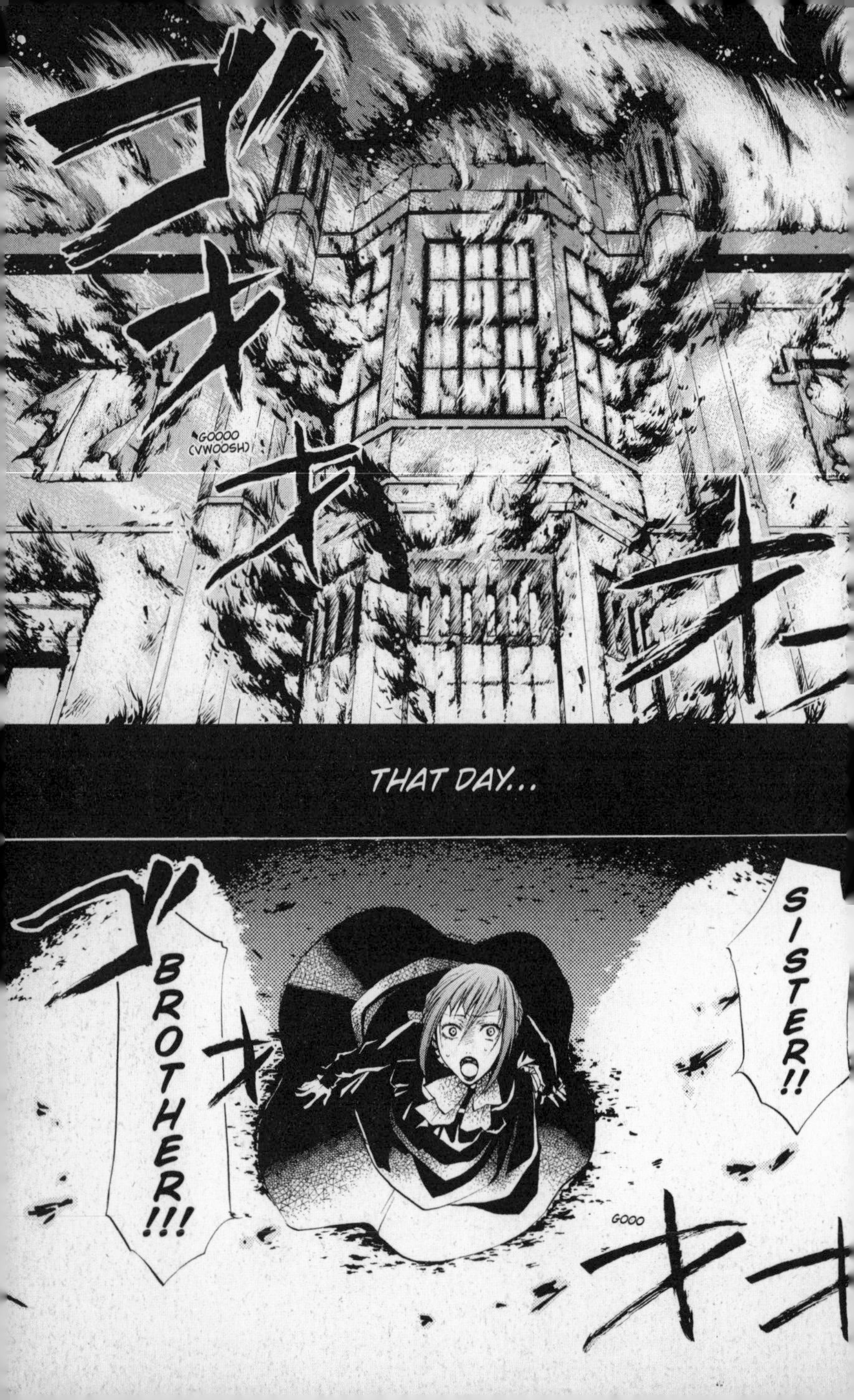
GOOOO (VWOOSH)
THAT DAY...
SISTER!!
BROTHER!!!
GOOO

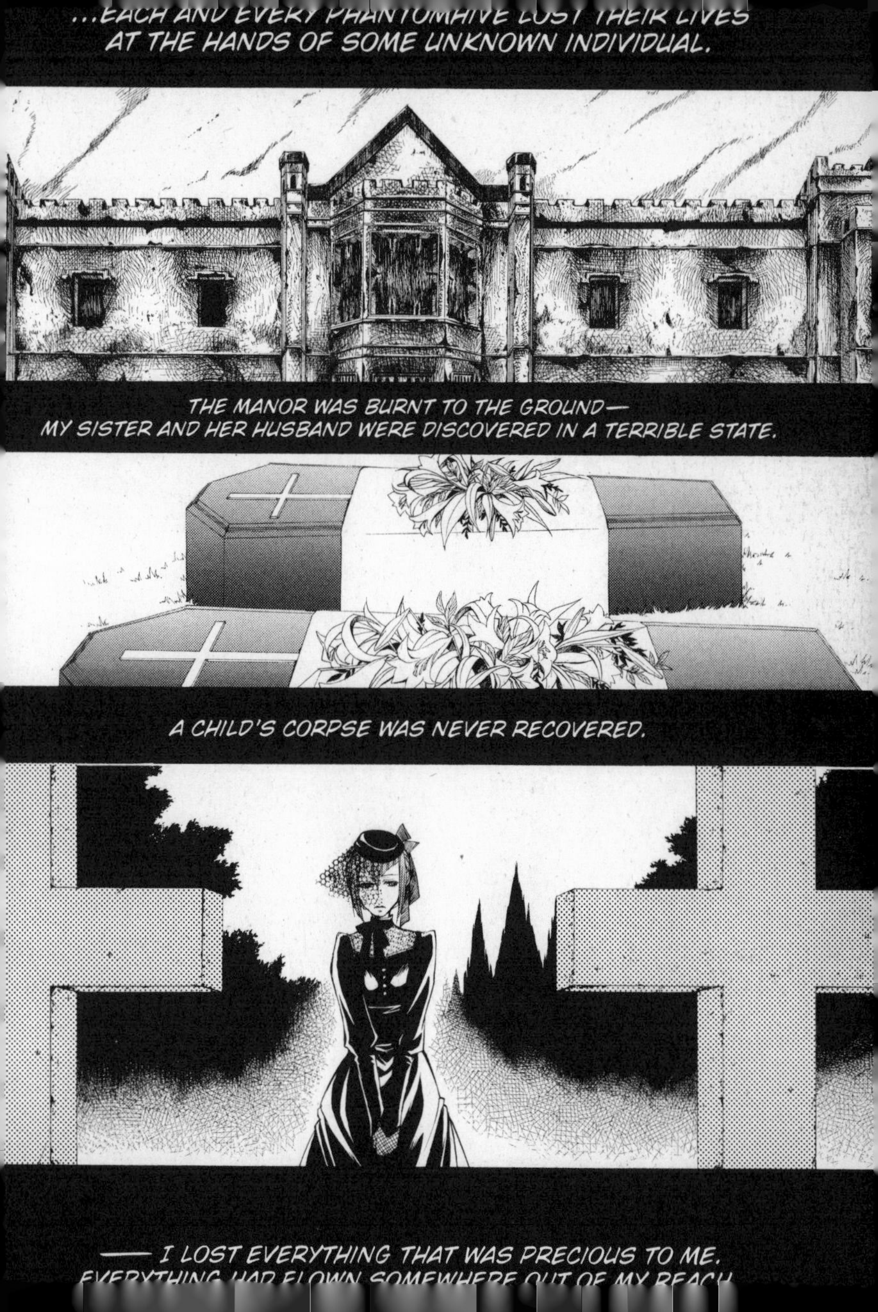
...EACH AND EVERY PHANTOMHIVE LOST THEIR LIVES AT THE HANDS OF SOME UNKNOWN INDIVIDUAL.
THE MANOR WAS BURNT TO THE GROUND— MY SISTER AND HER HUSBAND WERE DISCOVERED IN A TERRIBLE STATE.
A CHILD'S CORPSE WAS NEVER RECOVERED.
—— I LOST EVERYTHING THAT WAS PRECIOUS TO ME. EVERYTHING HAD FLOWN SOMEWHERE OUT OF MY REACH.

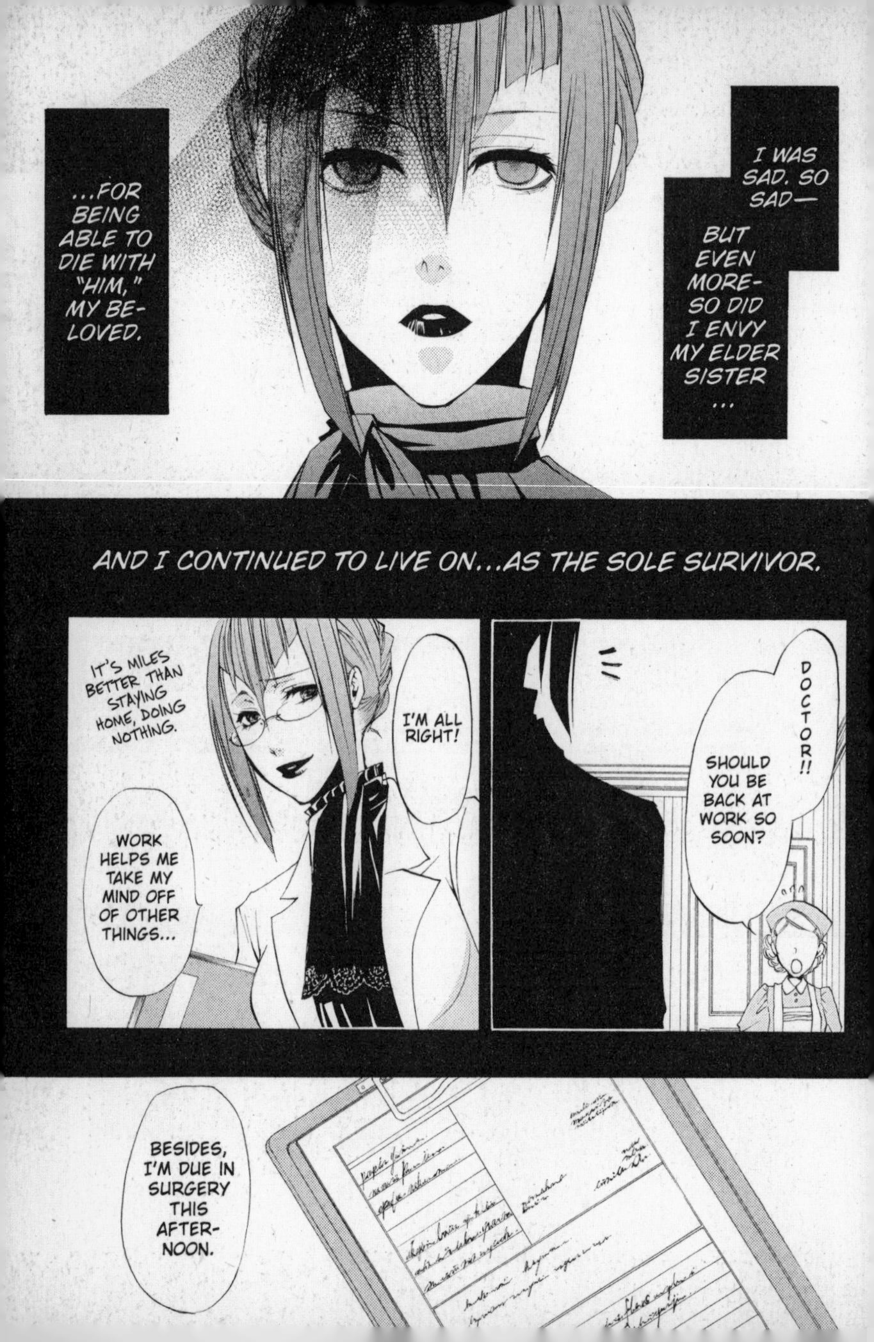
I WAS SAD. SO SAD—
BUT EVEN MORE-SO DID I ENVY MY ELDER SISTER...
...FOR BEING ABLE TO DIE WITH "HIM," MY BE-LOVED.
AND I CONTINUED TO LIVE ON...AS THE SOLE SURVIVOR.
DOCTOR!!
SHOULD YOU BE BACK AT WORK SO SOON?
I'M ALL RIGHT!
IT'S MILES BETTER THAN STAYING HOME, DOING NOTHING.
WORK HELPS ME TAKE MY MIND OFF OF OTHER THINGS...
BESIDES, I'M DUE IN SURGERY THIS AFTERNOON.

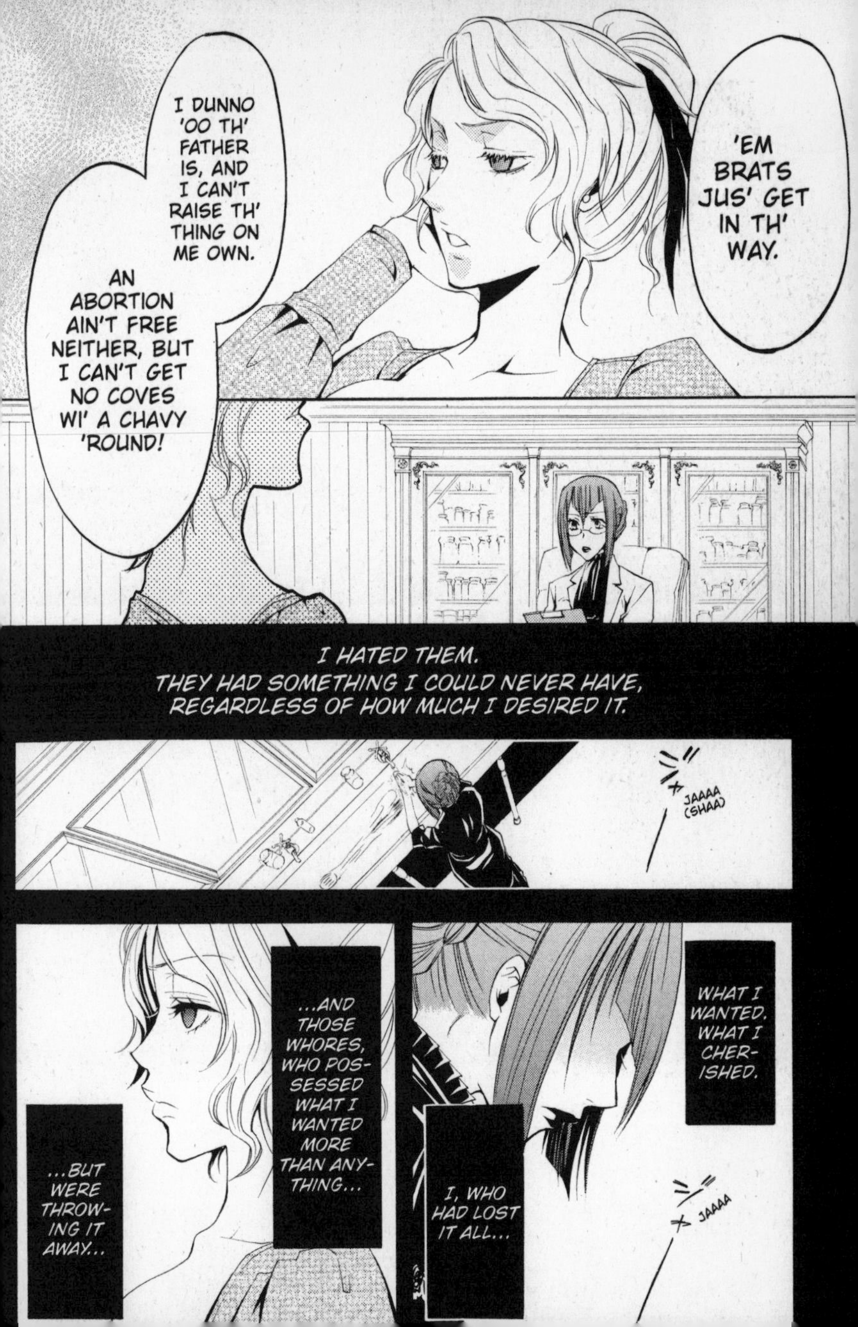
'EM BRATS JUS' GET IN TH' WAY.
I DUNNO 'OO TH' FATHER IS, AND I CAN'T RAISE TH' THING ON ME OWN.
AN ABORTION AIN'T FREE NEITHER, BUT I CAN'T GET NO COVES WI' A CHAVY 'ROUND!
I HATED THEM.
THEY HAD SOMETHING I COULD NEVER HAVE,
REGARDLESS OF HOW MUCH I DESIRED IT.
JAAAA (SHAA)
WHAT I WANTED. WHAT I CHER-ISHED.
I, WHO HAD LOST IT ALL...
JAAAA
...AND THOSE WHORES, WHO POS-SESSED WHAT I WANTED MORE THAN ANY-THING...
...BUT WERE THROWING IT AWAY...

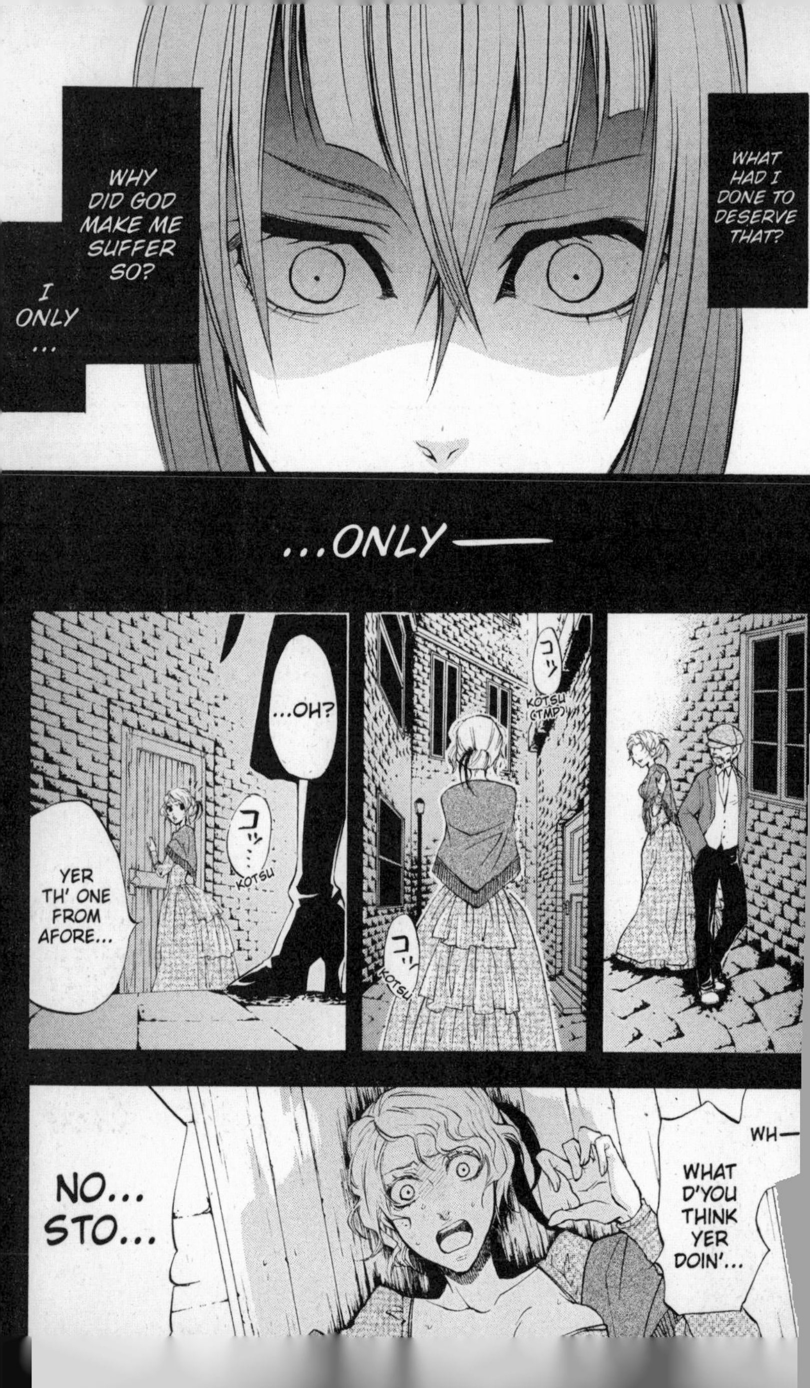
WHAT HAD I DONE TO DESERVE THAT?
WHY DID GOD MAKE ME SUFFER SO?
I ONLY ...
...ONLY—
コッ
KOTSU (TMP)
コッ
KOTSU
...OH?
コッ
KOTSU
YER TH' ONE FROM AFORE...
WH—
WHAT D'YOU THINK YER DOIN'...
NO... STO...

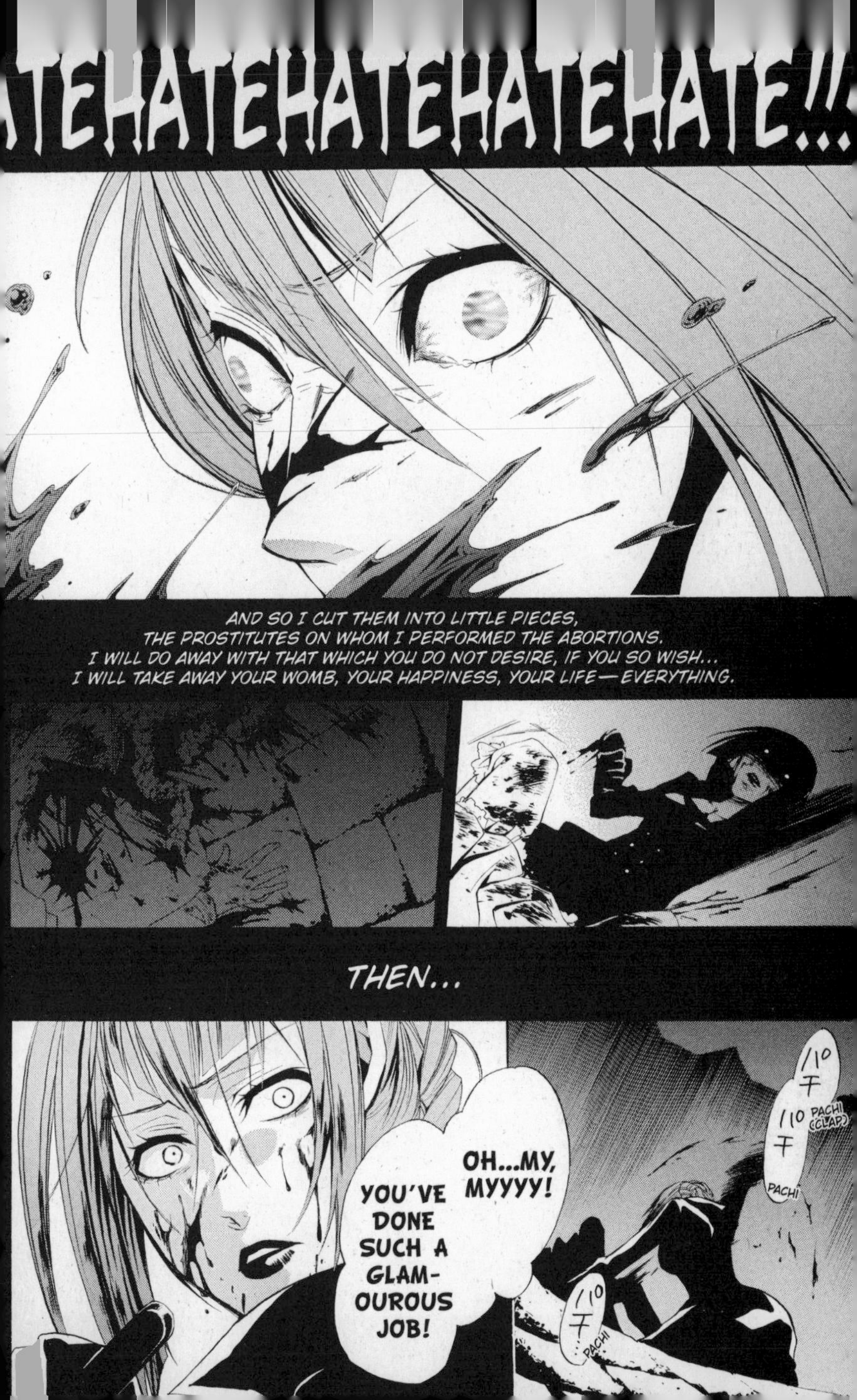
TEHATEHATEHATEHATE!!!
AND SO I CUT THEM INTO LITTLE PIECES,
THE PROSTITUTES ON WHOM I PERFORMED THE ABORTIONS.
I WILL DO AWAY WITH THAT WHICH YOU DO NOT DESIRE, IF YOU SO WISH...
I WILL TAKE AWAY YOUR WOMB, YOUR HAPPINESS, YOUR LIFE—EVERYTHING.
THEN...
PACHI (CLAP)
PACHI
PACHI
OH...MY, MYYYY!
YOU'VE DONE SUCH A GLAMOUROUS JOB!

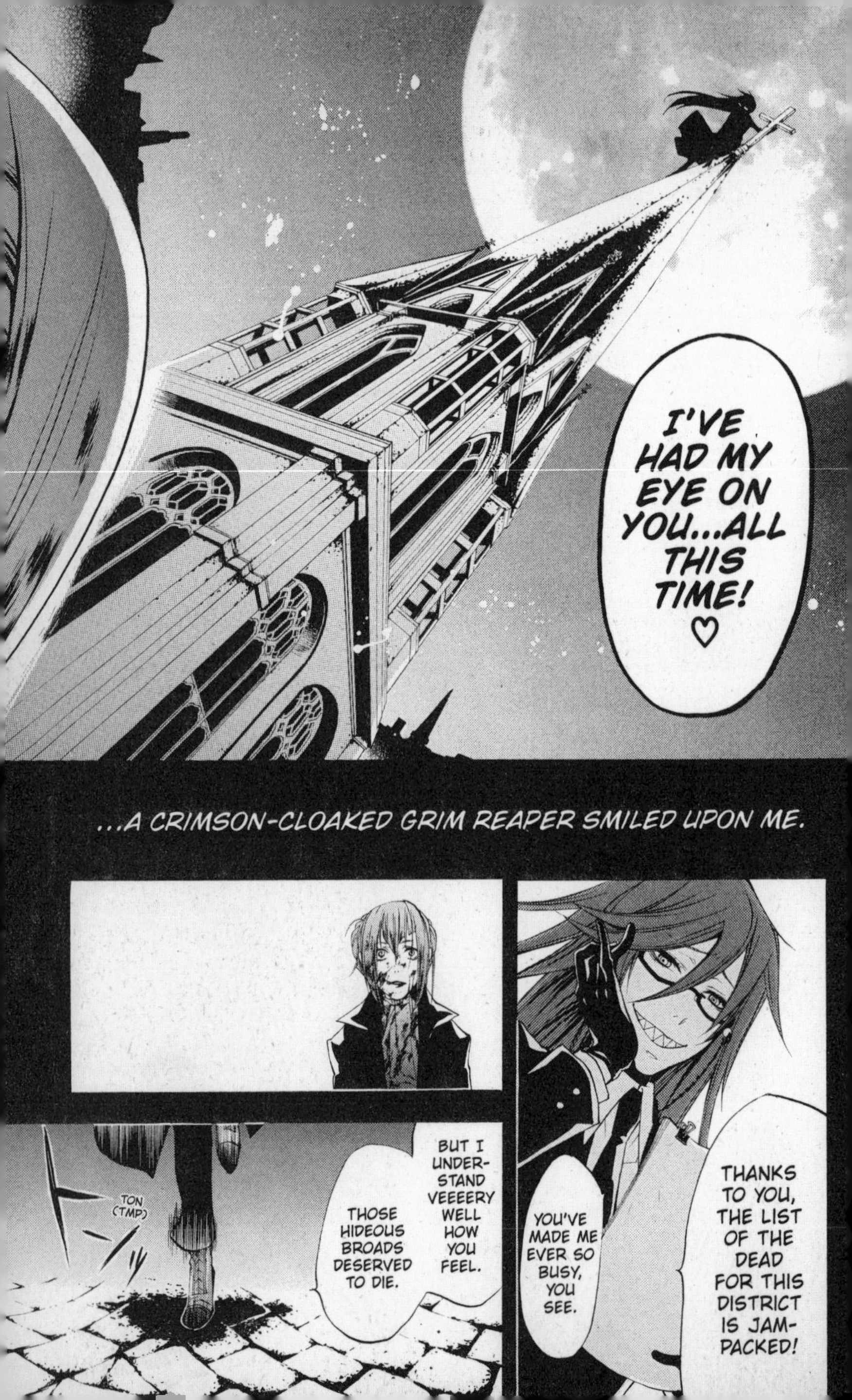
I'VE HAD MY EYE ON YOU...ALL THIS TIME! ♡
...A CRIMSON-CLOAKED GRIM REAPER SMILED UPON ME.
THANKS TO YOU, THE LIST OF THE DEAD FOR THIS DISTRICT IS JAM-PACKED!
YOU'VE MADE ME EVER SO BUSY, YOU SEE.
BUT I UNDER-STAND VEEEERY WELL HOW YOU FEEL.
THOSE HIDEOUS BROADS DESERVED TO DIE.
TON (TMP)

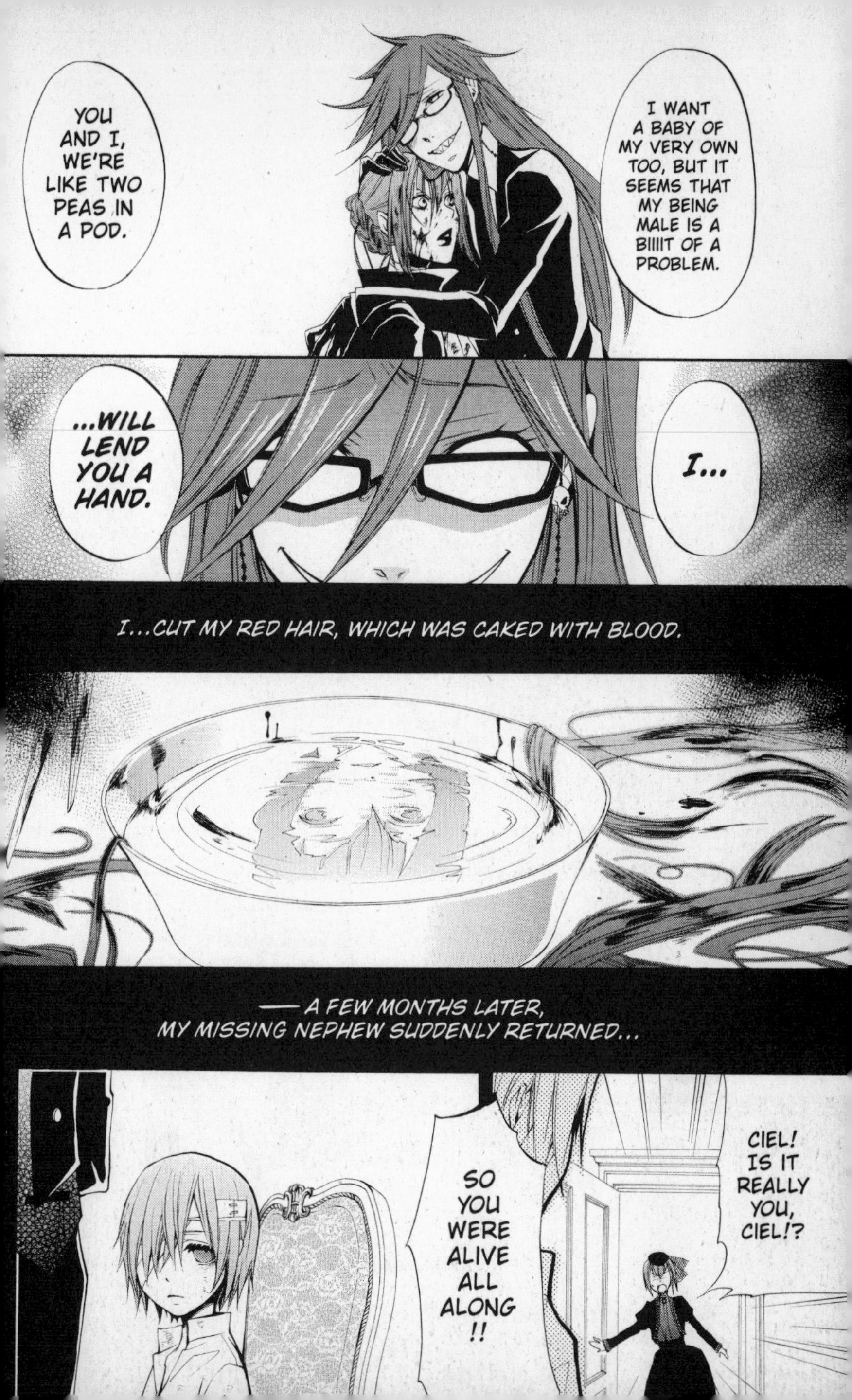
I WANT A BABY OF MY VERY OWN TOO, BUT IT SEEMS THAT MY BEING MALE IS A BIIIIT OF A PROBLEM.
YOU AND I, WE'RE LIKE TWO PEAS IN A POD.
I...
...WILL LEND YOU A HAND.
I...CUT MY RED HAIR, WHICH WAS CAKED WITH BLOOD.
—A FEW MONTHS LATER, MY MISSING NEPHEW SUDDENLY RETURNED...
CIEL! IS IT REALLY YOU, CIEL!?
SO YOU WERE ALIVE ALL ALONG!!

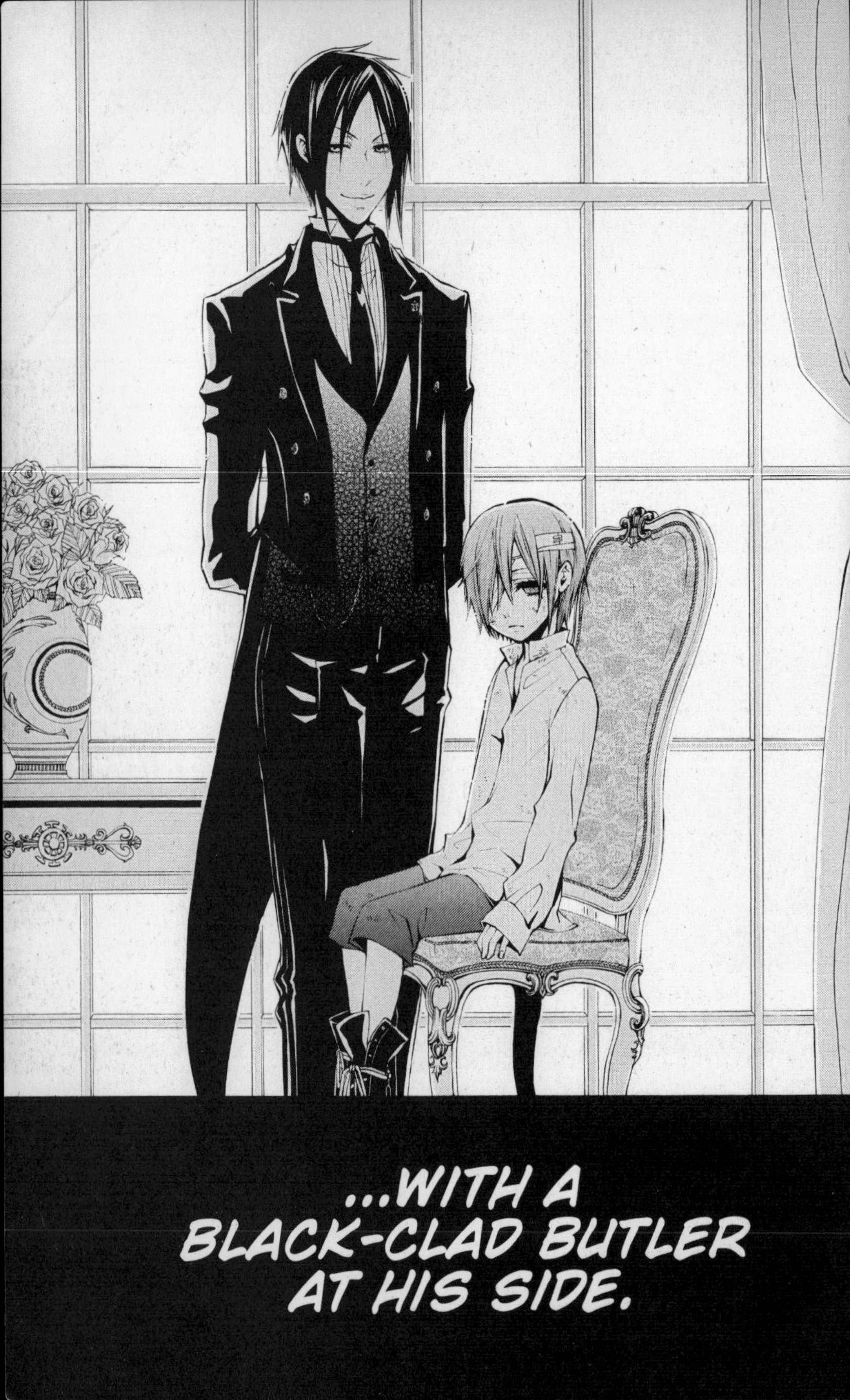

...WITH A
BLACK-CLAD BUTLER
AT HIS SIDE.

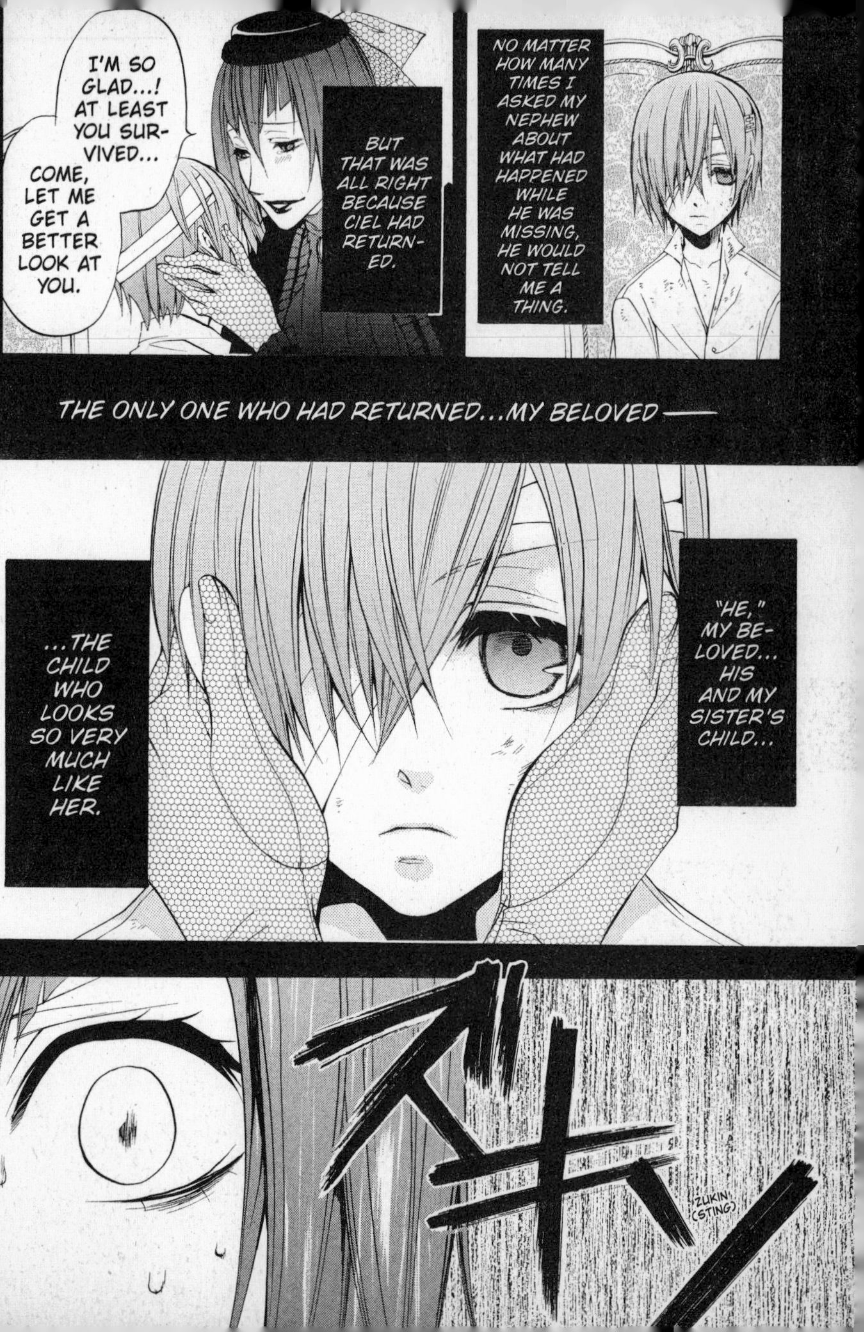
NO MATTER HOW MANY TIMES I ASKED MY NEPHEW ABOUT WHAT HAD HAPPENED WHILE HE WAS MISSING, HE WOULD NOT TELL ME A THING.
BUT THAT WAS ALL RIGHT BECAUSE CIEL HAD RETURN-ED.
I'M SO GLAD...! AT LEAST YOU SUR-VIVED...
COME, LET ME GET A BETTER LOOK AT YOU.
THE ONLY ONE WHO HAD RETURNED...MY BELOVED—
"HE," MY BE-LOVED... HIS AND MY SISTER'S CHILD...
...THE CHILD WHO LOOKS SO VERY MUCH LIKE HER.
ZUKIN (STING)

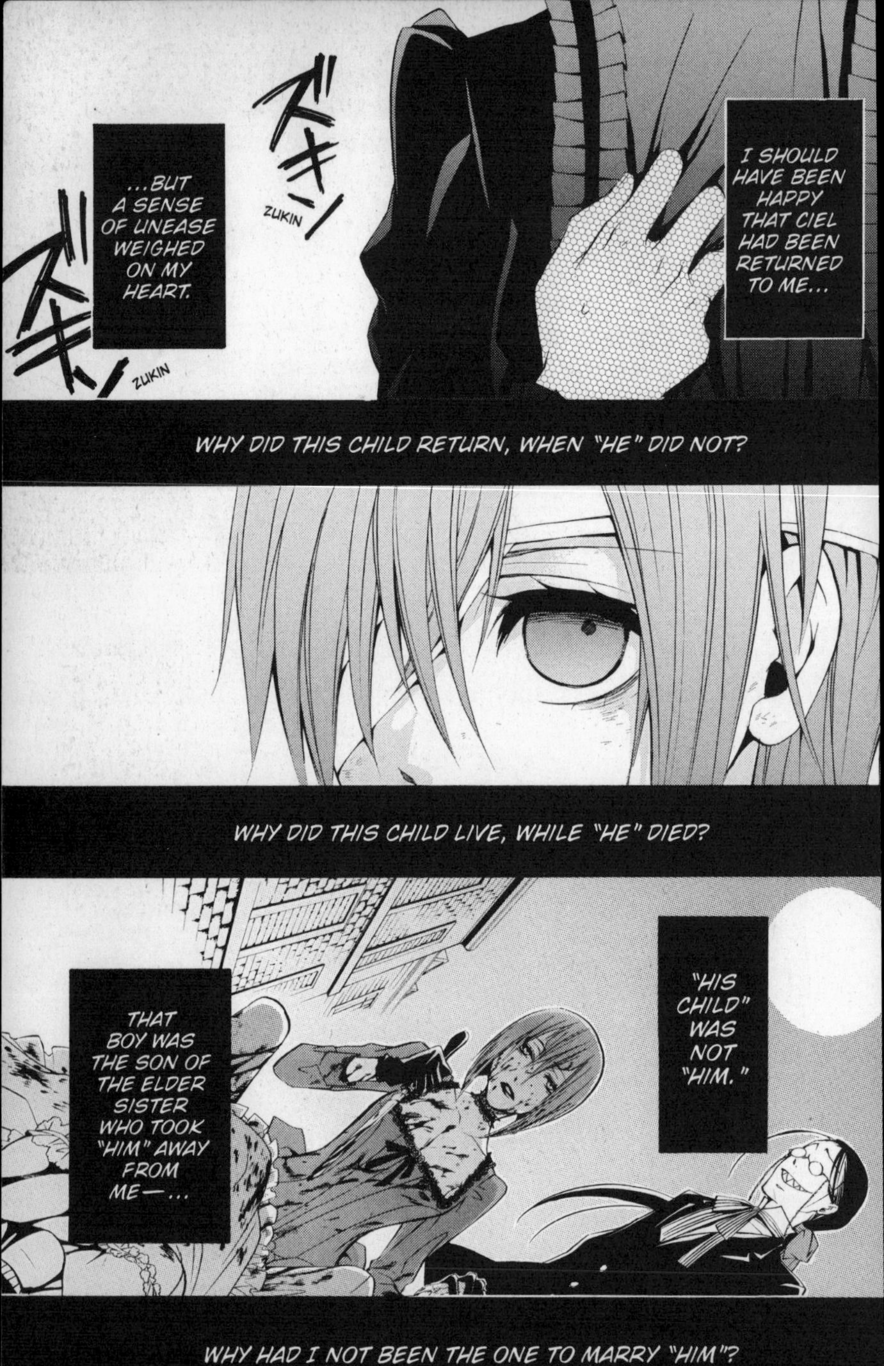
I SHOULD HAVE BEEN HAPPY THAT CIEL HAD BEEN RETURNED TO ME…
ズキン
ZUKIN
…BUT A SENSE OF UNEASE WEIGHED ON MY HEART.
ズキン
ZUKIN
WHY DID THIS CHILD RETURN, WHEN "HE" DID NOT?
WHY DID THIS CHILD LIVE, WHILE "HE" DIED?
"HIS CHILD" WAS NOT "HIM."
THAT BOY WAS THE SON OF THE ELDER SISTER WHO TOOK "HIM" AWAY FROM ME—…
WHY HAD I NOT BEEN THE ONE TO MARRY "HIM"?

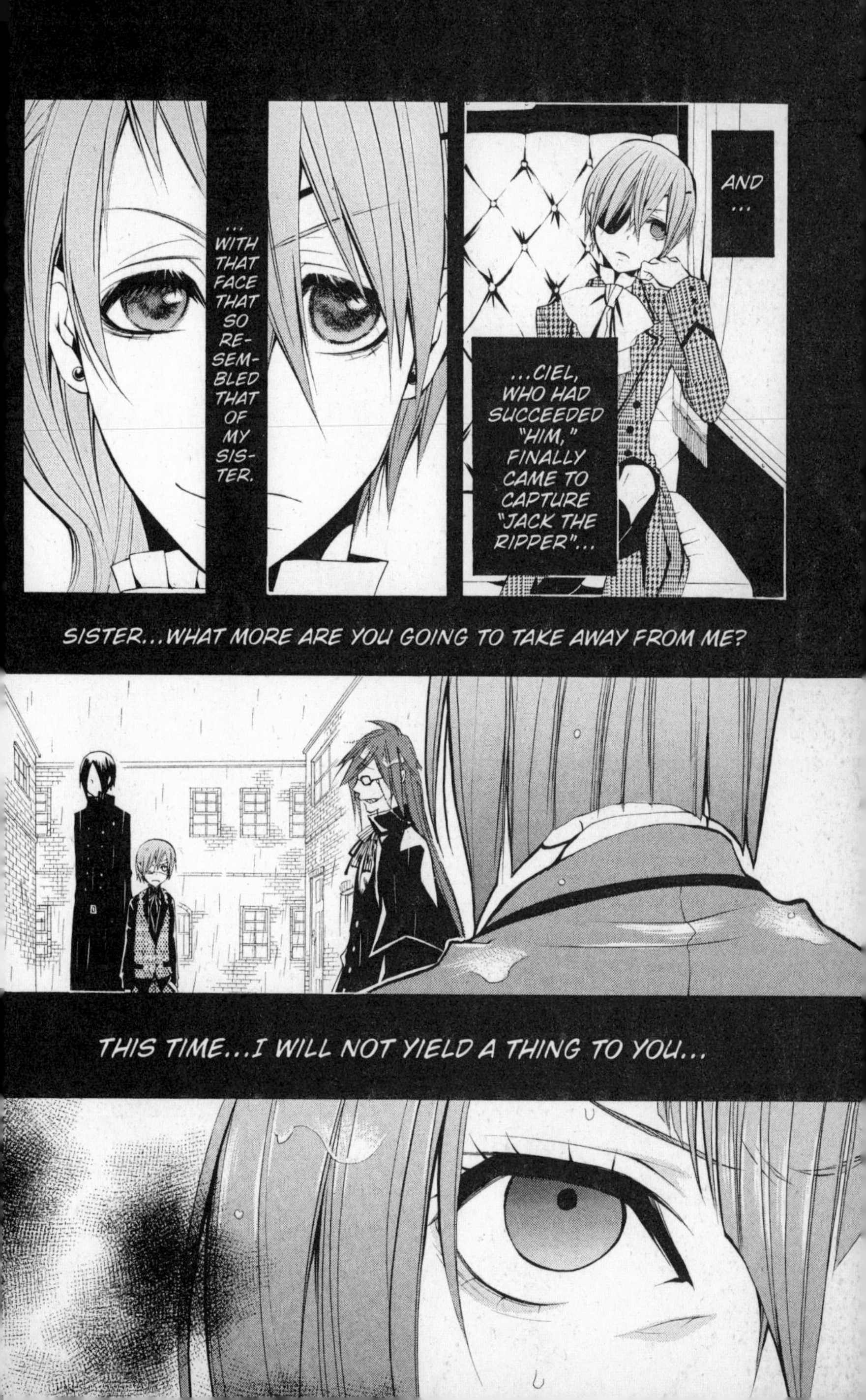
AND...
...CIEL, WHO HAD SUCCEEDED "HIM," FINALLY CAME TO CAPTURE "JACK THE RIPPER"...
...WITH THAT FACE THAT SO RE-SEM-BLED THAT OF MY SIS-TER.
SISTER...WHAT MORE ARE YOU GOING TO TAKE AWAY FROM ME?
THIS TIME...I WILL NOT YIELD A THING TO YOU...

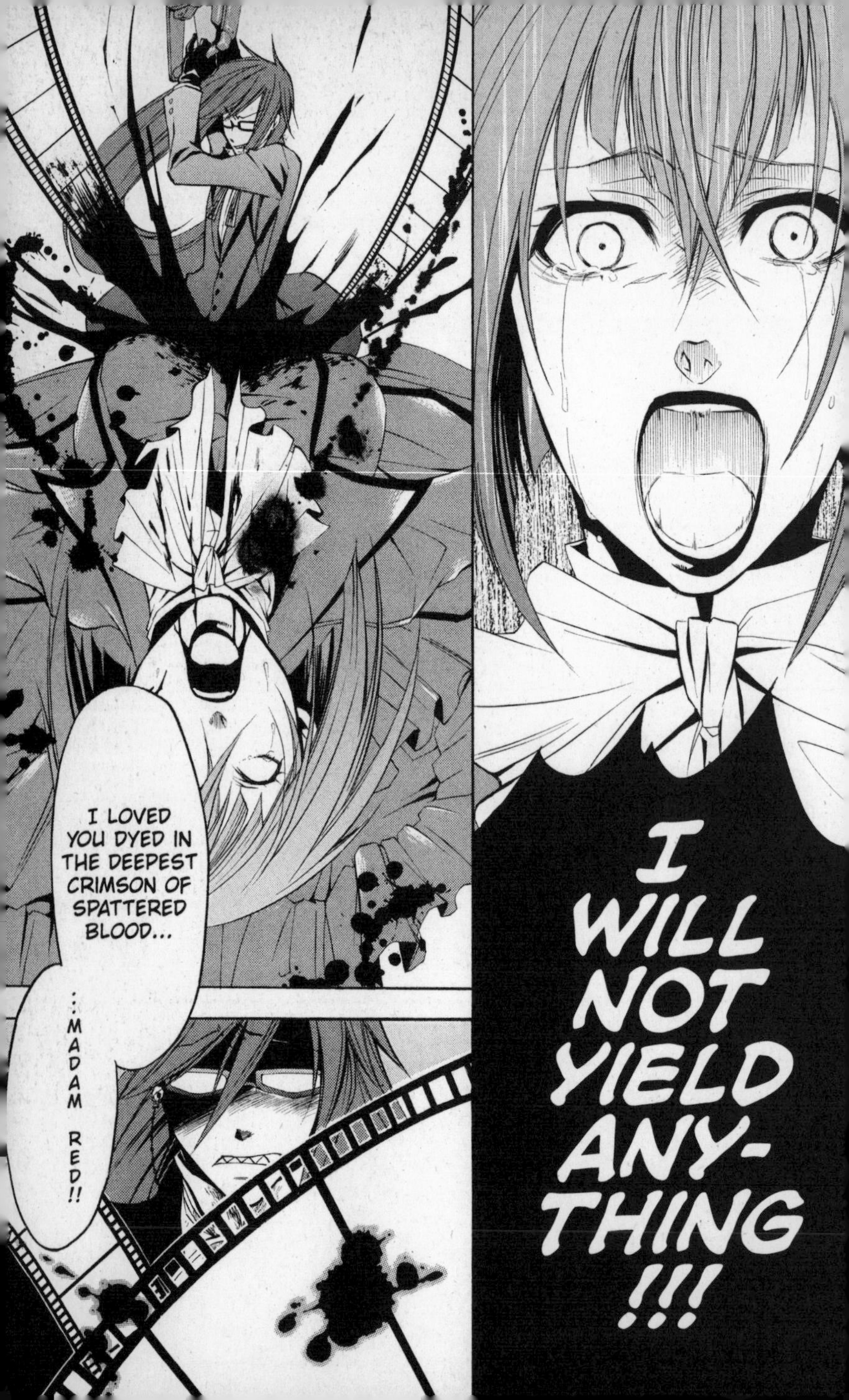
I WILL NOT YIELD ANYTHING!!!
I LOVED YOU DYED IN THE DEEPEST CRIMSON OF SPATTERED BLOOD...
...MADAM RED!!

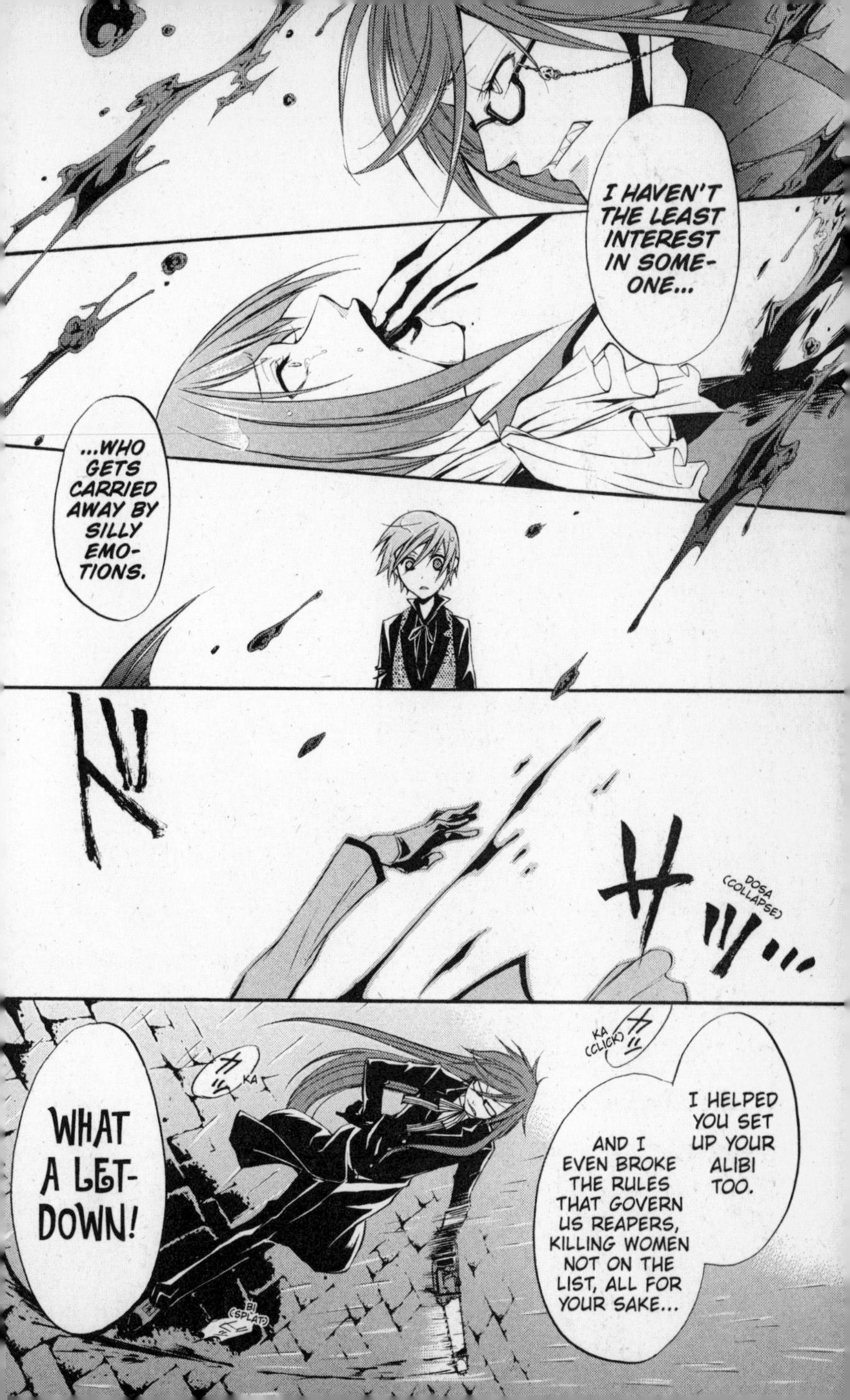
I HAVEN'T THE LEAST INTEREST IN SOME-ONE...
...WHO GETS CARRIED AWAY BY SILLY EMO-TIONS.
ドサッ
DOSA (COLLAPSE)
カッ
KA (CLICK)
I HELPED YOU SET UP YOUR ALIBI TOO.
AND I EVEN BROKE THE RULES THAT GOVERN US REAPERS, KILLING WOMEN NOT ON THE LIST, ALL FOR YOUR SAKE...
カッ
KA
WHAT A LET-DOWN!
BI (SPLAT)

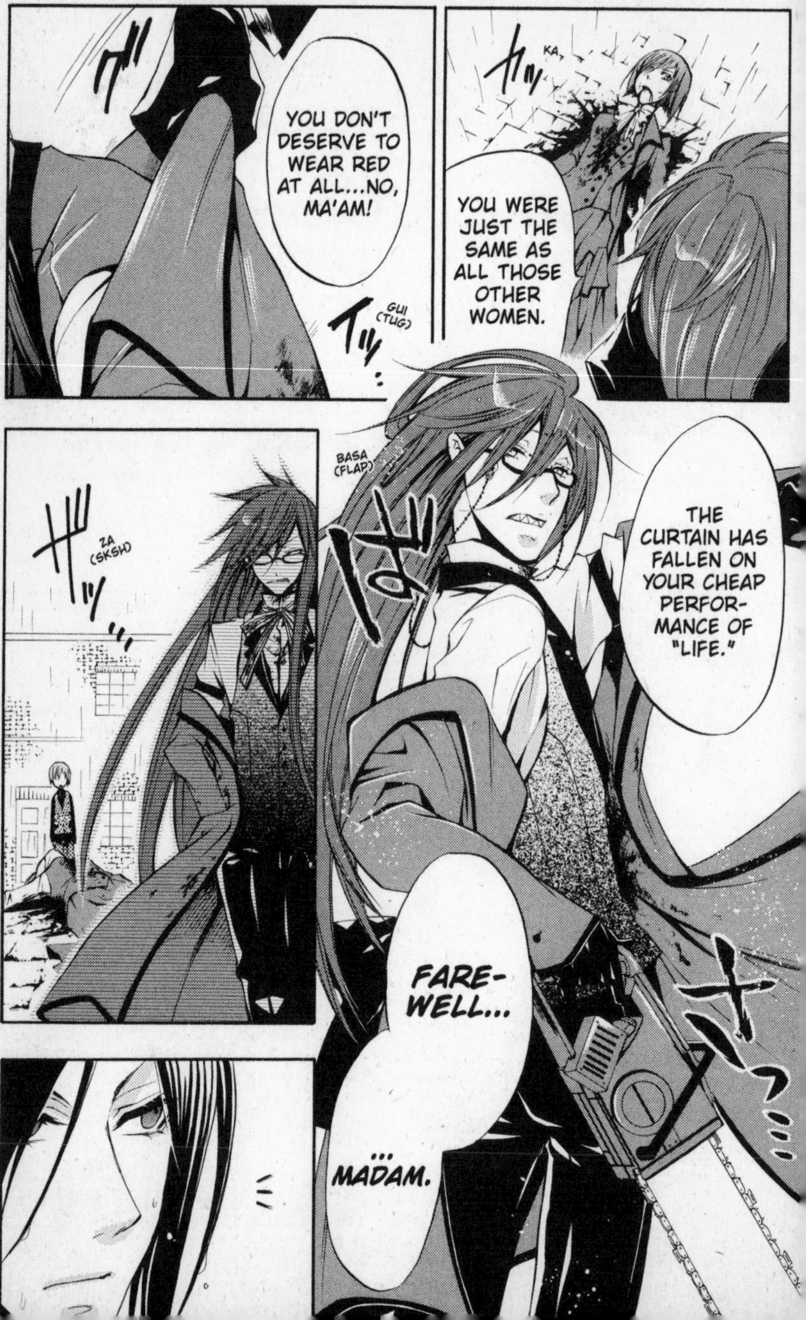
KA,
YOU WERE JUST THE SAME AS ALL THOSE OTHER WOMEN.
YOU DON'T DESERVE TO WEAR RED AT ALL...NO, MA'AM!
GUI (TUG)
THE CURTAIN HAS FALLEN ON YOUR CHEAP PERFOR-MANCE OF "LIFE."
BASA (FLAP)
FARE-WELL...
...MADAM.
ZA (SKSH)

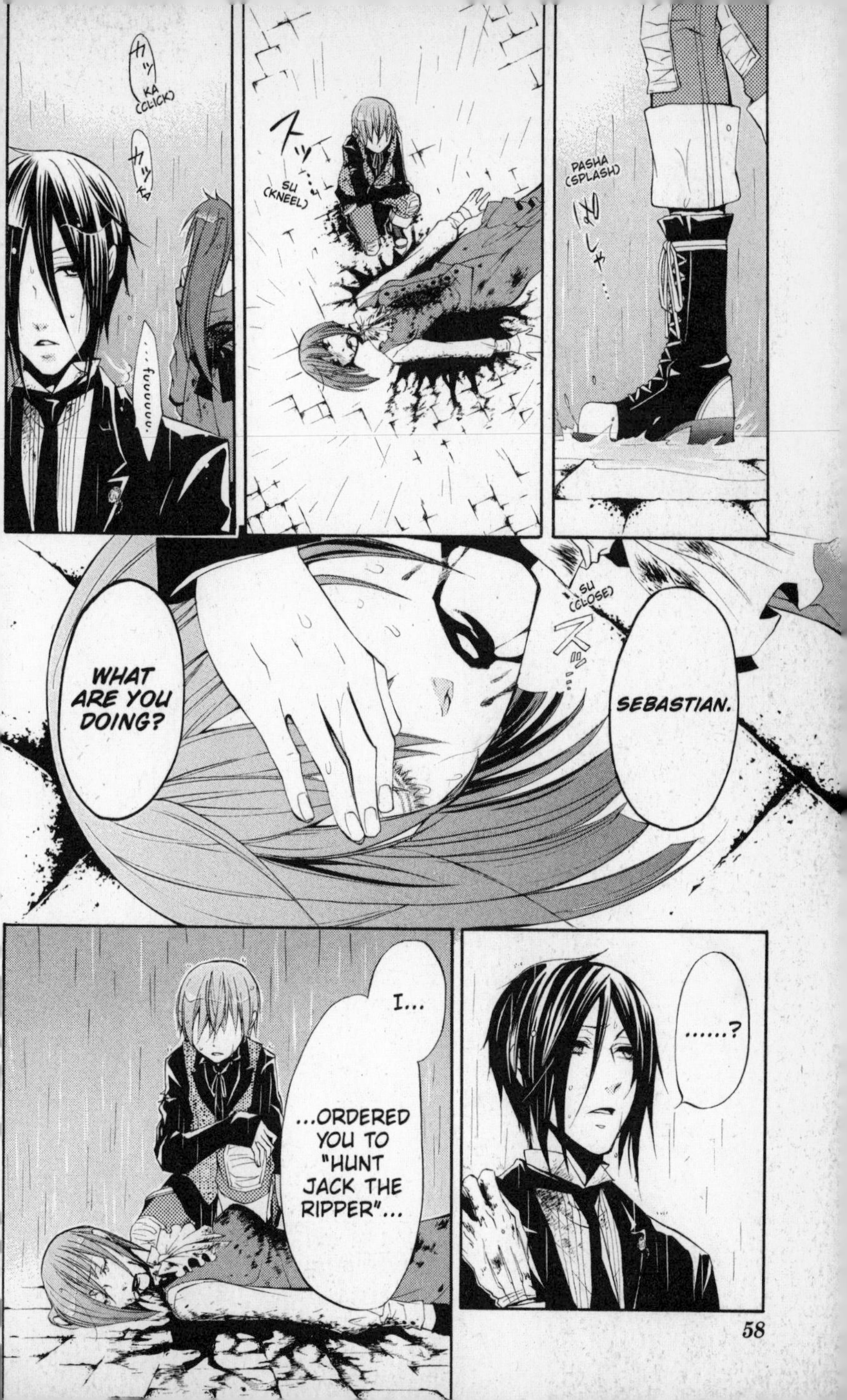

PASHA (SPLASH)
ぱしゃ…
スッ…
SU (KNEEL)
カッ
KA (CLICK)
カッ
KA
...fuuuuuu.
SU (CLOSE)
スッ…
SEBASTIAN.
WHAT ARE YOU DOING?
......?
I...
...ORDERED YOU TO "HUNT JACK THE RIPPER"...

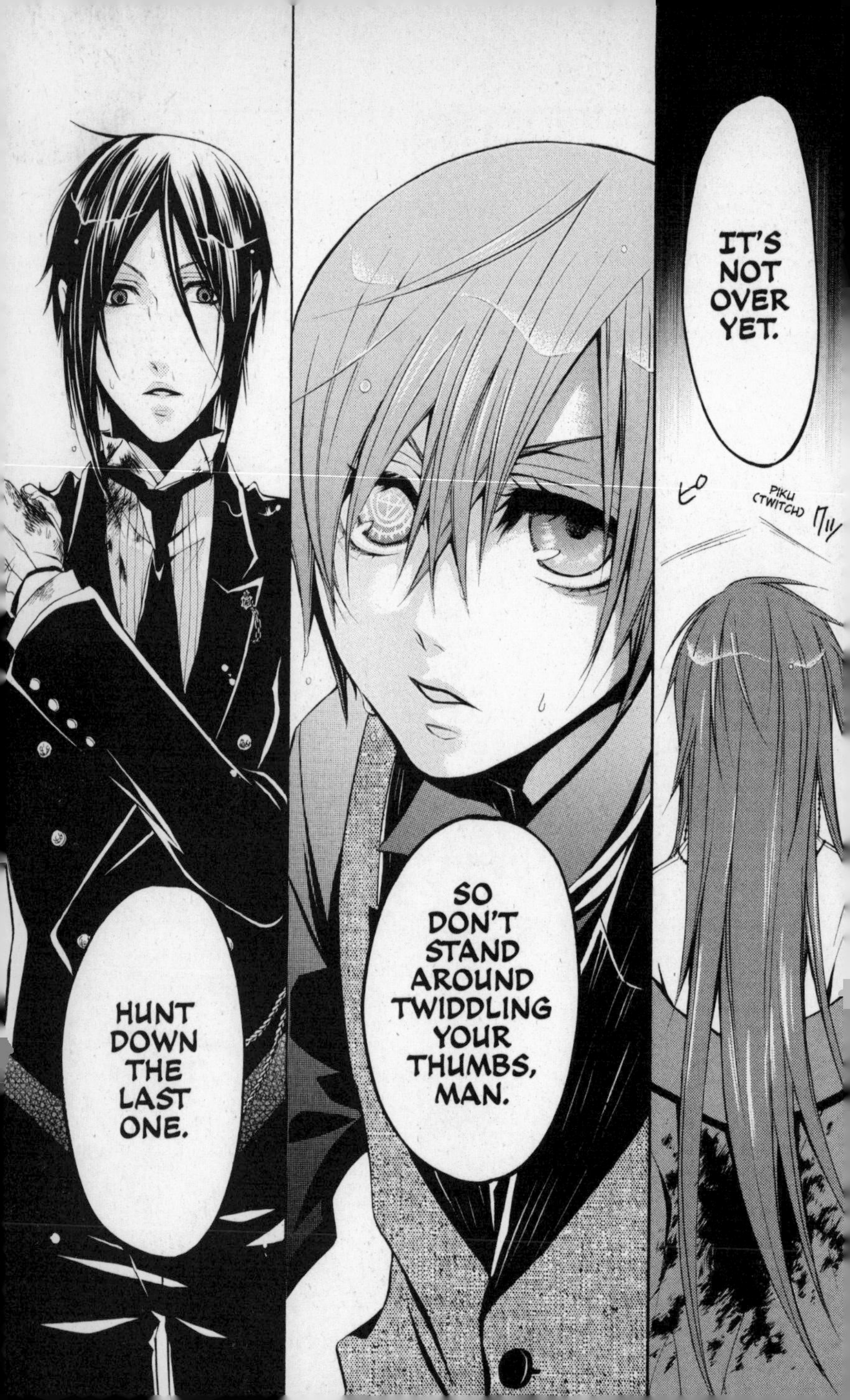
IT'S NOT OVER YET.
ピ
PIKU (TWITCH)
クッ
SO DON'T STAND AROUND TWIDDLING YOUR THUMBS, MAN.
HUNT DOWN THE LAST ONE.

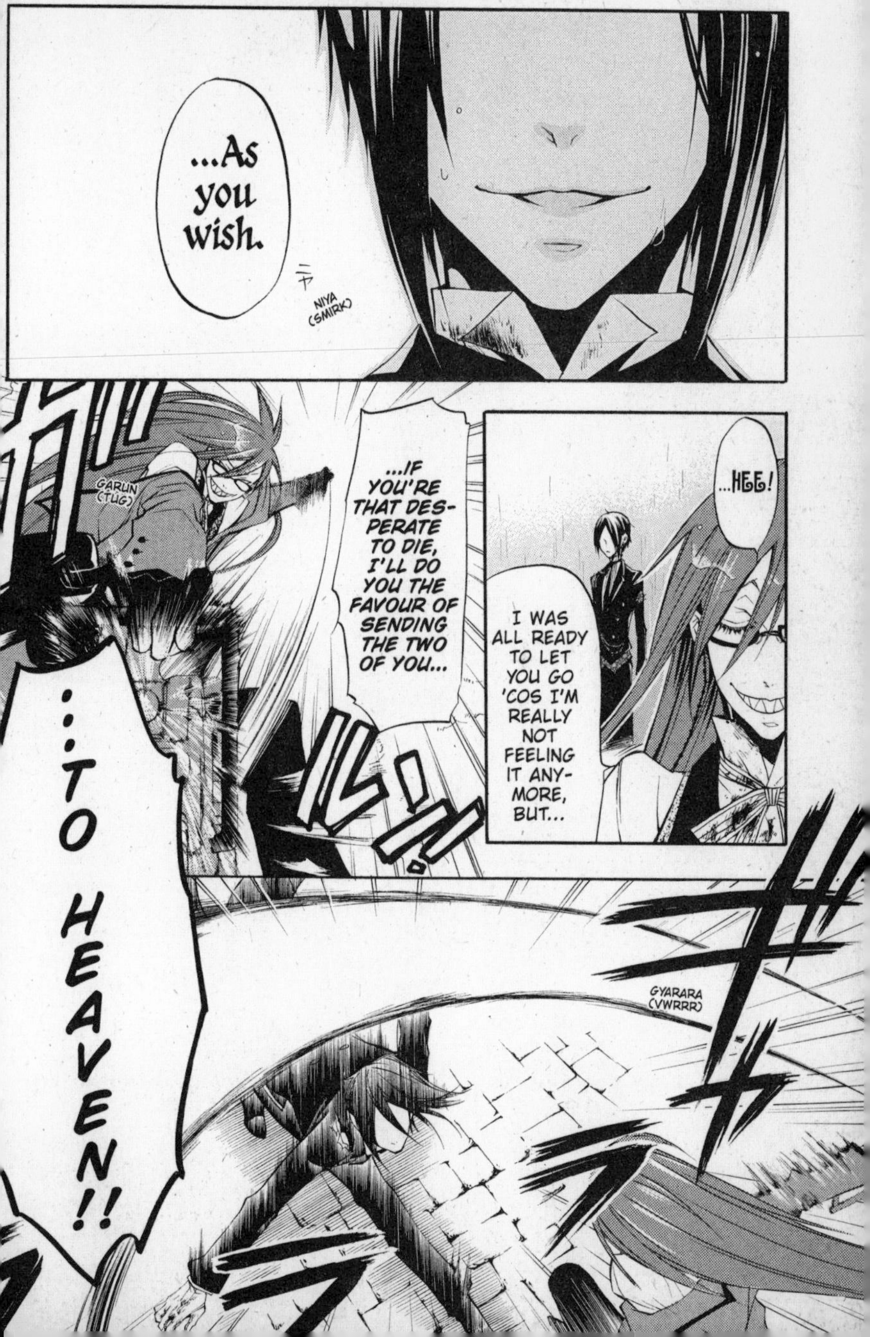
...As you wish.
ニヤ
NIYA (SMIRK)
...HEE!
I WAS ALL READY TO LET YOU GO 'COS I'M REALLY NOT FEELING IT ANY-MORE, BUT...
...IF YOU'RE THAT DES-PERATE TO DIE, I'LL DO YOU THE FAVOUR OF SENDING THE TWO OF YOU...
GARUN (TUG)
GYARARA (VWRRR)
...TO HEAVEN!!

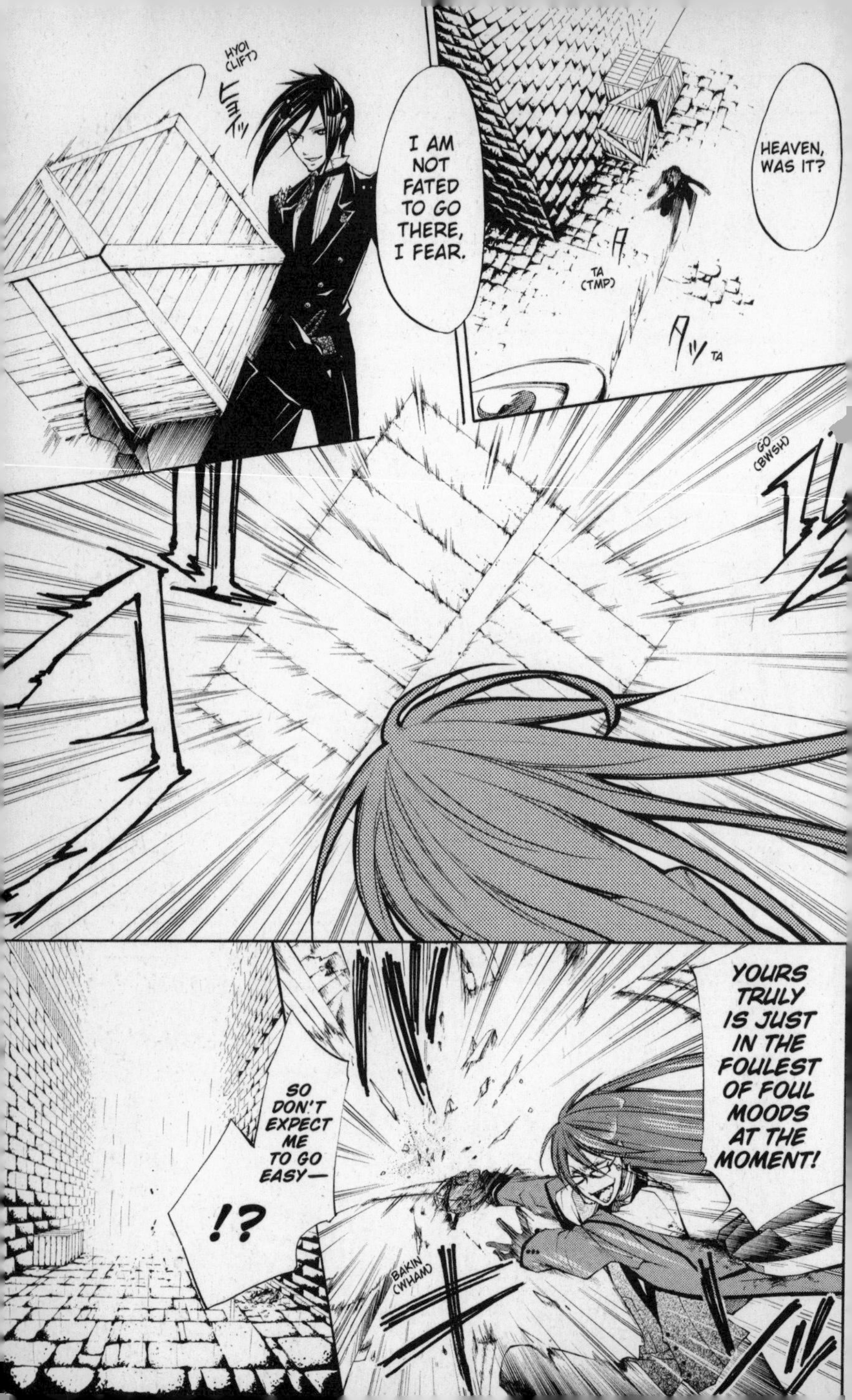
HEAVEN, WAS IT?
TA (TMP)
TA
HYOI (LIFT)
I AM NOT FATED TO GO THERE, I FEAR.
GO (BWSH)
YOURS TRULY IS JUST IN THE FOULEST OF FOUL MOODS AT THE MOMENT!
SO DON'T EXPECT ME TO GO EASY—
!?
BAKIN (WHAM)

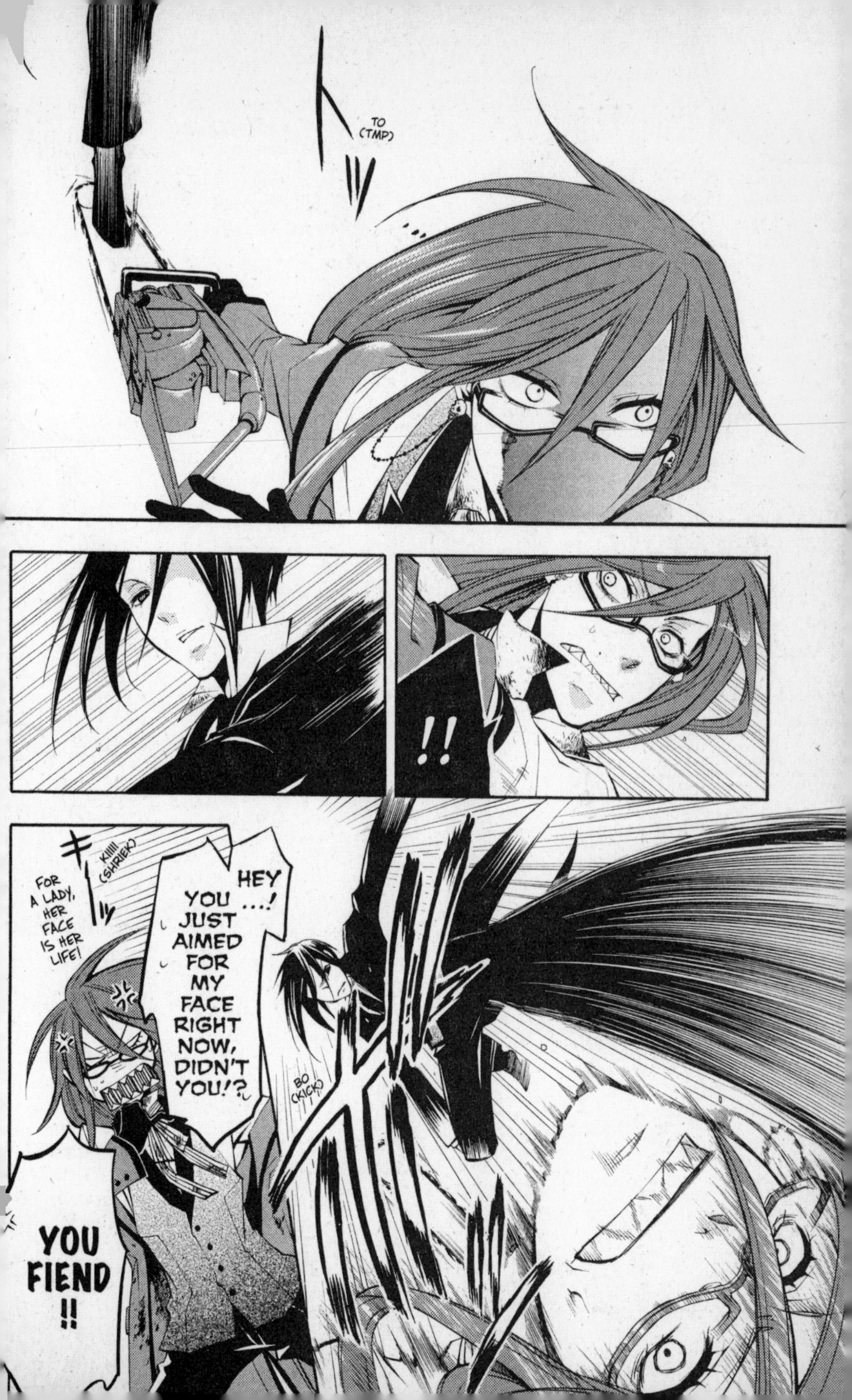
TO (TMP)
...
!!
HEY YOU ...! YOU JUST AIMED FOR MY FACE RIGHT NOW, DIDN'T YOU!?
KIIIII (SHRIEK)
FOR A LADY, HER FACE IS HER LIFE!
YOU FIEND!!
BO (KICK)

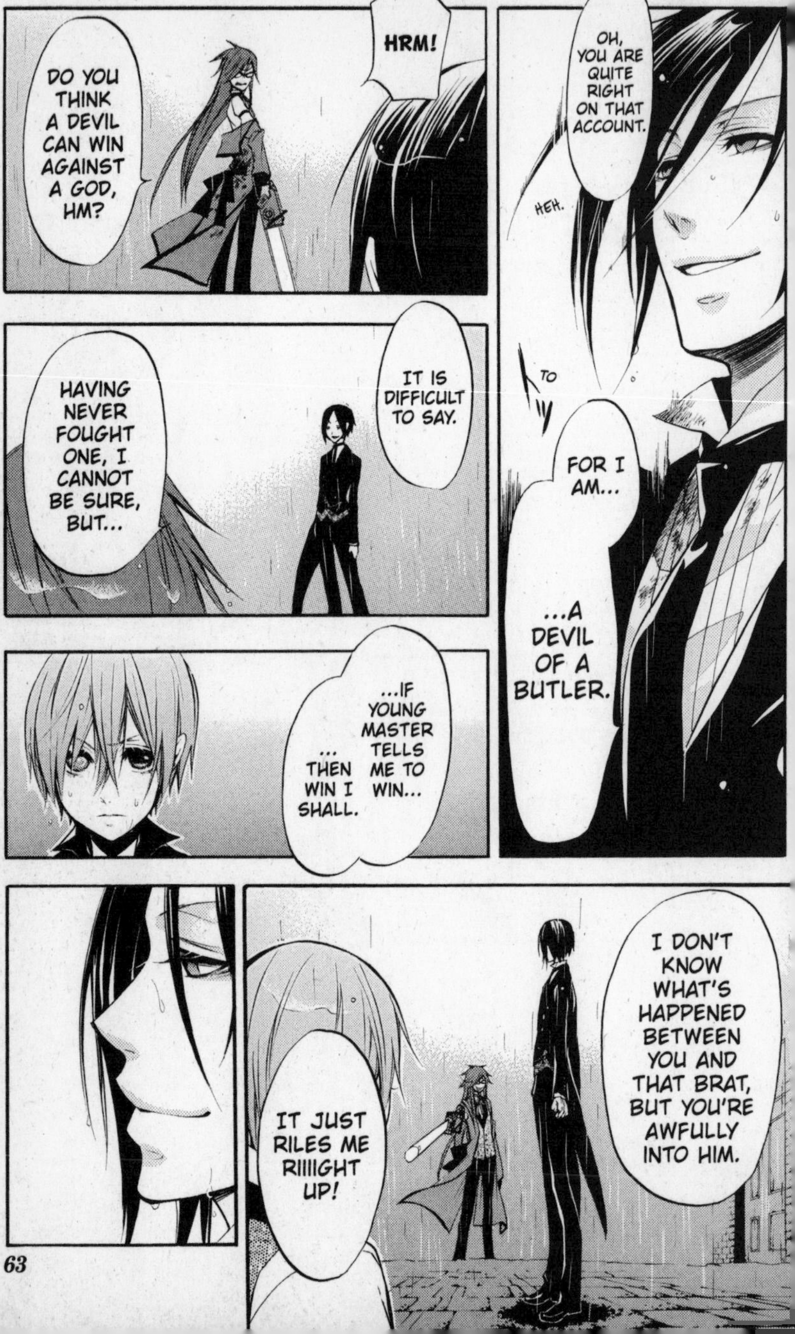

OH, YOU ARE QUITE RIGHT ON THAT ACCOUNT.
HEH.
TO
FOR I AM...
...A DEVIL OF A BUTLER.
HRM!
DO YOU THINK A DEVIL CAN WIN AGAINST A GOD, HM?
IT IS DIFFICULT TO SAY.
HAVING NEVER FOUGHT ONE, I CANNOT BE SURE, BUT...
...IF YOUNG MASTER TELLS ME TO WIN...
...THEN WIN I SHALL.
I DON'T KNOW WHAT'S HAPPENED BETWEEN YOU AND THAT BRAT, BUT YOU'RE AWFULLY INTO HIM.
IT JUST RILES ME RIIIIGHT UP!

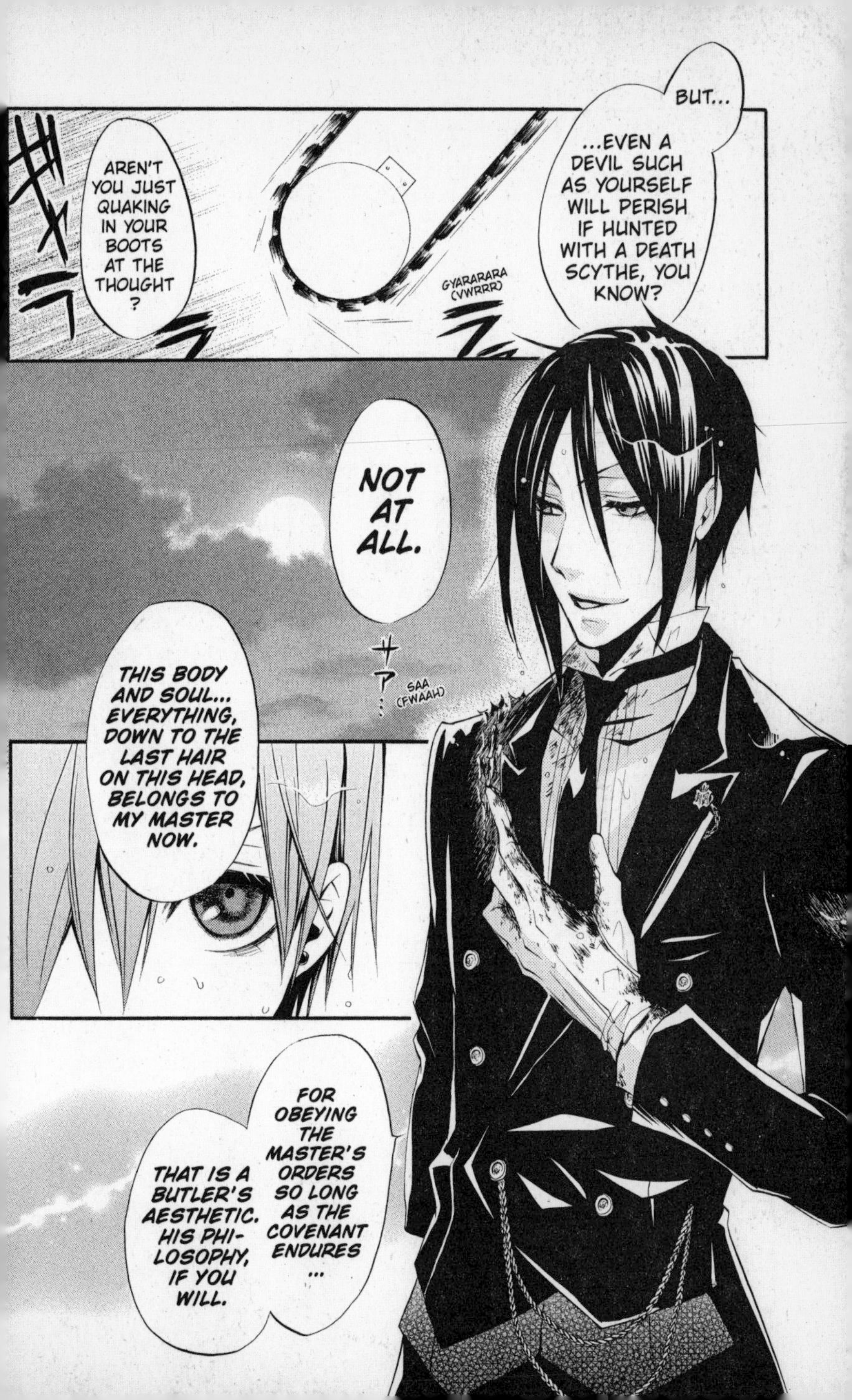
BUT...
...EVEN A DEVIL SUCH AS YOURSELF WILL PERISH IF HUNTED WITH A DEATH SCYTHE, YOU KNOW?
GYARARARA (VWRRR)
AREN'T YOU JUST QUAKING IN YOUR BOOTS AT THE THOUGHT?
NOT AT ALL.
SAA (FWAAH)
THIS BODY AND SOUL... EVERYTHING, DOWN TO THE LAST HAIR ON THIS HEAD, BELONGS TO MY MASTER NOW.
FOR OBEYING THE MASTER'S ORDERS SO LONG AS THE COVENANT ENDURES...
THAT IS A BUTLER'S AESTHETIC. HIS PHILOSOPHY, IF YOU WILL.

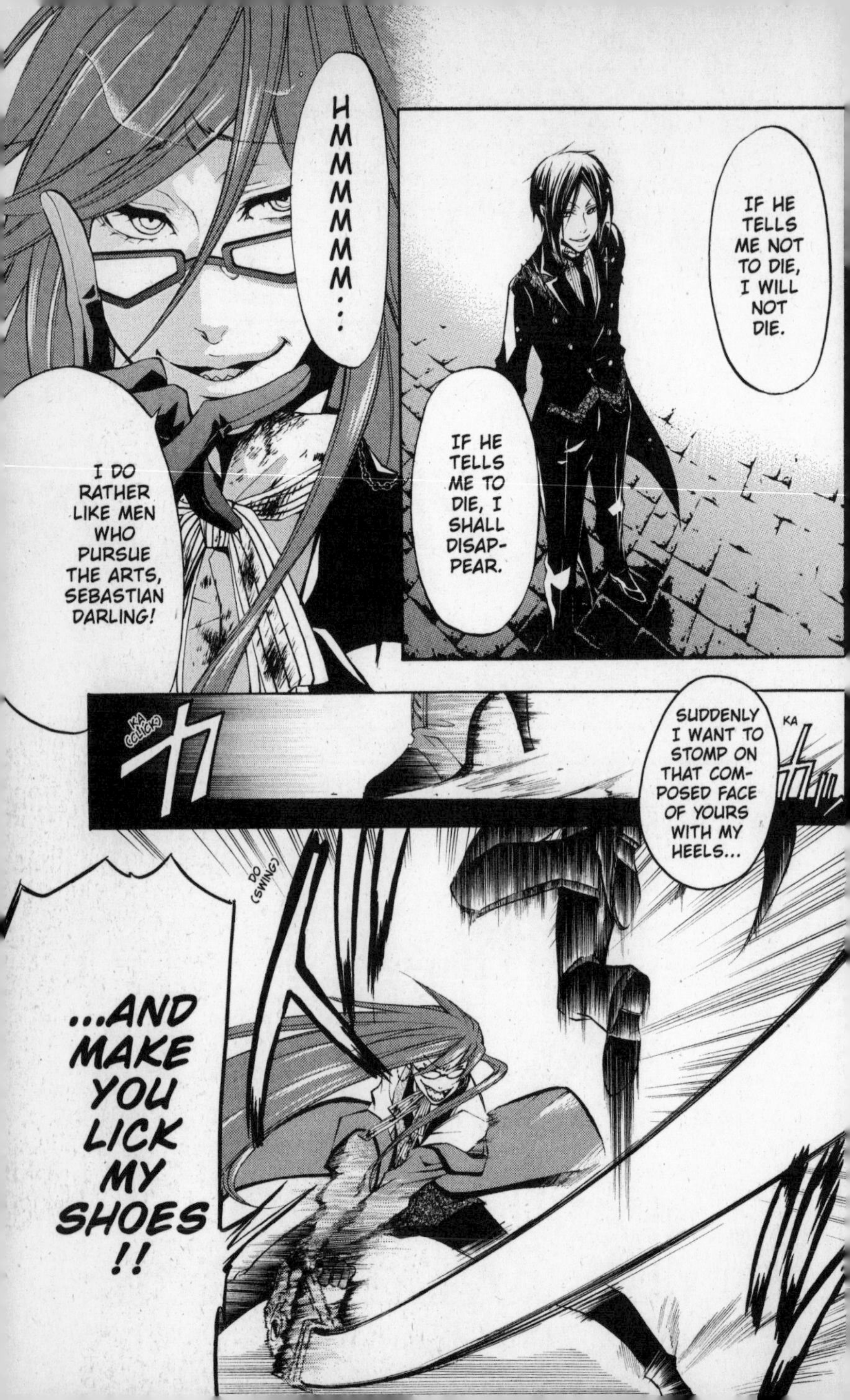
IF HE TELLS ME NOT TO DIE, I WILL NOT DIE.
IF HE TELLS ME TO DIE, I SHALL DISAPPEAR.
HMMMMMMM...
I DO RATHER LIKE MEN WHO PURSUE THE ARTS, SEBASTIAN DARLING!
KA
SUDDENLY I WANT TO STOMP ON THAT COMPOSED FACE OF YOURS WITH MY HEELS...
KA (CLICK)
DO (SWING)
...AND MAKE YOU LICK MY SHOES!!

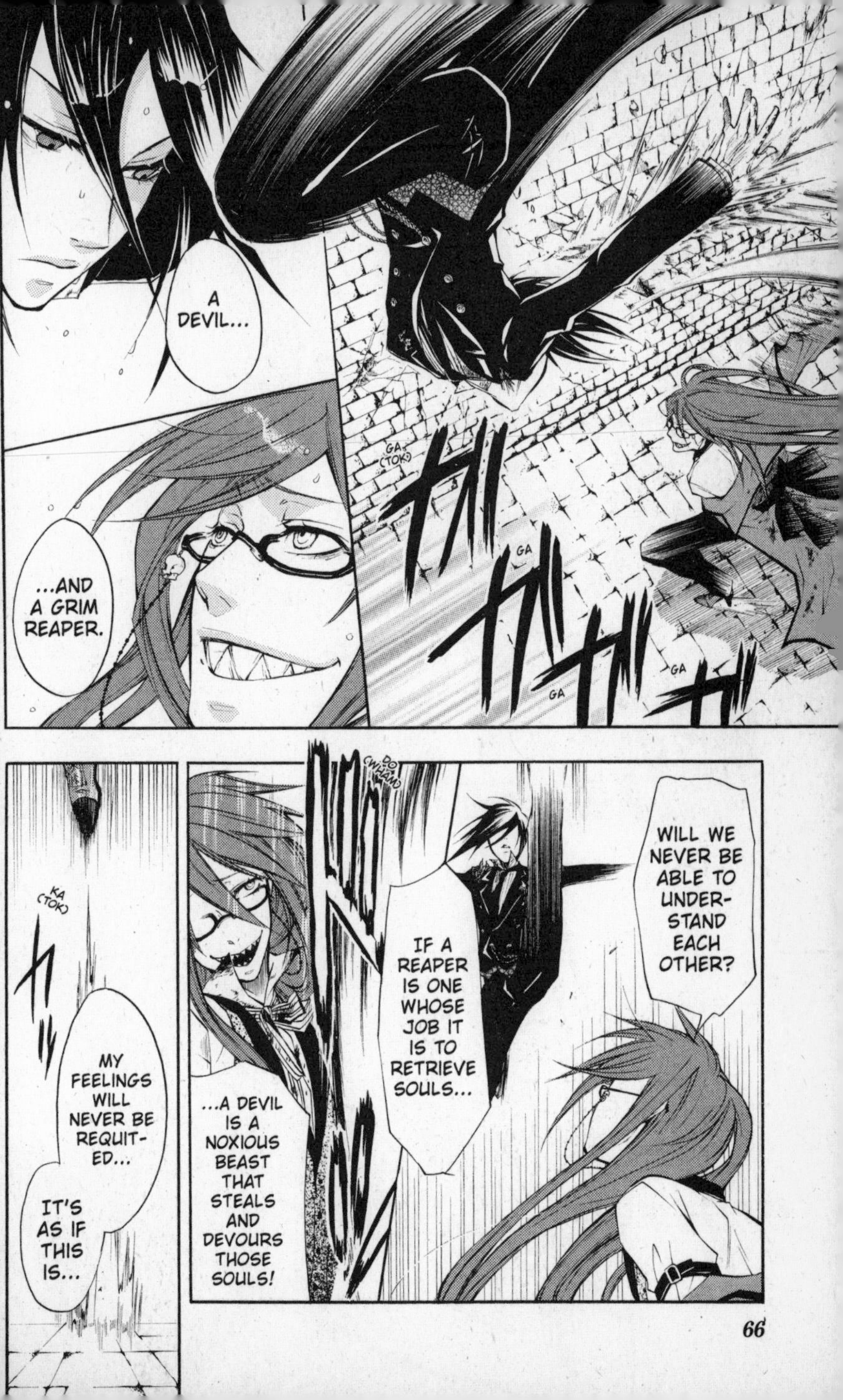
GA (TOK)
GA
GA
GA
A DEVIL...
...AND A GRIM REAPER.
DO (WHAM)
WILL WE NEVER BE ABLE TO UNDER-STAND EACH OTHER?
IF A REAPER IS ONE WHOSE JOB IT IS TO RETRIEVE SOULS...
...A DEVIL IS A NOXIOUS BEAST THAT STEALS AND DEVOURS THOSE SOULS!
KA (TOK)
MY FEELINGS WILL NEVER BE REQUIT-ED...
IT'S AS IF THIS IS...

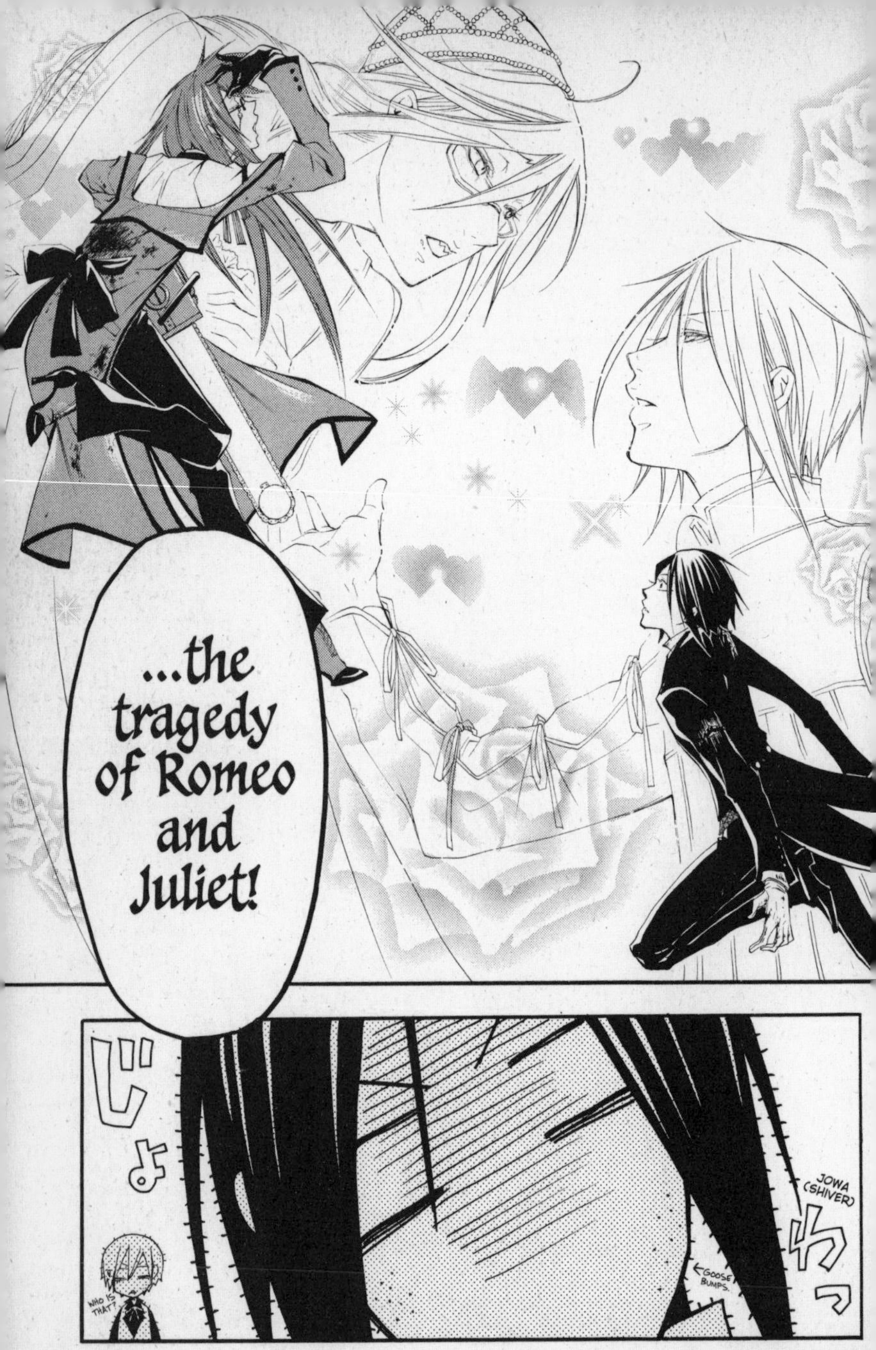
...the tragedy of Romeo and Juliet!
じょわっ
JOWA (SHIVER)
← GOOSE BUMPS.
WHO IS THAT?

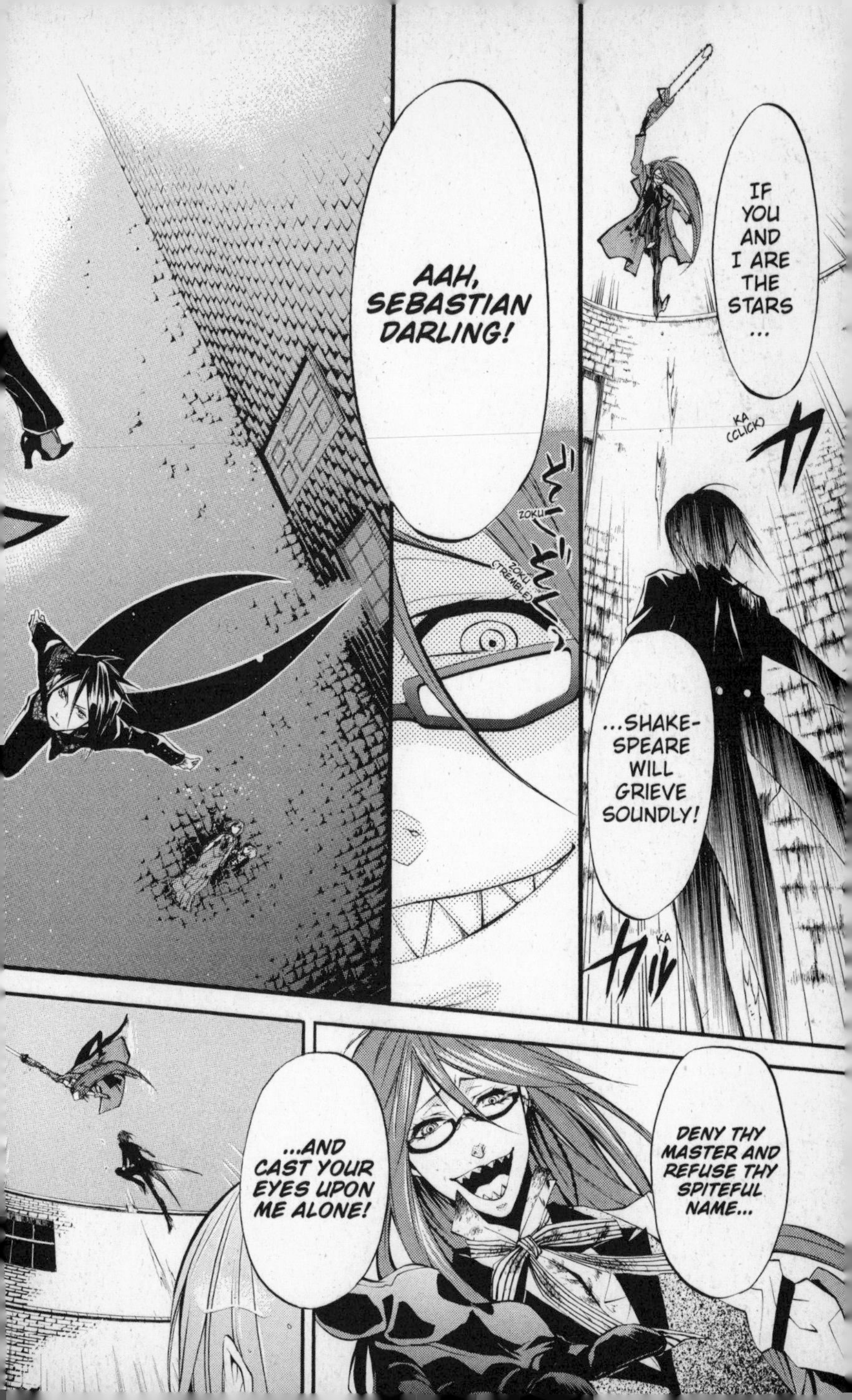
IF YOU AND I ARE THE STARS ...
KA (CLICK)
...SHAKE-SPEARE WILL GRIEVE SOUNDLY!
KA
AAH, SEBASTIAN DARLING!
ZOKU
ZOKU (TREMBLE)
DENY THY MASTER AND REFUSE THY SPITEFUL NAME...
...AND CAST YOUR EYES UPON ME ALONE!

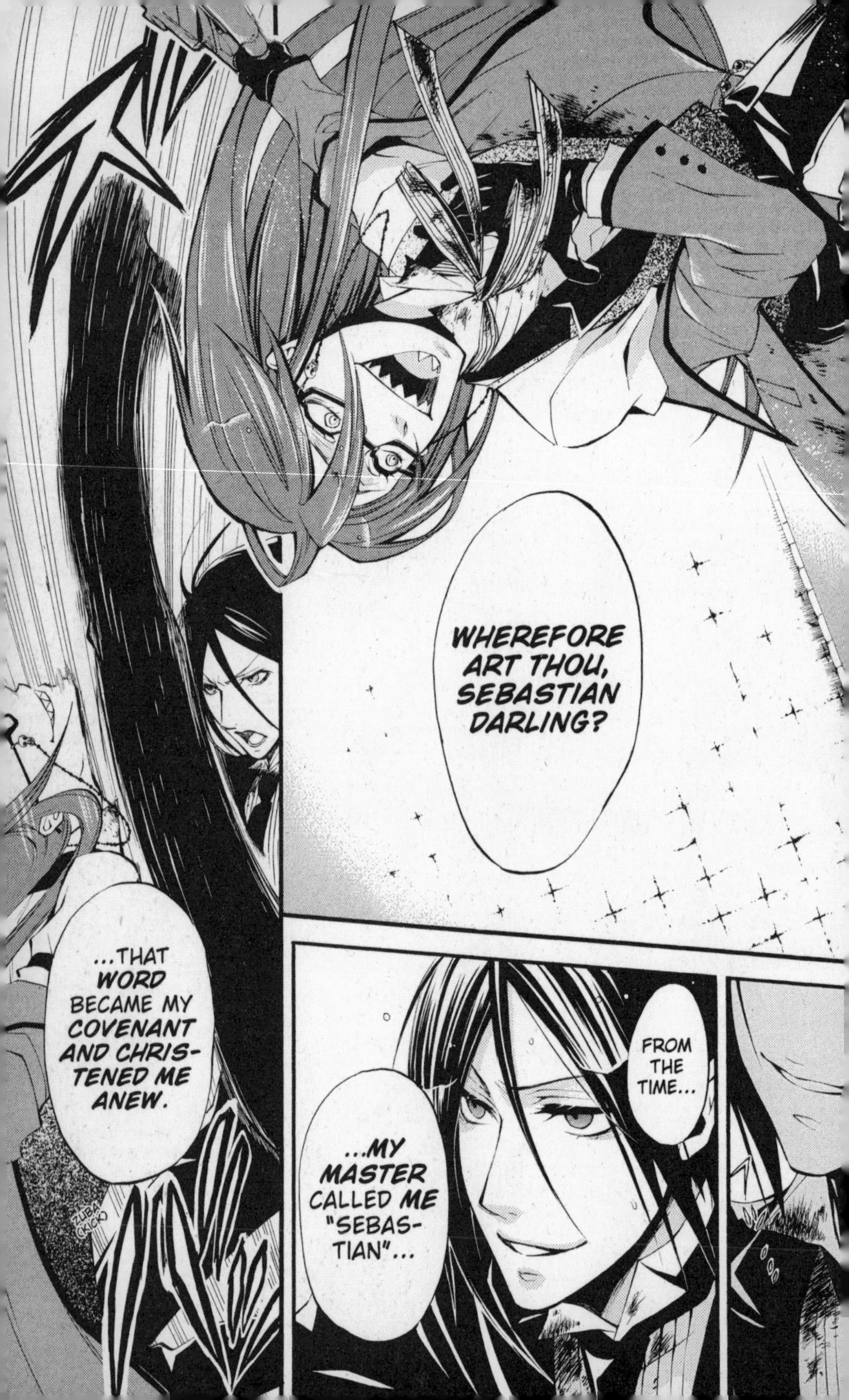
WHEREFORE ART THOU, SEBASTIAN DARLING?
FROM THE TIME...
...MY MASTER CALLED ME "SEBASTIAN"...
...THAT WORD BECAME MY COVENANT AND CHRISTENED ME ANEW.
ZUBA (KICK)

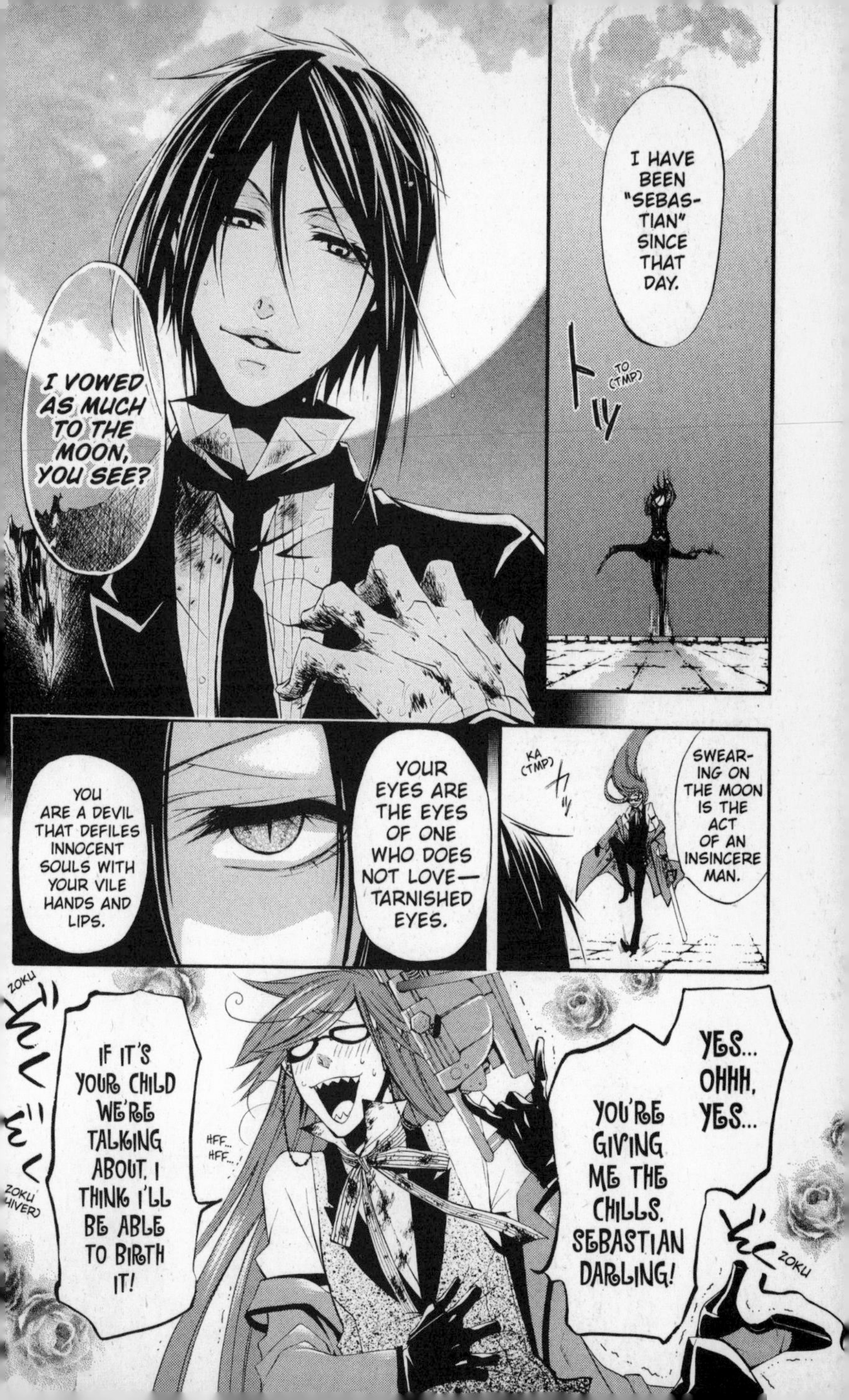
I HAVE BEEN "SEBASTIAN" SINCE THAT DAY.
TO (TMP)
I VOWED AS MUCH TO THE MOON, YOU SEE?
KA (TMP)
SWEARING ON THE MOON IS THE ACT OF AN INSINCERE MAN.
YOUR EYES ARE THE EYES OF ONE WHO DOES NOT LOVE—TARNISHED EYES.
YOU ARE A DEVIL THAT DEFILES INNOCENT SOULS WITH YOUR VILE HANDS AND LIPS.
YES... OHHH, YES...
YOU'RE GIVING ME THE CHILLS, SEBASTIAN DARLING!
ZOKU
HFF... HFF...
IF IT'S YOUR CHILD WE'RE TALKING ABOUT, I THINK I'LL BE ABLE TO BIRTH IT!
ZOKU
ZOKU (SHIVER)

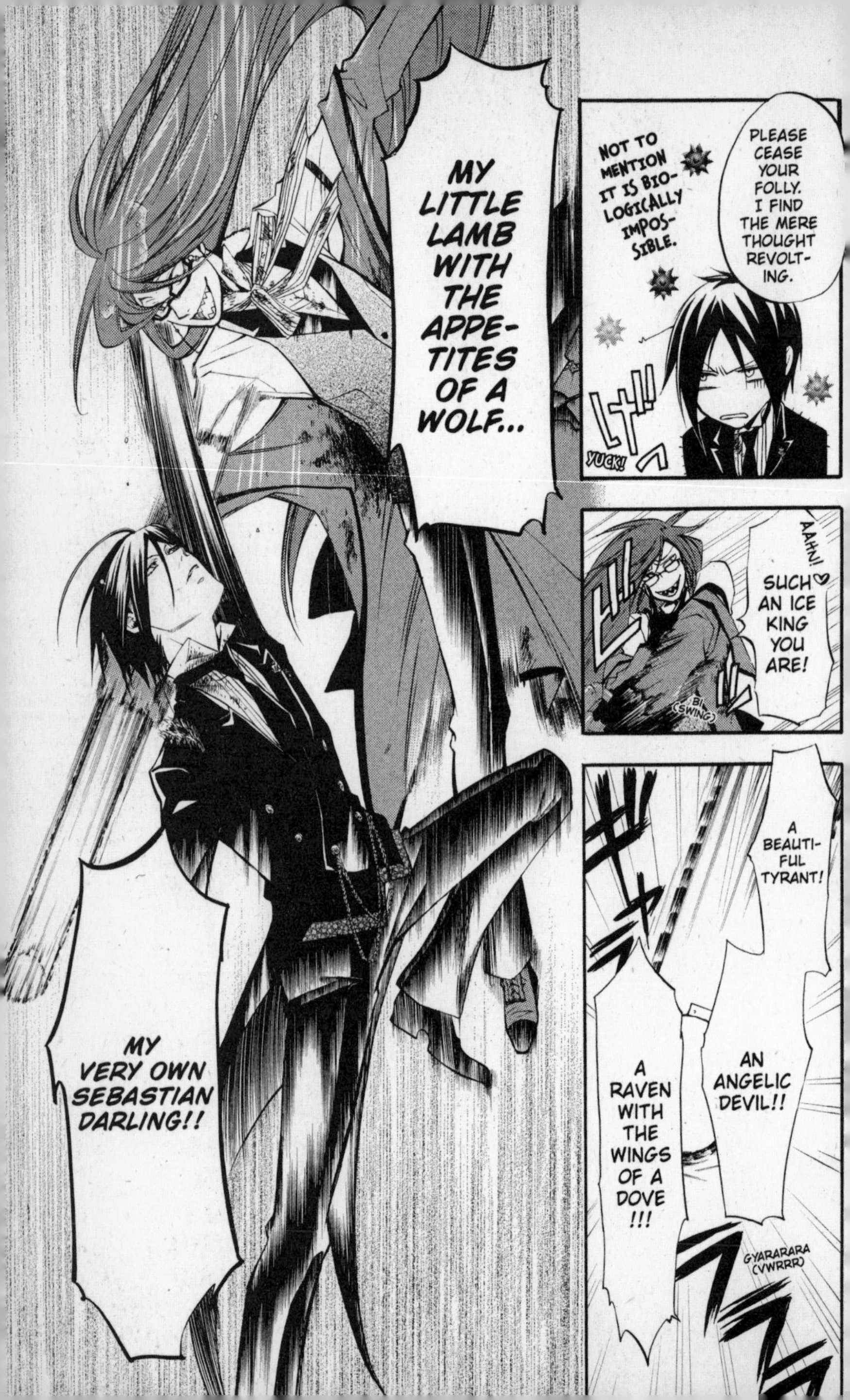
PLEASE CEASE YOUR FOLLY. I FIND THE MERE THOUGHT REVOLTING.
NOT TO MENTION IT IS BIOLOGICALLY IMPOSSIBLE.
YUCK!!
AAHN! ♡
SUCH AN ICE KING YOU ARE!
BI (SWING)
A BEAUTIFUL TYRANT!
AN ANGELIC DEVIL!!
A RAVEN WITH THE WINGS OF A DOVE!!!
GYARARARA (VWRRR)
MY LITTLE LAMB WITH THE APPETITES OF A WOLF...
MY VERY OWN SEBASTIAN DARLING!!

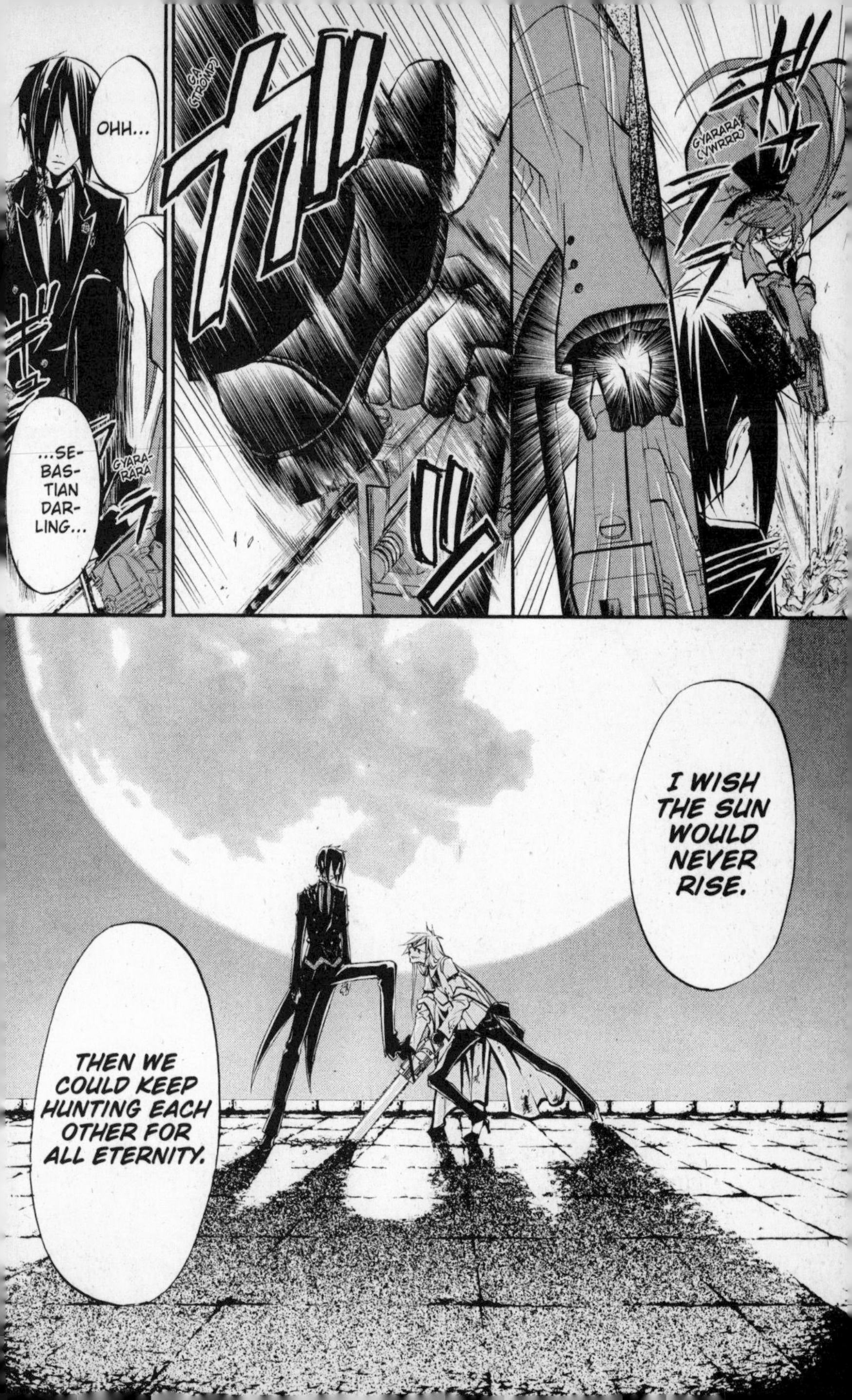
GYARARA (VWRRR)
GA (STOMP)
OHH...
...SEBASTIAN DARLING...
GYARARARA
I WISH THE SUN WOULD NEVER RISE.
THEN WE COULD KEEP HUNTING EACH OTHER FOR ALL ETERNITY.

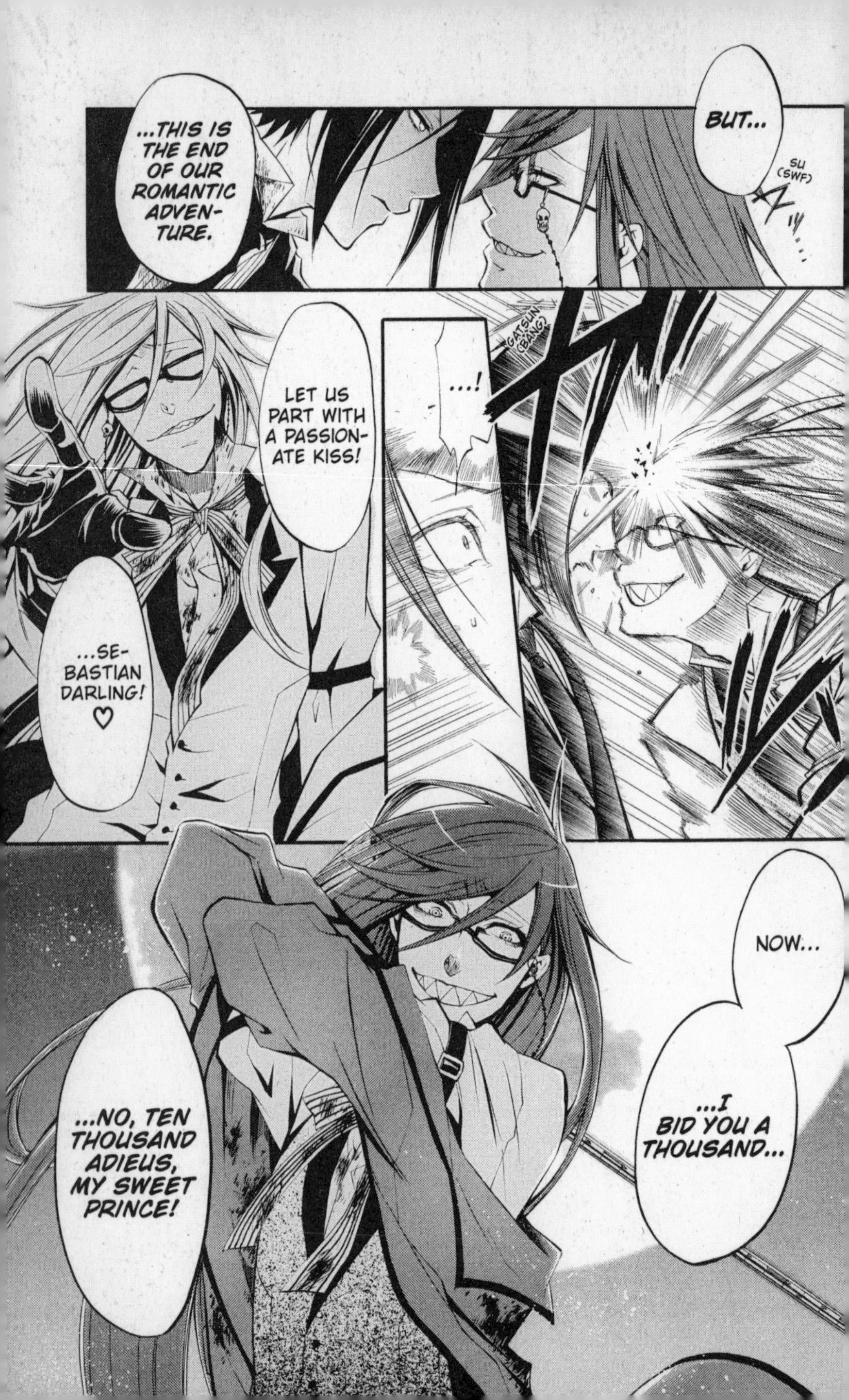
BUT...
SU (SWF)
...THIS IS THE END OF OUR ROMANTIC ADVEN-TURE.
GATSUN (BANG)
...!
LET US PART WITH A PASSION-ATE KISS!
...SE-BASTIAN DARLING! ♡
NOW...
...I BID YOU A THOUSAND...
...NO, TEN THOUSAND ADIEUS, MY SWEET PRINCE!

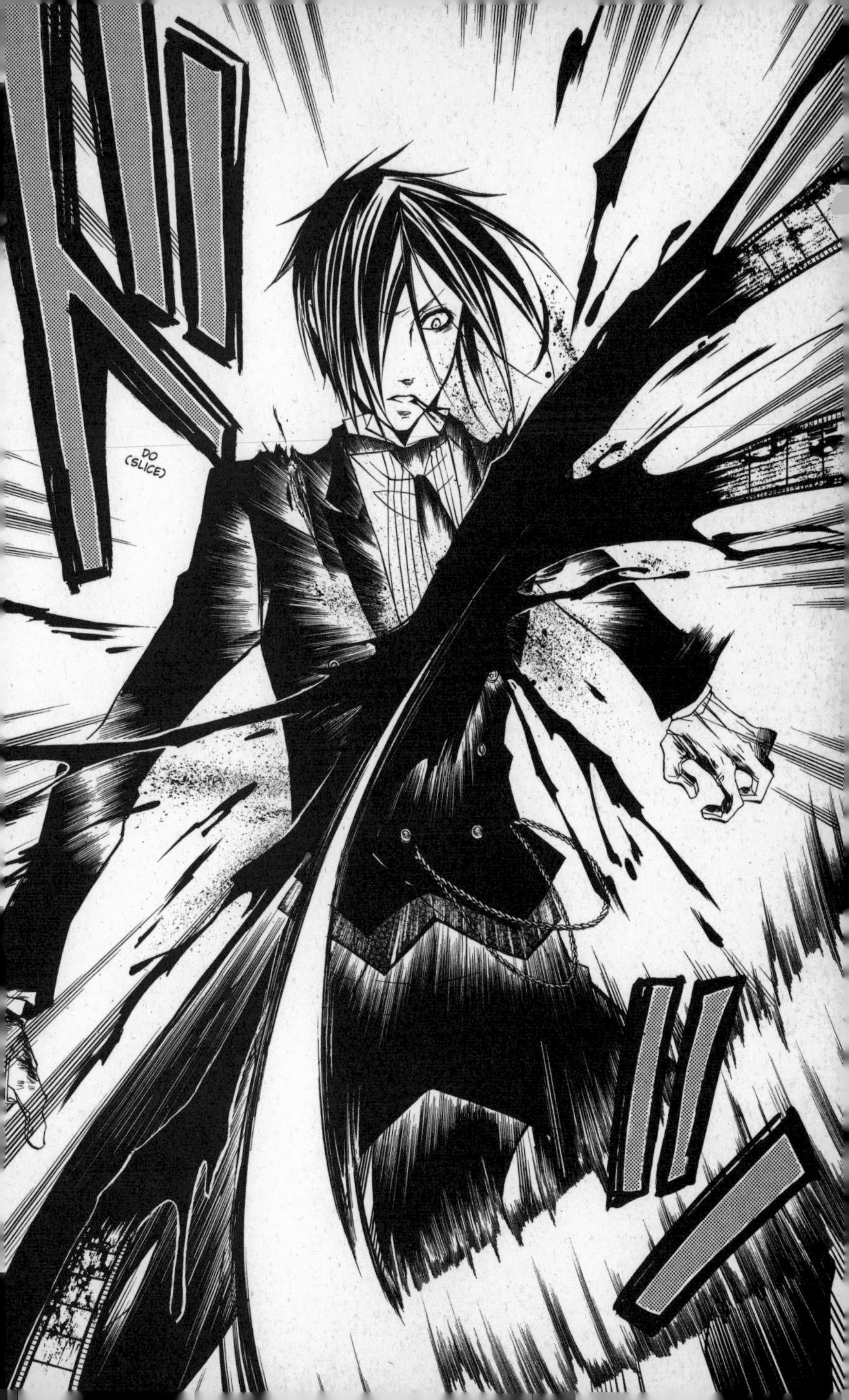
DO
(SLICE)

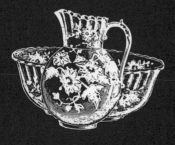

Black Butler

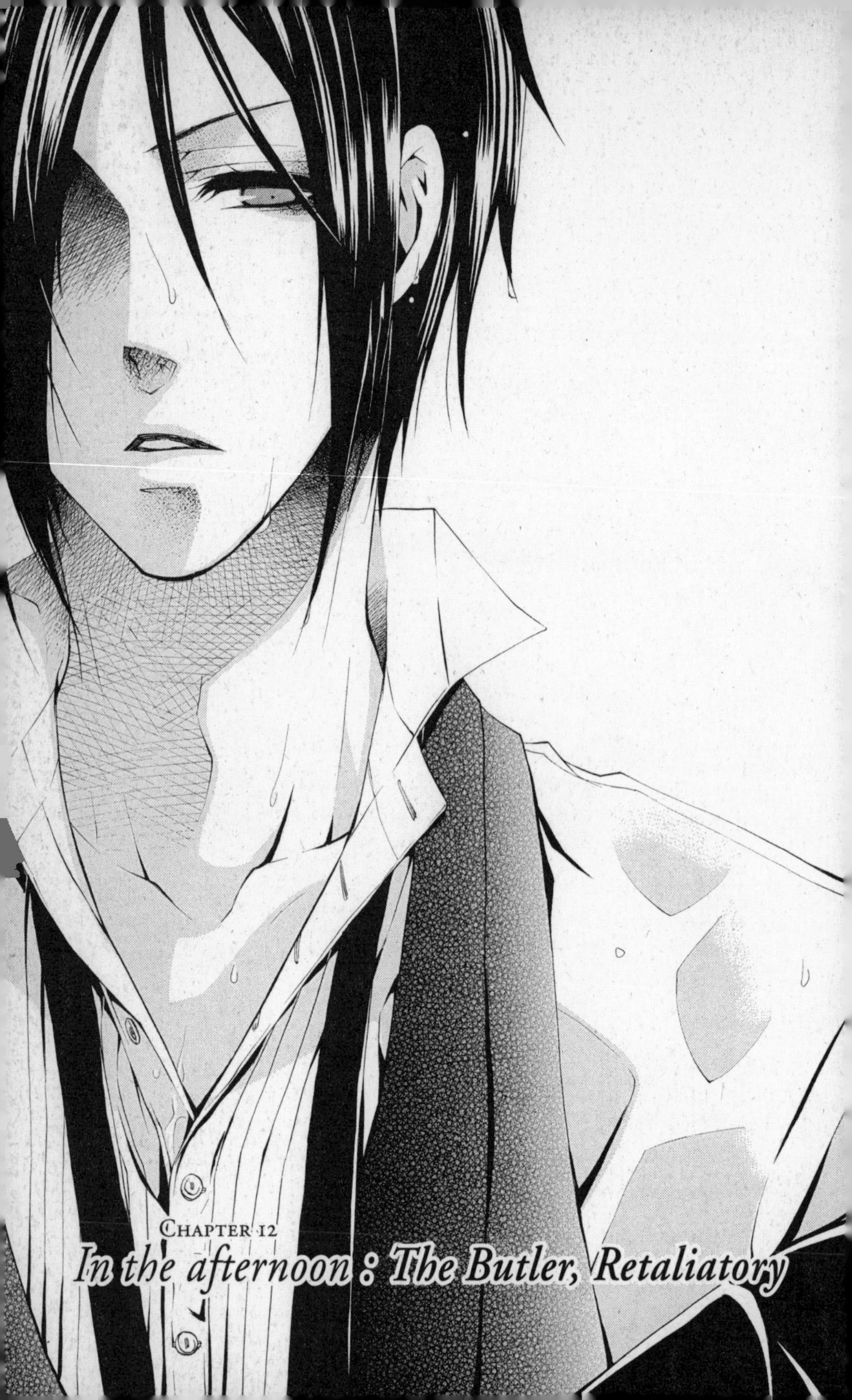

Chapter 12

In the afternoon : The Butler, Retaliatory

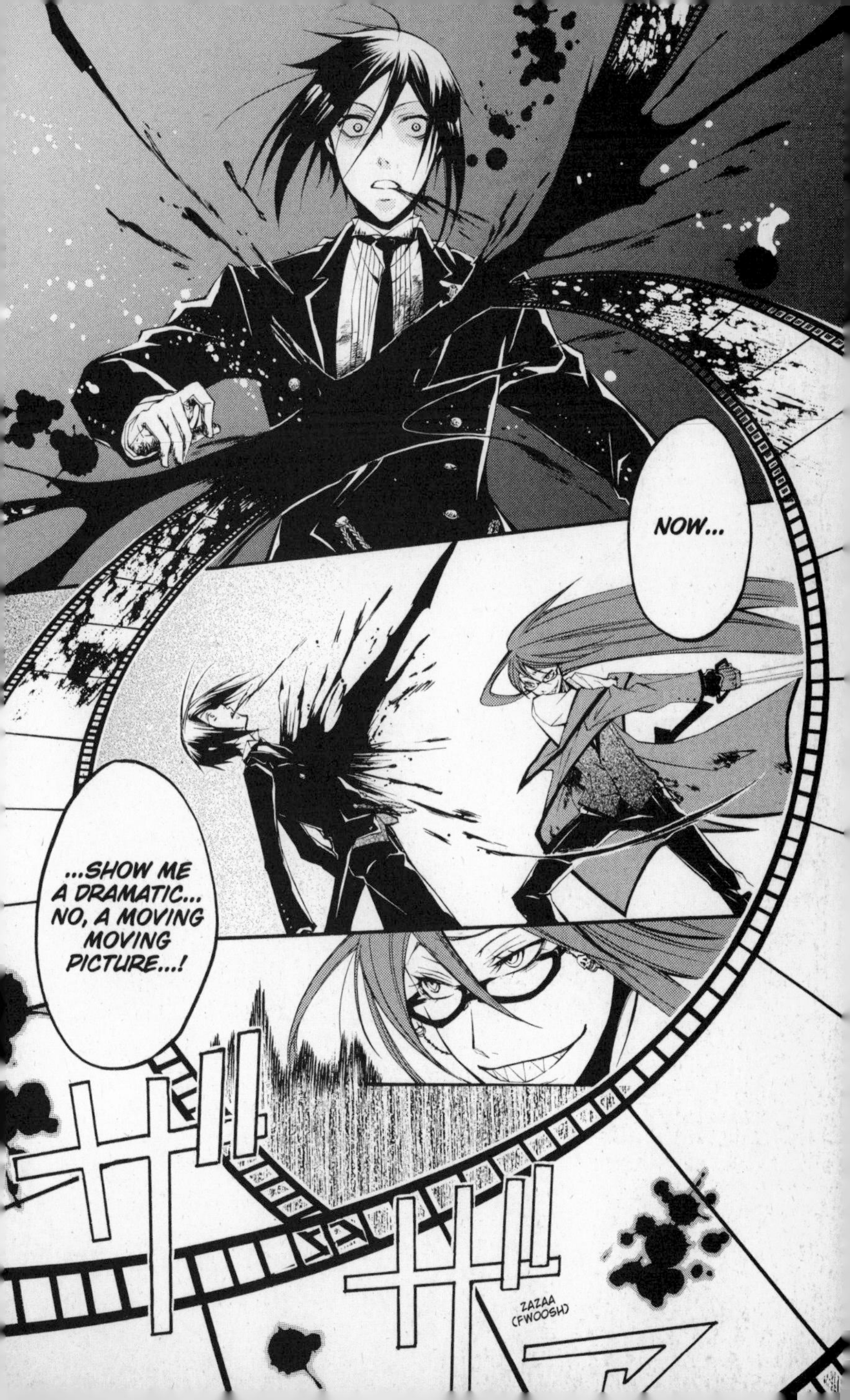
NOW...
...SHOW ME A DRAMATIC... NO, A MOVING MOVING PICTURE...!
ZAZAA (FWOOSH)

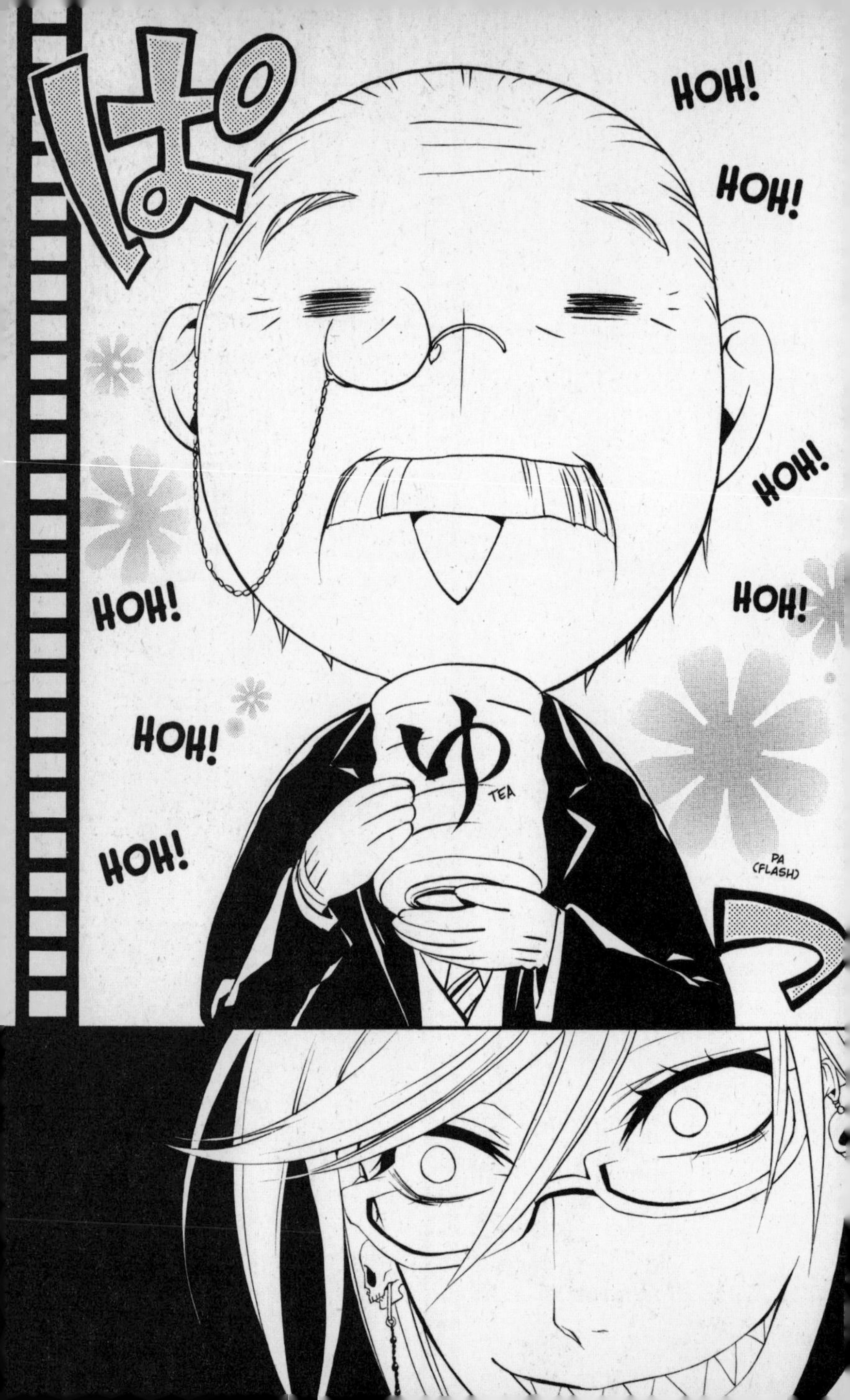

HOH!
HOH!
HOH!
HOH!
HOH!
HOH!
HOH!
ゆ
TEA
PA (FLASH)

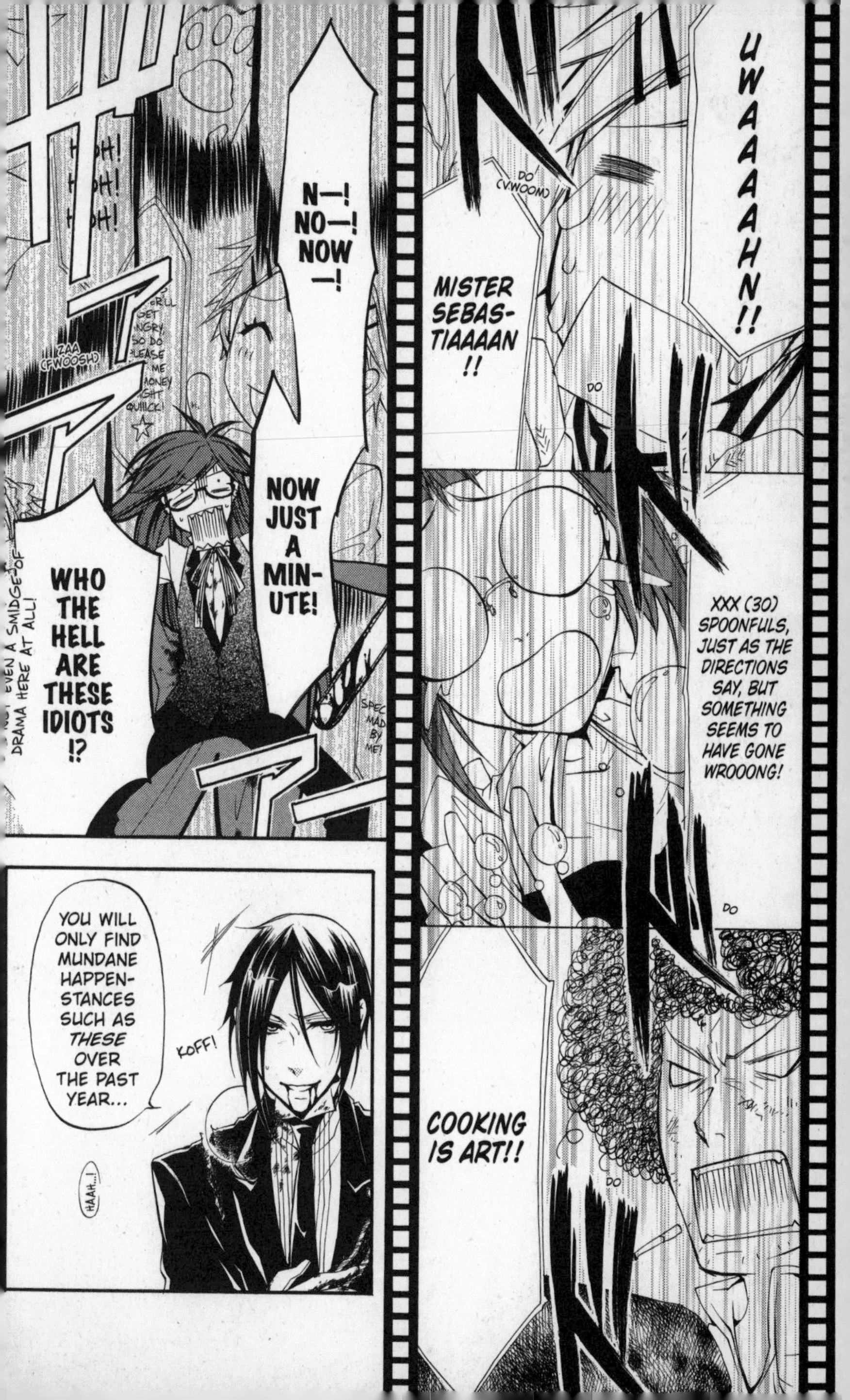
UWAAAAAHN!!
DO (VWOOM)
MISTER SEBASTIAAAAN!!
DO
XXX (30) SPOONFULS, JUST AS THE DIRECTIONS SAY, BUT SOMETHING SEEMS TO HAVE GONE WROOONG!
DO
COOKING IS ART!!
DO
N—! NO—! NOW —!
ZAA (FWOOSH)
NOW JUST A MINUTE!
WHO THE HELL ARE THESE IDIOTS !?
EVEN A SMIDGE OF DRAMA HERE AT ALL!
YOU WILL ONLY FIND MUNDANE HAPPENSTANCES SUCH AS *THESE* OVER THE PAST YEAR...
KOFF!
HAAH...!

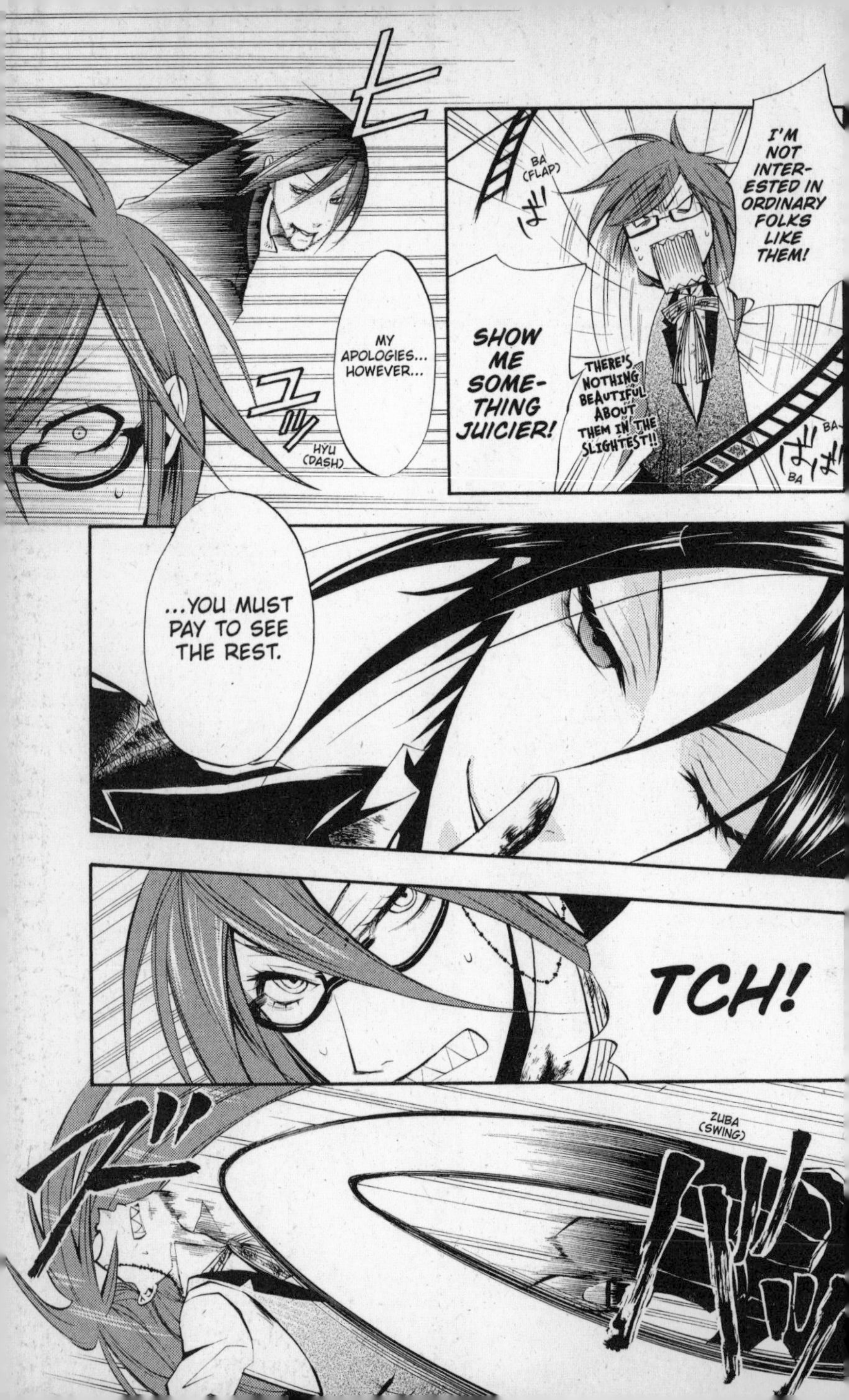

I'M NOT INTERESTED IN ORDINARY FOLKS LIKE THEM!
BA (FLAP)
THERE'S NOTHING BEAUTIFUL ABOUT THEM IN THE SLIGHTEST!!
SHOW ME SOMETHING JUICIER!
BA BA
MY APOLOGIES... HOWEVER...
HYU (DASH)
...YOU MUST PAY TO SEE THE REST.
TCH!
ZUBA (SWING)

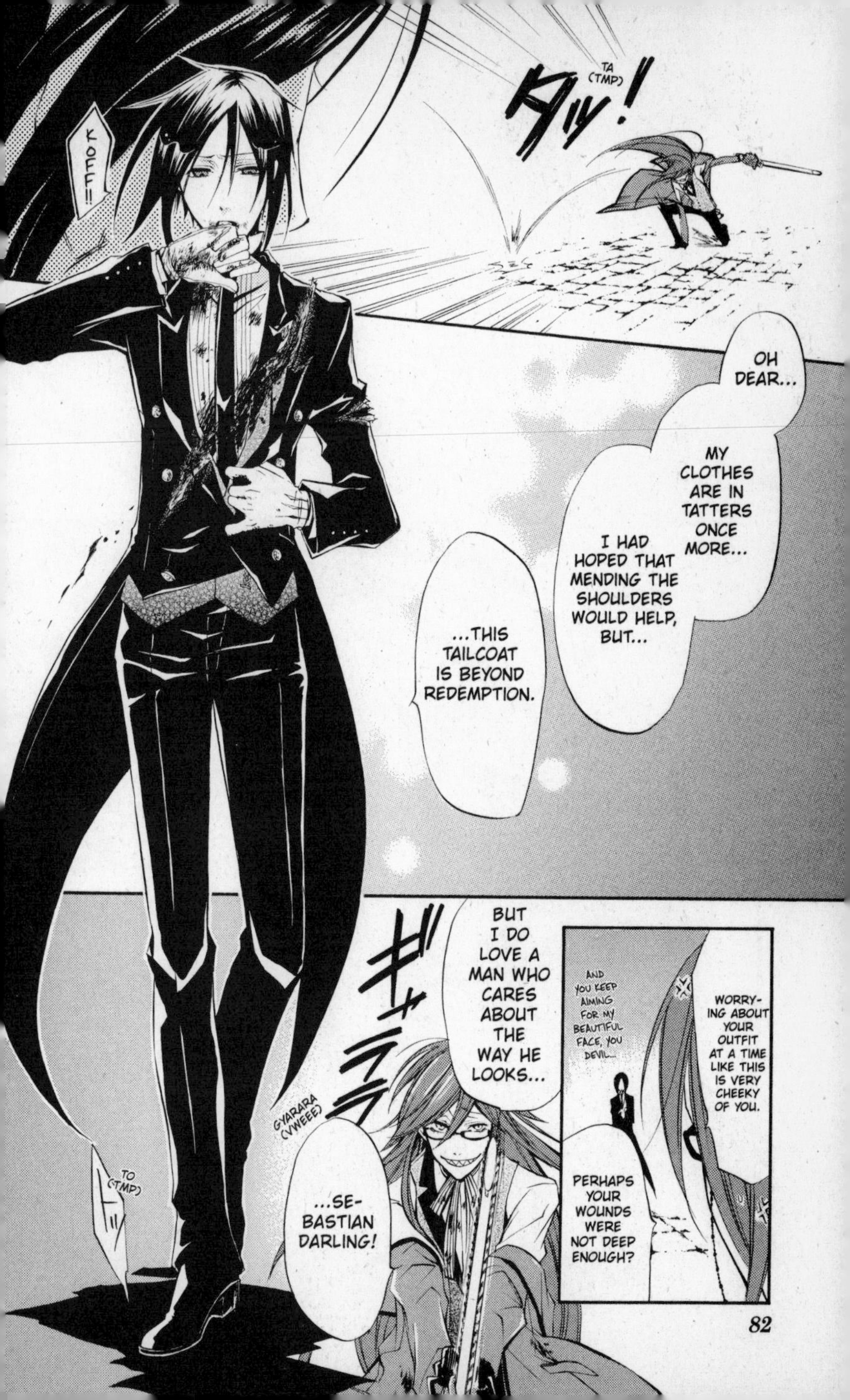
TA (TMP)
タッ!
OH DEAR...
MY CLOTHES ARE IN TATTERS ONCE MORE...
I HAD HOPED THAT MENDING THE SHOULDERS WOULD HELP, BUT...
...THIS TAILCOAT IS BEYOND REDEMPTION.
WORRYING ABOUT YOUR OUTFIT AT A TIME LIKE THIS IS VERY CHEEKY OF YOU.
AND YOU KEEP AIMING FOR MY BEAUTIFUL FACE, YOU DEVIL...
PERHAPS YOUR WOUNDS WERE NOT DEEP ENOUGH?
BUT I DO LOVE A MAN WHO CARES ABOUT THE WAY HE LOOKS...
GYARARA (VWEEE)
...SE-BASTIAN DARLING!
KOFF!!
TO (TMP)

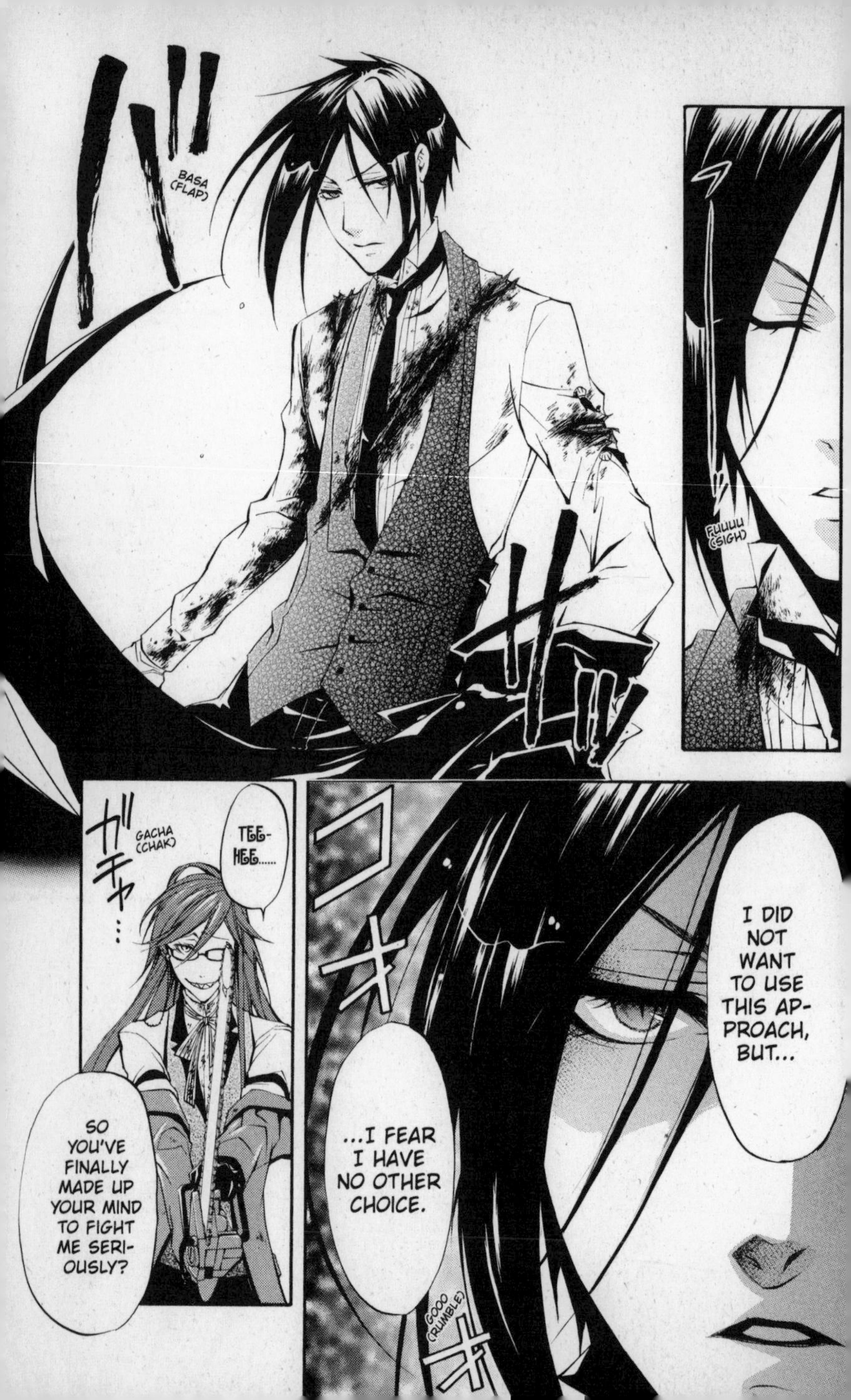
FUUUU (SIGH)
BASA (FLAP)
I DID NOT WANT TO USE THIS AP-PROACH, BUT...
...I FEAR I HAVE NO OTHER CHOICE.
GOOO (RUMBLE)
GACHA (CHAK)
TEE-HEE......
SO YOU'VE FINALLY MADE UP YOUR MIND TO FIGHT ME SERI-OUSLY?

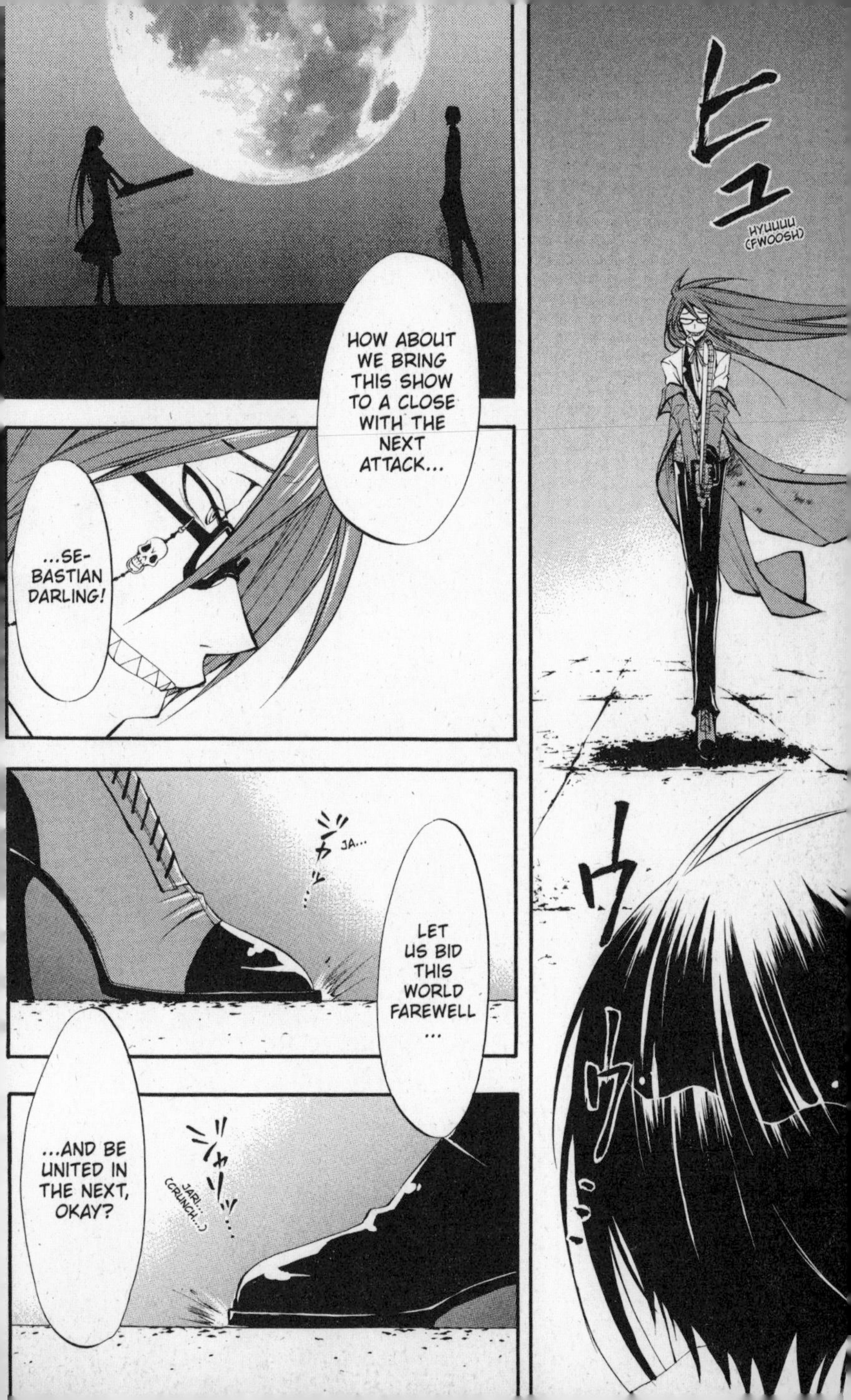
HYUUUU (FWOOSH)
HOW ABOUT WE BRING THIS SHOW TO A CLOSE WITH THE NEXT ATTACK...
...SE-BASTIAN DARLING!
JA...
LET US BID THIS WORLD FAREWELL...
JARI... (CRUNCH...)
...AND BE UNITED IN THE NEXT, OKAY?

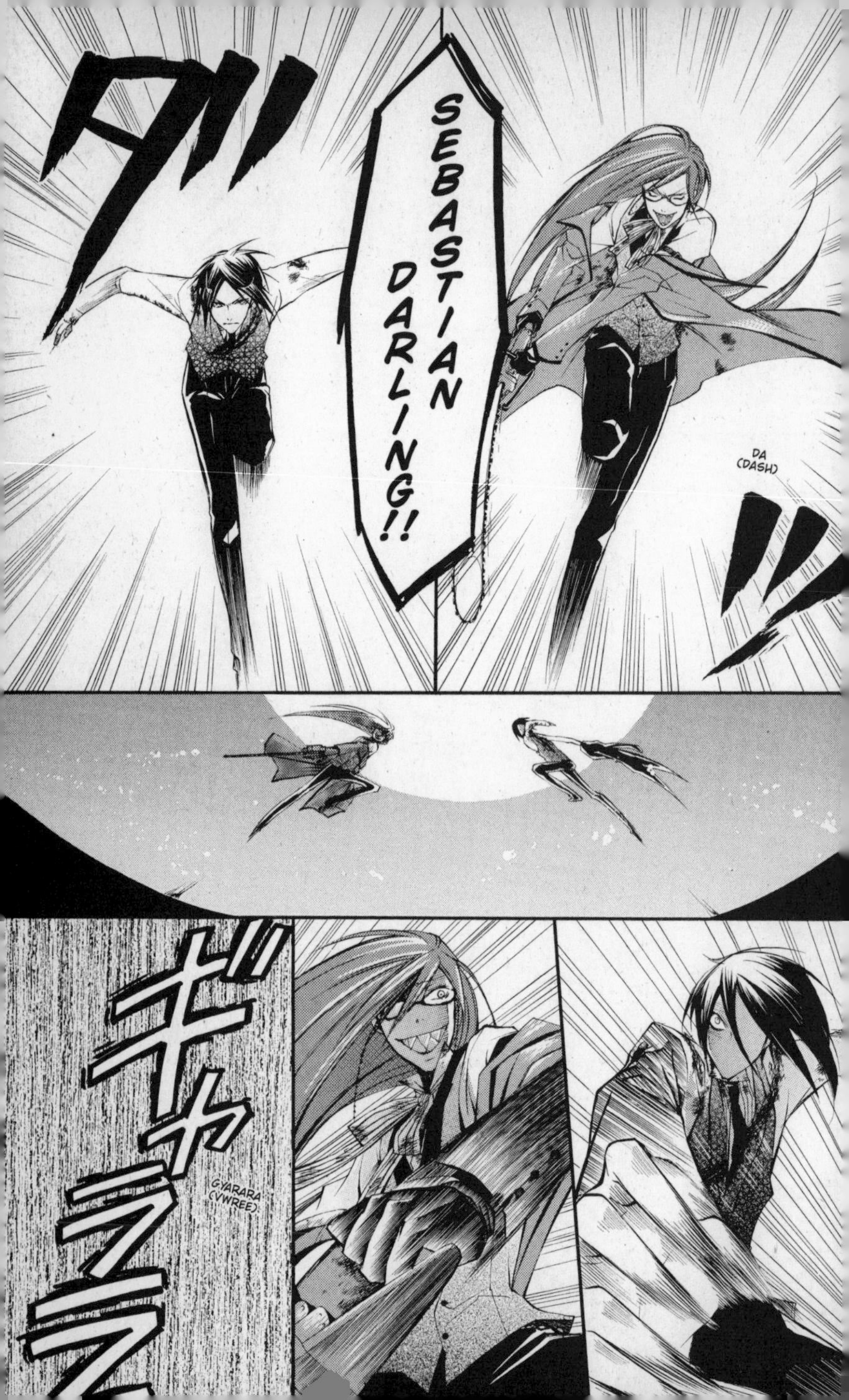
DA (DASH)
SEBASTIAN DARLING!!
GYARARA (VWREE)

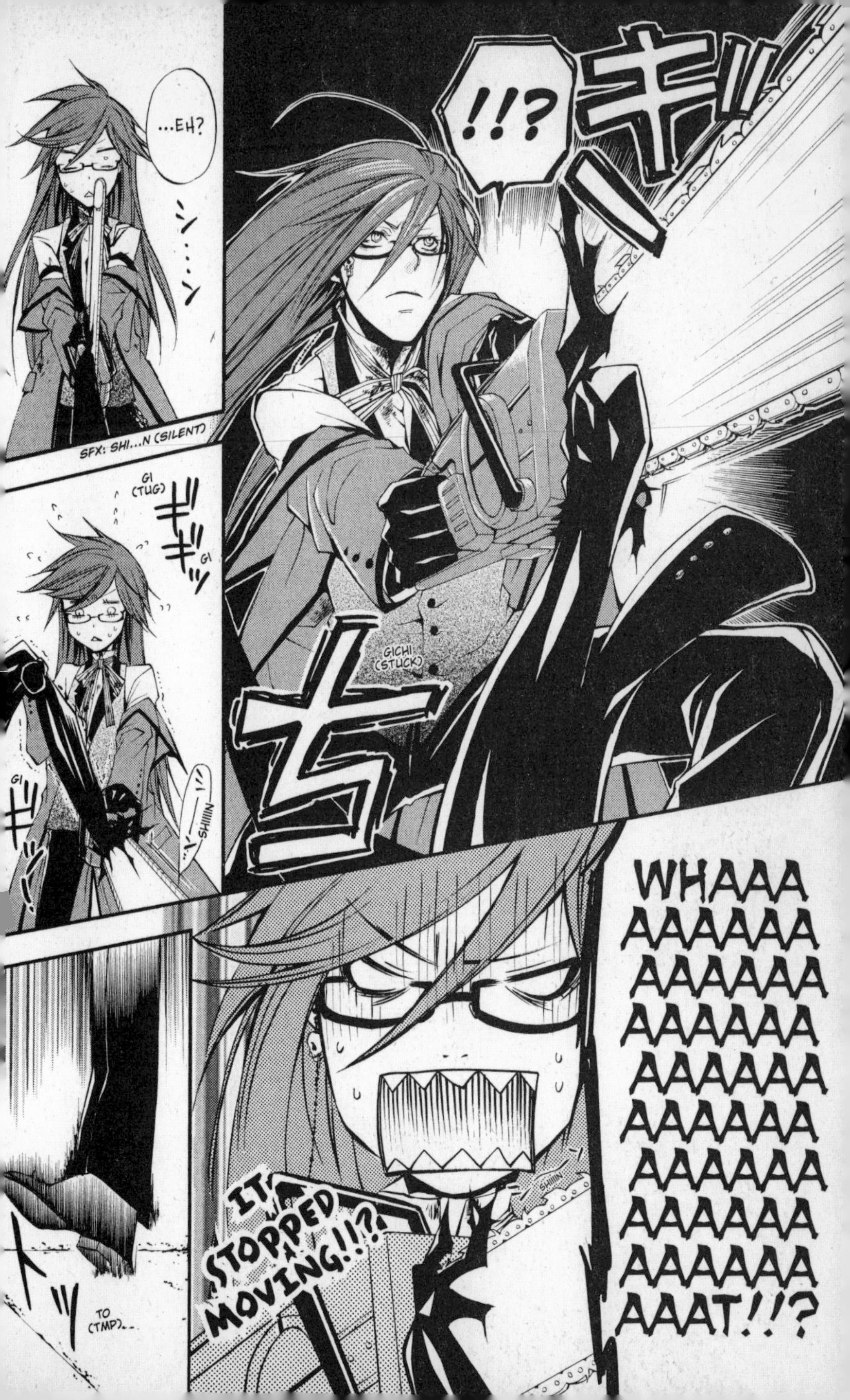
!!?
GICHI (STUCK)
...EH?
SFX: SHI...N (SILENT)
GI (TUG)
GI
GI
SHIIIN
WHAAAAAAAAAAAAAAAAAAAAAAAAAAAAAAAAAAAAAAAAAAAAAAAAAAAAAAT!!?
IT STOPPED MOVING!!?
SHIIIN
TO (TMP)

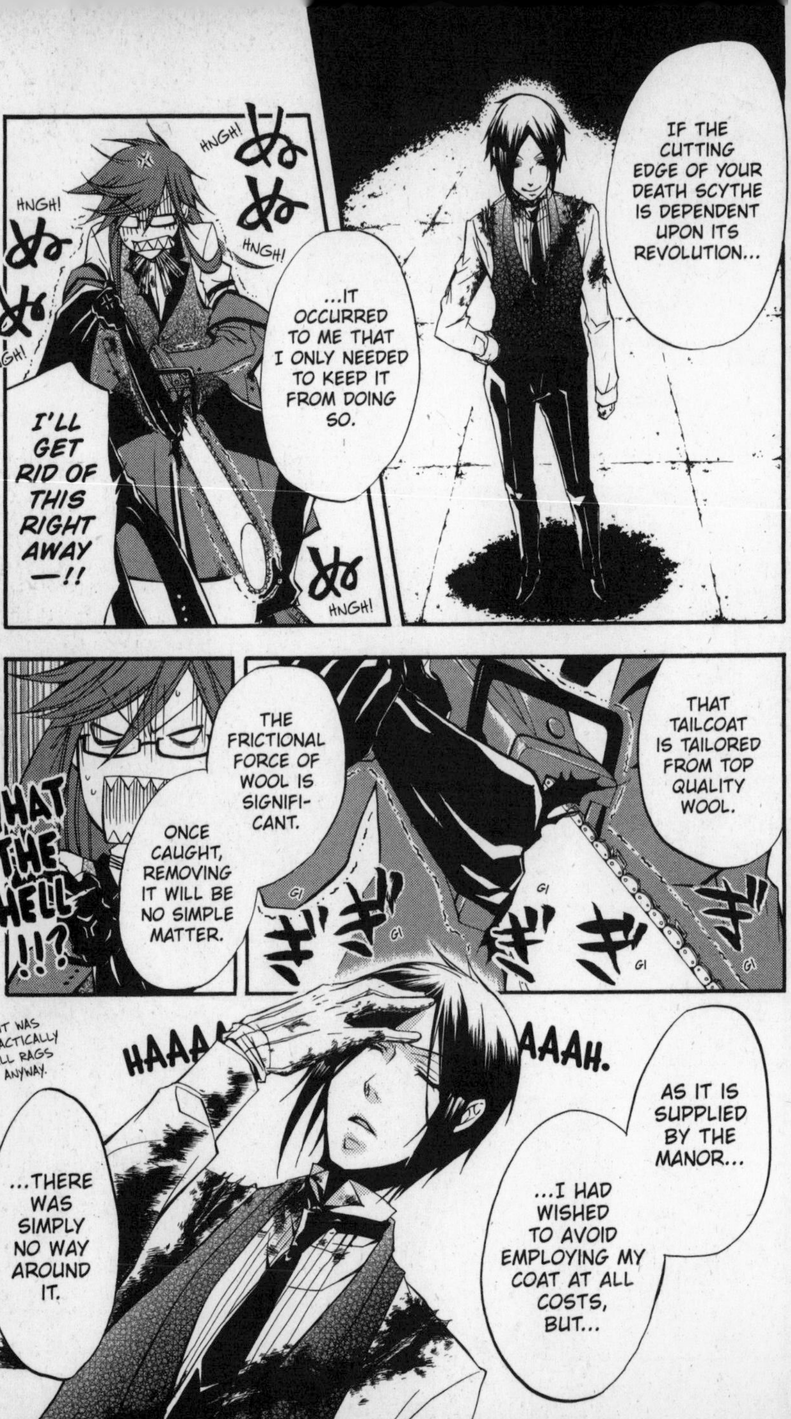
IF THE CUTTING EDGE OF YOUR DEATH SCYTHE IS DEPENDENT UPON ITS REVOLUTION...
...IT OCCURRED TO ME THAT I ONLY NEEDED TO KEEP IT FROM DOING SO.
ぬ HNGH!
ぬ HNGH!
ぬ HNGH!
ぬ HNGH!
ぬ HNGH!
I'LL GET RID OF THIS RIGHT AWAY—!!
THAT TAILCOAT IS TAILORED FROM TOP QUALITY WOOL.
ぎ GI
ぎ GI
ぎ GI
ぎ GI
THE FRICTIONAL FORCE OF WOOL IS SIGNIFI-CANT.
ONCE CAUGHT, REMOVING IT WILL BE NO SIMPLE MATTER.
WHAT THE HELL!!?
HAAAAAAH.
AS IT IS SUPPLIED BY THE MANOR...
...I HAD WISHED TO AVOID EMPLOYING MY COAT AT ALL COSTS, BUT...
...THERE WAS SIMPLY NO WAY AROUND IT.
IT WAS PRACTICALLY ALL RAGS ANYWAY.

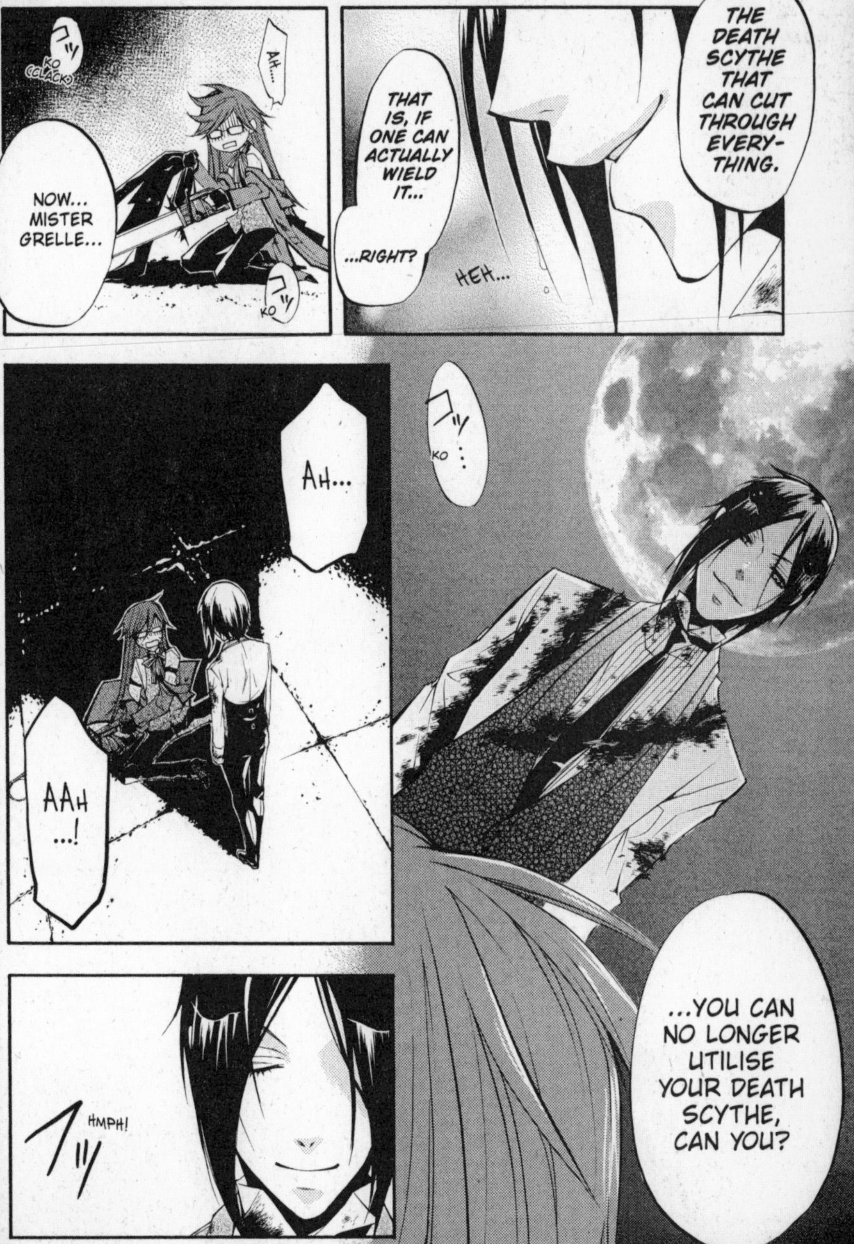
THE DEATH SCYTHE THAT CAN CUT THROUGH EVERY-THING.
THAT IS, IF ONE CAN ACTUALLY WIELD IT...
...RIGHT?
HEH...
AH...
KO (CLACK)
NOW... MISTER GRELLE...
KO
KO...
...YOU CAN NO LONGER UTILISE YOUR DEATH SCYTHE, CAN YOU?
AH...
AAH ...!
HMPH!

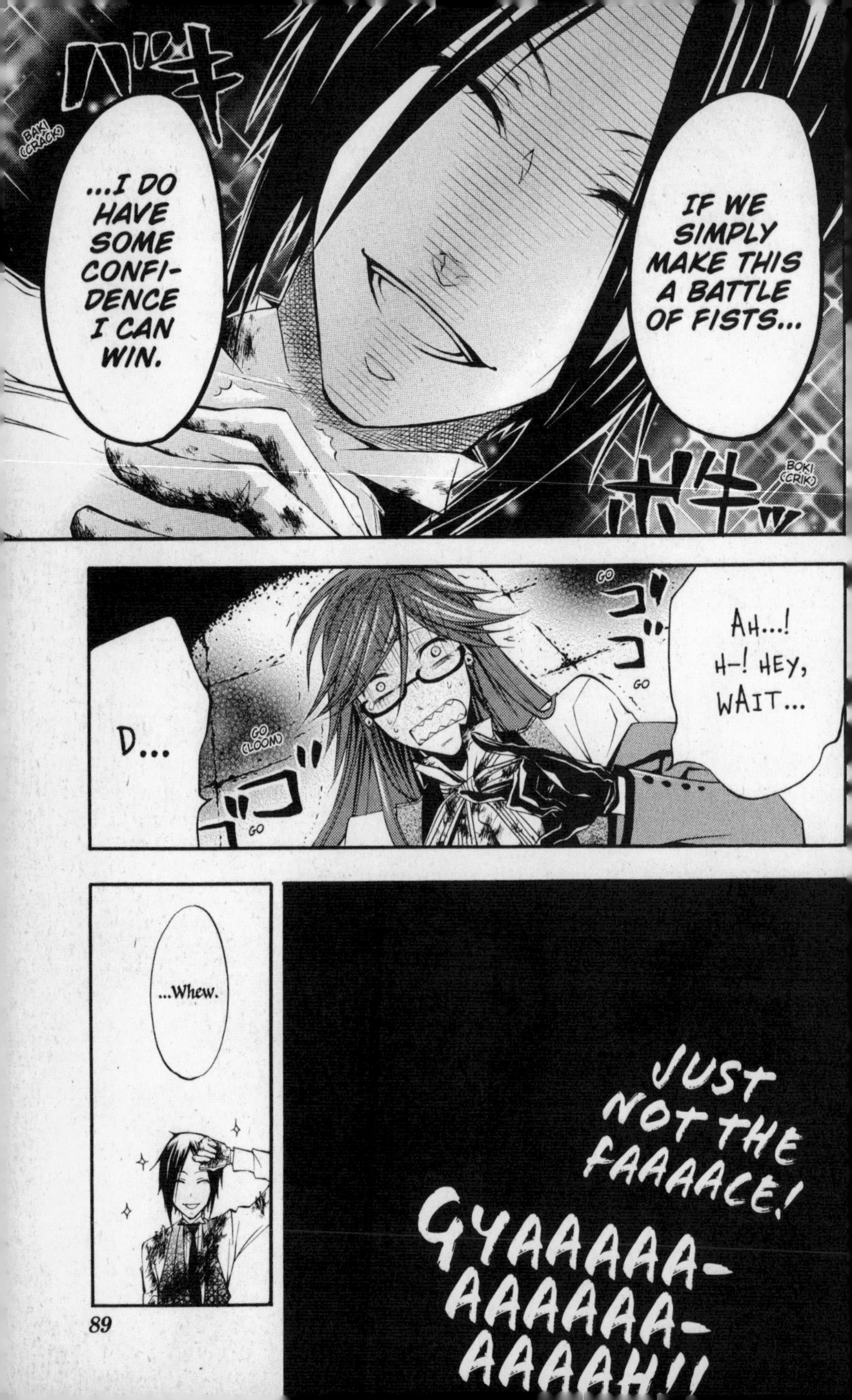
IF WE SIMPLY MAKE THIS A BATTLE OF FISTS...
BOKI (CRIK)
BAKI (CRACK)
...I DO HAVE SOME CONFIDENCE I CAN WIN.
GO
AH...! H-! HEY, WAIT...
GO
GO (LOOM)
D...
GO
JUST NOT THE FAAAACE!
GYAAAAAA-AAAAAA-AAAAH!!
...Whew.

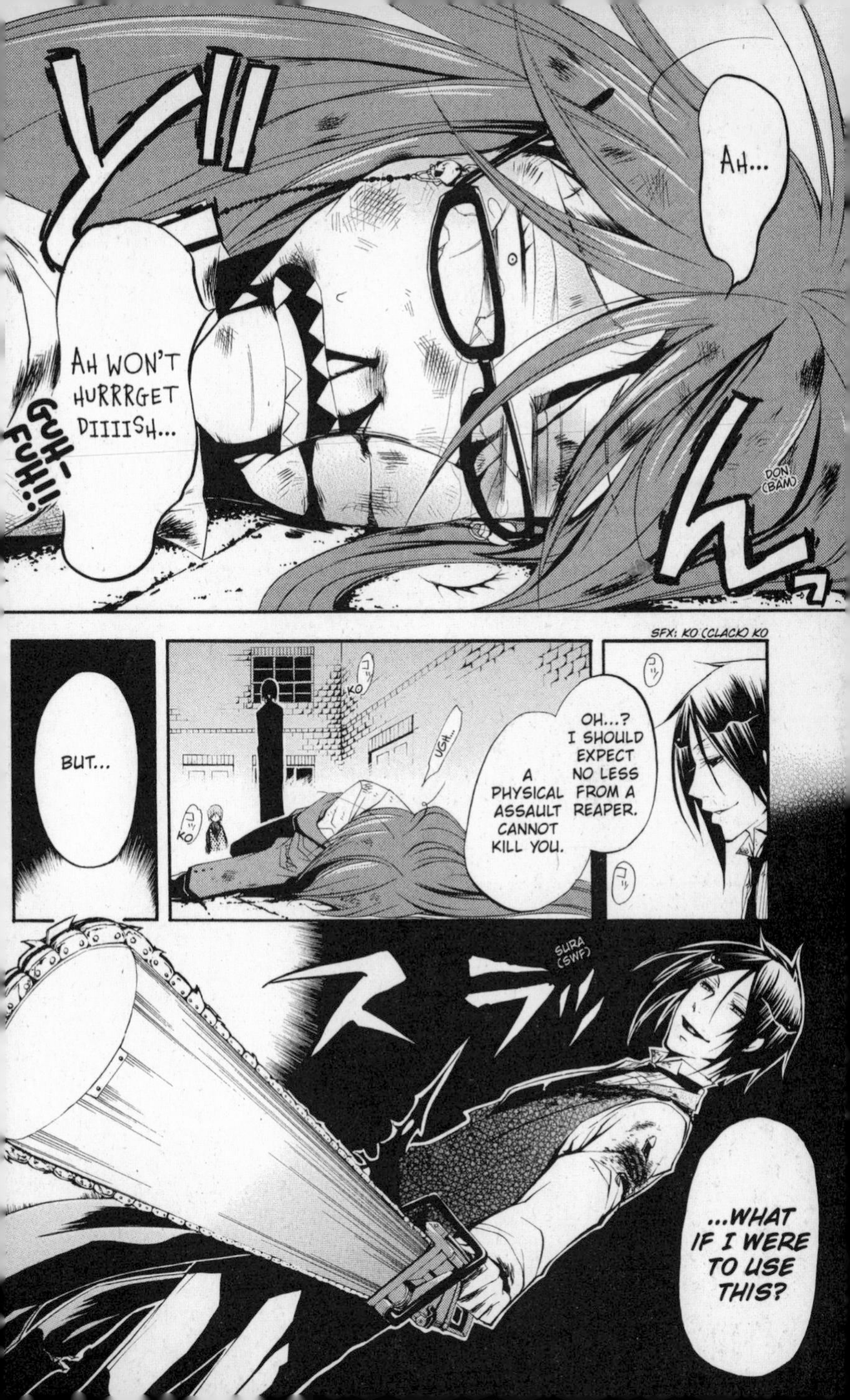
AH...
DON (BAM)
AH WON'T HURRRGET DIIIISH...
GUH-FUH!!!
SFX: KO (CLACK) KO
KO
OH...? I SHOULD EXPECT NO LESS FROM A REAPER.
A PHYSICAL ASSAULT CANNOT KILL YOU.
UGH...
KO
BUT...
SURA (SWF)
...WHAT IF I WERE TO USE THIS?

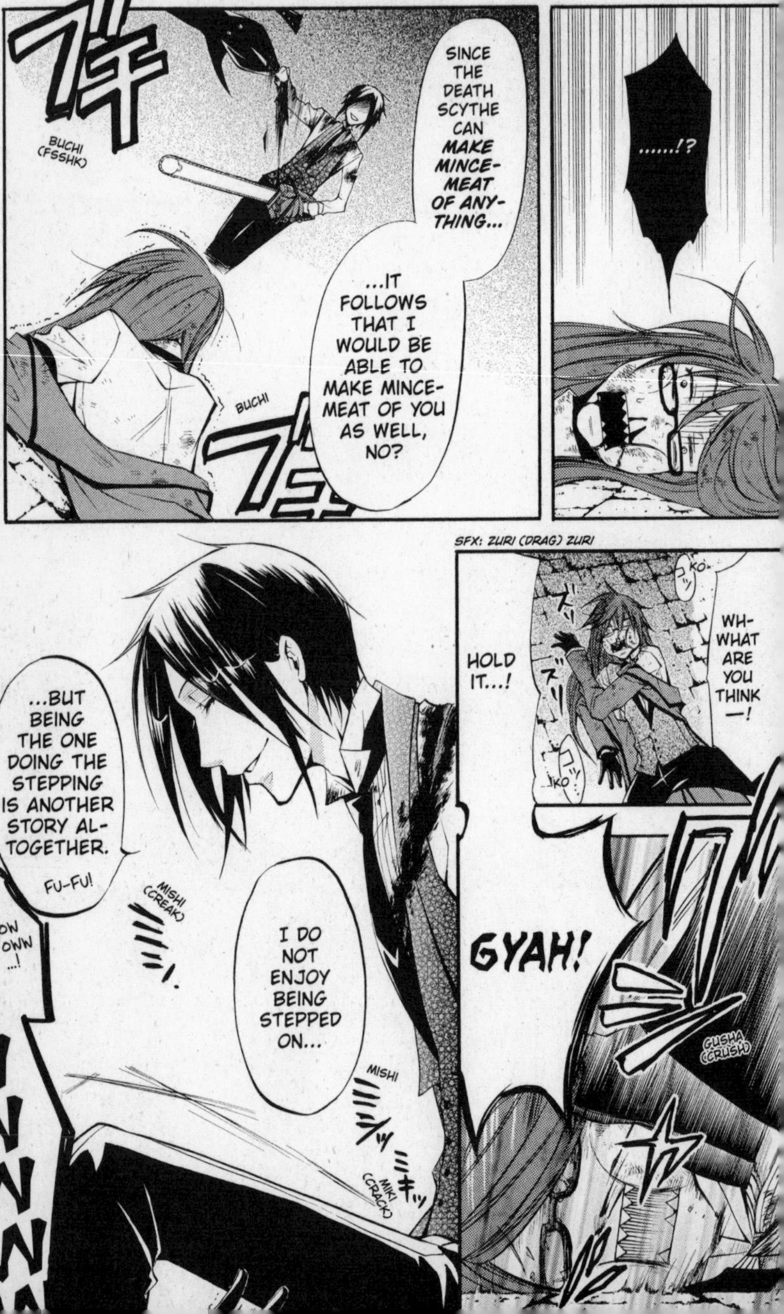

......!?
SINCE THE DEATH SCYTHE CAN MAKE MINCE-MEAT OF ANY-THING...
BUCHI (FSSHK)
...IT FOLLOWS THAT I WOULD BE ABLE TO MAKE MINCE-MEAT OF YOU AS WELL, NO?
BUCHI
SFX: ZURI (DRAG) ZURI
KO
WH-WHAT ARE YOU THINK—!
HOLD IT...!
KO
GYAH!
GUSHA (CRUSH)
MISHI (CREAK)
I DO NOT ENJOY BEING STEPPED ON...
...BUT BEING THE ONE DOING THE STEPPING IS ANOTHER STORY AL-TOGETHER.
FU-FU!
MISHI
MIKI (CRACK)
OW D'OWN ...!
OWWW...!

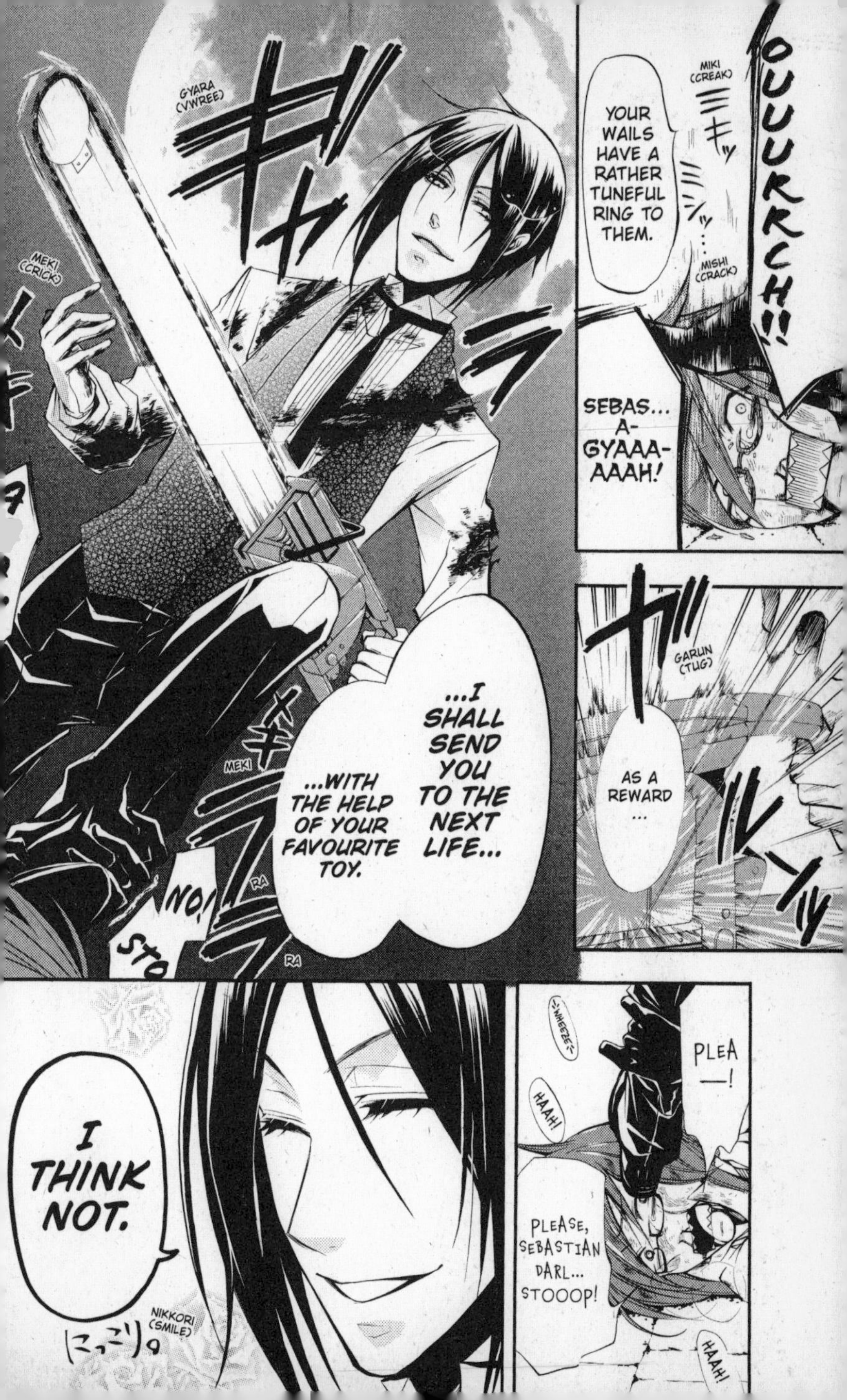
OUUURRCH!!
MIKI (CREAK)
YOUR WAILS HAVE A RATHER TUNEFUL RING TO THEM.
MISHI (CRACK)
SEBAS... A-GYAAA-AAAH!
GARUN (TUG)
AS A REWARD ...
GYARA (VWREE)
...I SHALL SEND YOU TO THE NEXT LIFE...
...WITH THE HELP OF YOUR FAVOURITE TOY.
MEKI (CRICK)
MEKI
RA
RA
NO!
STO
PLEA —!
WHEEZE
HAAH!
PLEASE, SEBASTIAN DARL... STOOOP!
HAAH!
I THINK NOT.
NIKKORI (SMILE)

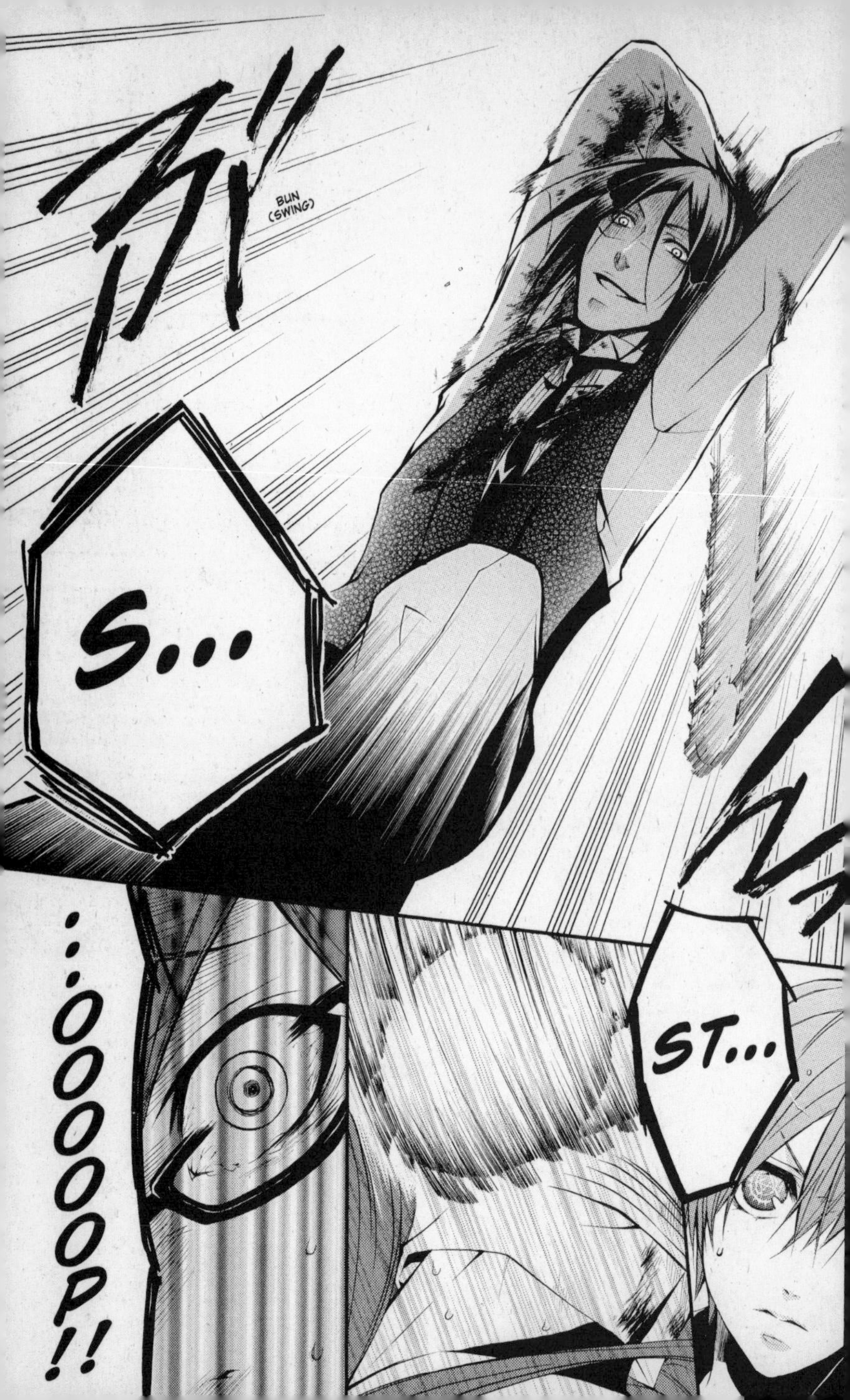
BUN (SWING)
S...
ST...
...OOOOOOP!!

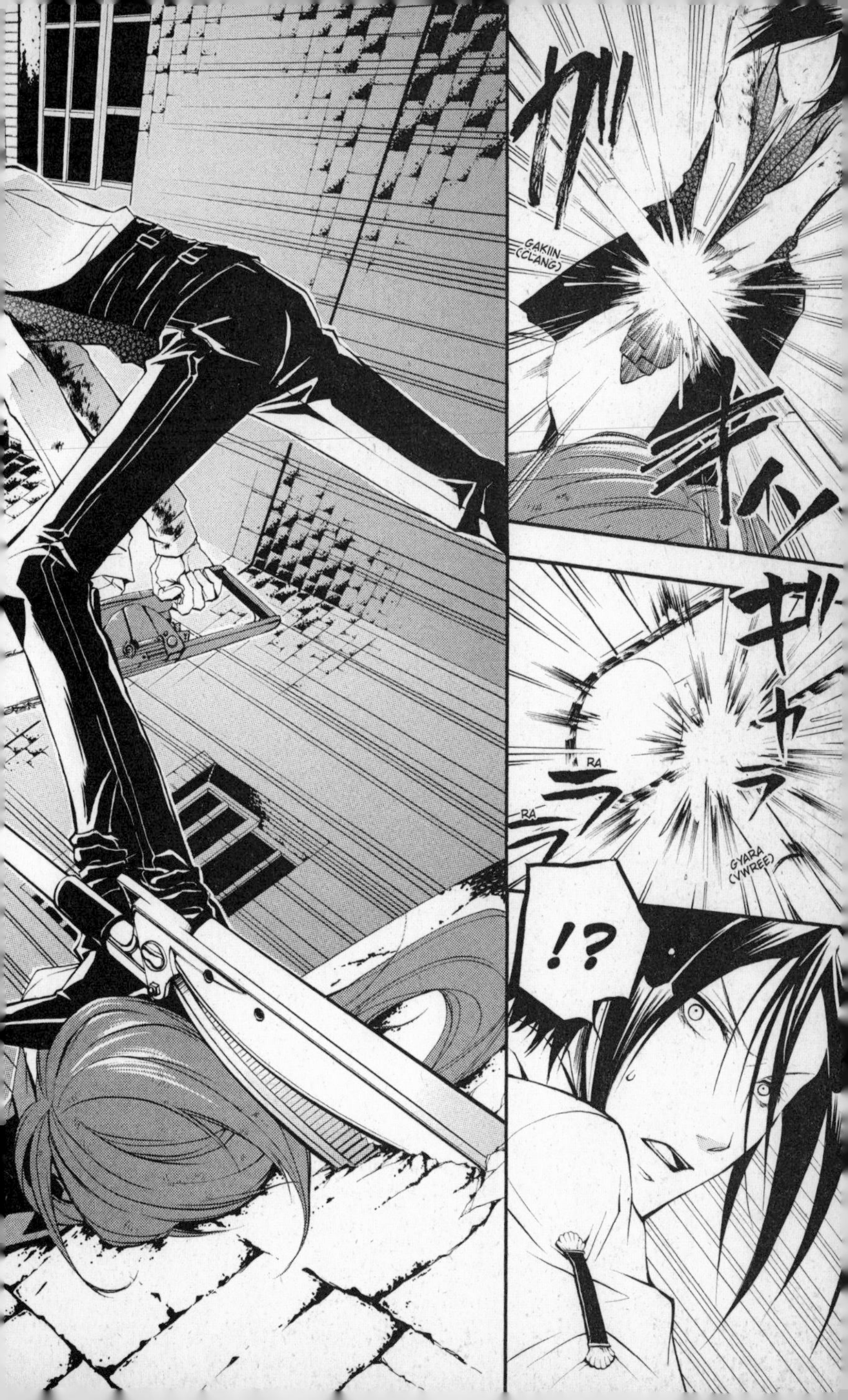
GAKIIN (CLANG)
RA
RA
GYARA (VWREE)
!?

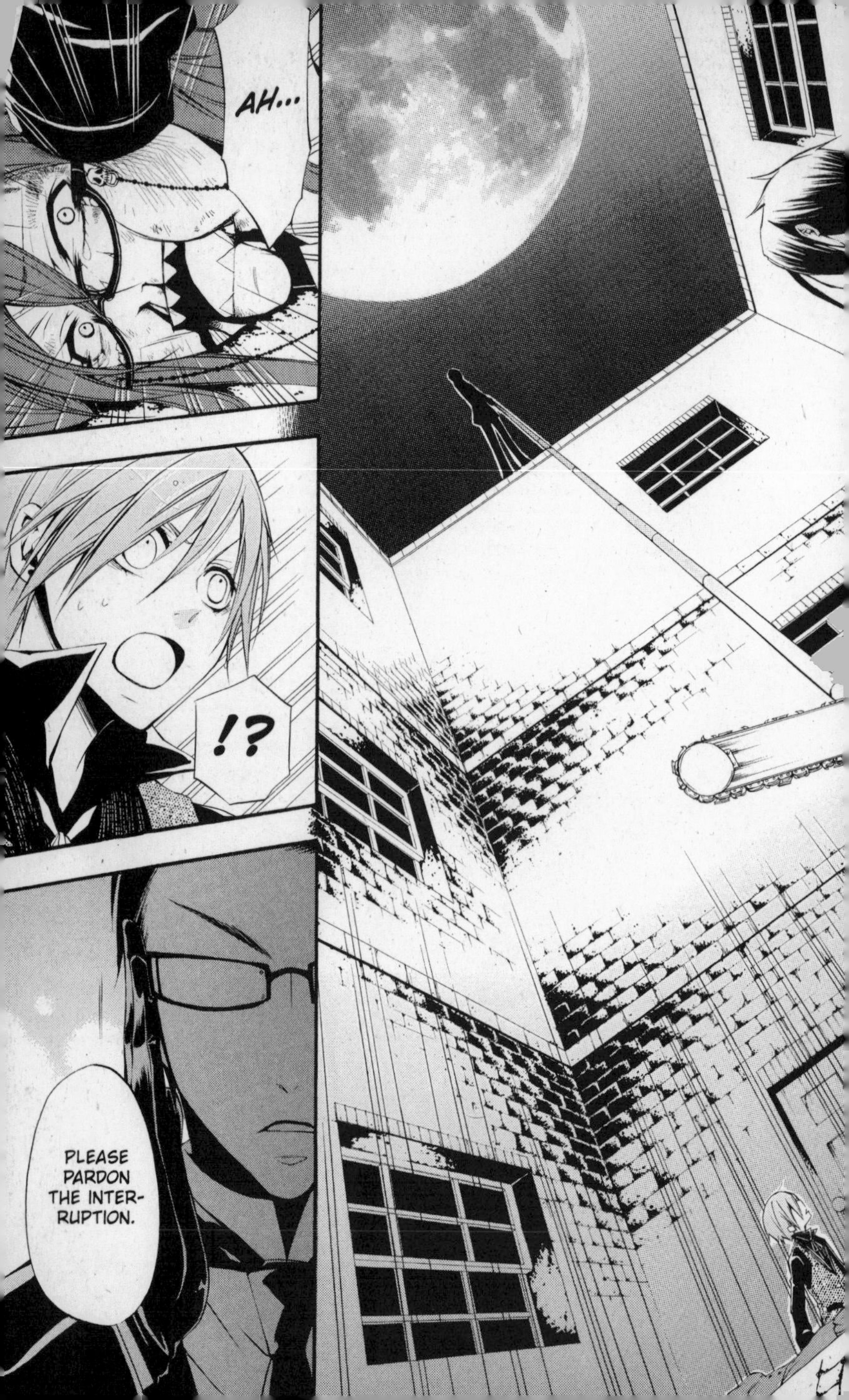
AH...
!?
PLEASE PARDON THE INTER-RUPTION.

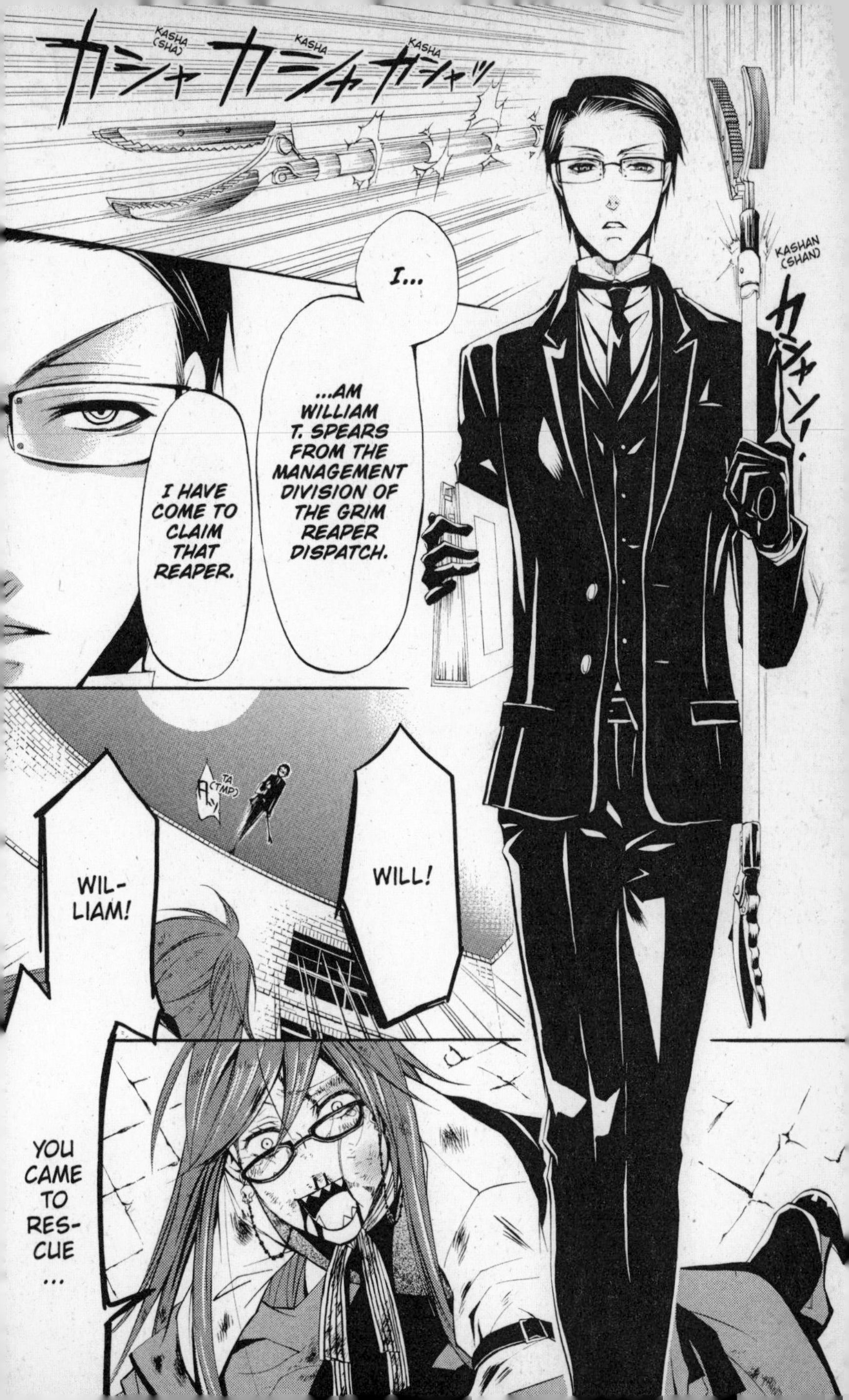
KASHA (SHA)
KASHA
KASHA
KASHAN (SHAN)
I...
...AM WILLIAM T. SPEARS FROM THE MANAGEMENT DIVISION OF THE GRIM REAPER DISPATCH.
I HAVE COME TO CLAIM THAT REAPER.
TA (TMP)
WILL!
WIL-LIAM!
YOU CAME TO RES-CUE ...

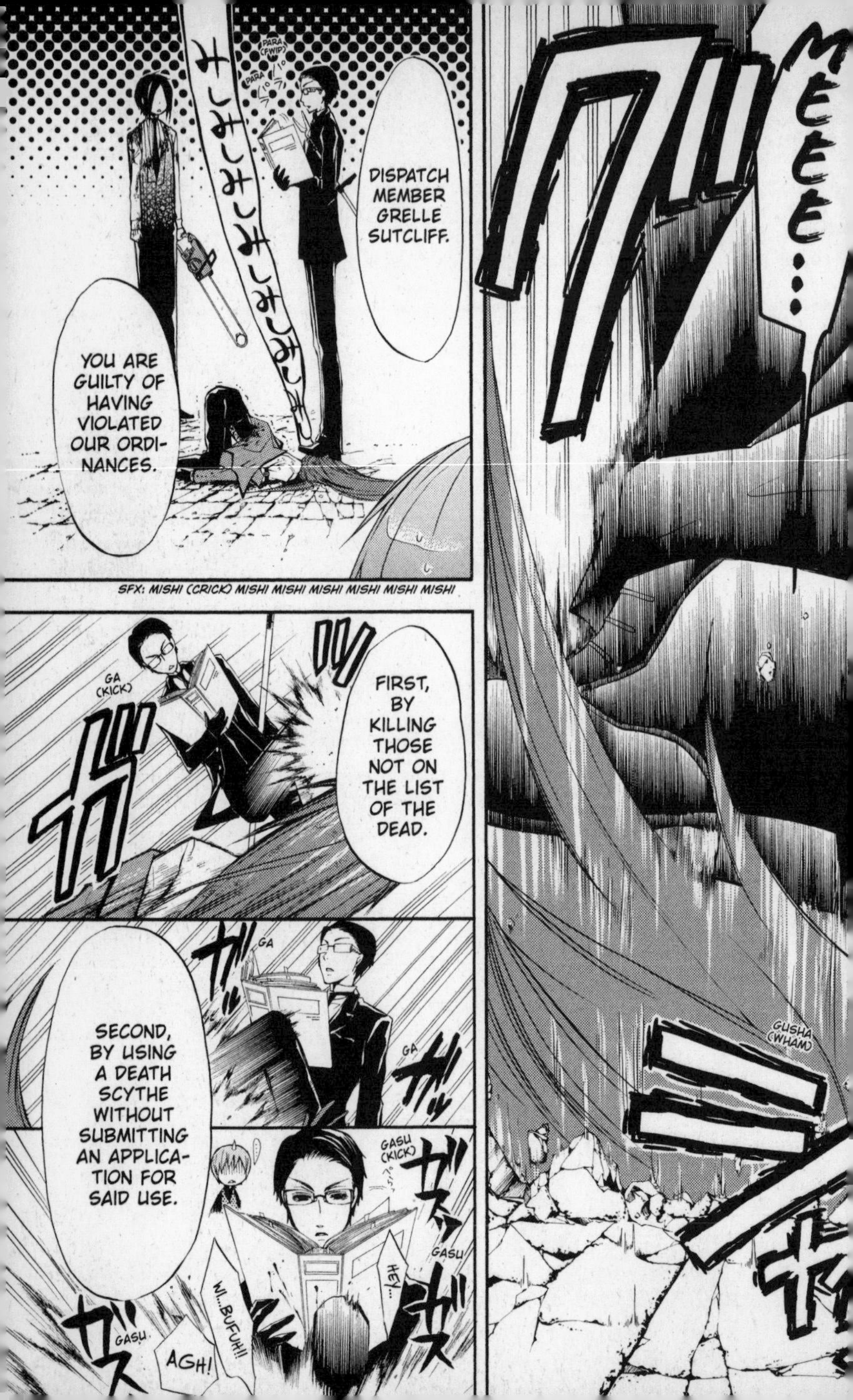
MEEEE...
GUSHA (WHAM)
PARA (FWIP) PARA
DISPATCH MEMBER GRELLE SUTCLIFF.
YOU ARE GUILTY OF HAVING VIOLATED OUR ORDINANCES.
SFX: MISHI (CRICK) MISHI MISHI MISHI MISHI MISHI MISHI
FIRST, BY KILLING THOSE NOT ON THE LIST OF THE DEAD.
GA (KICK)
GA
GA
SECOND, BY USING A DEATH SCYTHE WITHOUT SUBMITTING AN APPLICATION FOR SAID USE.
GASU (KICK)
GASU
HEY...
WI...BUFUH!!
AGH!
GASU

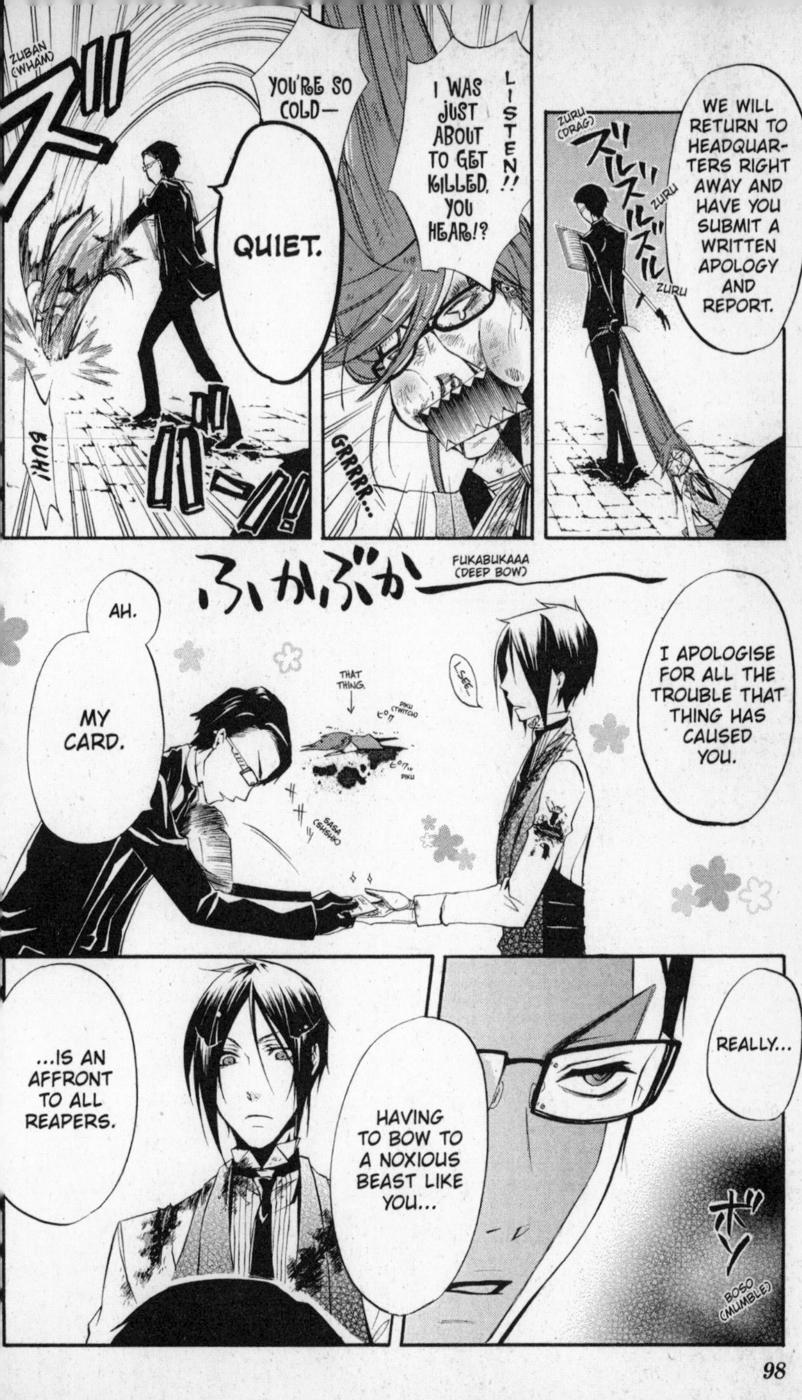
WE WILL RETURN TO HEADQUARTERS RIGHT AWAY AND HAVE YOU SUBMIT A WRITTEN APOLOGY AND REPORT.
ZURU (DRAG)
ZURU
ZURU
LISTEN!!
I WAS JUST ABOUT TO GET KILLED, YOU HEAR!?
GRRRRR...
YOU'RE SO COLD—
QUIET.
ZUBAN (WHAM)
BUH!
ふかぶか
FUKABUKAAA (DEEP BOW)
I APOLOGISE FOR ALL THE TROUBLE THAT THING HAS CAUSED YOU.
I SEE...
THAT THING.
PIKU (TWITCH)
PIKU
SASA (SHSHK)
AH.
MY CARD.
REALLY...
HAVING TO BOW TO A NOXIOUS BEAST LIKE YOU...
ボソ
BOSO (MUMBLE)
...IS AN AFFRONT TO ALL REAPERS.

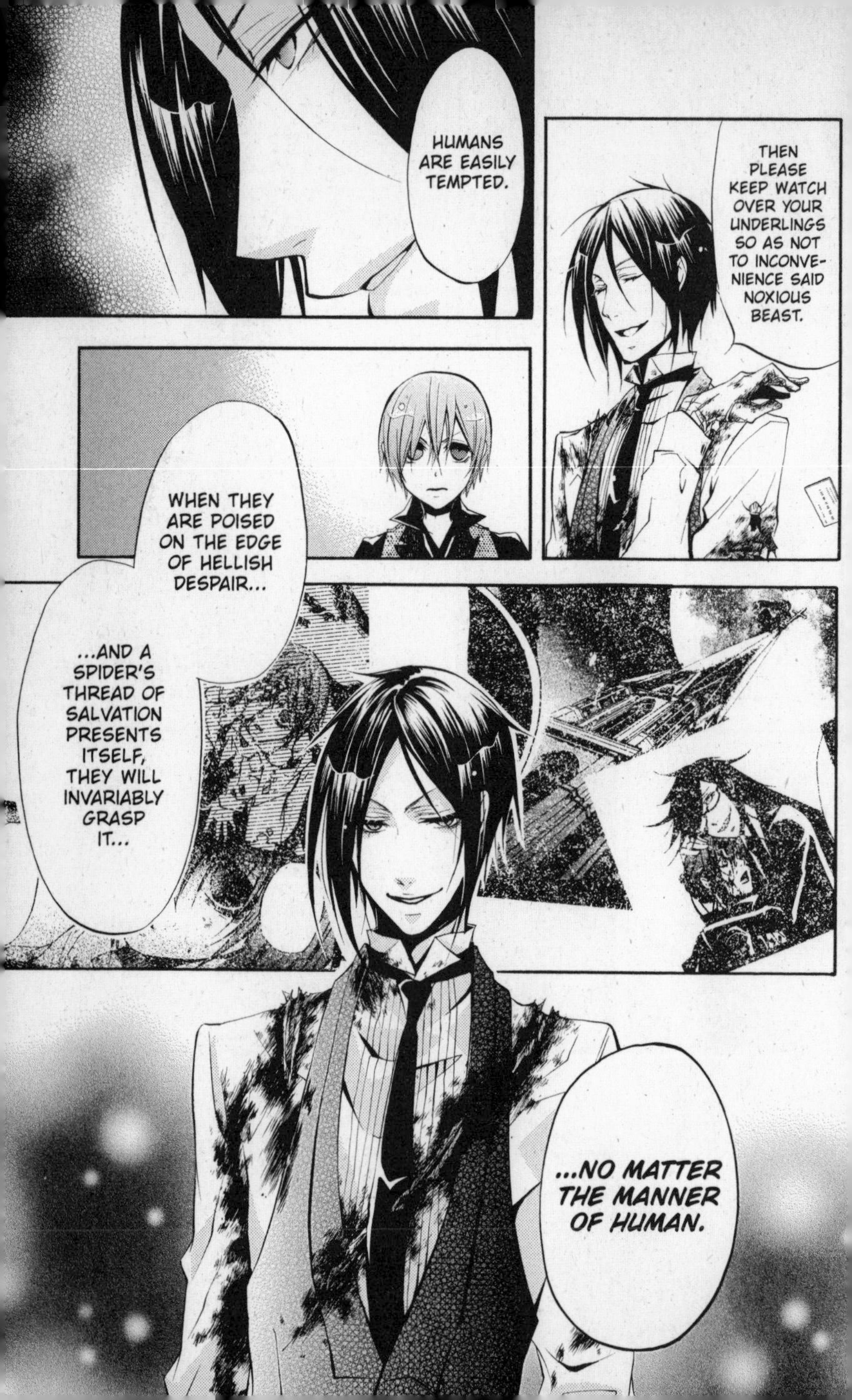
THEN PLEASE KEEP WATCH OVER YOUR UNDERLINGS SO AS NOT TO INCONVE-NIENCE SAID NOXIOUS BEAST.
HUMANS ARE EASILY TEMPTED.
WHEN THEY ARE POISED ON THE EDGE OF HELLISH DESPAIR...
...AND A SPIDER'S THREAD OF SALVATION PRESENTS ITSELF, THEY WILL INVARIABLY GRASP IT...
...NO MATTER THE MANNER OF HUMAN.

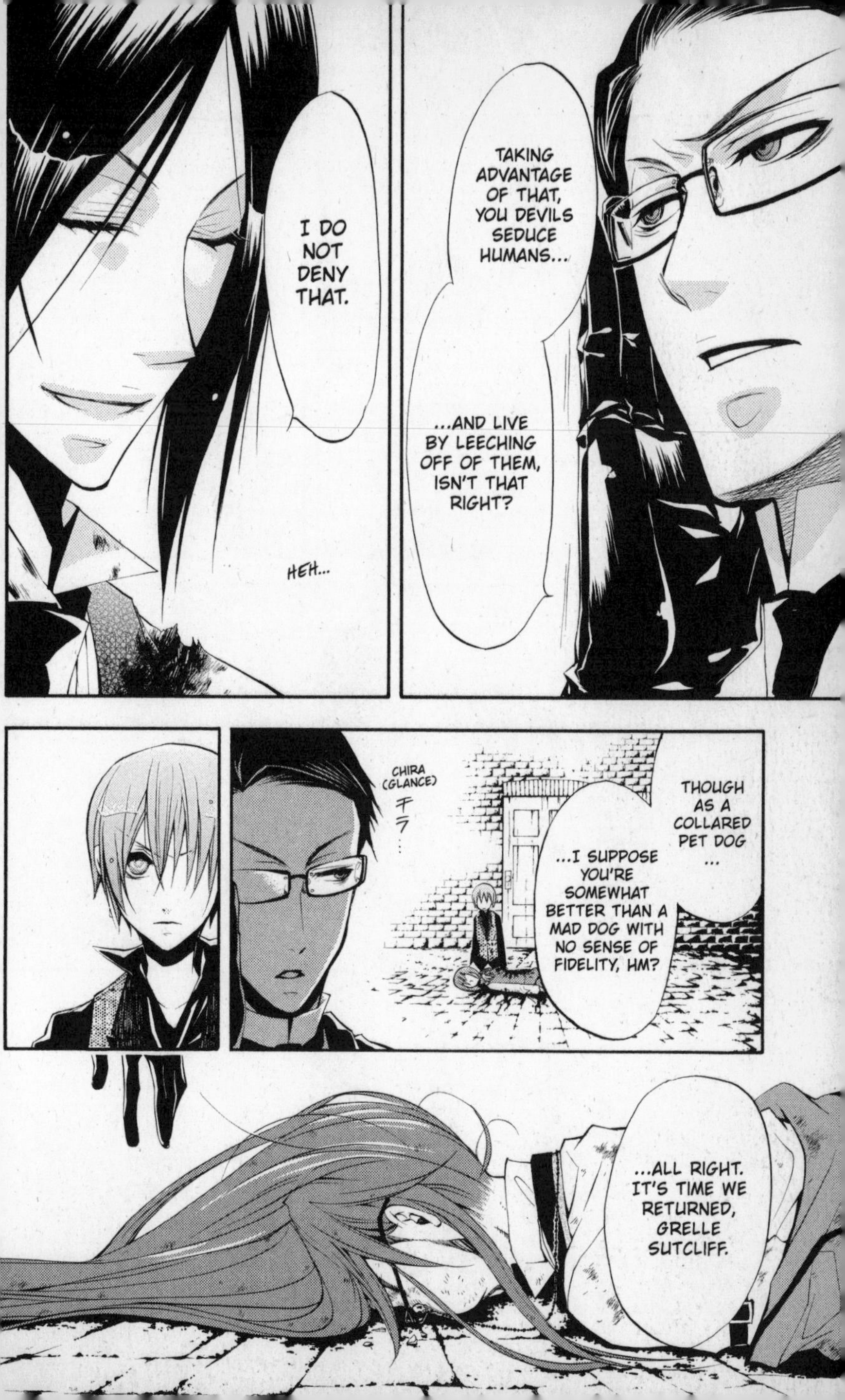
TAKING ADVANTAGE OF THAT, YOU DEVILS SEDUCE HUMANS...
...AND LIVE BY LEECHING OFF OF THEM, ISN'T THAT RIGHT?
I DO NOT DENY THAT.
HEH...
THOUGH AS A COLLARED PET DOG ...
...I SUPPOSE YOU'RE SOMEWHAT BETTER THAN A MAD DOG WITH NO SENSE OF FIDELITY, HM?
CHIRA (GLANCE)
...ALL RIGHT. IT'S TIME WE RETURNED, GRELLE SUTCLIFF.

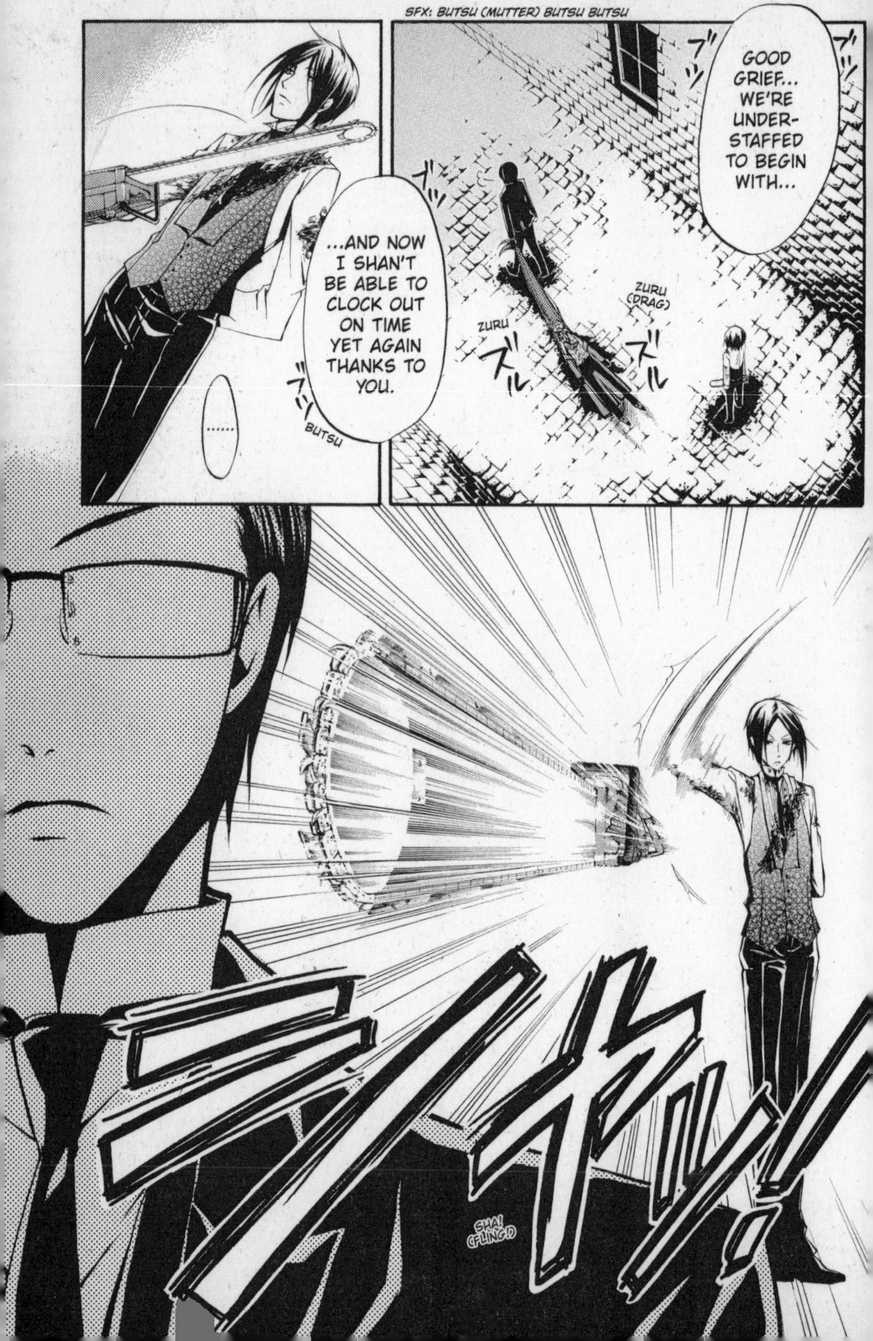
SFX: BUTSU (MUTTER) BUTSU BUTSU
GOOD GRIEF... WE'RE UNDER-STAFFED TO BEGIN WITH...
ZURU (DRAG)
ZURU
...AND NOW I SHAN'T BE ABLE TO CLOCK OUT ON TIME YET AGAIN THANKS TO YOU.
BUTSU
......
SHA! (FLING!)

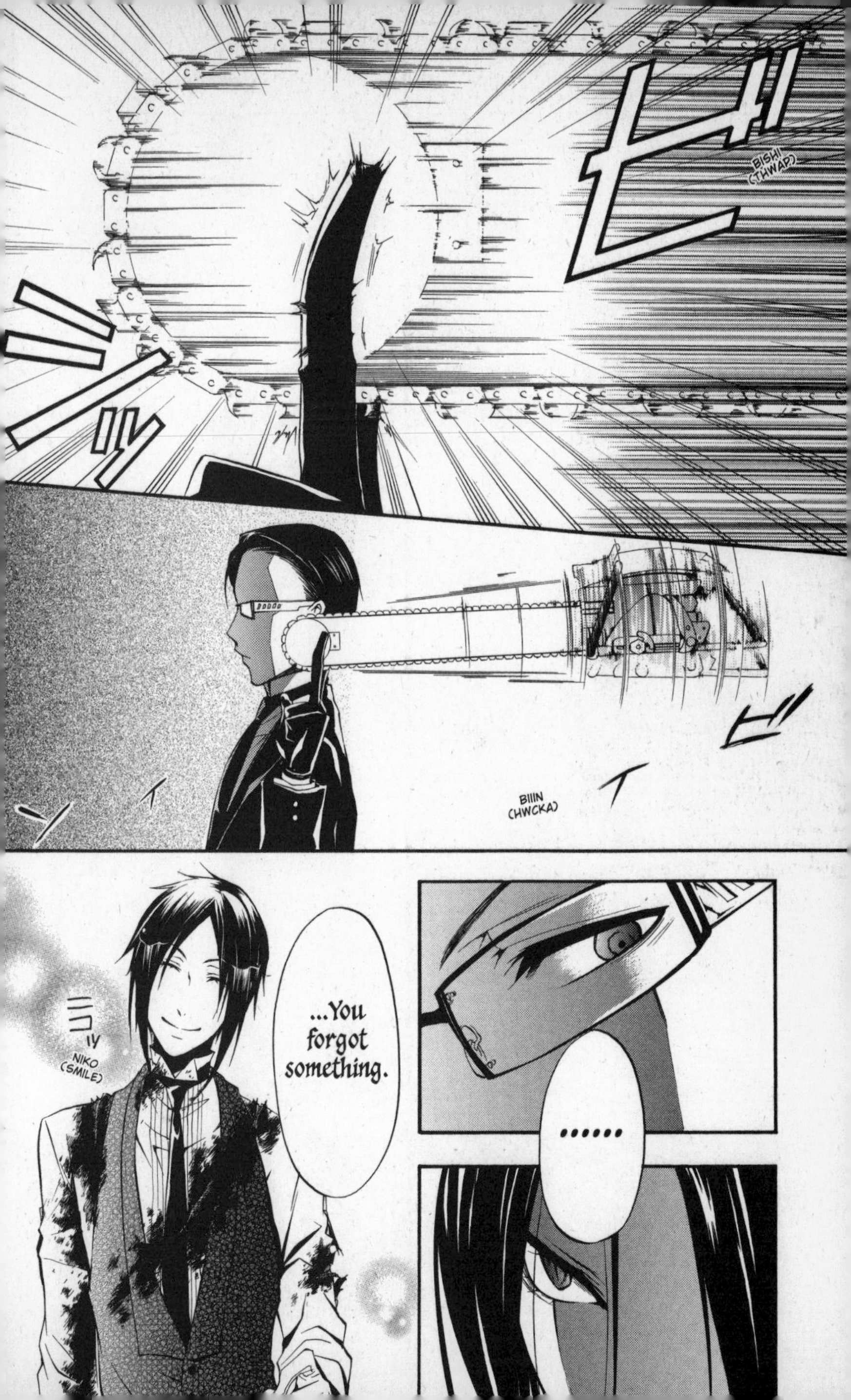
BISHI (THWAP)
BIIN (HWCKA)
......
...You forgot something.
NIKO (SMILE)

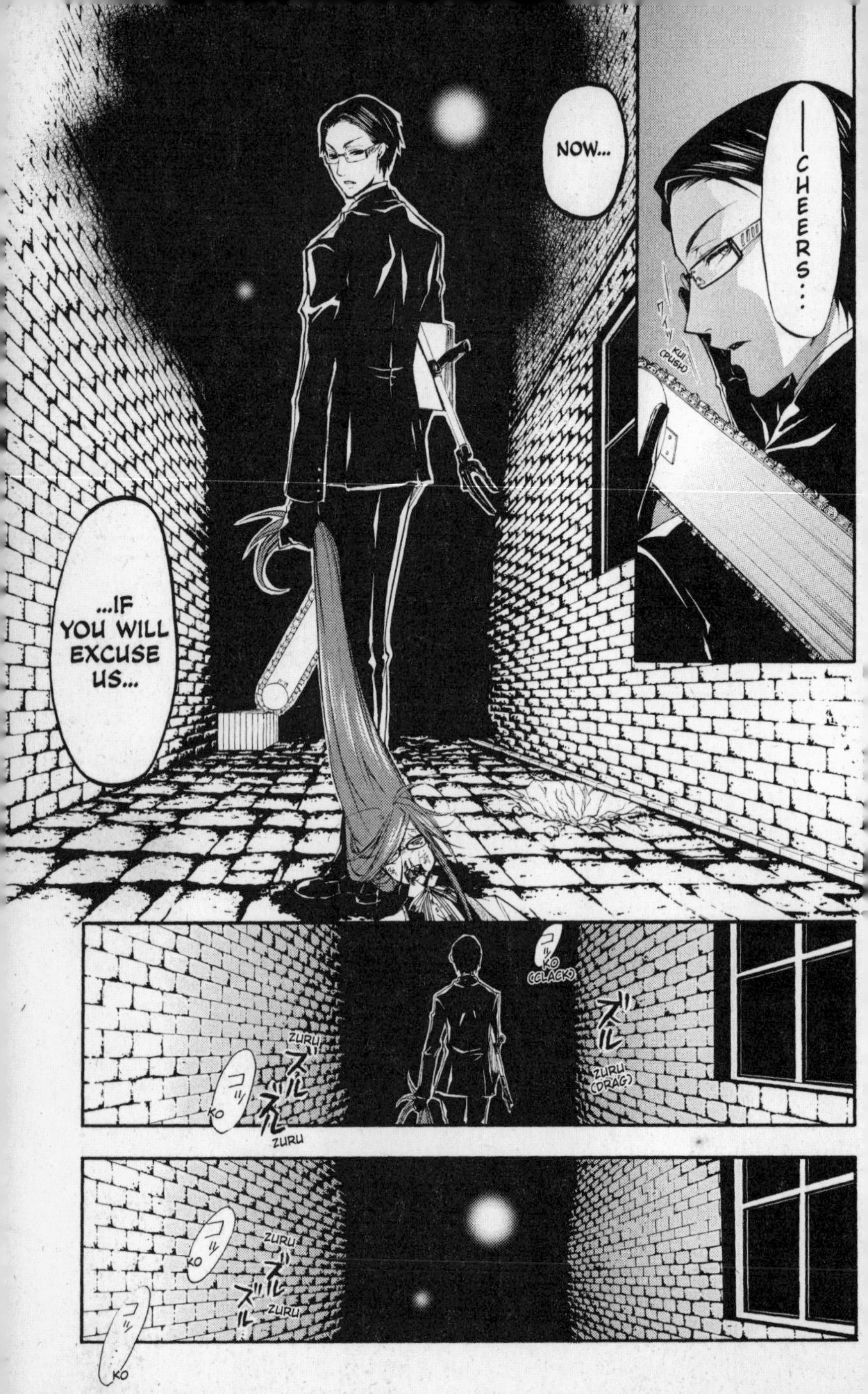

—CHEERS...
KUI (PUSH)
NOW...
...IF YOU WILL EXCUSE US...
KO (CLACK)
ZURU (DRAG)
ZURU
KO
ZURU
ZURU
KO
ZURU
KO

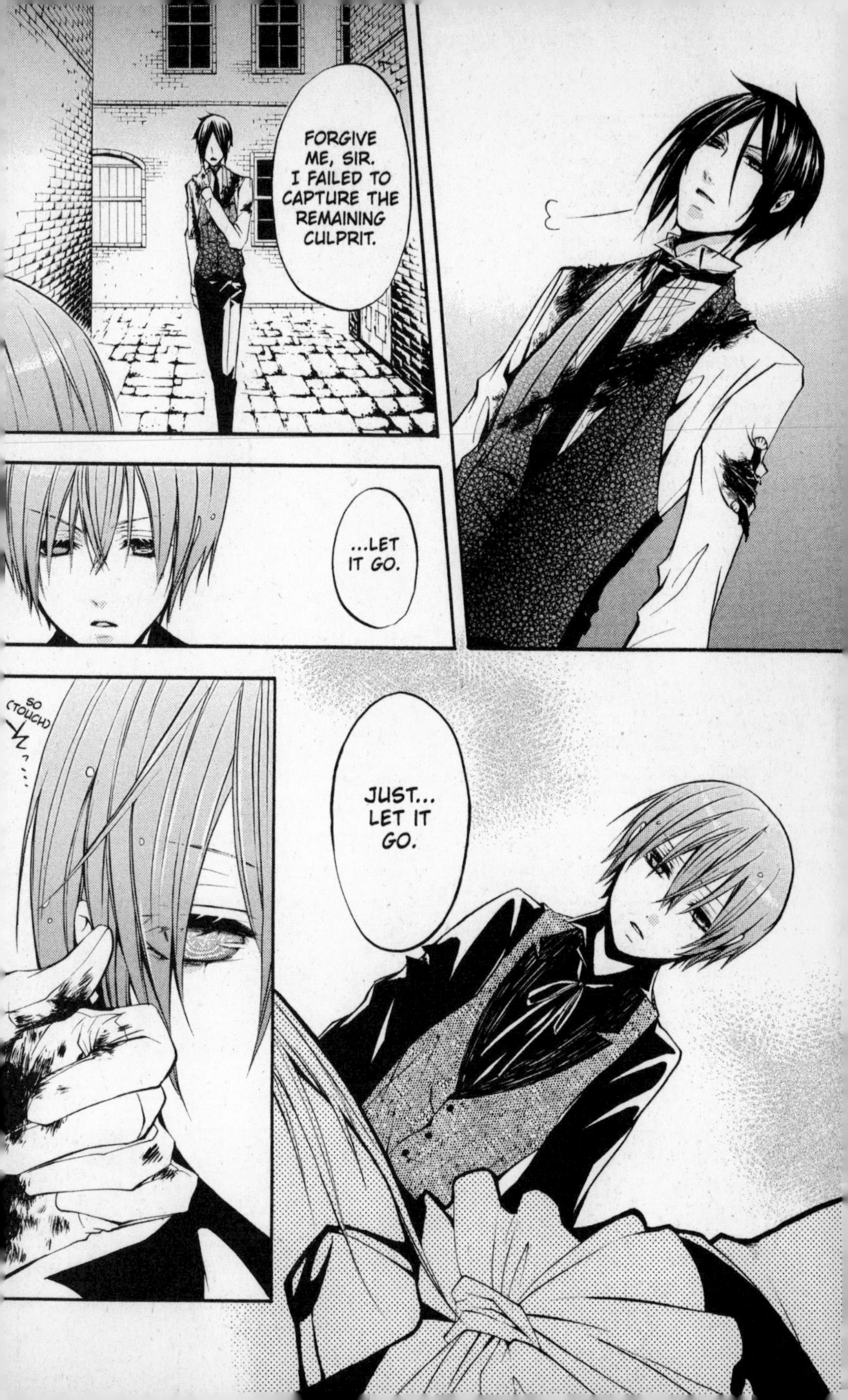
FORGIVE ME, SIR. I FAILED TO CAPTURE THE REMAINING CULPRIT.
...LET IT GO.
JUST... LET IT GO.
SO (TOUCH)

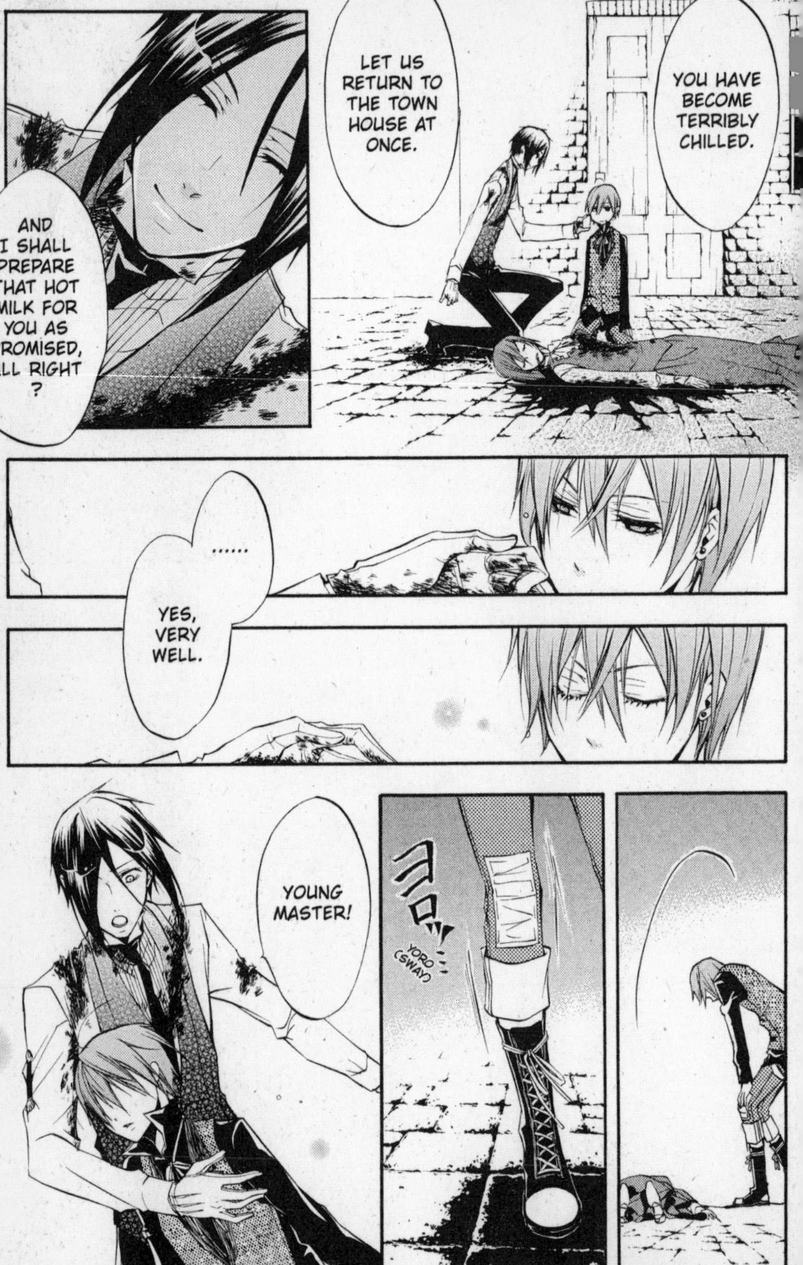
YOU HAVE BECOME TERRIBLY CHILLED.
LET US RETURN TO THE TOWN HOUSE AT ONCE.
AND I SHALL PREPARE THAT HOT MILK FOR YOU AS PROMISED, ALL RIGHT?
......
YES, VERY WELL.
ヨロッ
YORO (SWAY)
YOUNG MASTER!

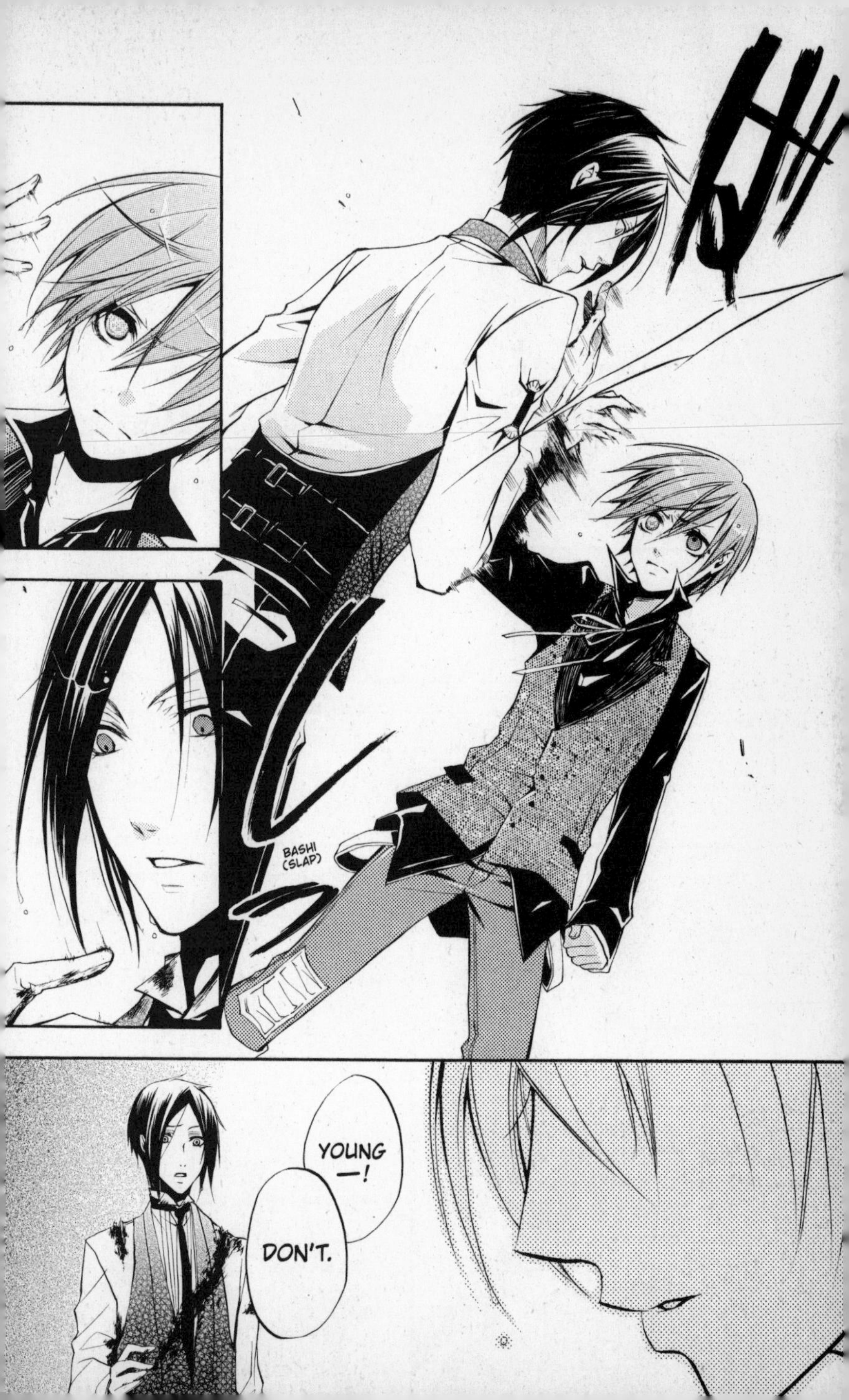
BASHI (SLAP)
YOUNG—!
DON'T.

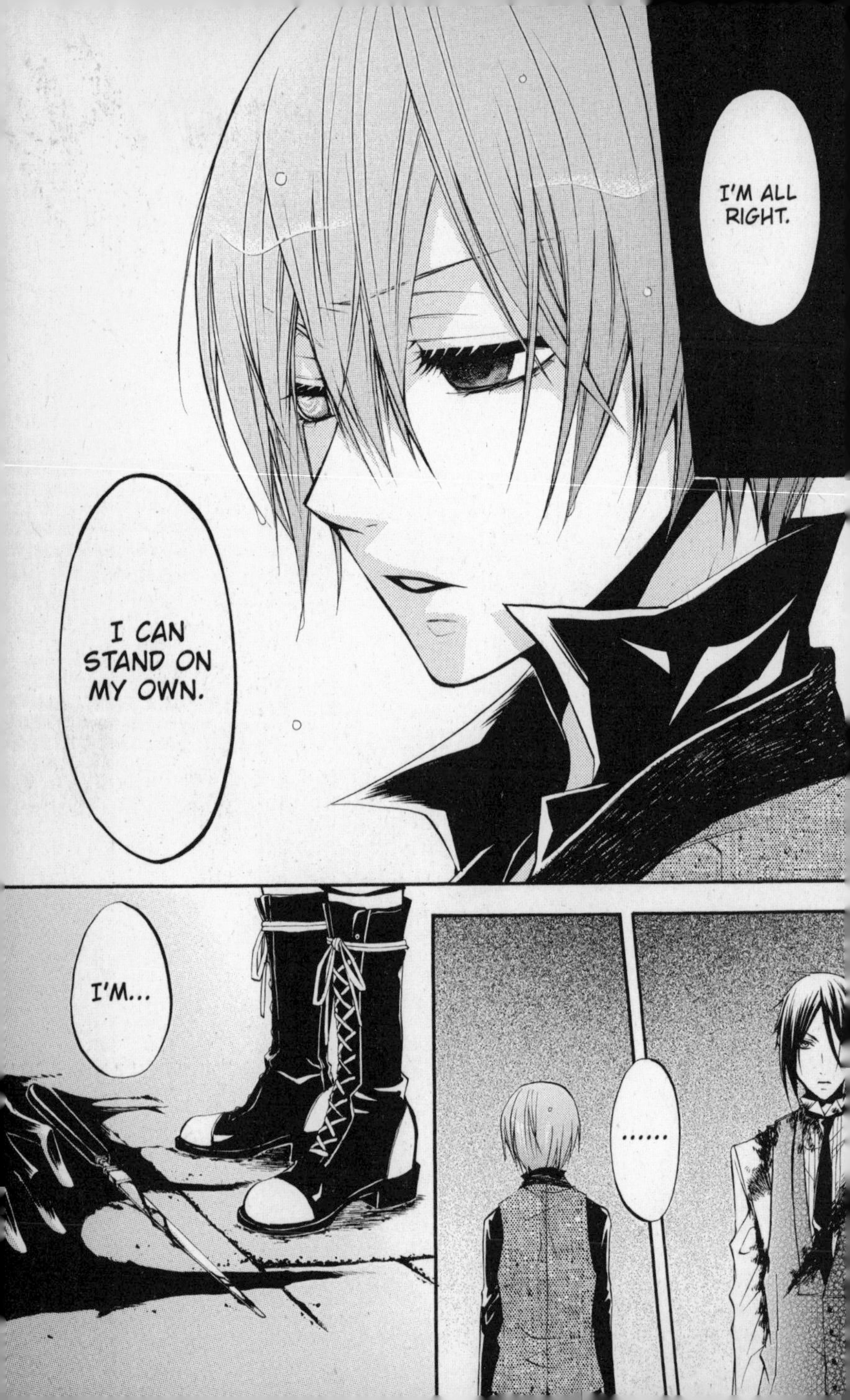
I'M ALL RIGHT.
I CAN STAND ON MY OWN.
......
I'M...

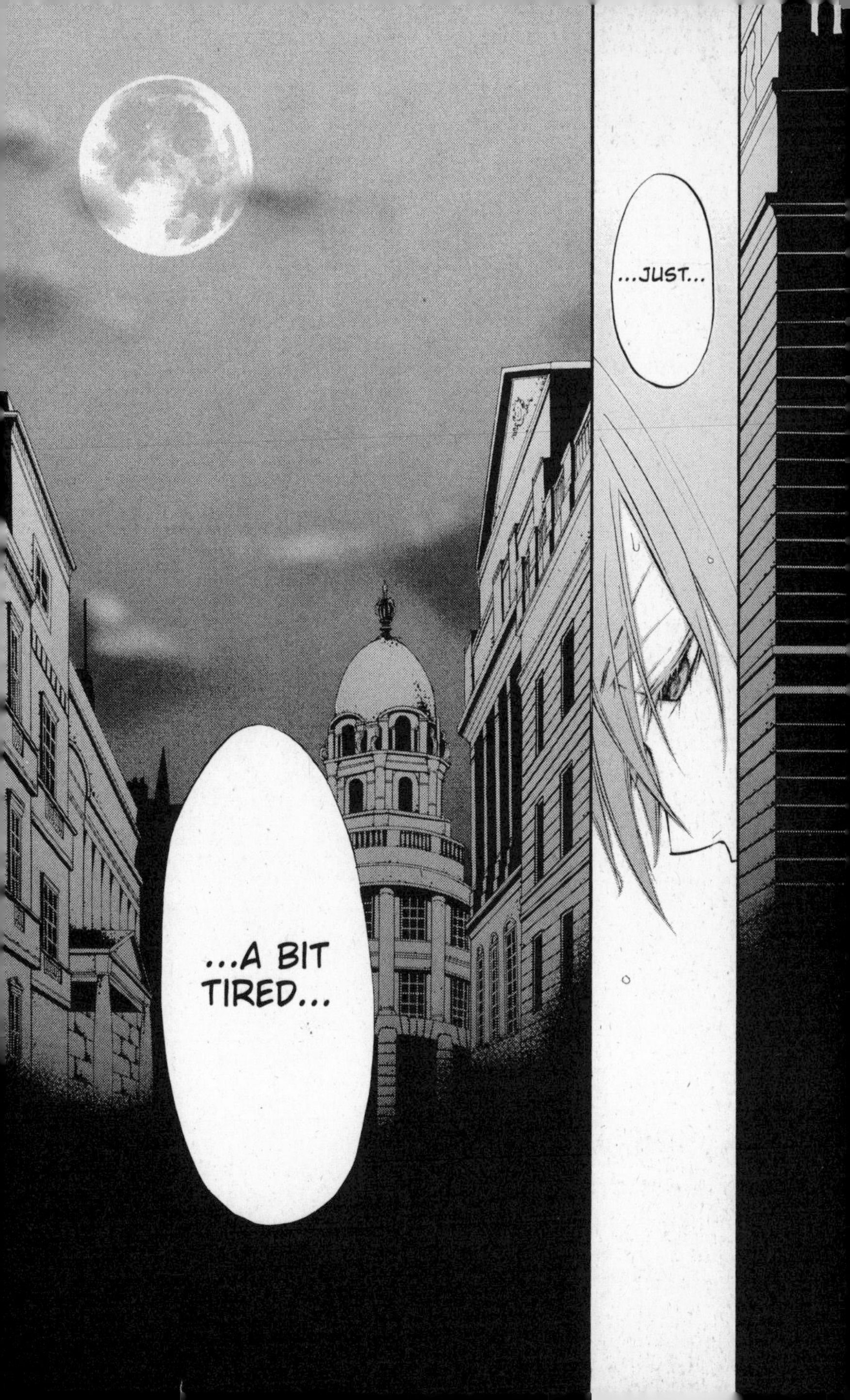
...JUST...
...A BIT TIRED...

Black Butler

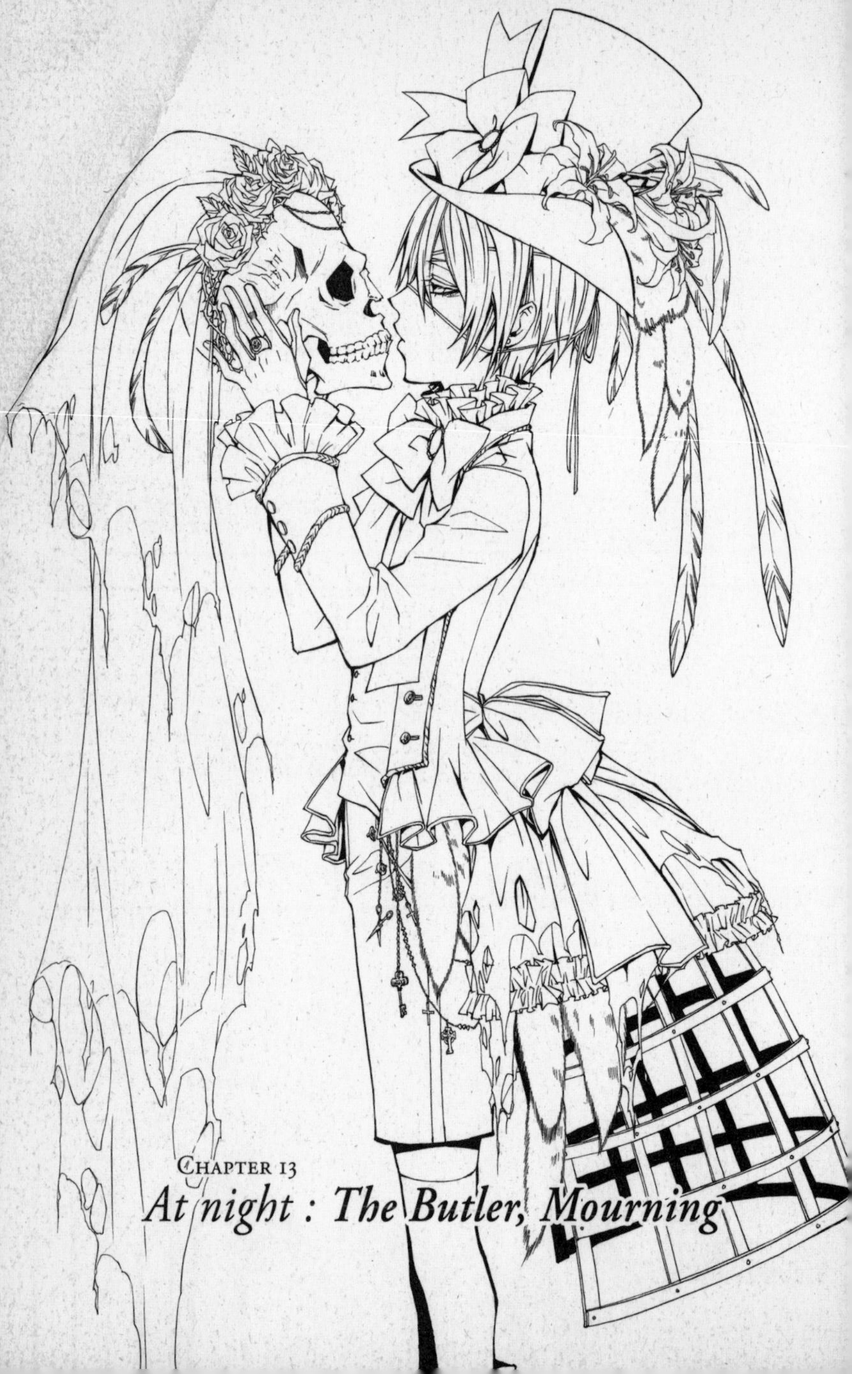

Chapter 13

At night : The Butler, Mourning

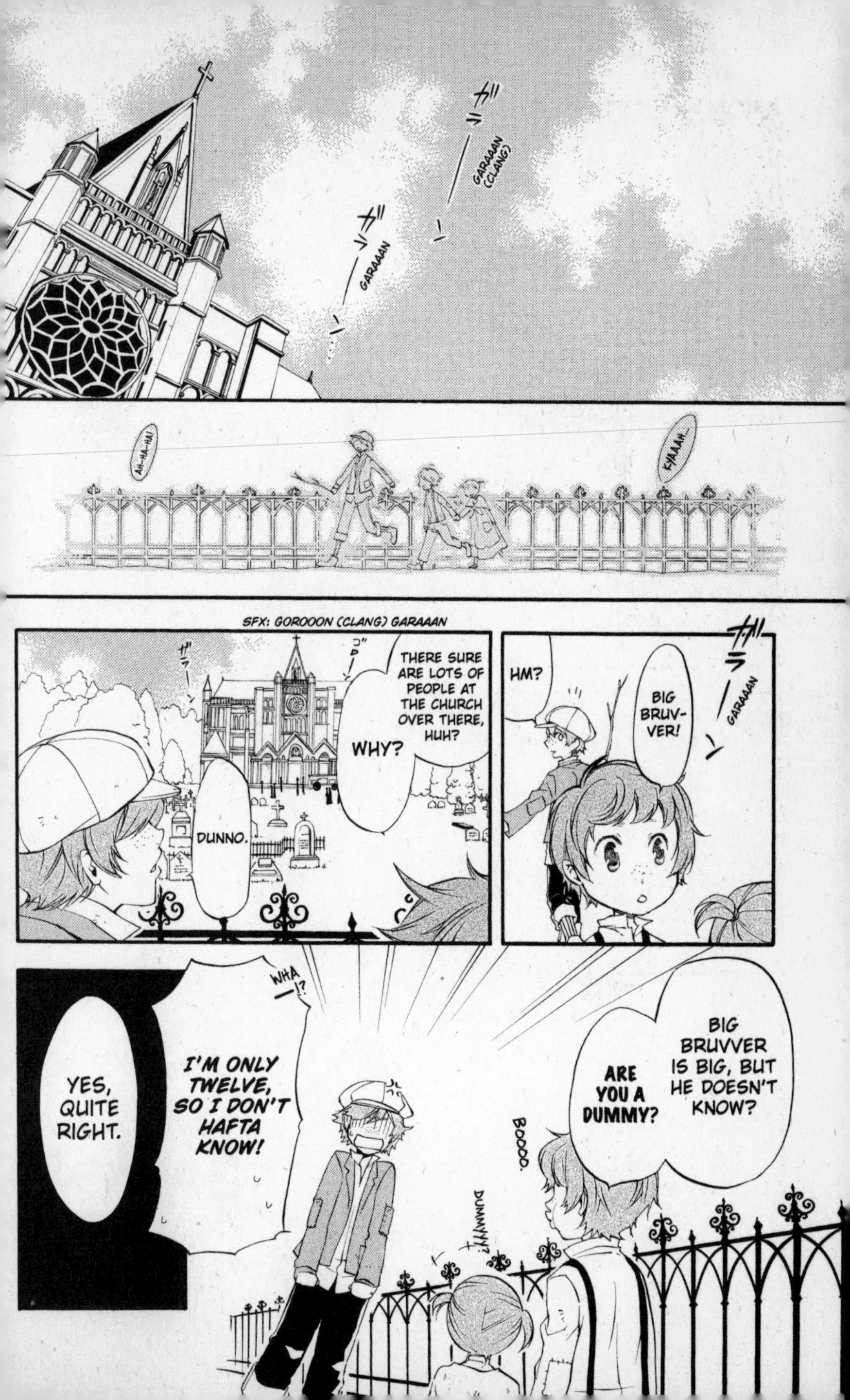
GARAAAN (CLANG)
GARAAAN
KYAAAH...
AH-HA-HA!
SFX: GOROOON (CLANG) GARAAAN
GARAAAN
BIG BRUVVER!
HM?
THERE SURE ARE LOTS OF PEOPLE AT THE CHURCH OVER THERE, HUH?
WHY?
DUNNO.
BIG BRUVVER IS BIG, BUT HE DOESN'T KNOW?
ARE YOU A DUMMY?
BOOOO.
DUMMYY!
WHA—!?
I'M ONLY TWELVE, SO I DON'T HAFTA KNOW!
YES, QUITE RIGHT.

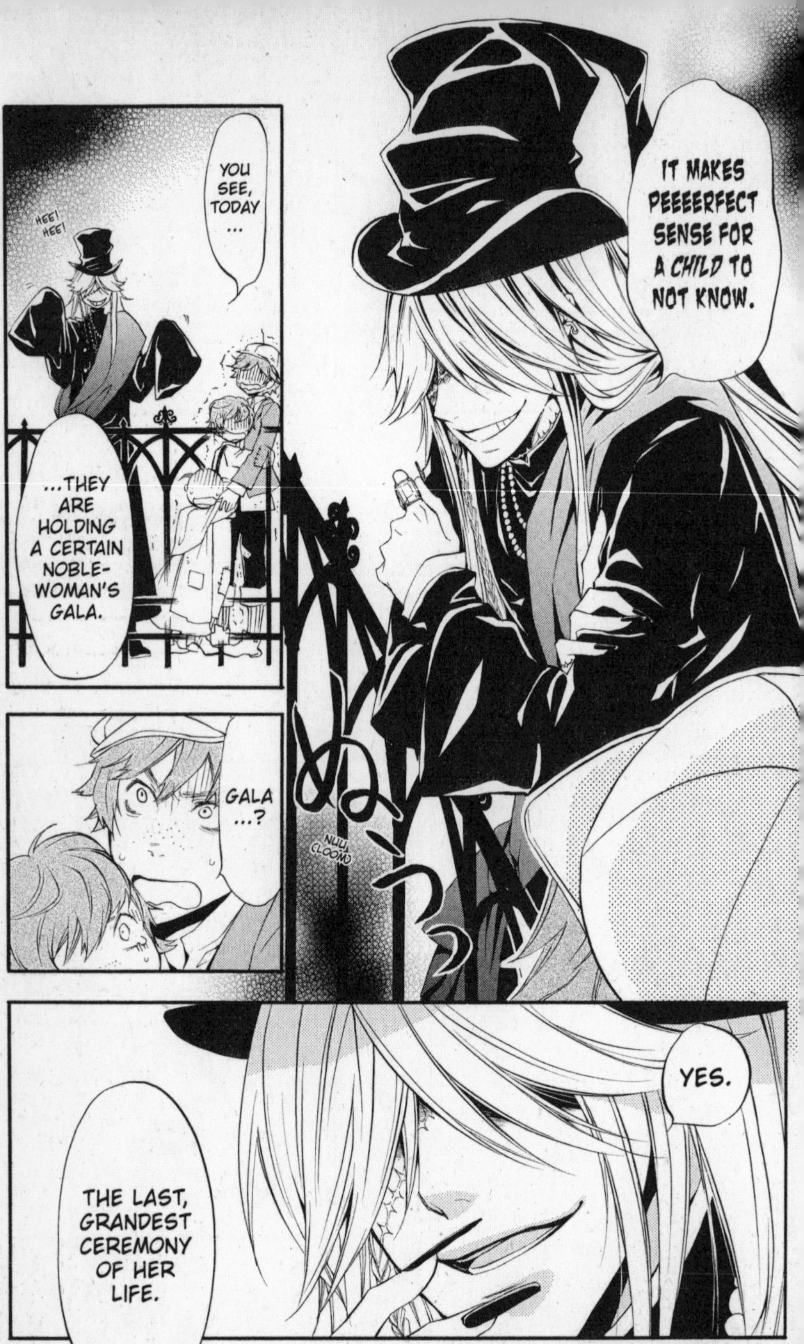

IT MAKES PEEEERFECT SENSE FOR A *CHILD* TO NOT KNOW.
NUU (LOOM)
YOU SEE, TODAY...
HEE! HEE!
...THEY ARE HOLDING A CERTAIN NOBLE-WOMAN'S GALA.
GALA...?
YES.
THE LAST, GRANDEST CEREMONY OF HER LIFE.

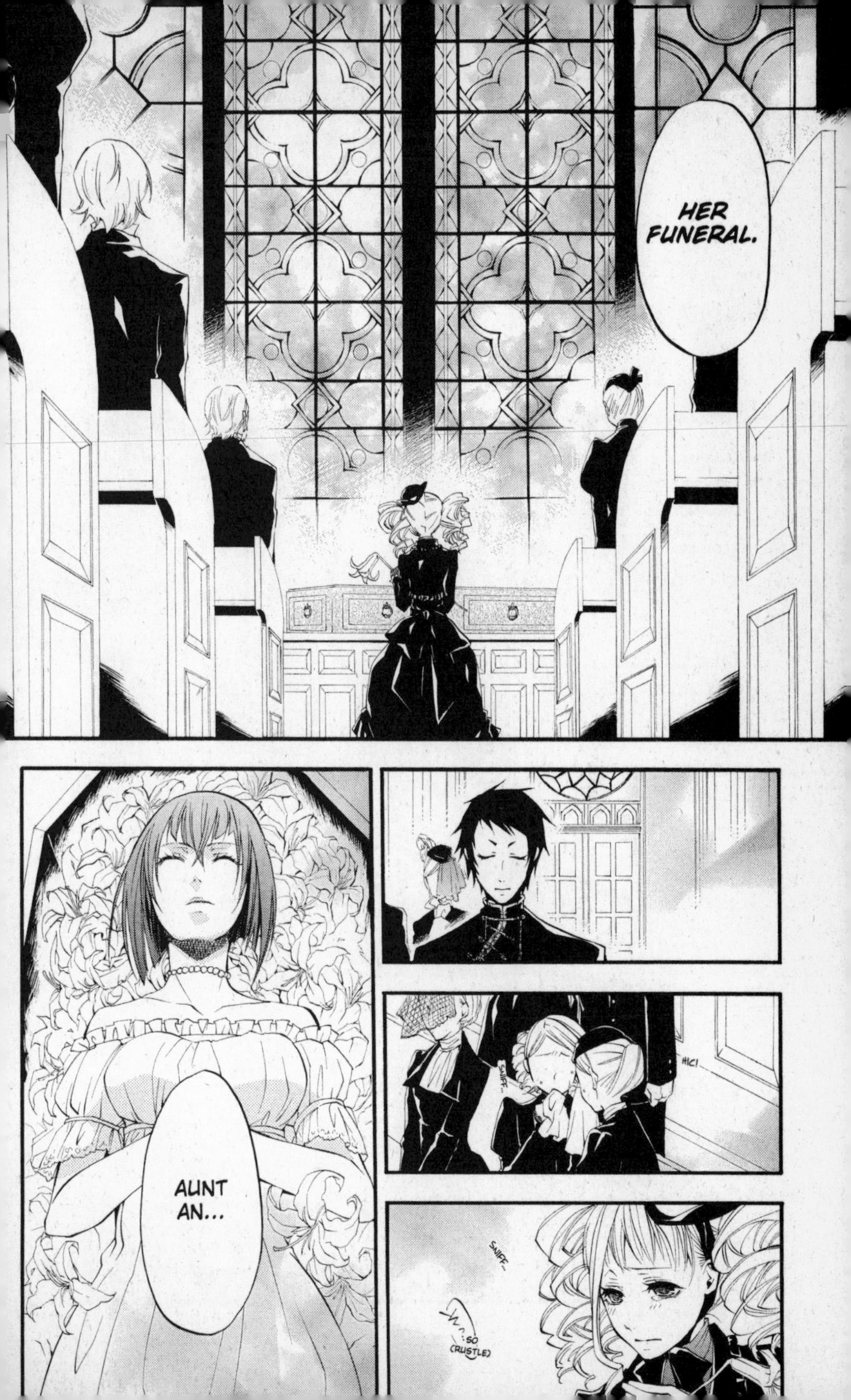
HER FUNERAL.
HIC!
SNIFF...
SNIFF...
SO (RUSTLE)
AUNT AN...

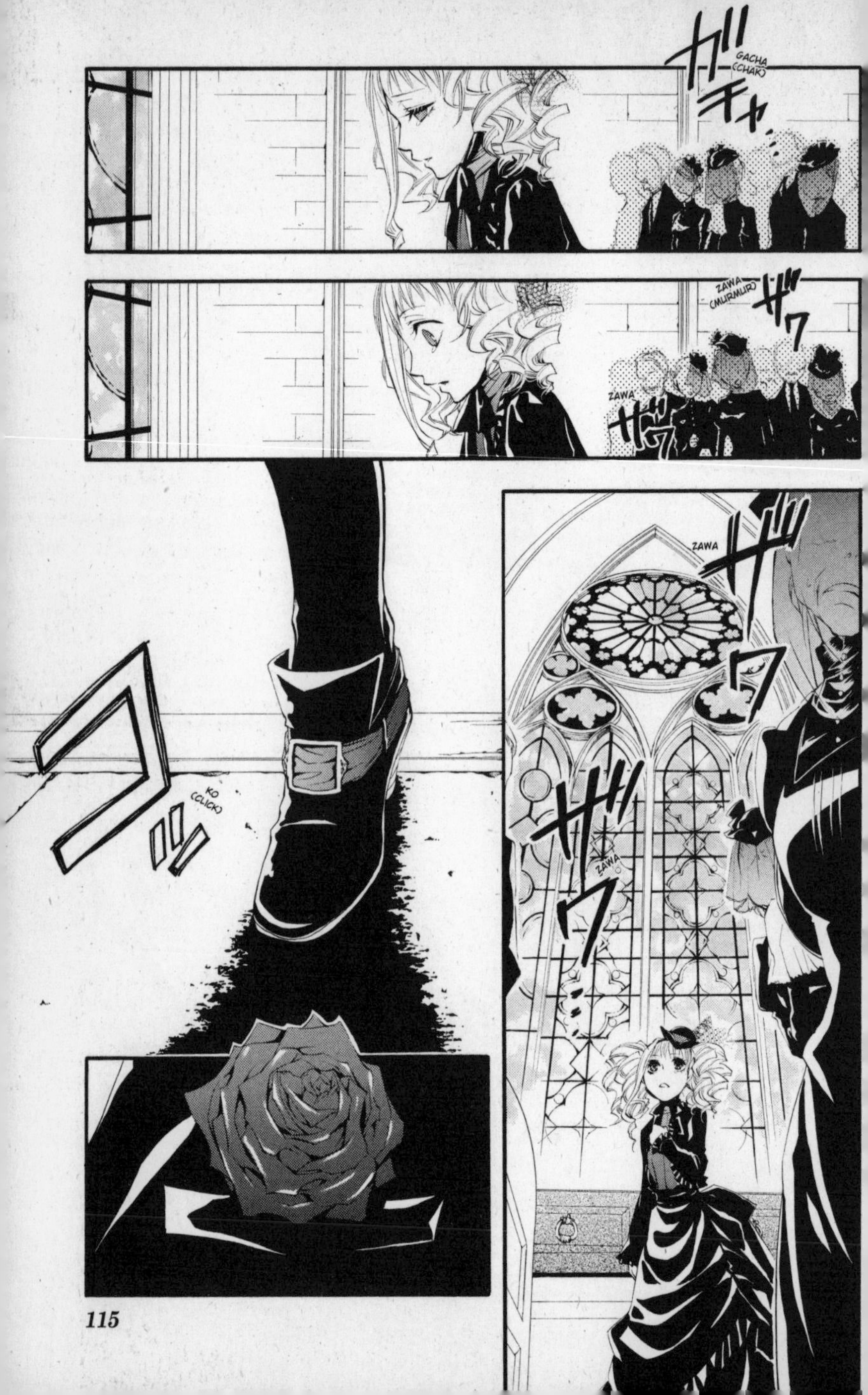
GACHA (CHAK)
ZAWA (MURMUR)
ZAWA
ZAWA
ZAWA
KO (CLICK)

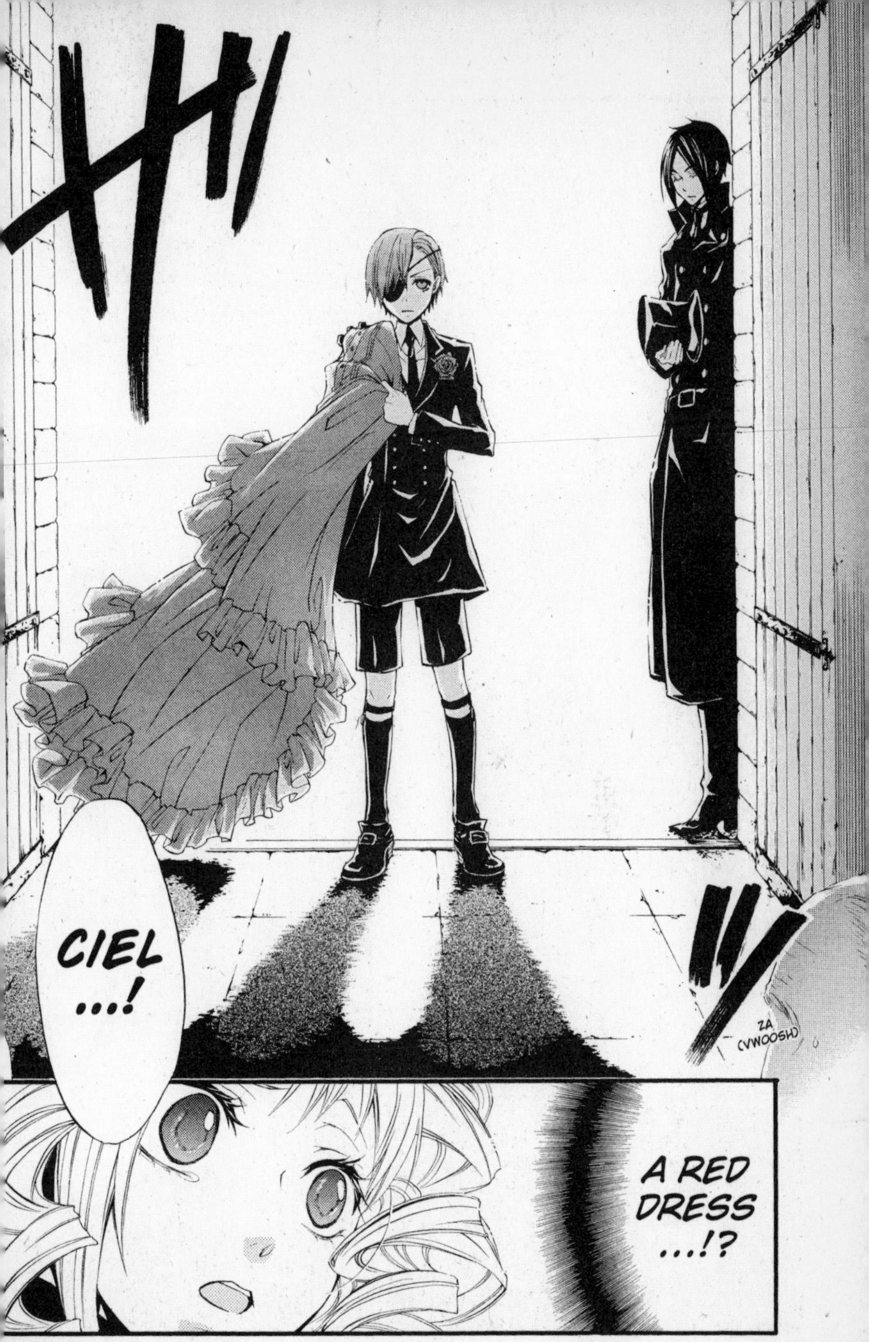
ZA (VWOOSH)
CIEL ...!
A RED DRESS ...!?

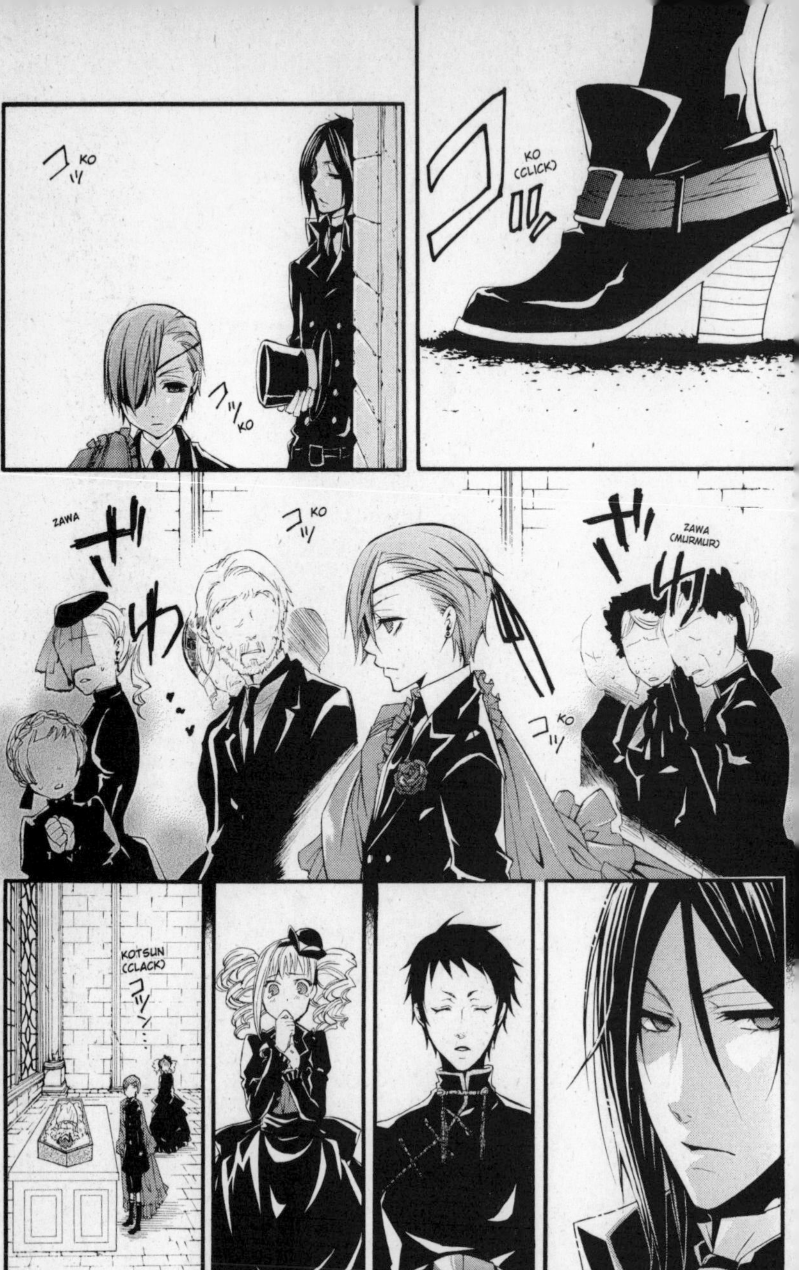
コッ
KO (CLICK)
コッ
KO
コッ
KO
ざわ
ZAWA (MURMUR)
コッ
KO
コッ
KO
ざわ
ZAWA
コツン…
KOTSUN (CLACK)

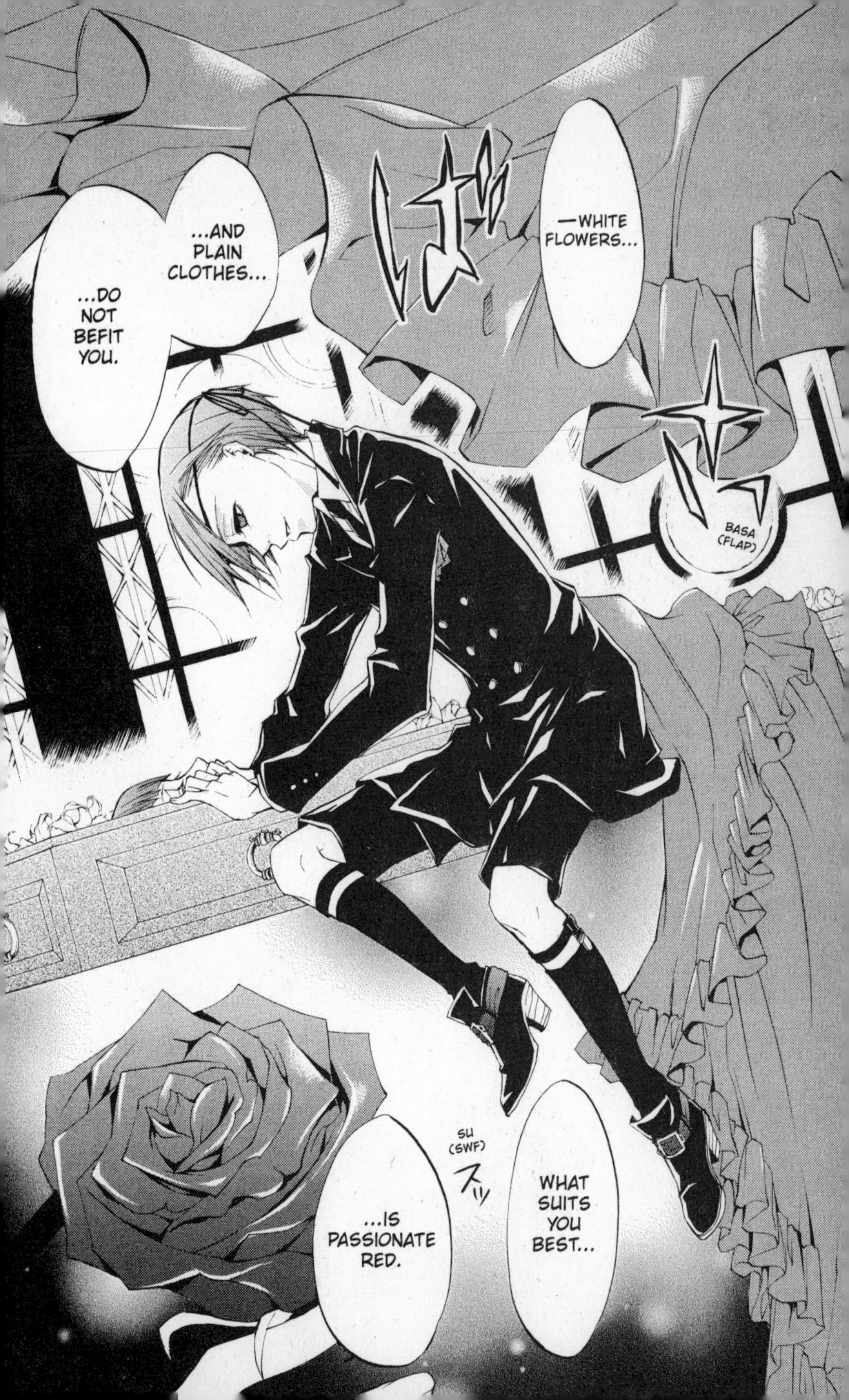
—WHITE FLOWERS...
...AND PLAIN CLOTHES...
...DO NOT BEFIT YOU.
BASA (FLAP)
WHAT SUITS YOU BEST...
SU (SWF)
スッ
...IS PASSIONATE RED.

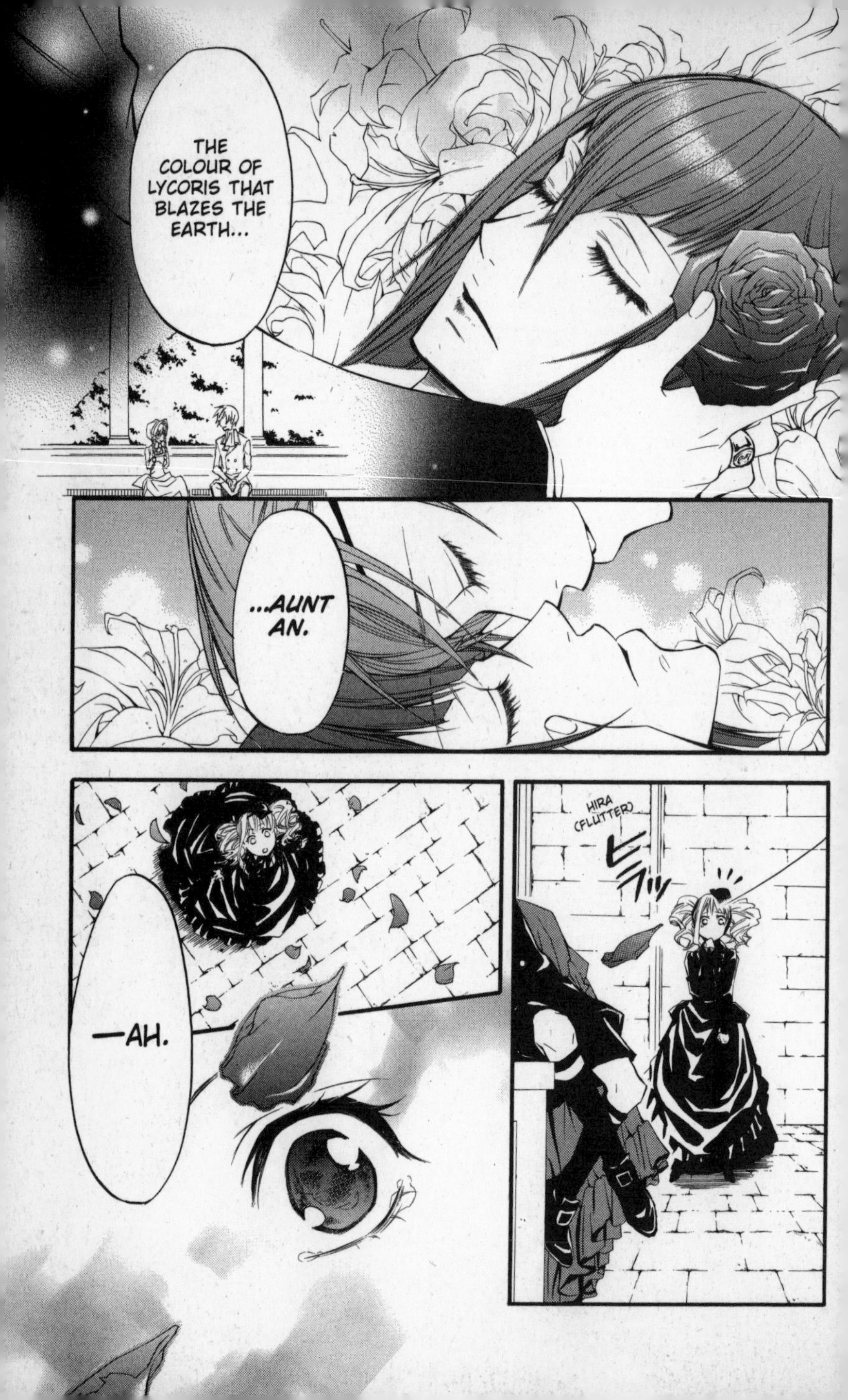
THE COLOUR OF LYCORIS THAT BLAZES THE EARTH...
...AUNT AN.
HIRA (FLUTTER)
—AH.

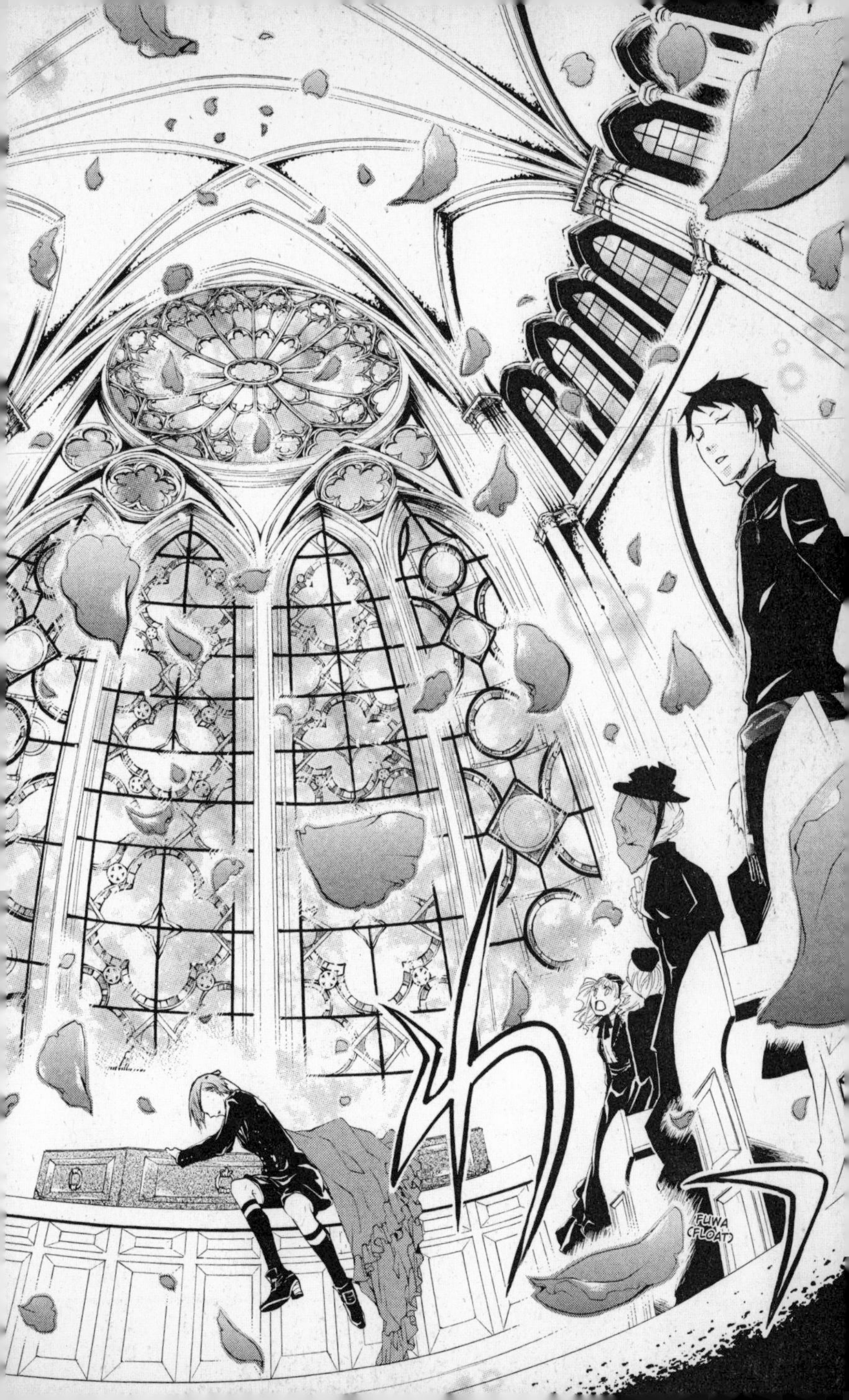
FUWA (FLOAT)

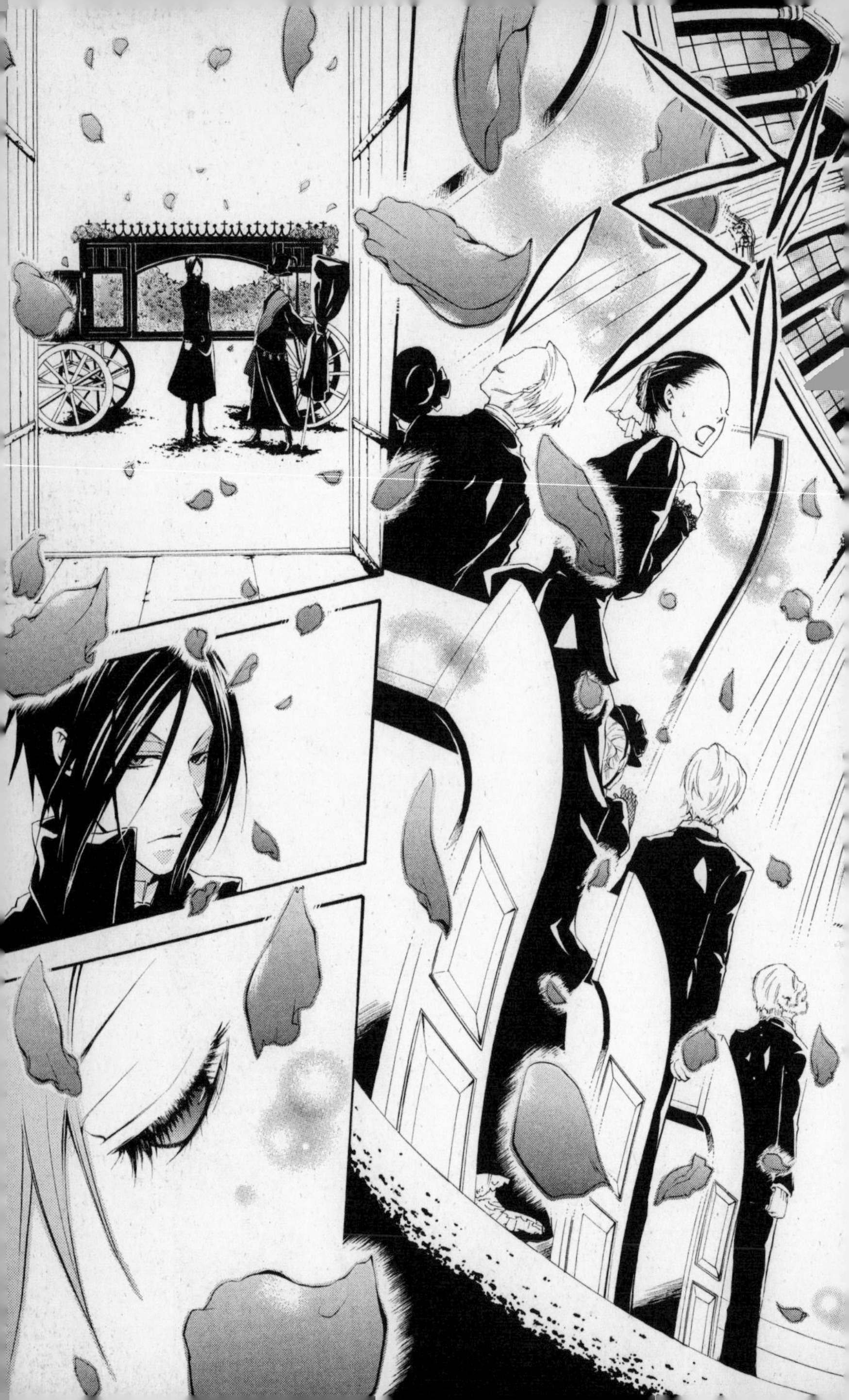

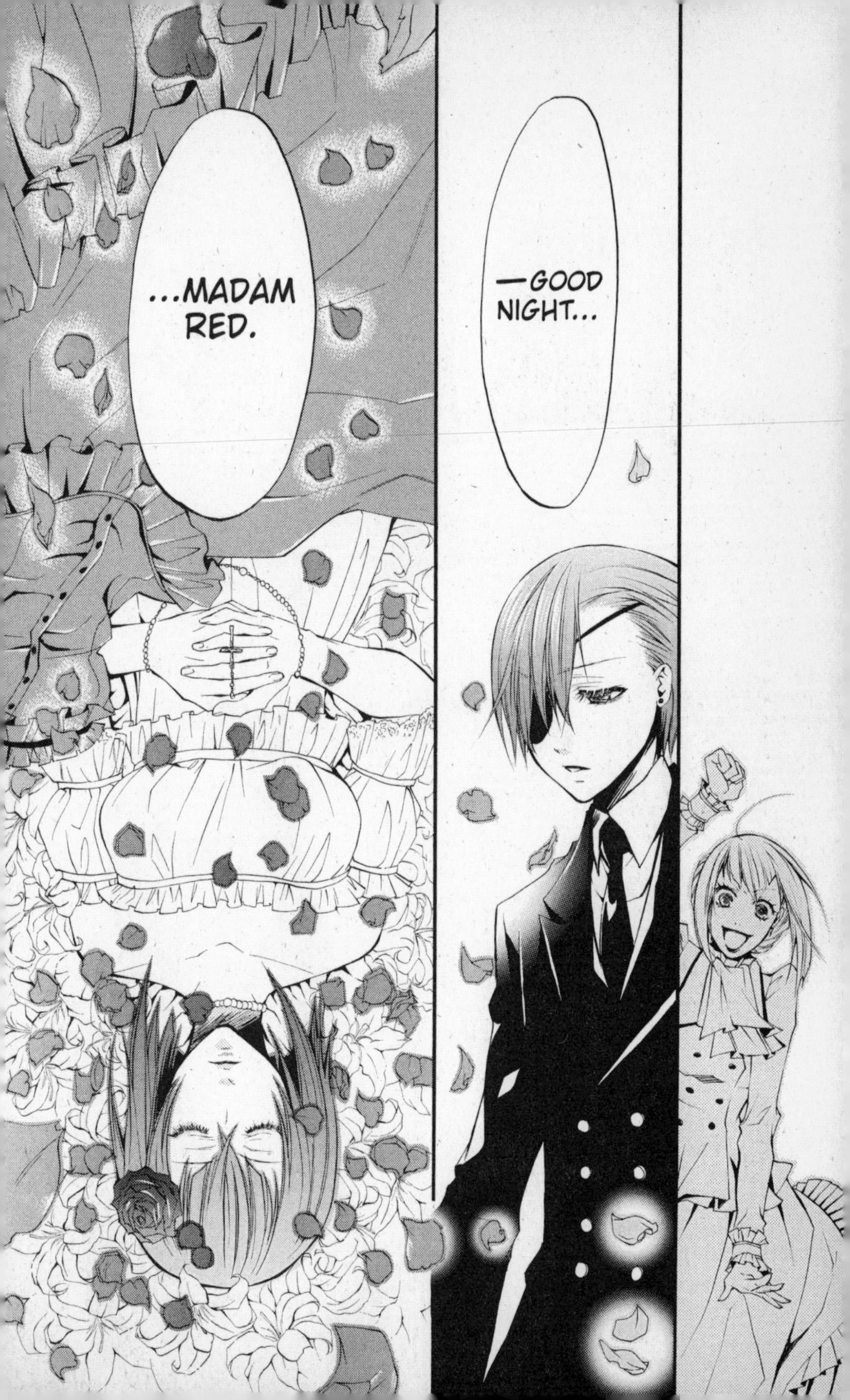
—GOOD NIGHT...
...MADAM RED.

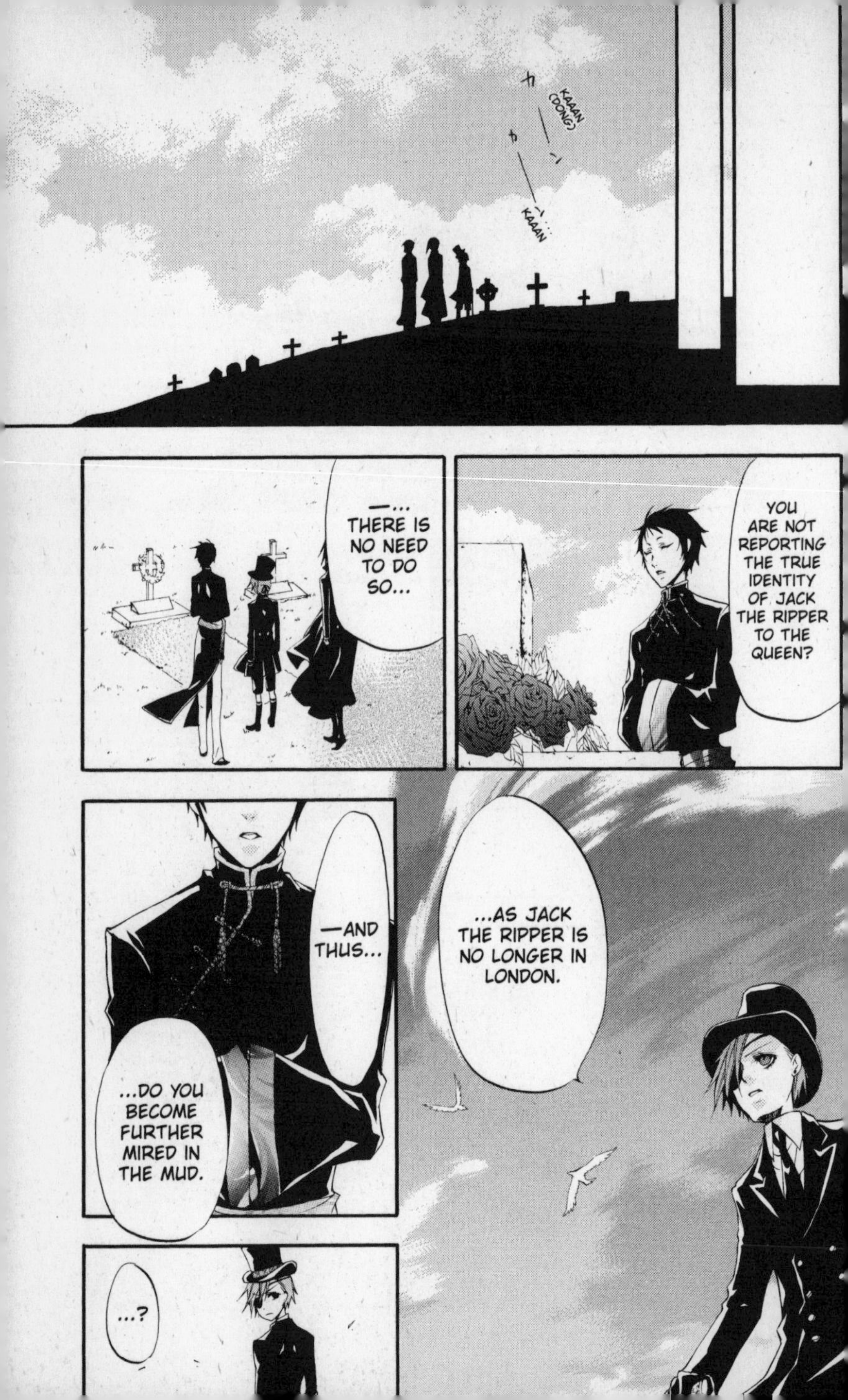
KAAAN (DONG)
KAAAN
YOU ARE NOT REPORTING THE TRUE IDENTITY OF JACK THE RIPPER TO THE QUEEN?
—... THERE IS NO NEED TO DO SO...
...AS JACK THE RIPPER IS NO LONGER IN LONDON.
—AND THUS...
...DO YOU BECOME FURTHER MIRED IN THE MUD.
...?

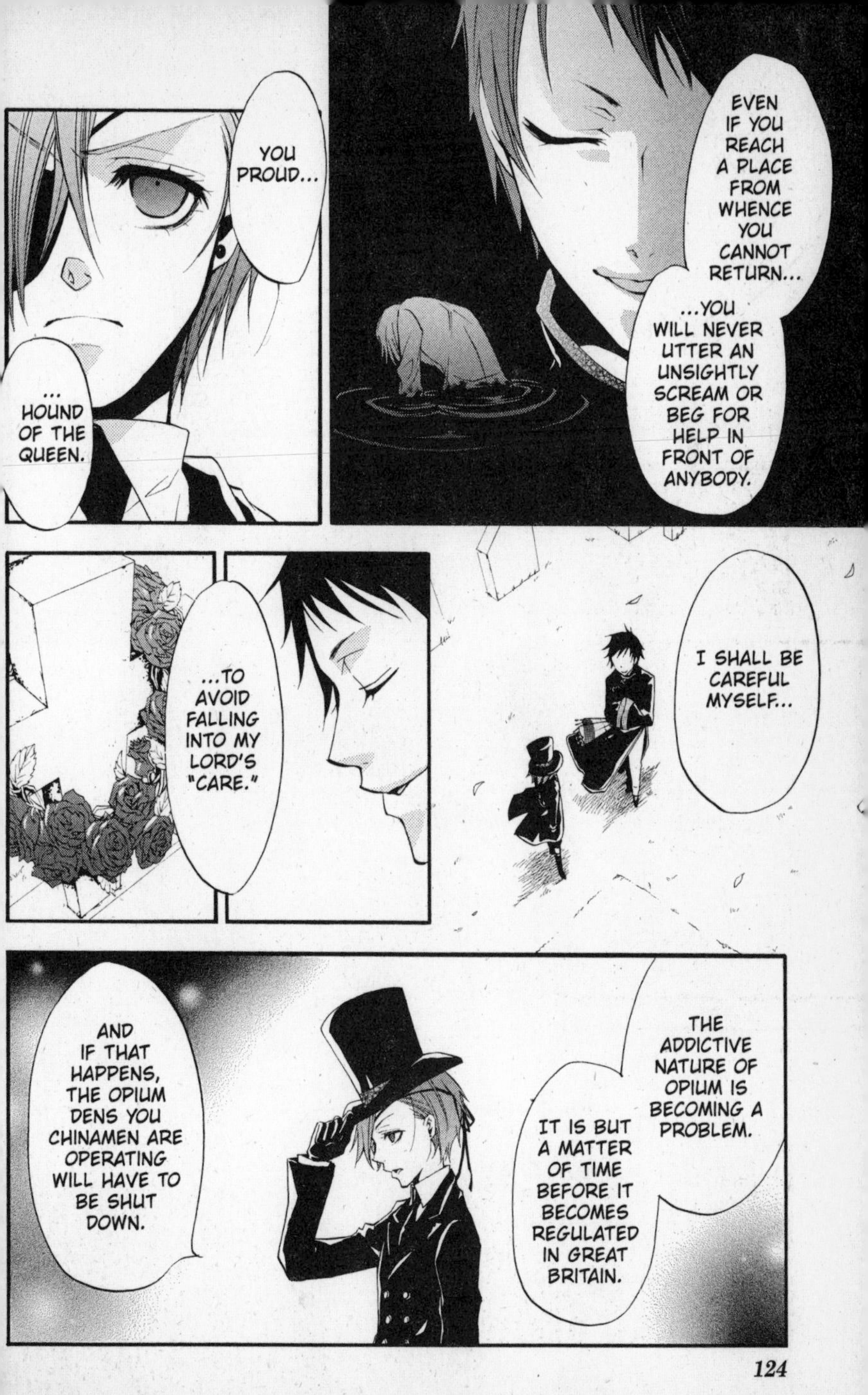
EVEN IF YOU REACH A PLACE FROM WHENCE YOU CANNOT RETURN...
...YOU WILL NEVER UTTER AN UNSIGHTLY SCREAM OR BEG FOR HELP IN FRONT OF ANYBODY.
YOU PROUD...
...HOUND OF THE QUEEN.
I SHALL BE CAREFUL MYSELF...
...TO AVOID FALLING INTO MY LORD'S "CARE."
THE ADDICTIVE NATURE OF OPIUM IS BECOMING A PROBLEM.
IT IS BUT A MATTER OF TIME BEFORE IT BECOMES REGULATED IN GREAT BRITAIN.
AND IF THAT HAPPENS, THE OPIUM DENS YOU CHINAMEN ARE OPERATING WILL HAVE TO BE SHUT DOWN.

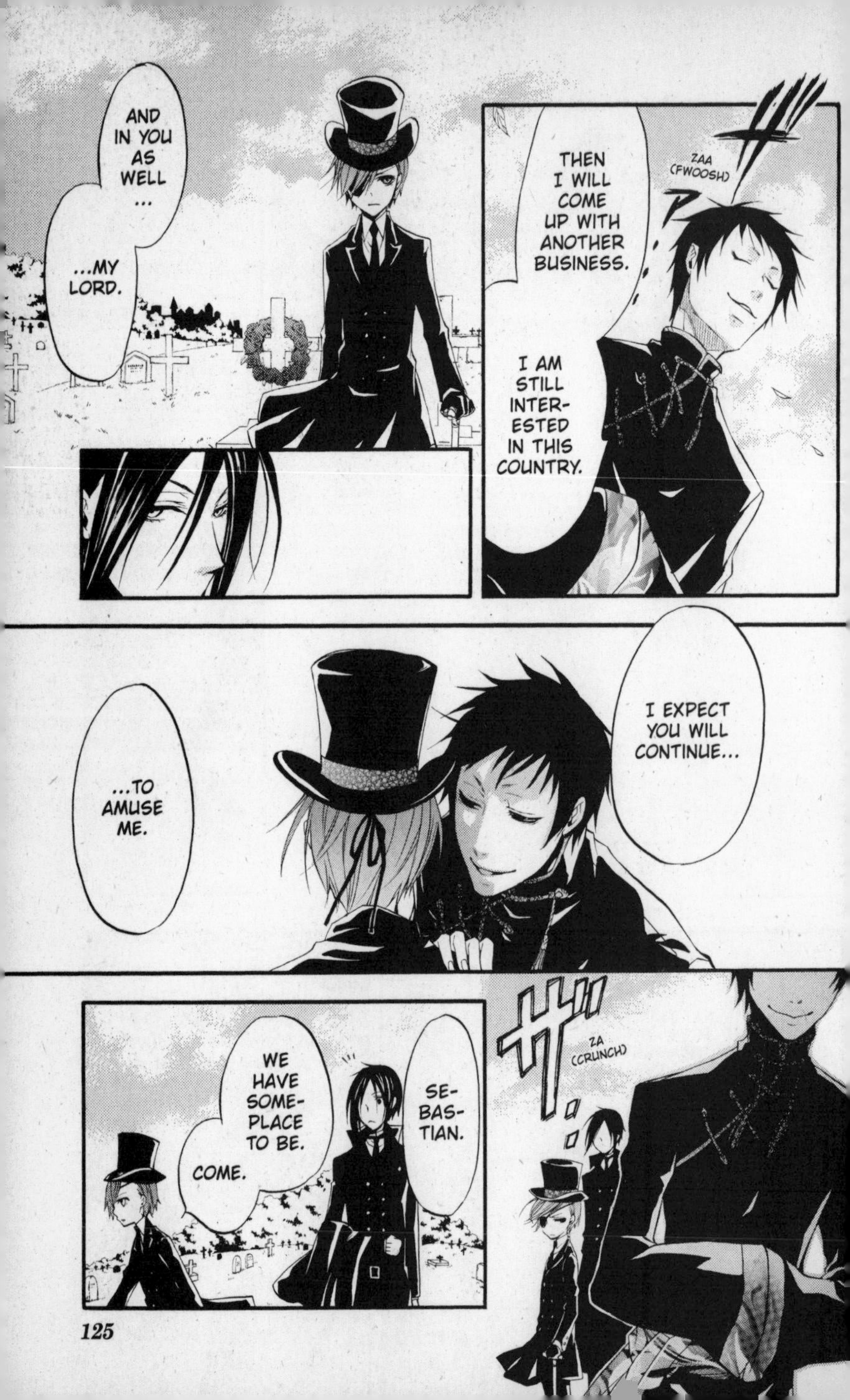
ZAA (FWOOSH)
THEN I WILL COME UP WITH ANOTHER BUSINESS.
I AM STILL INTER-ESTED IN THIS COUNTRY.
AND IN YOU AS WELL ...
...MY LORD.
I EXPECT YOU WILL CONTINUE...
...TO AMUSE ME.
ZA (CRUNCH)
SE-BAS-TIAN.
WE HAVE SOME-PLACE TO BE.
COME.

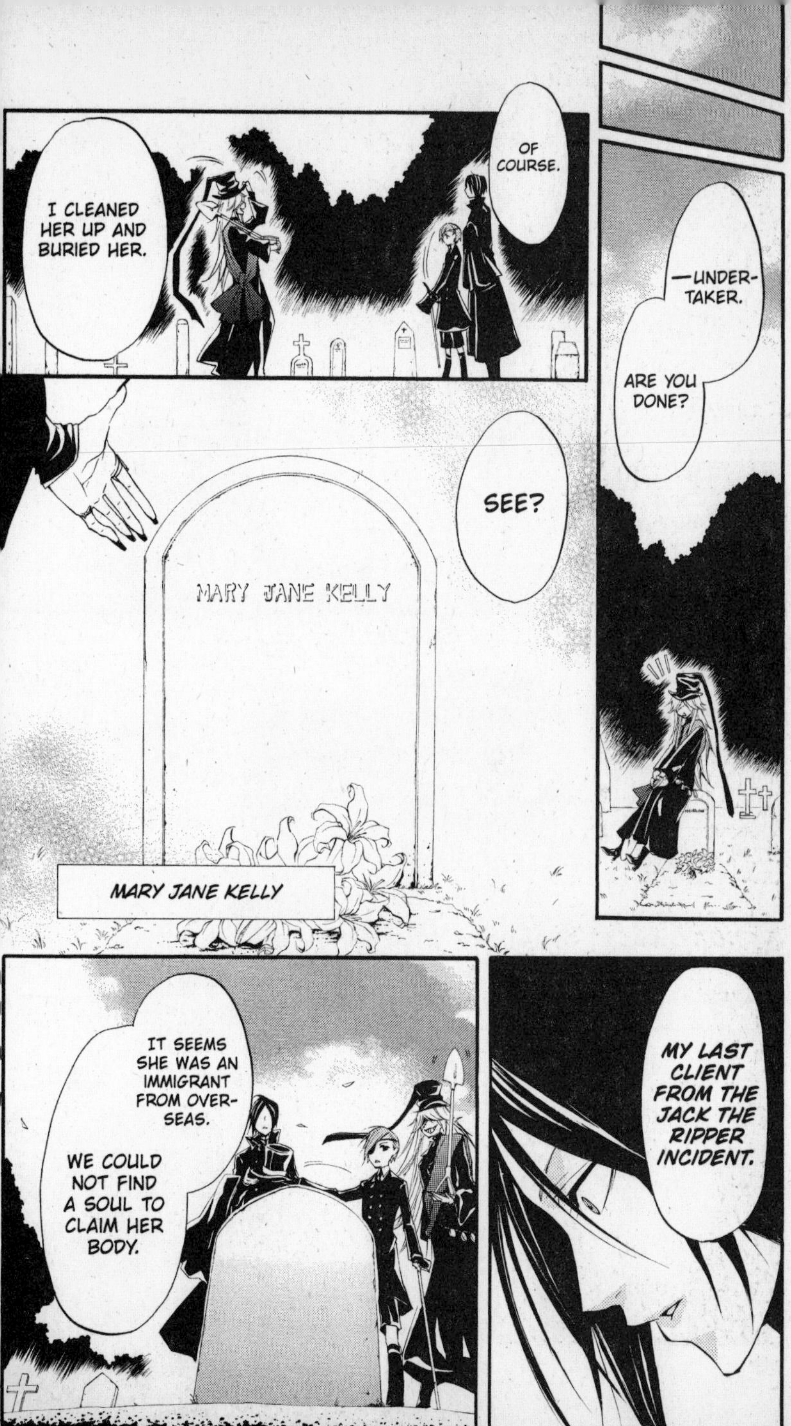
—UNDER-TAKER.
ARE YOU DONE?
OF COURSE.
I CLEANED HER UP AND BURIED HER.
SEE?
MARY JANE KELLY
MARY JANE KELLY
MY LAST CLIENT FROM THE JACK THE RIPPER INCIDENT.
IT SEEMS SHE WAS AN IMMIGRANT FROM OVER-SEAS.
WE COULD NOT FIND A SOUL TO CLAIM HER BODY.

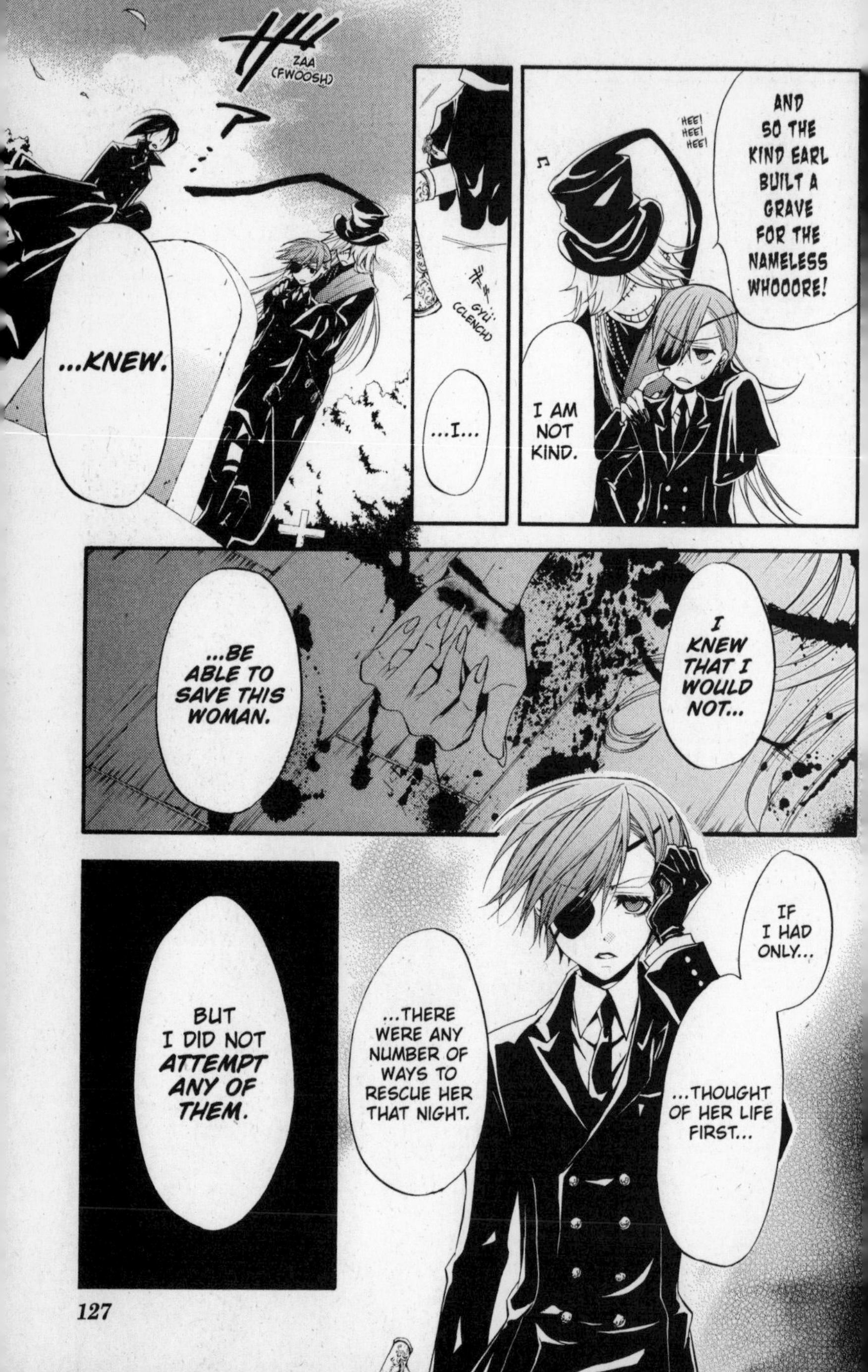
HEE! HEE! HEE!
AND SO THE KIND EARL BUILT A GRAVE FOR THE NAMELESS WHOOORE!
I AM NOT KIND.
GYU (CLENCH)
...I...
ZAA (FWOOSH)
...KNEW.
I KNEW THAT I WOULD NOT...
...BE ABLE TO SAVE THIS WOMAN.
IF I HAD ONLY...
...THOUGHT OF HER LIFE FIRST...
...THERE WERE ANY NUMBER OF WAYS TO RESCUE HER THAT NIGHT.
BUT I DID NOT ATTEMPT ANY OF THEM.

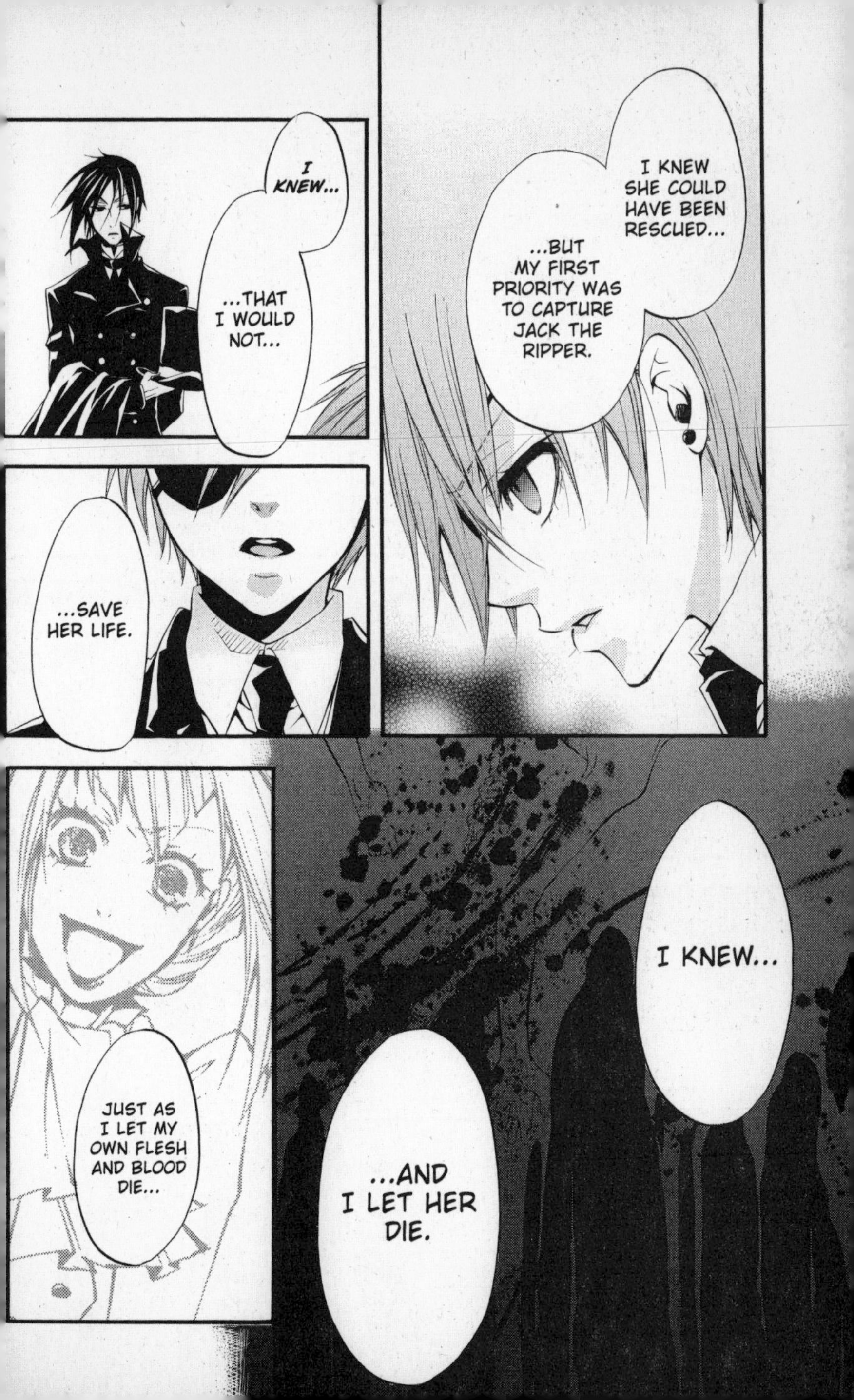

I KNEW SHE COULD HAVE BEEN RESCUED...
...BUT MY FIRST PRIORITY WAS TO CAPTURE JACK THE RIPPER.
I KNEW...
...THAT I WOULD NOT...
...SAVE HER LIFE.
I KNEW...
...AND I LET HER DIE.
JUST AS I LET MY OWN FLESH AND BLOOD DIE...

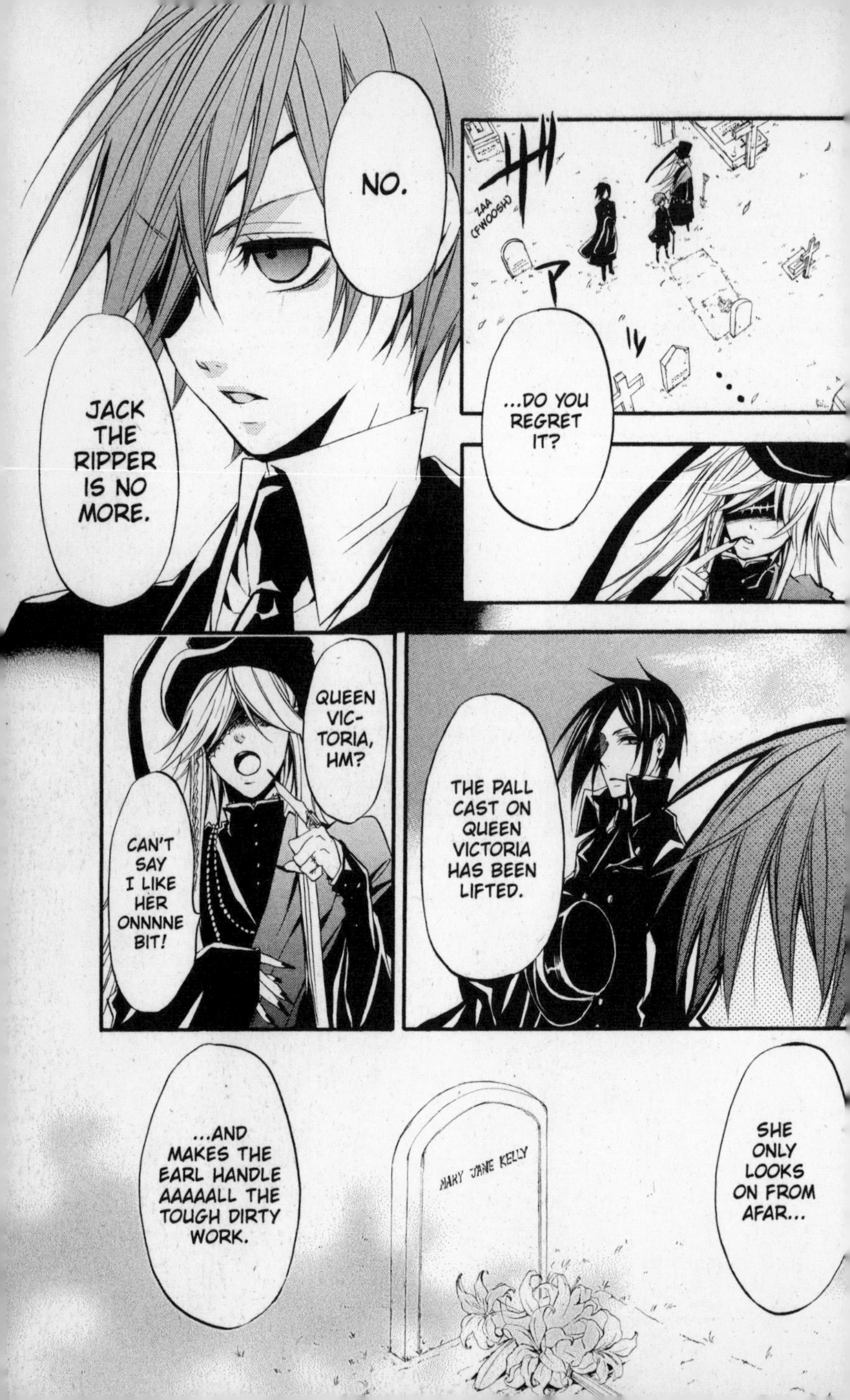
ZAA (FWOOSH)
...DO YOU REGRET IT?
NO.
JACK THE RIPPER IS NO MORE.
THE PALL CAST ON QUEEN VICTORIA HAS BEEN LIFTED.
QUEEN VICTORIA, HM?
CAN'T SAY I LIKE HER ONNNNE BIT!
SHE ONLY LOOKS ON FROM AFAR...
...AND MAKES THE EARL HANDLE AAAAALL THE TOUGH DIRTY WORK.
MARY JANE KELLY

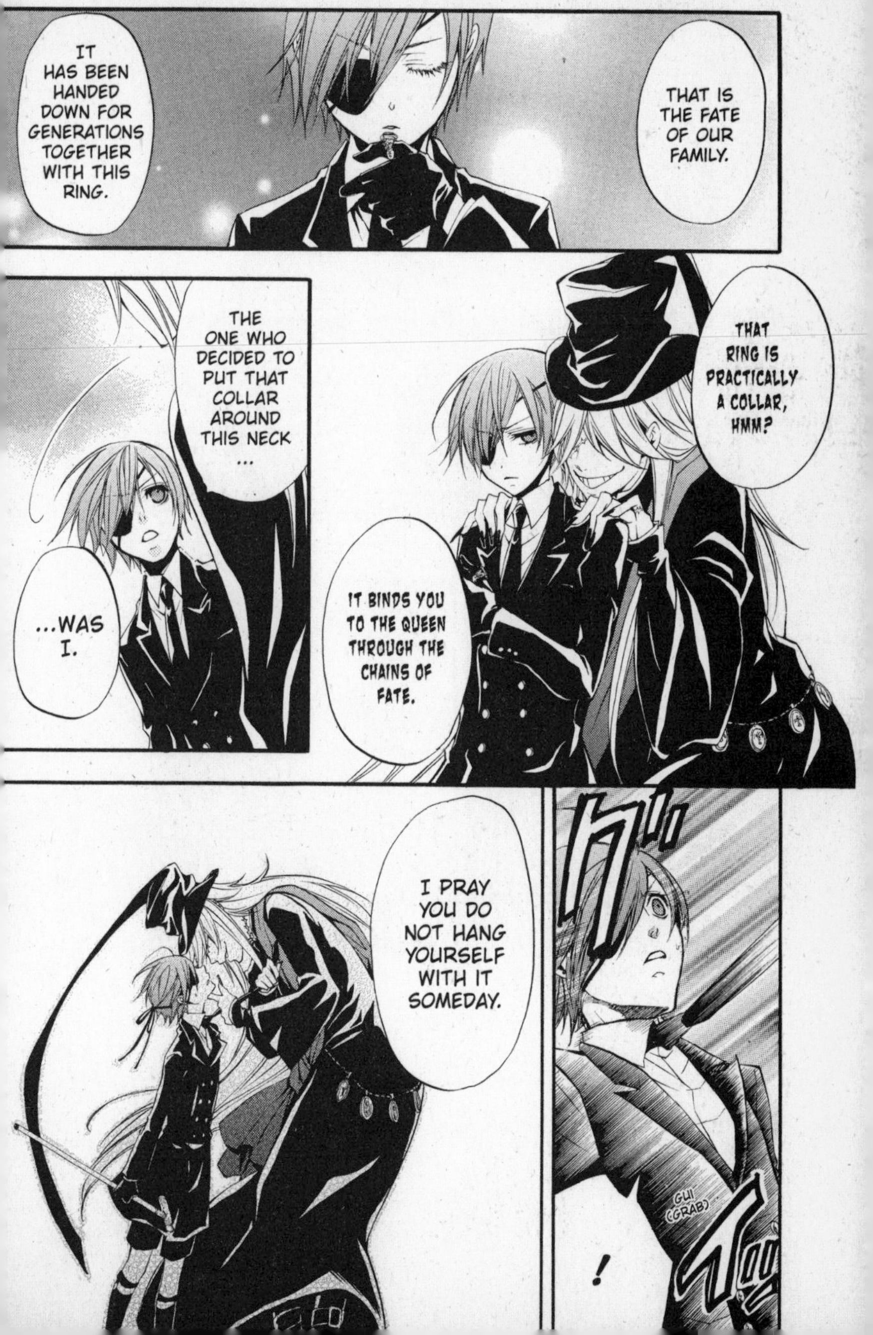
THAT IS THE FATE OF OUR FAMILY.
IT HAS BEEN HANDED DOWN FOR GENERATIONS TOGETHER WITH THIS RING.
THAT RING IS PRACTICALLY A COLLAR, HMM?
IT BINDS YOU TO THE QUEEN THROUGH THE CHAINS OF FATE.
THE ONE WHO DECIDED TO PUT THAT COLLAR AROUND THIS NECK ...
...WAS I.
GUI (GRAB)
!
I PRAY YOU DO NOT HANG YOURSELF WITH IT SOMEDAY.

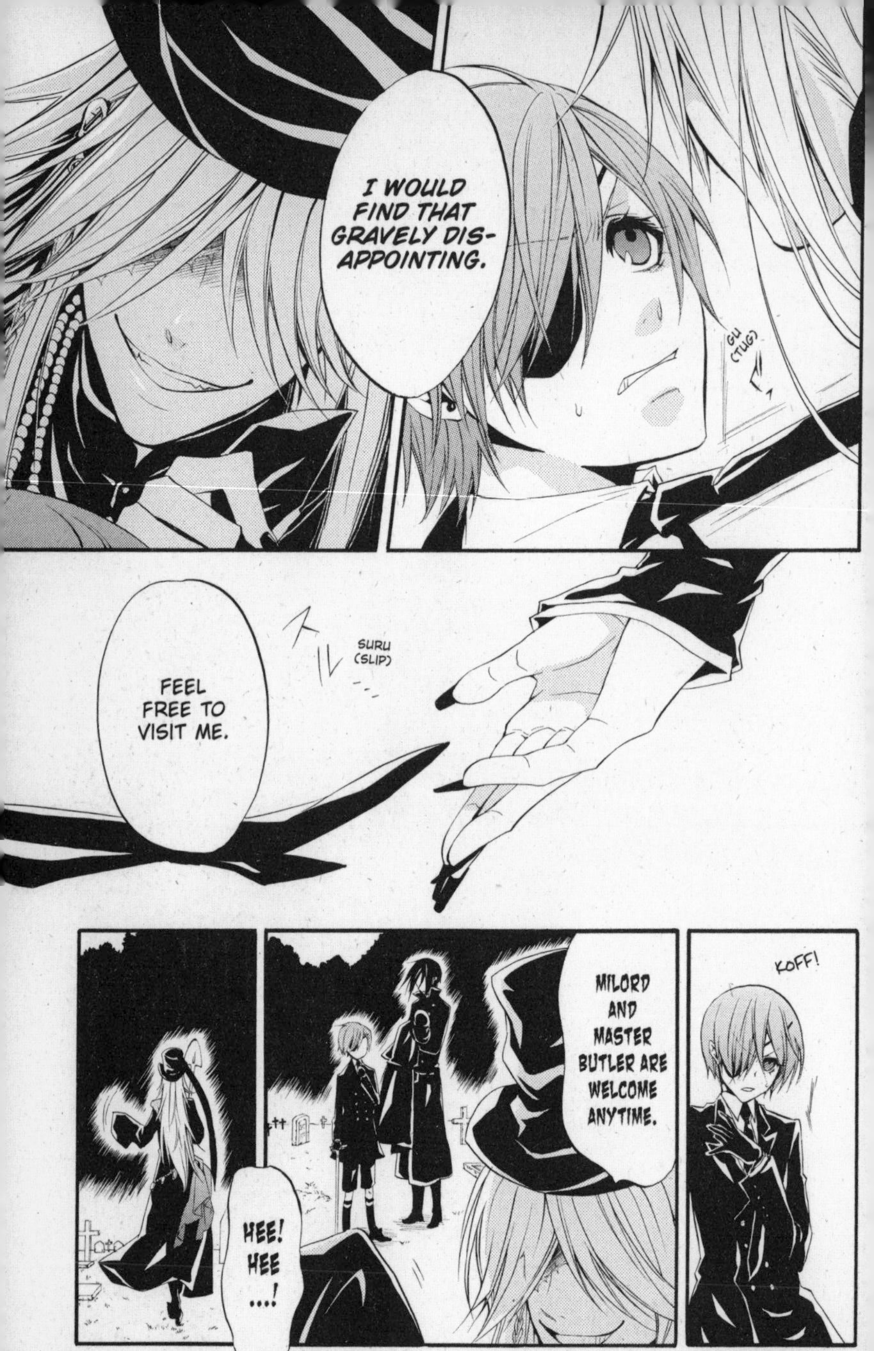
I WOULD FIND THAT GRAVELY DIS-APPOINTING.
GU (TUG)
SURU (SLIP)
FEEL FREE TO VISIT ME.
KOFF!
MILORD AND MASTER BUTLER ARE WELCOME ANYTIME.
HEE! HEE ...!

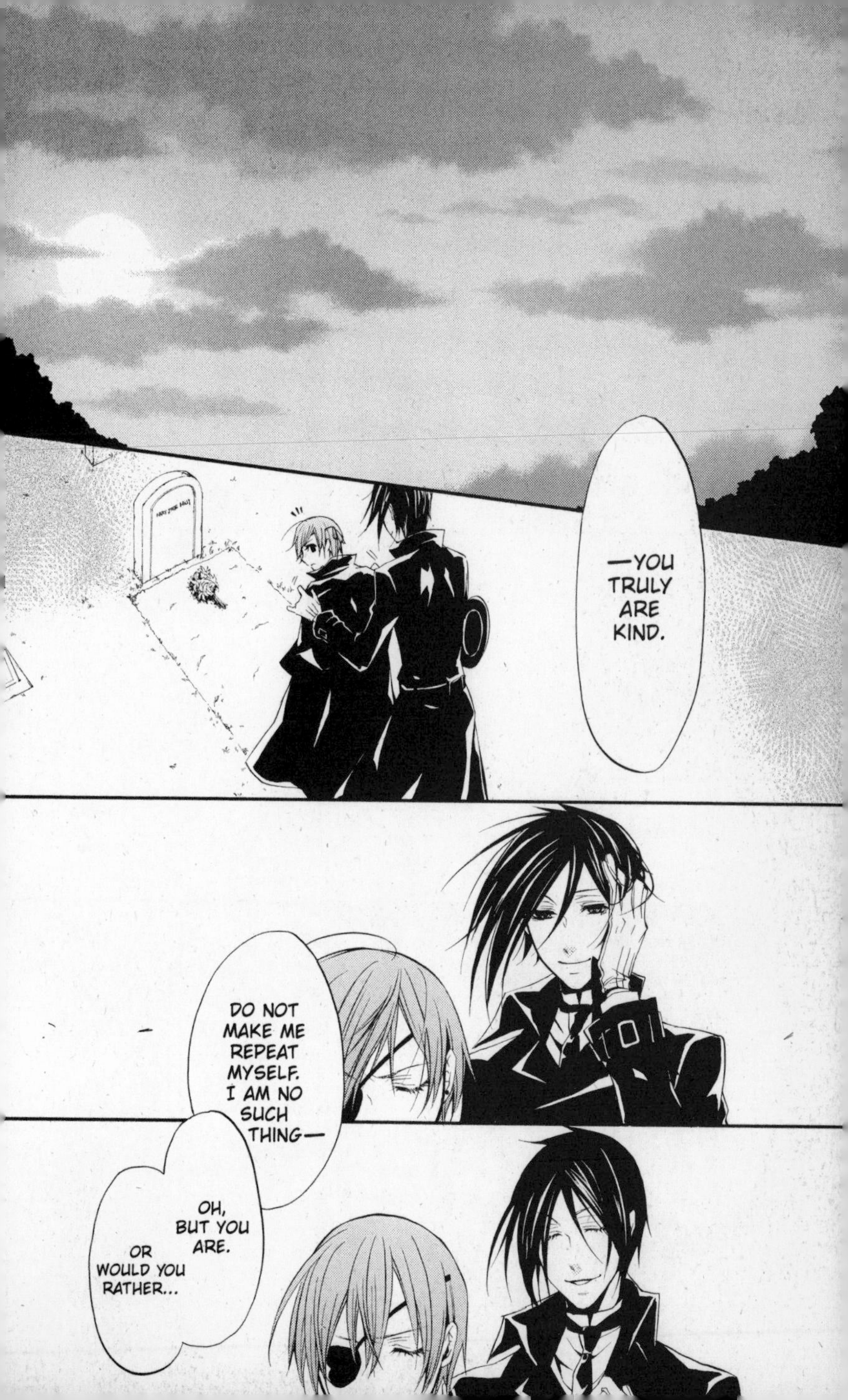
—YOU TRULY ARE KIND.
DO NOT MAKE ME REPEAT MYSELF. I AM NO SUCH THING—
OH, BUT YOU ARE.
OR WOULD YOU RATHER...

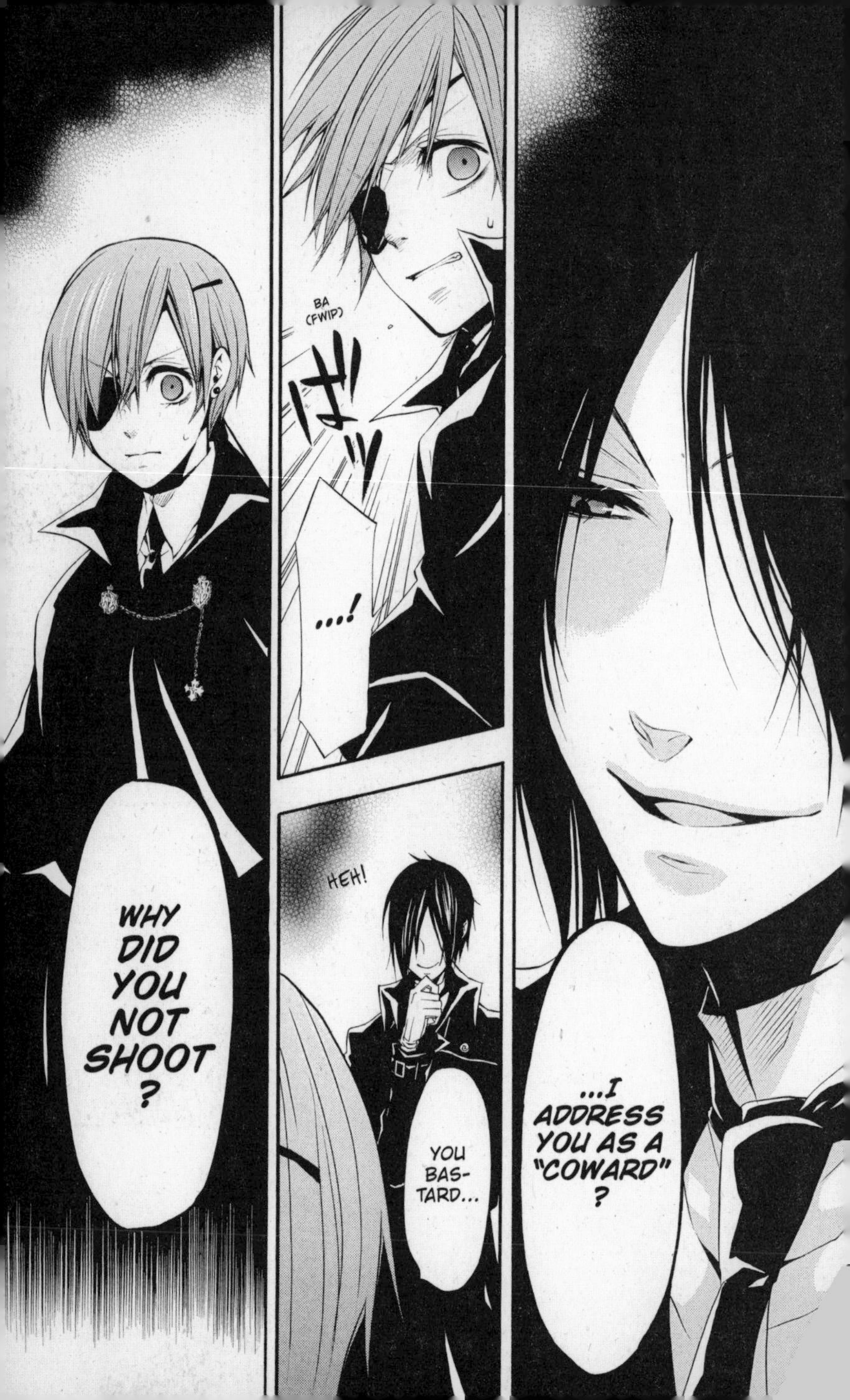

...I ADDRESS YOU AS A "COWARD"?
BA (FWIP)
...!
HEH!
YOU BASTARD...
WHY DID YOU NOT SHOOT?

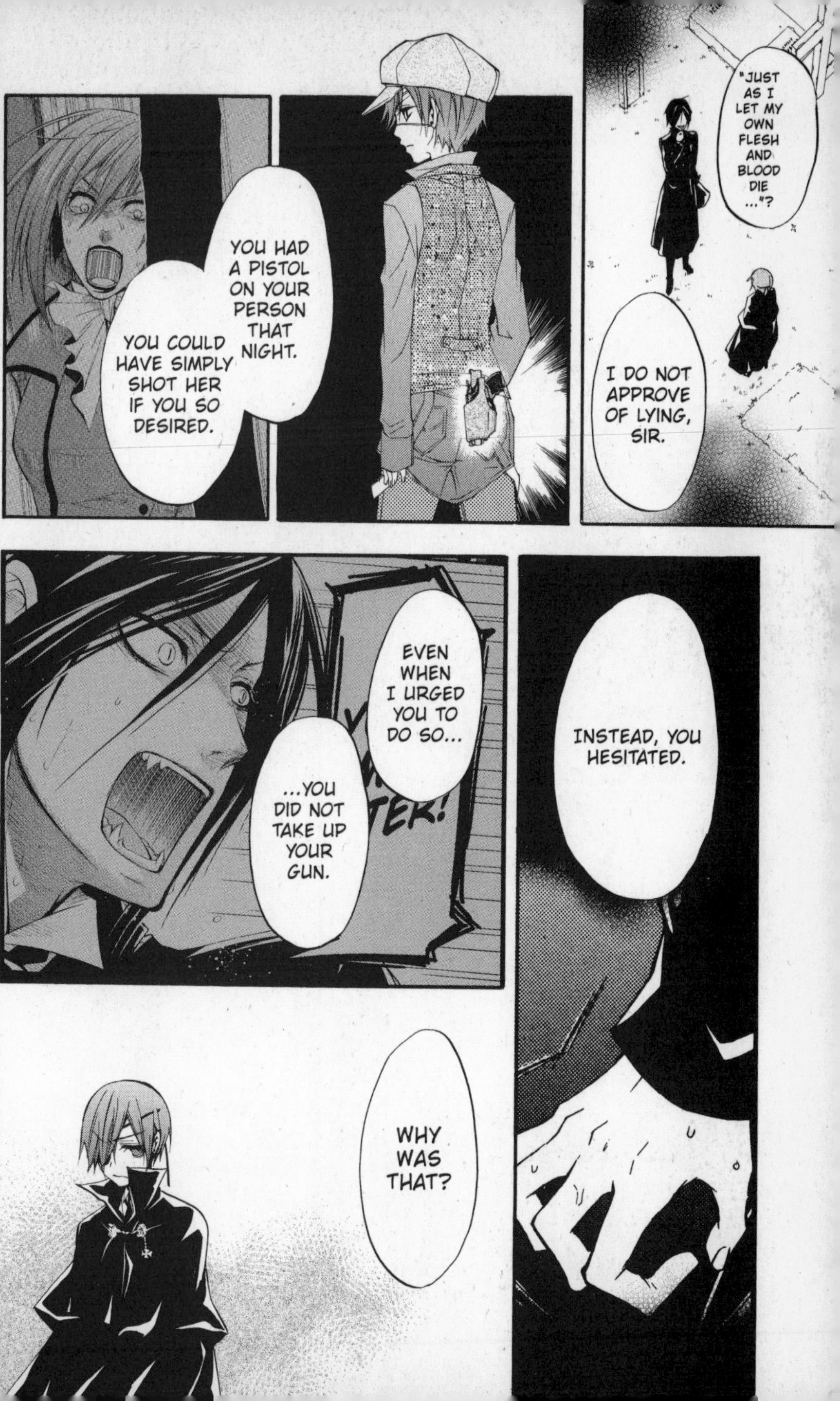
"JUST AS I LET MY OWN FLESH AND BLOOD DIE ..."?
I DO NOT APPROVE OF LYING, SIR.
YOU HAD A PISTOL ON YOUR PERSON THAT NIGHT.
YOU COULD HAVE SIMPLY SHOT HER IF YOU SO DESIRED.
INSTEAD, YOU HESITATED.
EVEN WHEN I URGED YOU TO DO SO...
...YOU DID NOT TAKE UP YOUR GUN.
WHY WAS THAT?

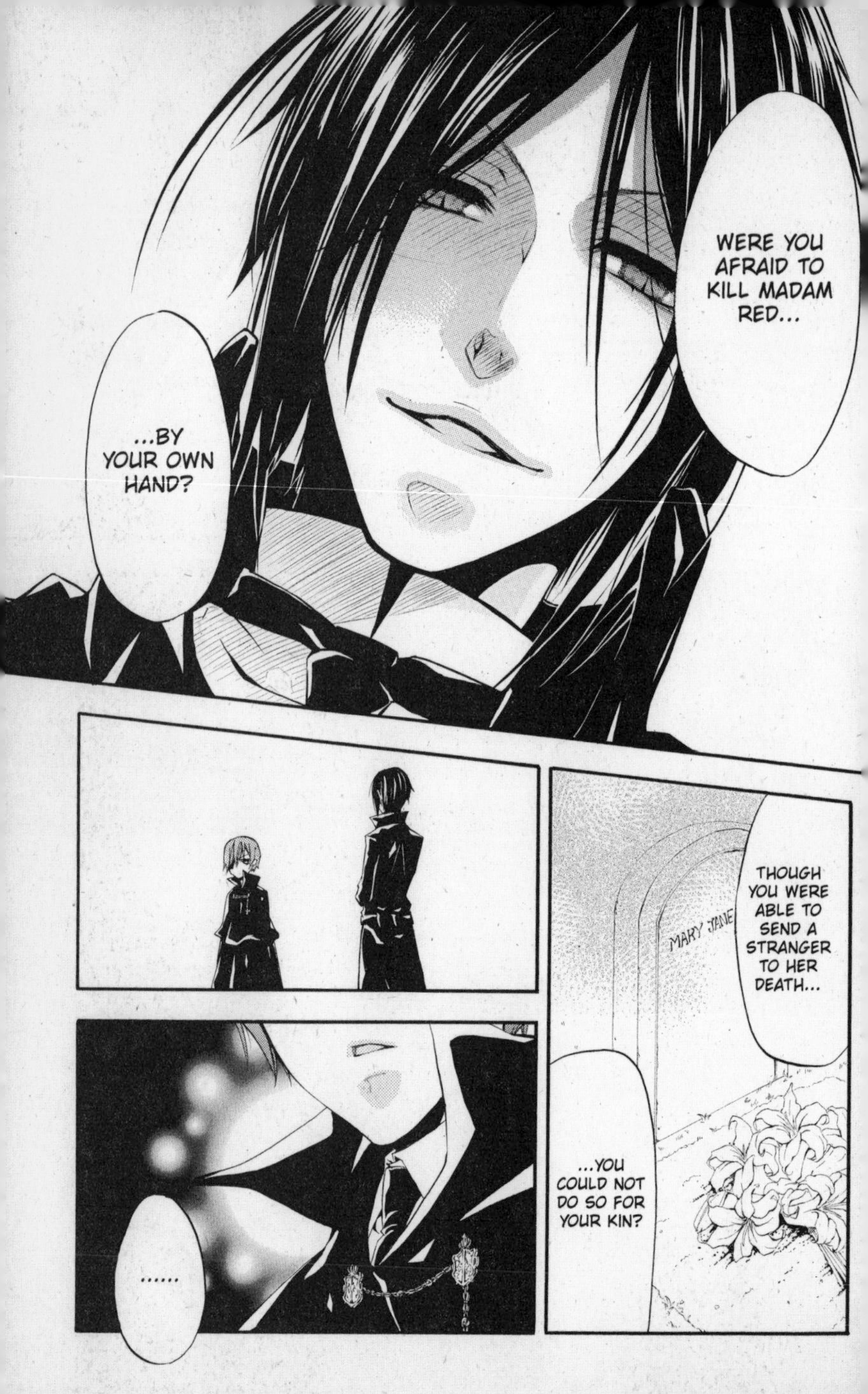
WERE YOU AFRAID TO KILL MADAM RED...
...BY YOUR OWN HAND?
THOUGH YOU WERE ABLE TO SEND A STRANGER TO HER DEATH...
MARY JANE
...YOU COULD NOT DO SO FOR YOUR KIN?
......

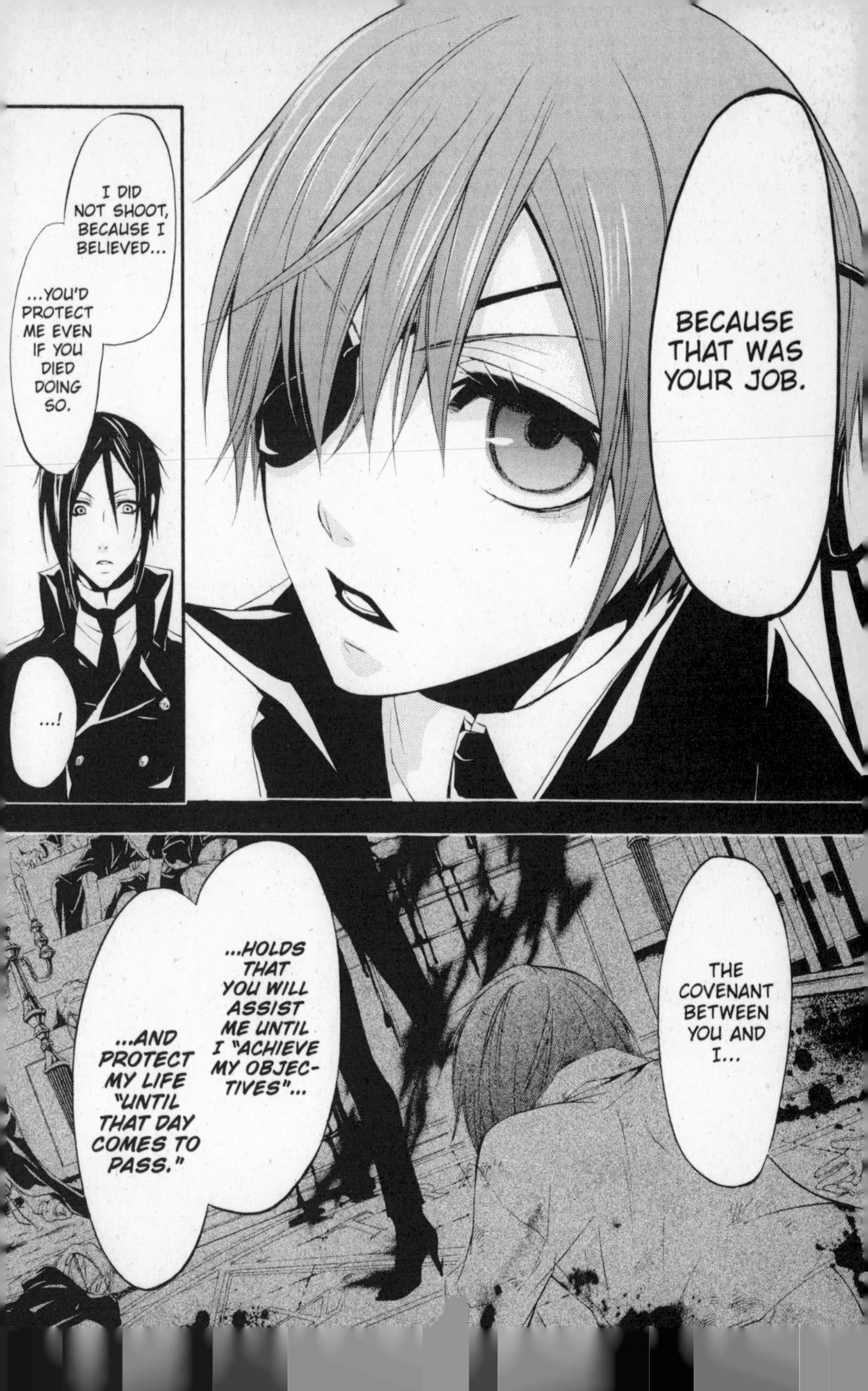
I DID NOT SHOOT, BECAUSE I BELIEVED...
...YOU'D PROTECT ME EVEN IF YOU DIED DOING SO.
...!
BECAUSE THAT WAS YOUR JOB.
THE COVENANT BETWEEN YOU AND I...
...HOLDS THAT YOU WILL ASSIST ME UNTIL I "ACHIEVE MY OBJECTIVES"...
...AND PROTECT MY LIFE "UNTIL THAT DAY COMES TO PASS."

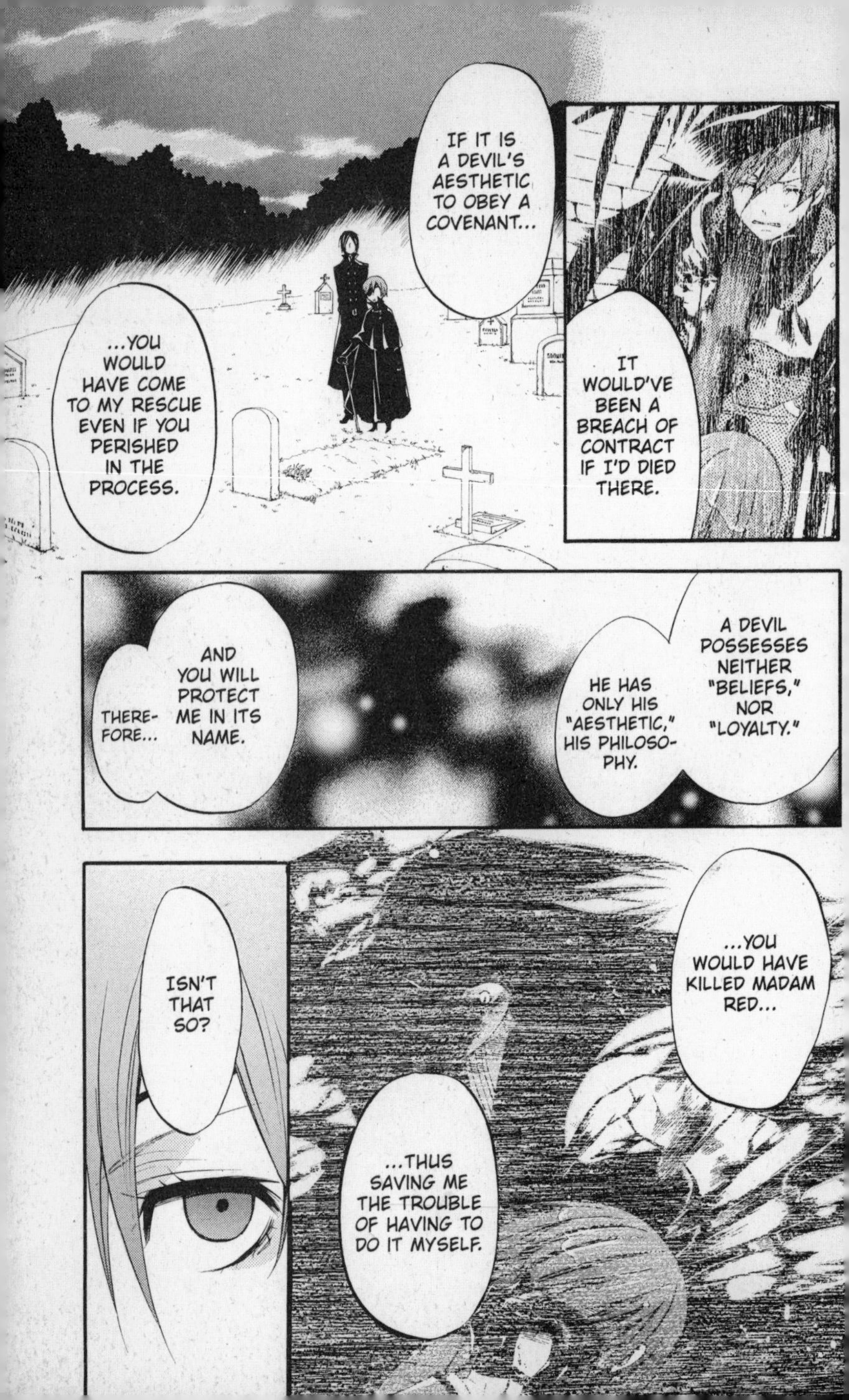
IT WOULD'VE BEEN A BREACH OF CONTRACT IF I'D DIED THERE.
IF IT IS A DEVIL'S AESTHETIC TO OBEY A COVENANT...
...YOU WOULD HAVE COME TO MY RESCUE EVEN IF YOU PERISHED IN THE PROCESS.
A DEVIL POSSESSES NEITHER "BELIEFS," NOR "LOYALTY."
HE HAS ONLY HIS "AESTHETIC," HIS PHILOSO-PHY.
AND YOU WILL PROTECT ME IN ITS NAME.
THERE-FORE...
...YOU WOULD HAVE KILLED MADAM RED...
...THUS SAVING ME THE TROUBLE OF HAVING TO DO IT MYSELF.
ISN'T THAT SO?

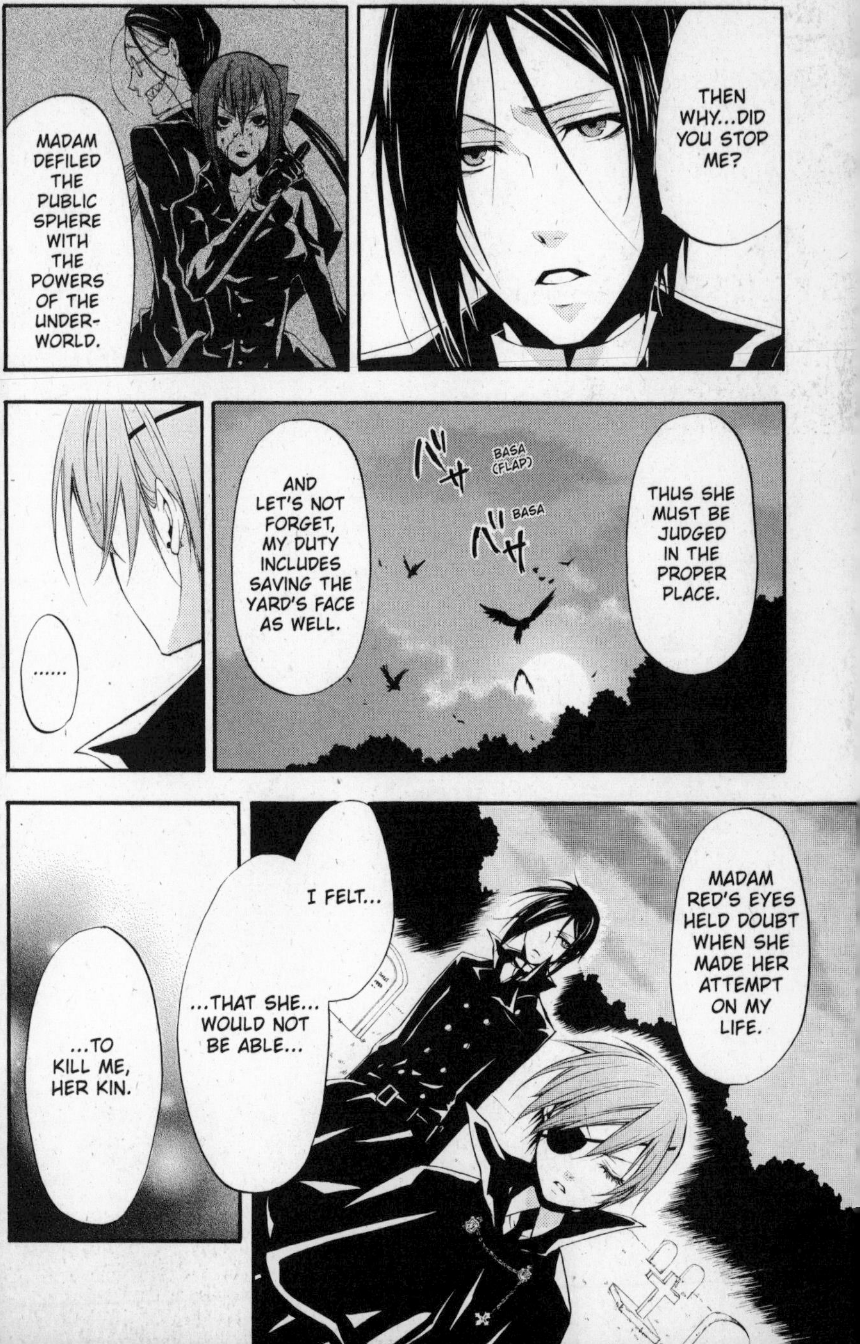
THEN WHY...DID YOU STOP ME?
MADAM DEFILED THE PUBLIC SPHERE WITH THE POWERS OF THE UNDER-WORLD.
THUS SHE MUST BE JUDGED IN THE PROPER PLACE.
BASA (FLAP)
BASA
AND LET'S NOT FORGET, MY DUTY INCLUDES SAVING THE YARD'S FACE AS WELL.
......
MADAM RED'S EYES HELD DOUBT WHEN SHE MADE HER ATTEMPT ON MY LIFE.
I FELT...
...THAT SHE... WOULD NOT BE ABLE...
...TO KILL ME, HER KIN.

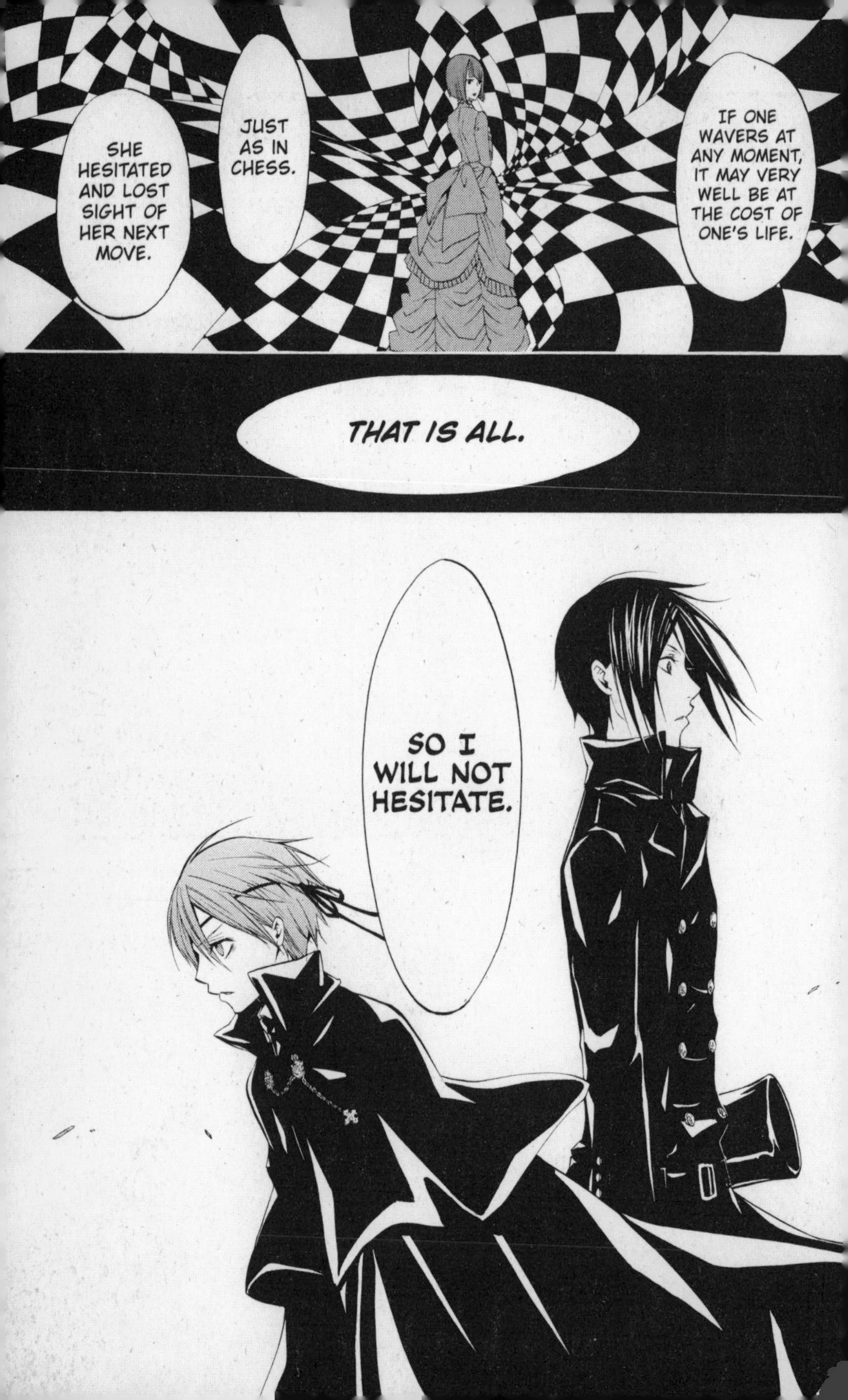
IF ONE WAVERS AT ANY MOMENT, IT MAY VERY WELL BE AT THE COST OF ONE'S LIFE.
JUST AS IN CHESS.
SHE HESITATED AND LOST SIGHT OF HER NEXT MOVE.
THAT IS ALL.
SO I WILL NOT HESITATE.

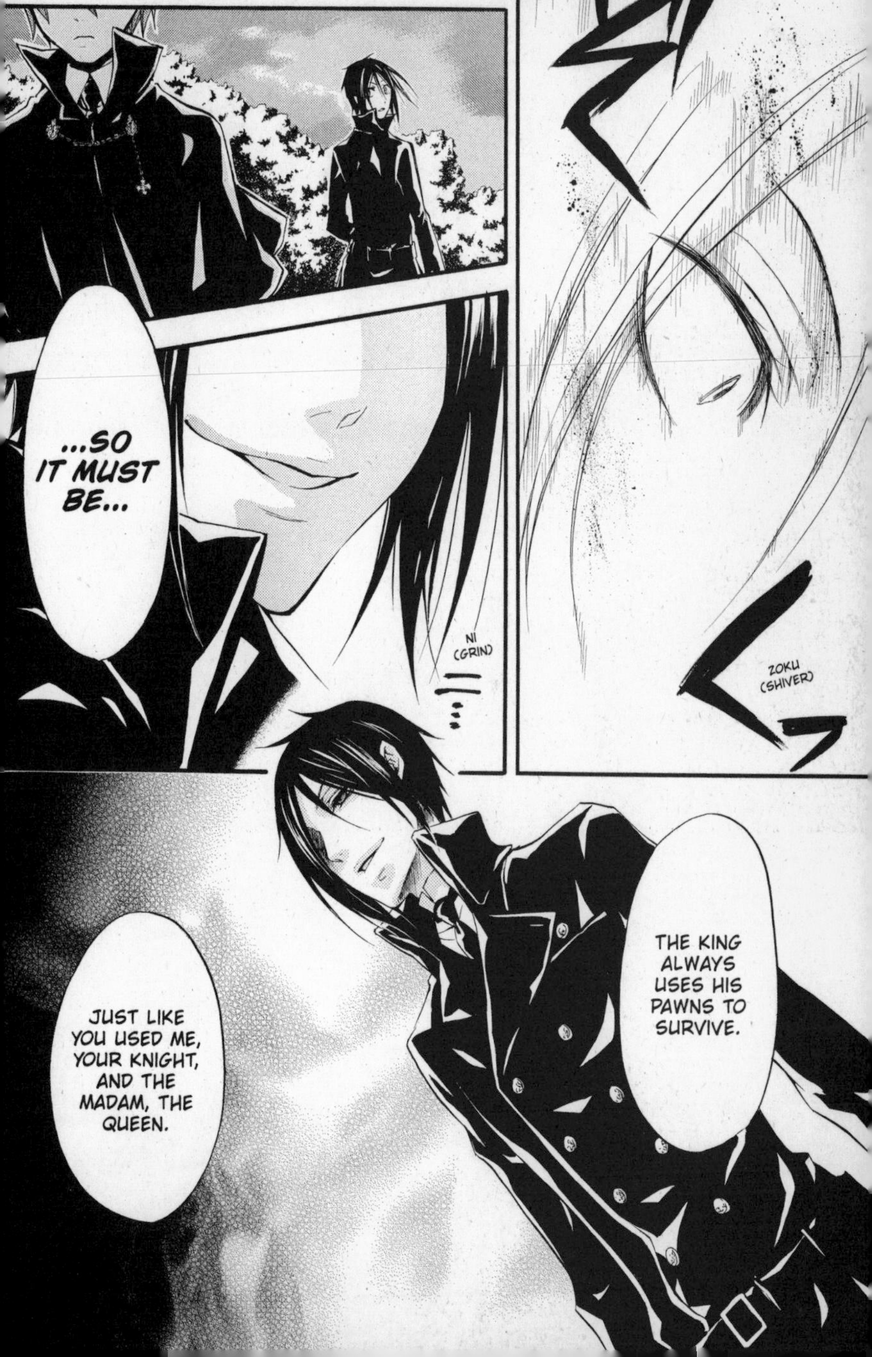
ZOKU (SHIVER)
...SO IT MUST BE...
NI (GRIN)
THE KING ALWAYS USES HIS PAWNS TO SURVIVE.
JUST LIKE YOU USED ME, YOUR KNIGHT, AND THE MADAM, THE QUEEN.

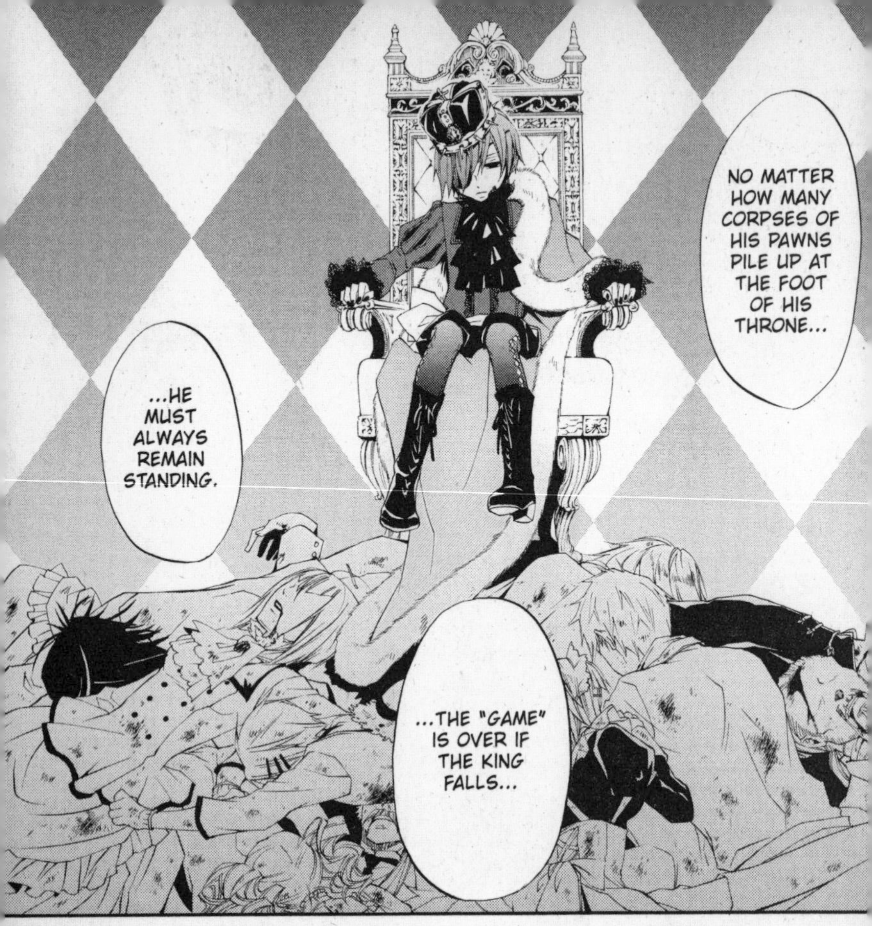
NO MATTER HOW MANY CORPSES OF HIS PAWNS PILE UP AT THE FOOT OF HIS THRONE...
...HE MUST ALWAYS REMAIN STANDING.
...THE "GAME" IS OVER IF THE KING FALLS...
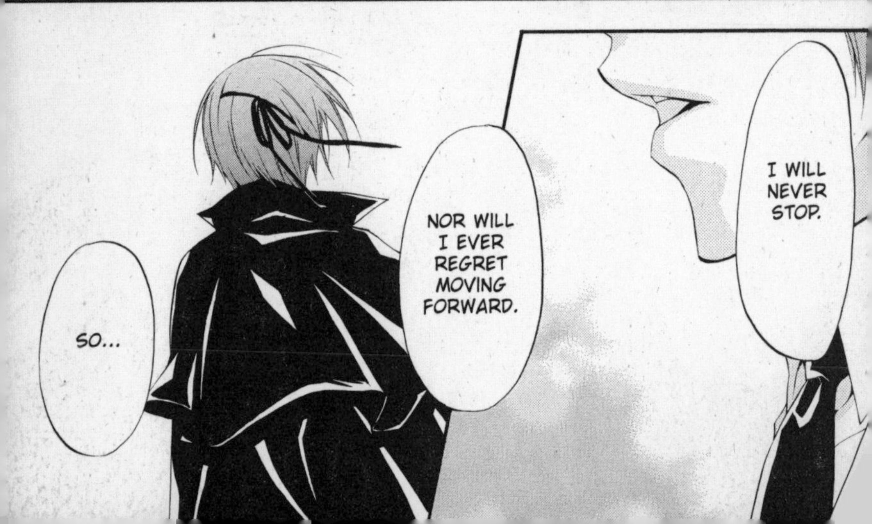
I WILL NEVER STOP.
NOR WILL I EVER REGRET MOVING FORWARD.
SO...

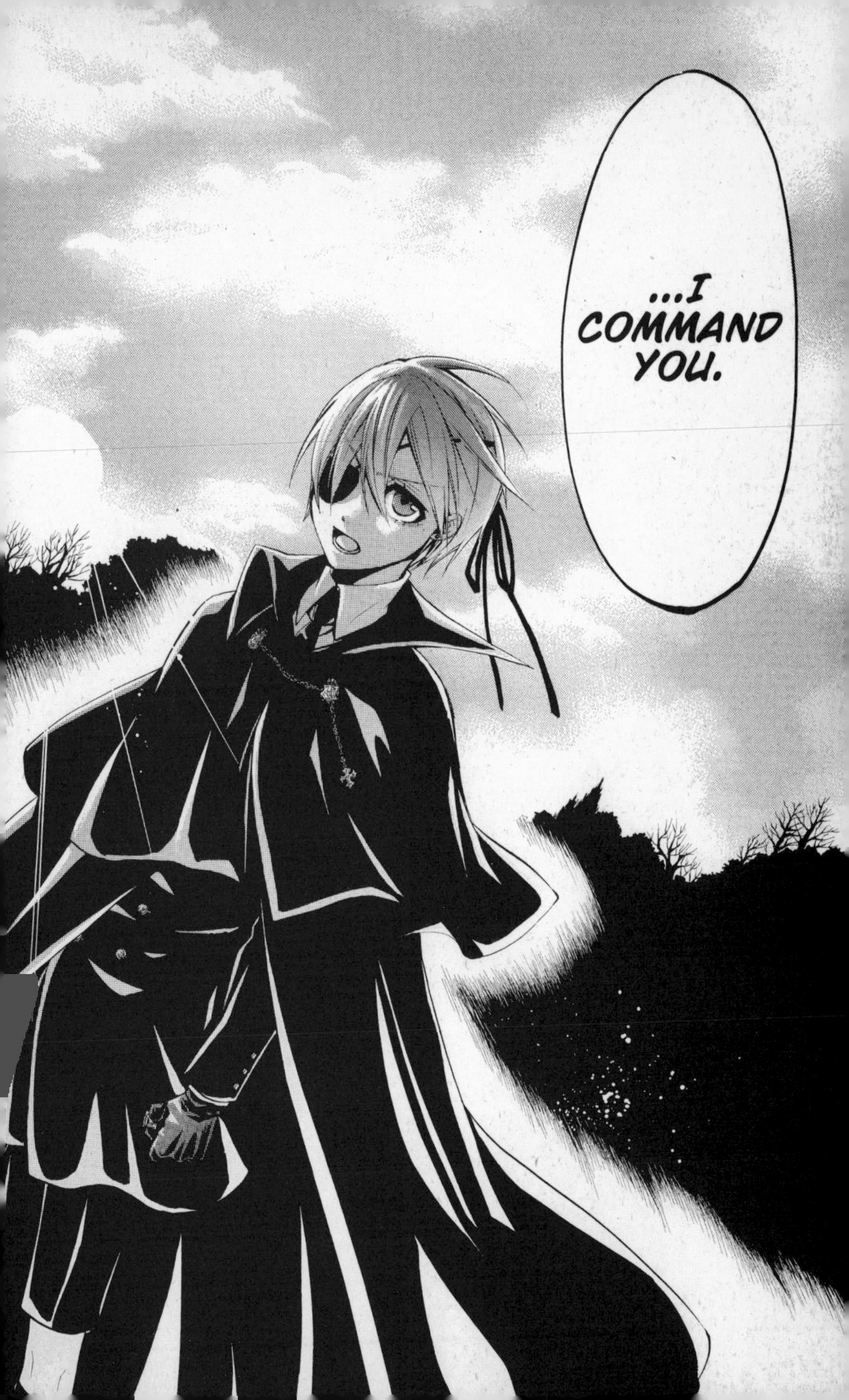
...I COMMAND YOU.

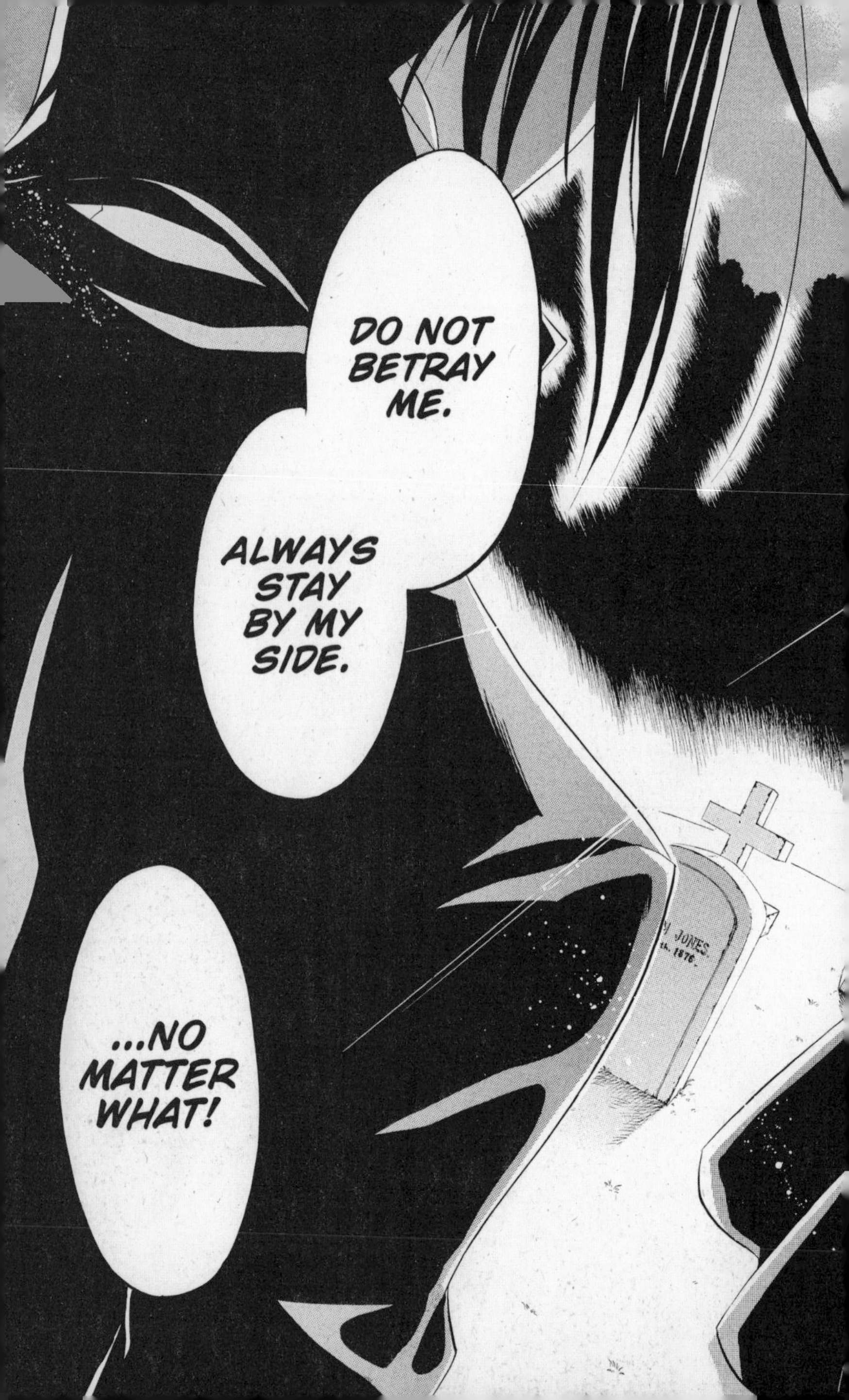
DO NOT BETRAY ME.
ALWAYS STAY BY MY SIDE.
...NO MATTER WHAT!

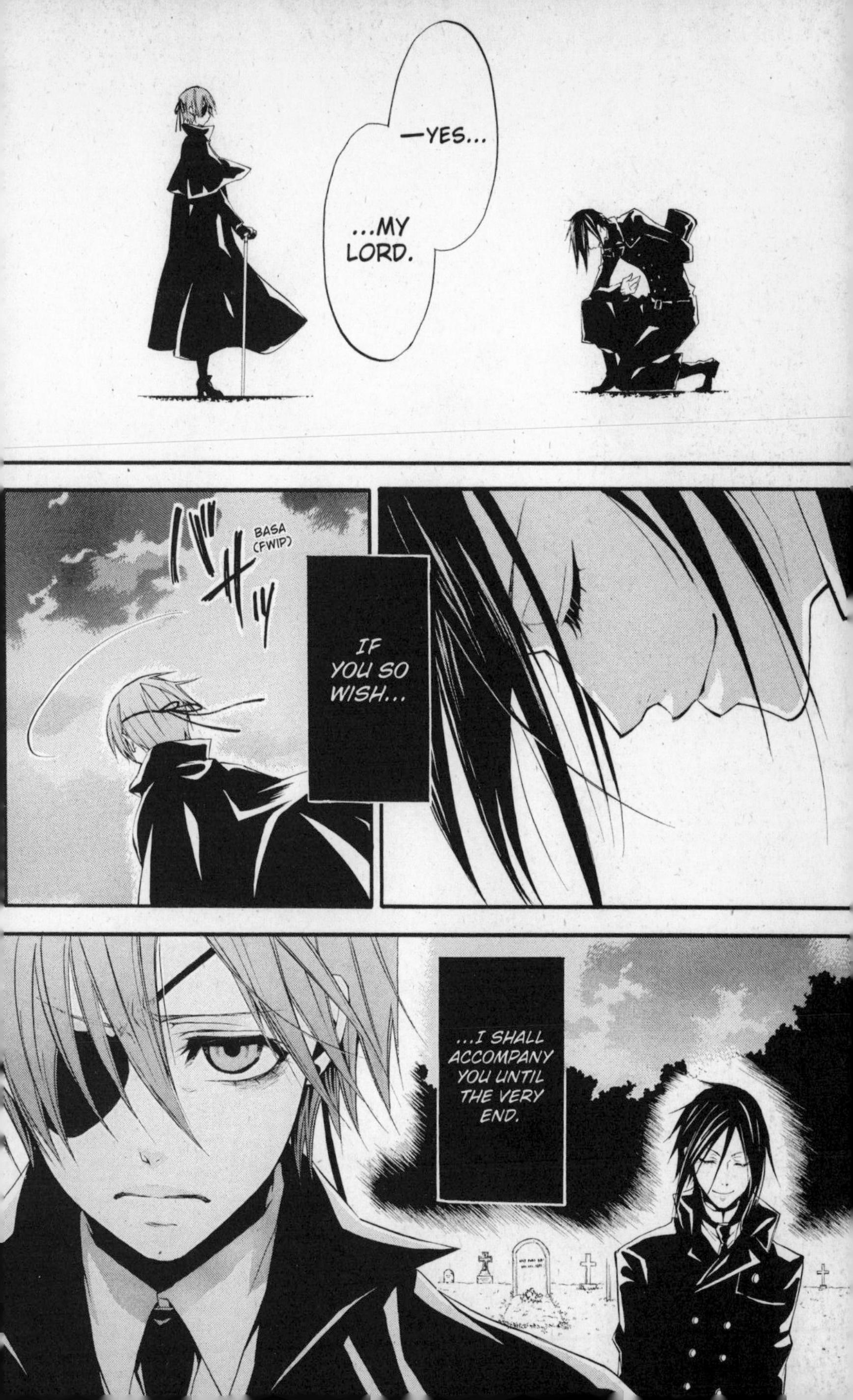
—YES...
...MY LORD.
IF YOU SO WISH...
BASA (FWIP)
...I SHALL ACCOMPANY YOU UNTIL THE VERY END.

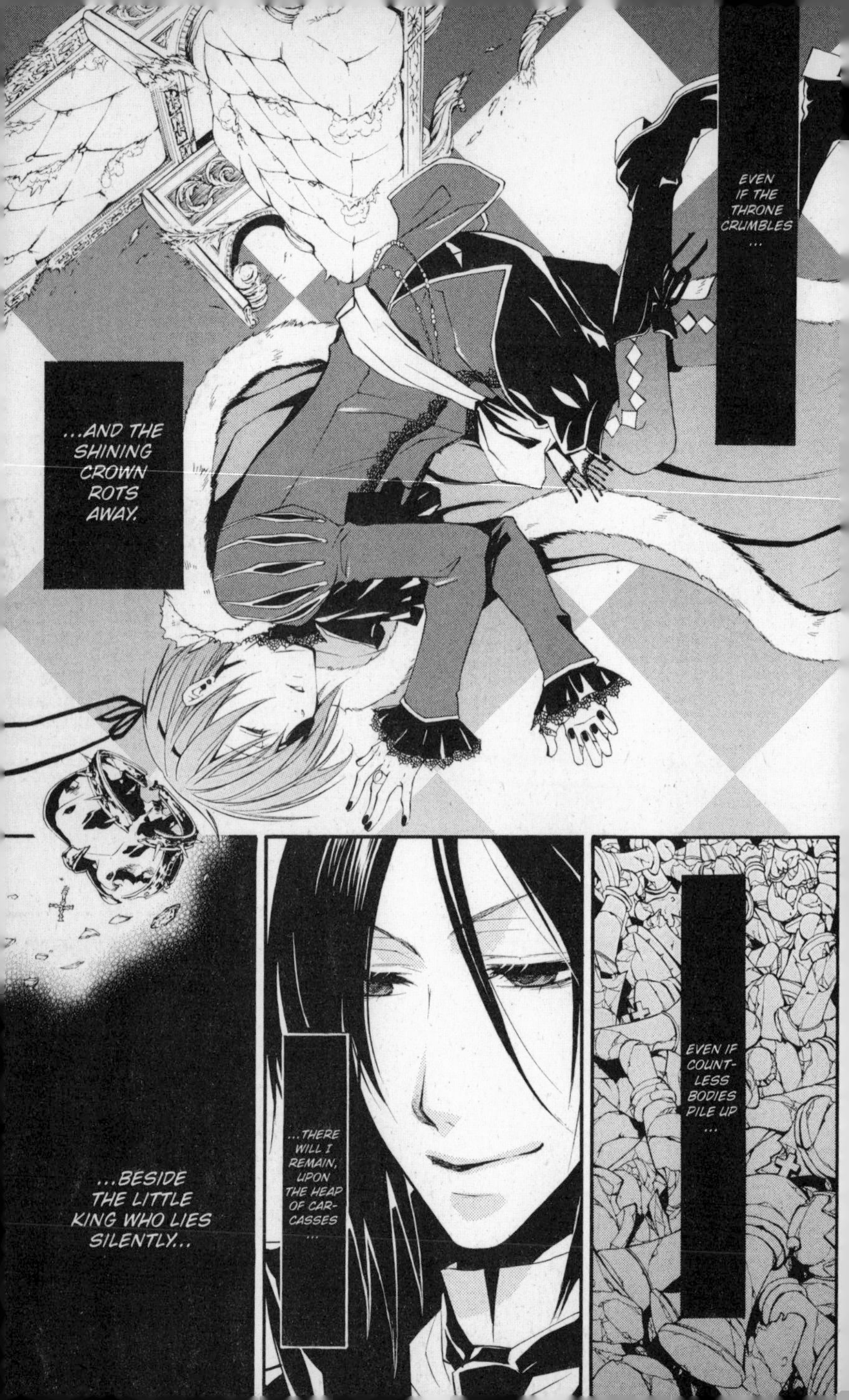
EVEN IF THE THRONE CRUMBLES...
...AND THE SHINING CROWN ROTS AWAY.
EVEN IF COUNT-LESS BODIES PILE UP...
...THERE WILL I REMAIN, UPON THE HEAP OF CAR-CASSES...
...BESIDE THE LITTLE KING WHO LIES SILENTLY...

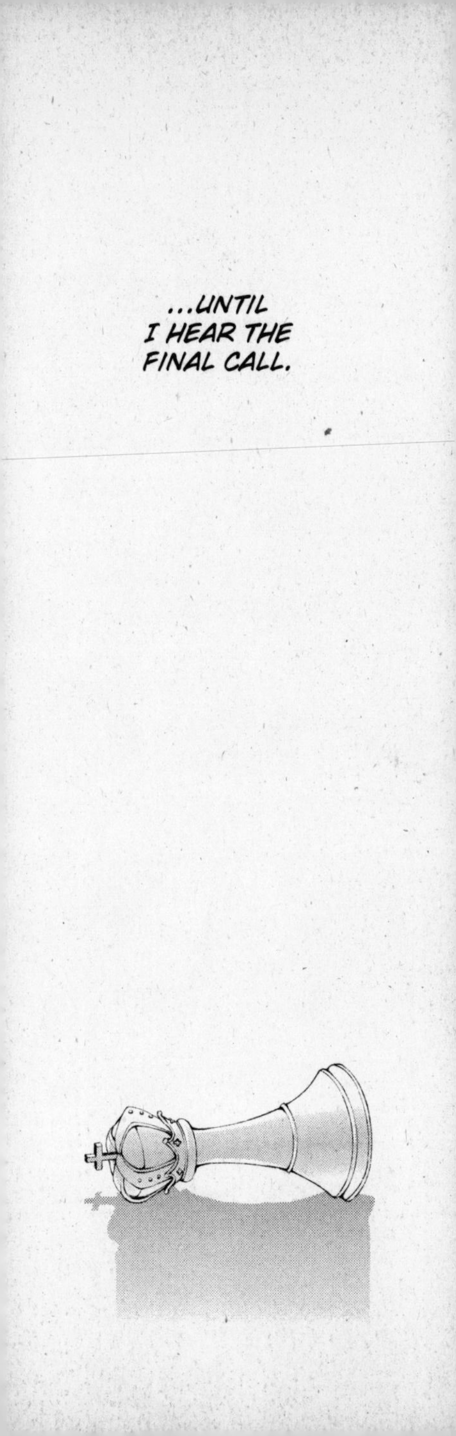
...UNTIL I HEAR THE FINAL CALL.

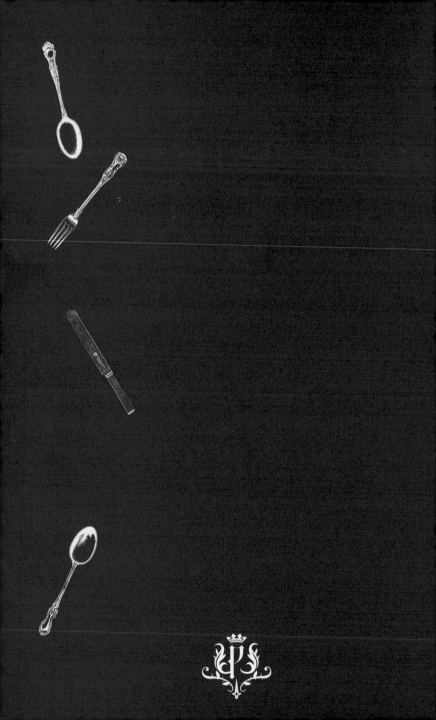

Black Butler

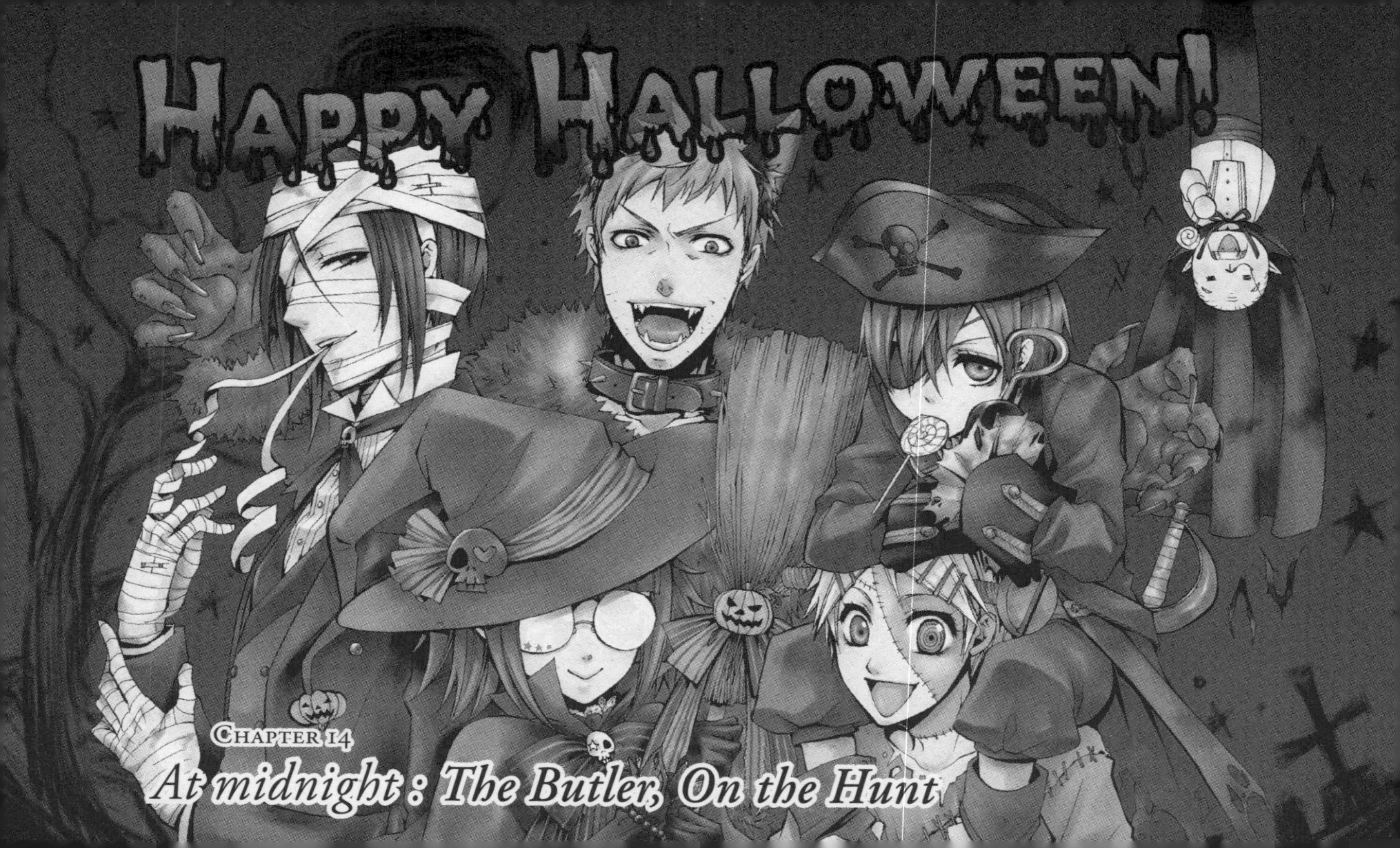
HAPPY HALLOWEEN!
CHAPTER 14
At midnight : The Butler, On the Hunt

Black Butler

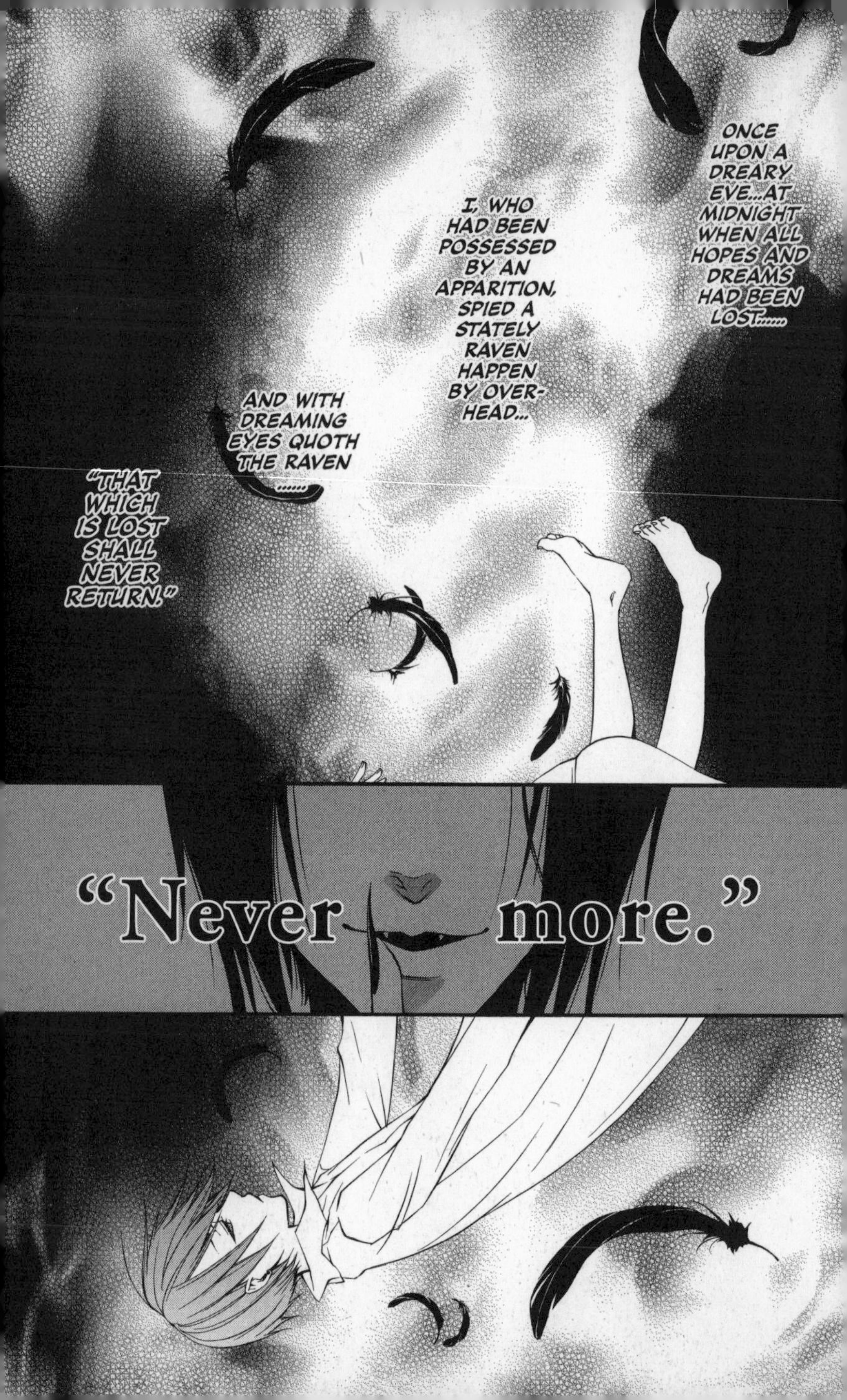
ONCE UPON A DREARY EVE...AT MIDNIGHT WHEN ALL HOPES AND DREAMS HAD BEEN LOST......
I, WHO HAD BEEN POSSESSED BY AN APPARITION, SPIED A STATELY RAVEN HAPPEN BY OVER-HEAD...
AND WITH DREAMING EYES QUOTH THE RAVEN ......
"THAT WHICH IS LOST SHALL NEVER RETURN."
"Never more."

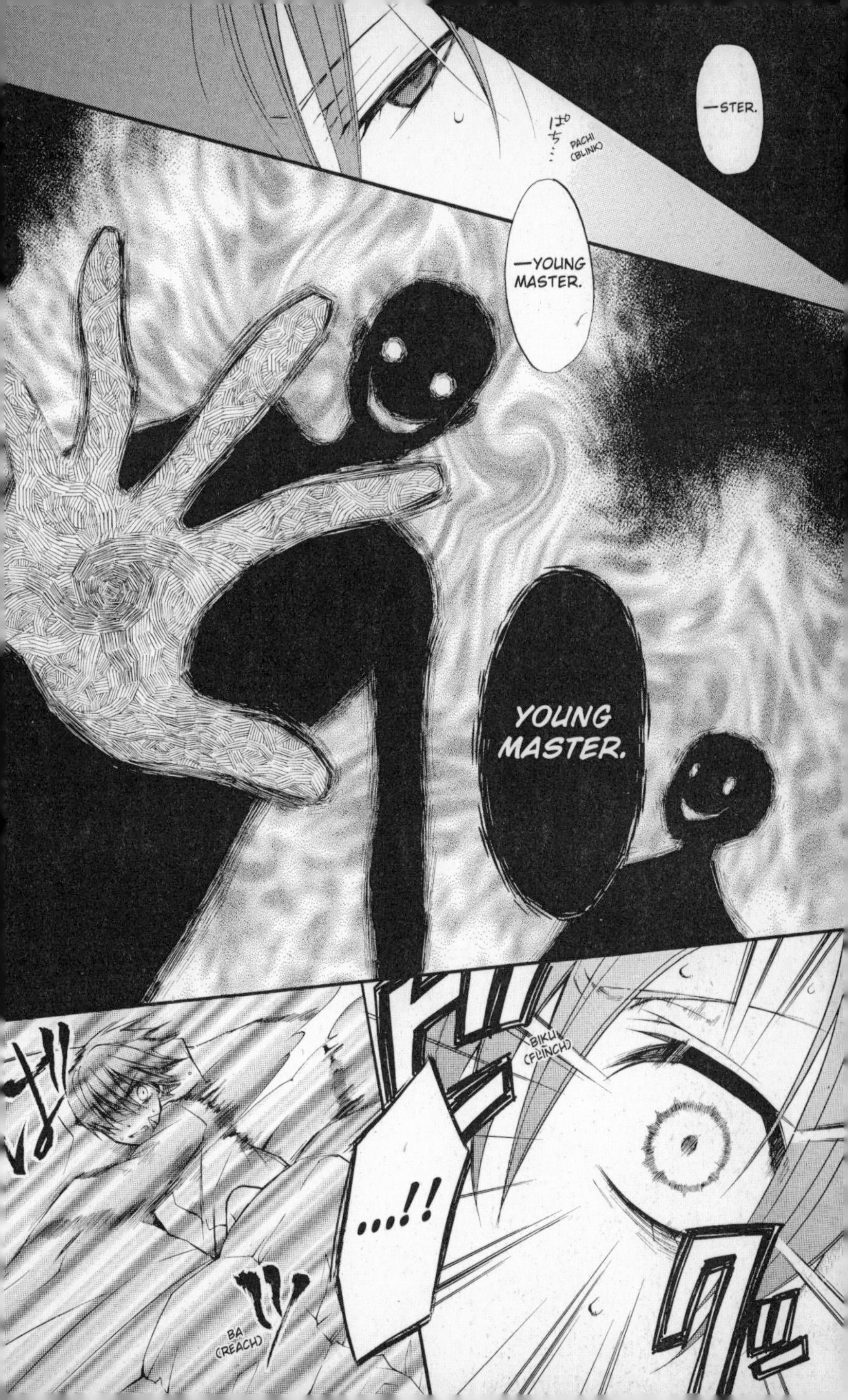
—STER.
ぱち… PACHI (BLINK)
—YOUNG MASTER.
YOUNG MASTER.
BIKU (FLINCH)
…!!
BA (REACH)

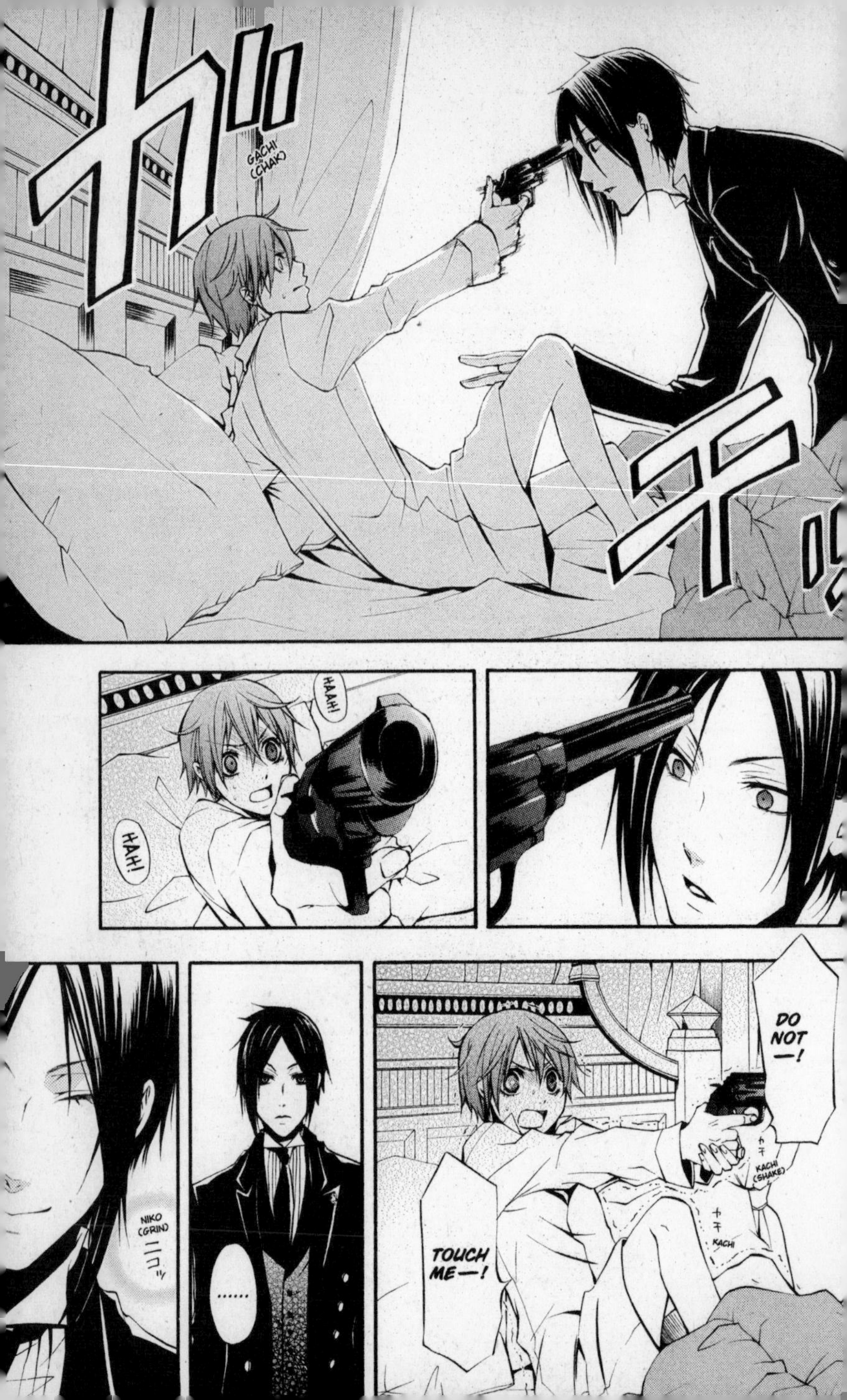
GACHI (CHAK)
HAAH!
HAH!
DO NOT—!
KACHI (SHAKE)
KACHI
TOUCH ME—!
......
NIKO (GRIN)

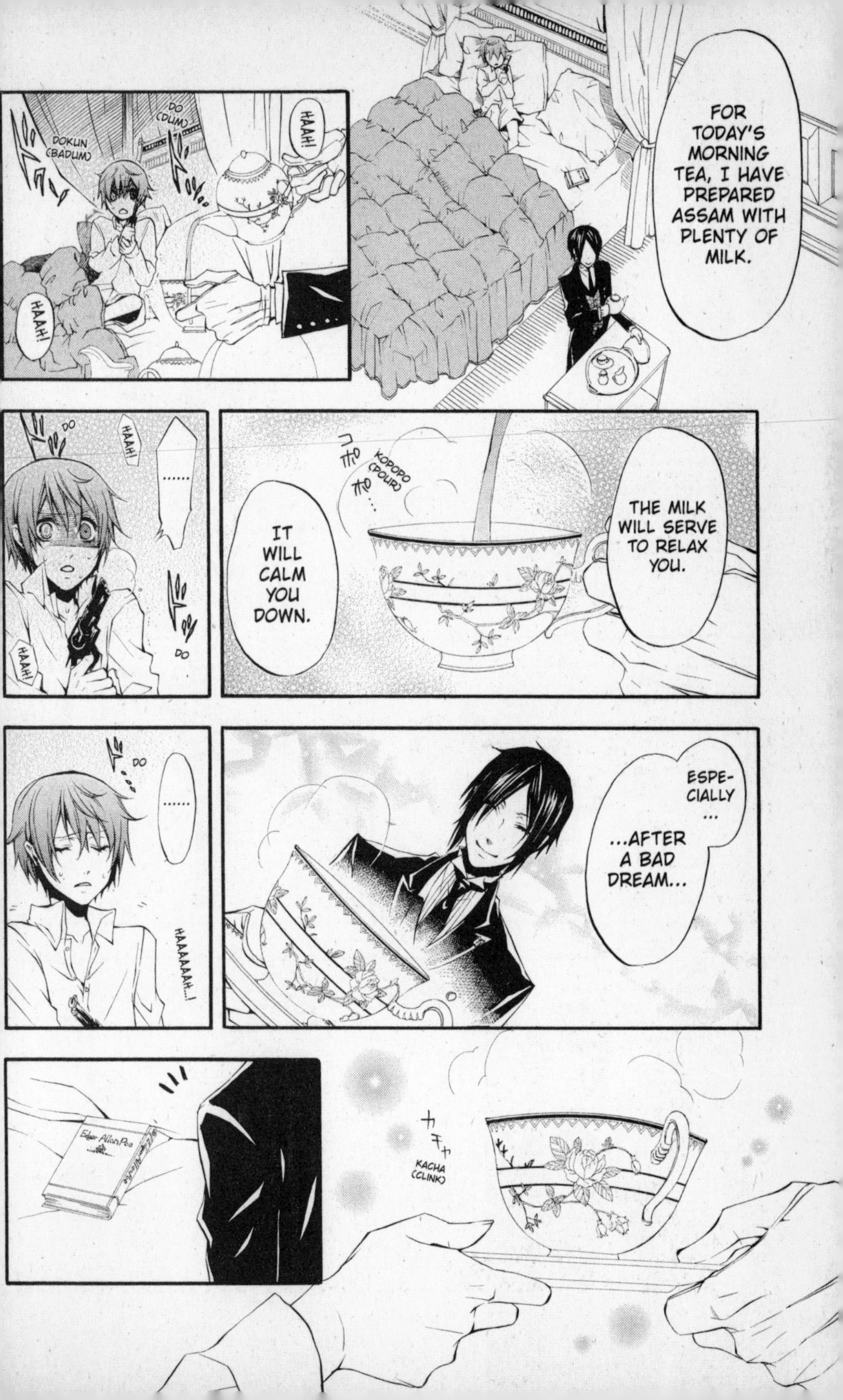
FOR TODAY'S MORNING TEA, I HAVE PREPARED ASSAM WITH PLENTY OF MILK.
HAAH!
DO (DUM)
DOKUN (BADUM)
HAAH!
THE MILK WILL SERVE TO RELAX YOU.
KOPOPO (POUR)
IT WILL CALM YOU DOWN.
HAAH!
......
DO
HAAH!
DO
ESPE-CIALLY...
...AFTER A BAD DREAM...
DO
......
HAAAAAAH...!
KACHA (CLINK)
Edgar Allan Poe

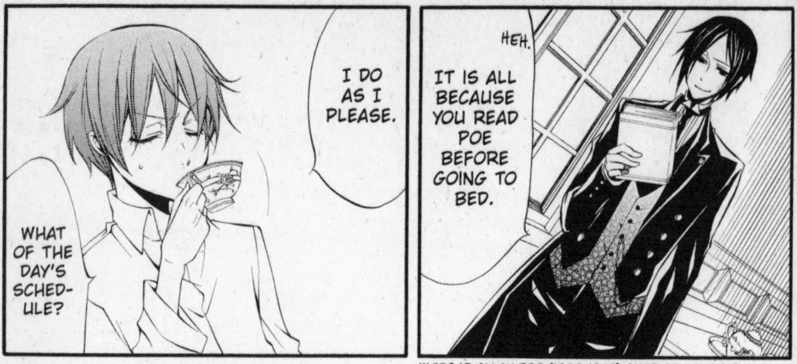
HEH.
IT IS ALL BECAUSE YOU READ POE BEFORE GOING TO BED.
I DO AS I PLEASE.
WHAT OF THE DAY'S SCHEDULE?

※EDGAR ALLAN POE (1809-1849) AMERICAN AUTHOR

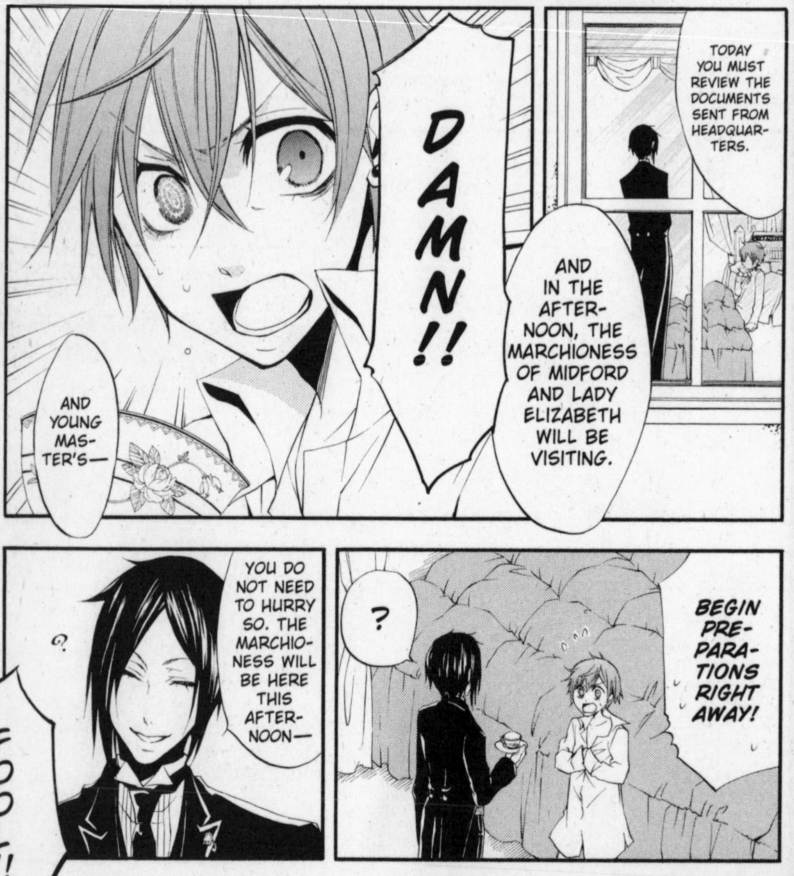
TODAY YOU MUST REVIEW THE DOCUMENTS SENT FROM HEADQUARTERS.
AND IN THE AFTERNOON, THE MARCHIONESS OF MIDFORD AND LADY ELIZABETH WILL BE VISITING.
AND YOUNG MASTER'S—
DAMN!!
?
BEGIN PREPARATIONS RIGHT AWAY!
YOU DO NOT NEED TO HURRY SO. THE MARCHIONESS WILL BE HERE THIS AFTERNOON—
FOOL!!

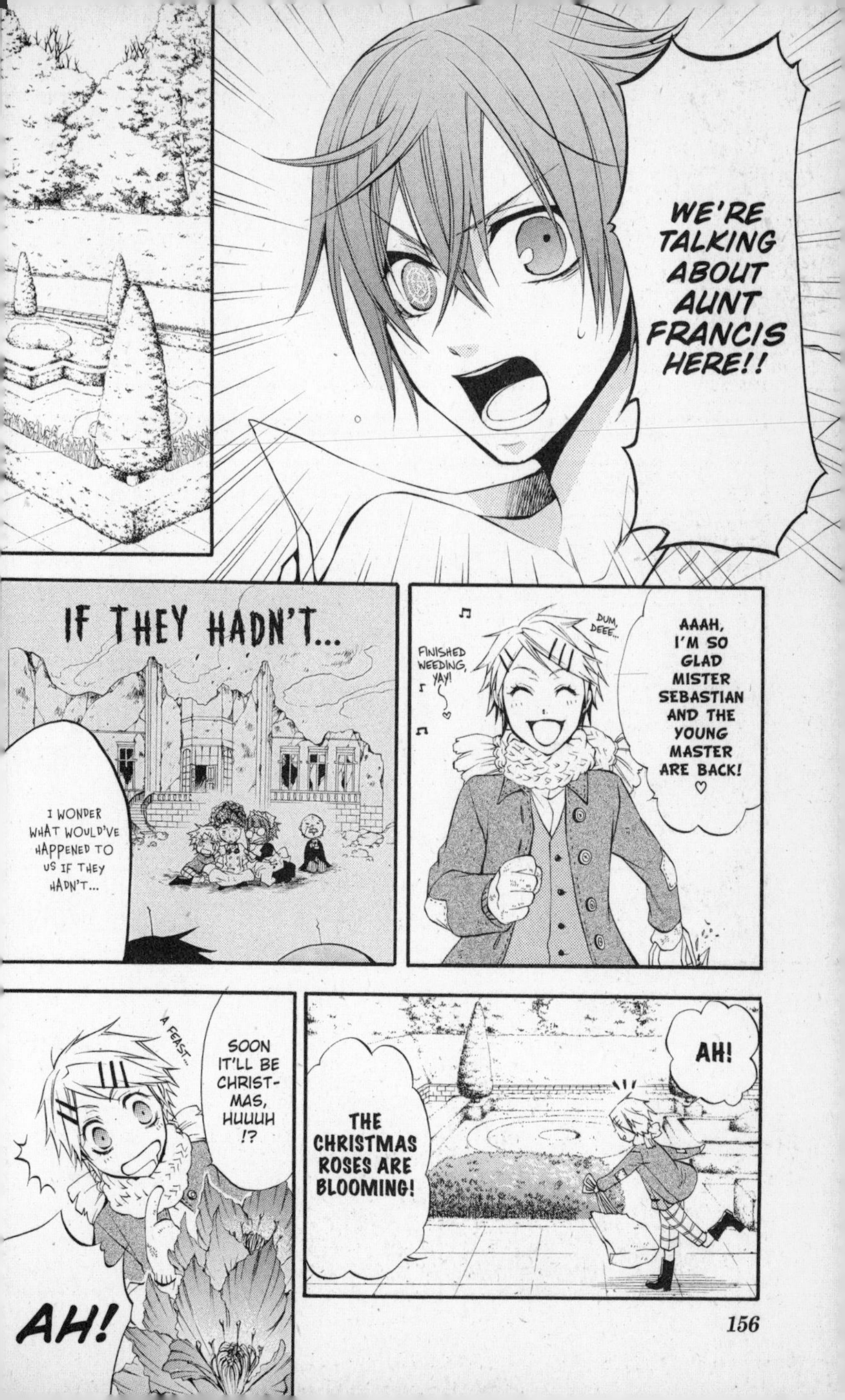
WE'RE TALKING ABOUT AUNT FRANCIS HERE!!
DUM, DEEE...
FINISHED WEEDING, YAY!
AAAH, I'M SO GLAD MISTER SEBASTIAN AND THE YOUNG MASTER ARE BACK! ♡
IF THEY HADN'T...
I WONDER WHAT WOULD'VE HAPPENED TO US IF THEY HADN'T...
AH!
THE CHRISTMAS ROSES ARE BLOOMING!
A FEAST...
SOON IT'LL BE CHRIST-MAS, HUUUH !?
AH!

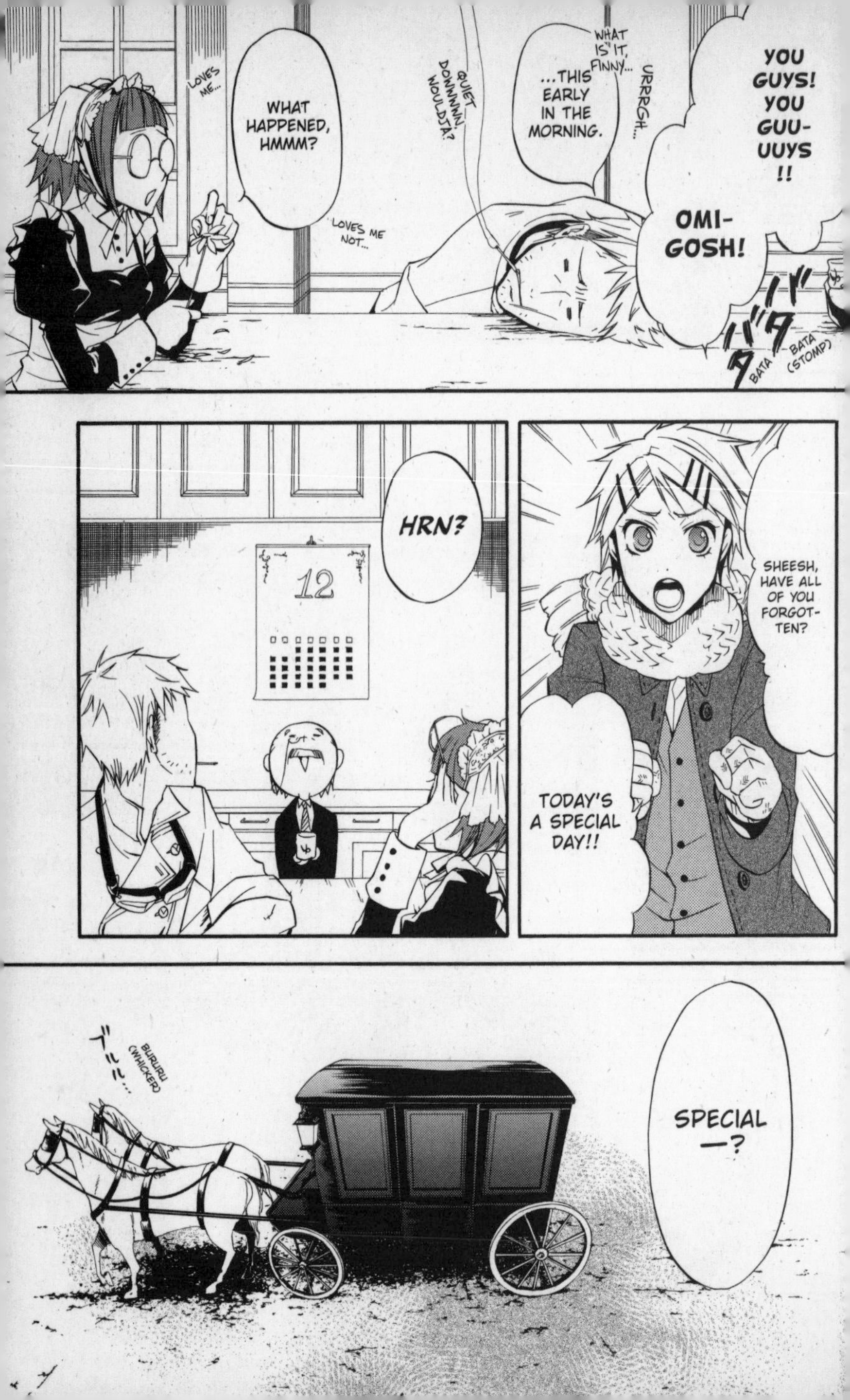
YOU GUYS! YOU GUU-UUYS!!
OMI-GOSH!
BATA BATA (STOMP)
URRGH...
WHAT IS IT, FINNY... ...THIS EARLY IN THE MORNING.
QUIET DOWWWN, WOULDJA?
LOVES ME NOT...
WHAT HAPPENED, HMMM?
LOVES ME...
SHEESH, HAVE ALL OF YOU FORGOT-TEN?
TODAY'S A SPECIAL DAY!!
HRN?
12
SPECIAL —?
BURURU (WHICKER)

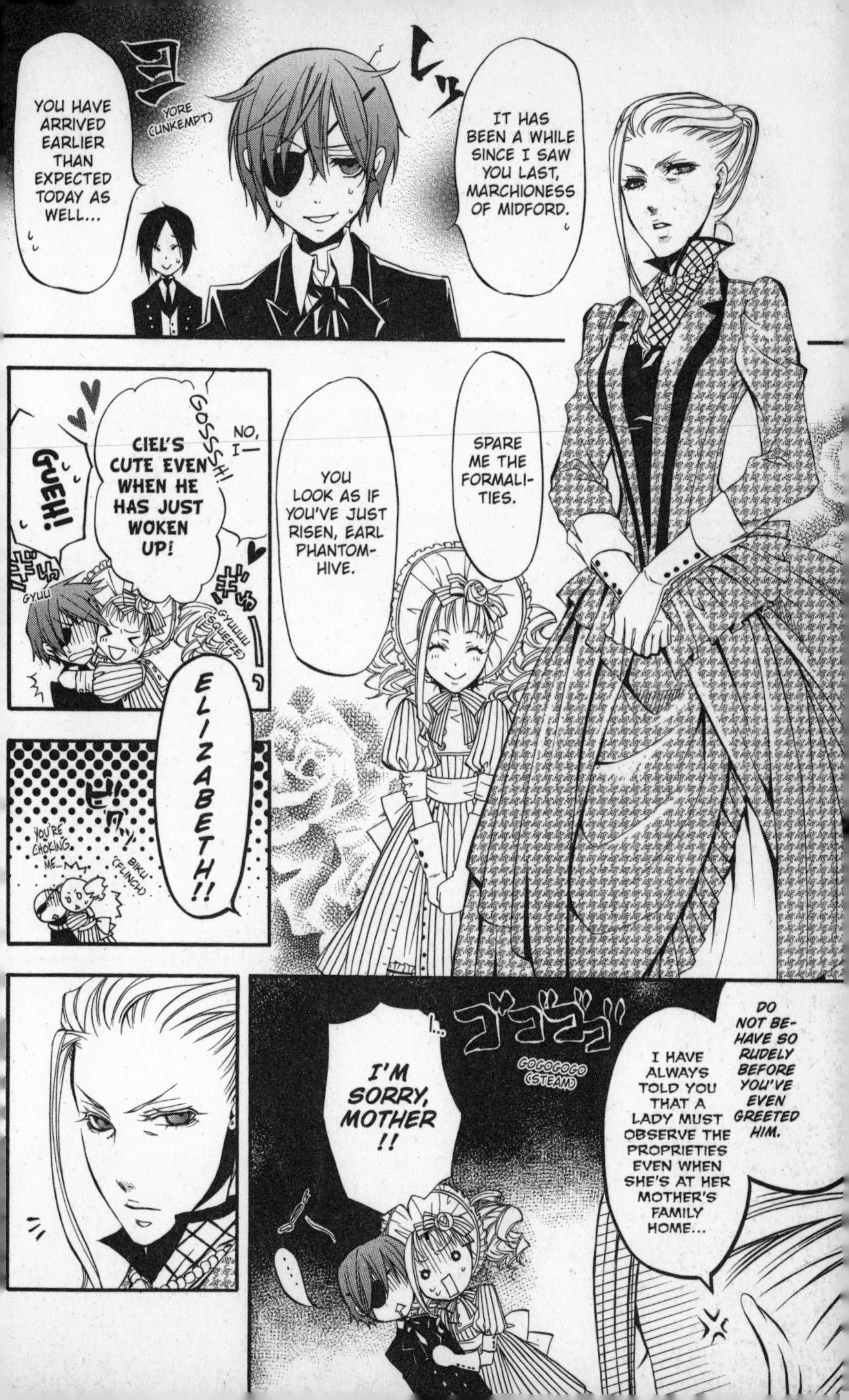
IT HAS BEEN A WHILE SINCE I SAW YOU LAST, MARCHIONESS OF MIDFORD.
YORE (UNKEMPT)
YOU HAVE ARRIVED EARLIER THAN EXPECTED TODAY AS WELL...
SPARE ME THE FORMALITIES.
YOU LOOK AS IF YOU'VE JUST RISEN, EARL PHANTOMHIVE.
NO, I—
GOSSSH!
CIEL'S CUTE EVEN WHEN HE HAS JUST WOKEN UP!
GUEH!
GYUUUU (SQUEEZE)
GYUU
ELIZABETH!!
BIKU (FLINCH)
YOU'RE CHOKING ME...
DO NOT BEHAVE SO RUDELY BEFORE YOU'VE EVEN GREETED HIM.
I HAVE ALWAYS TOLD YOU THAT A LADY MUST OBSERVE THE PROPRIETIES EVEN WHEN SHE'S AT HER MOTHER'S FAMILY HOME...
GOGOGOGO (STEAM)
I...
I'M SORRY, MOTHER!!

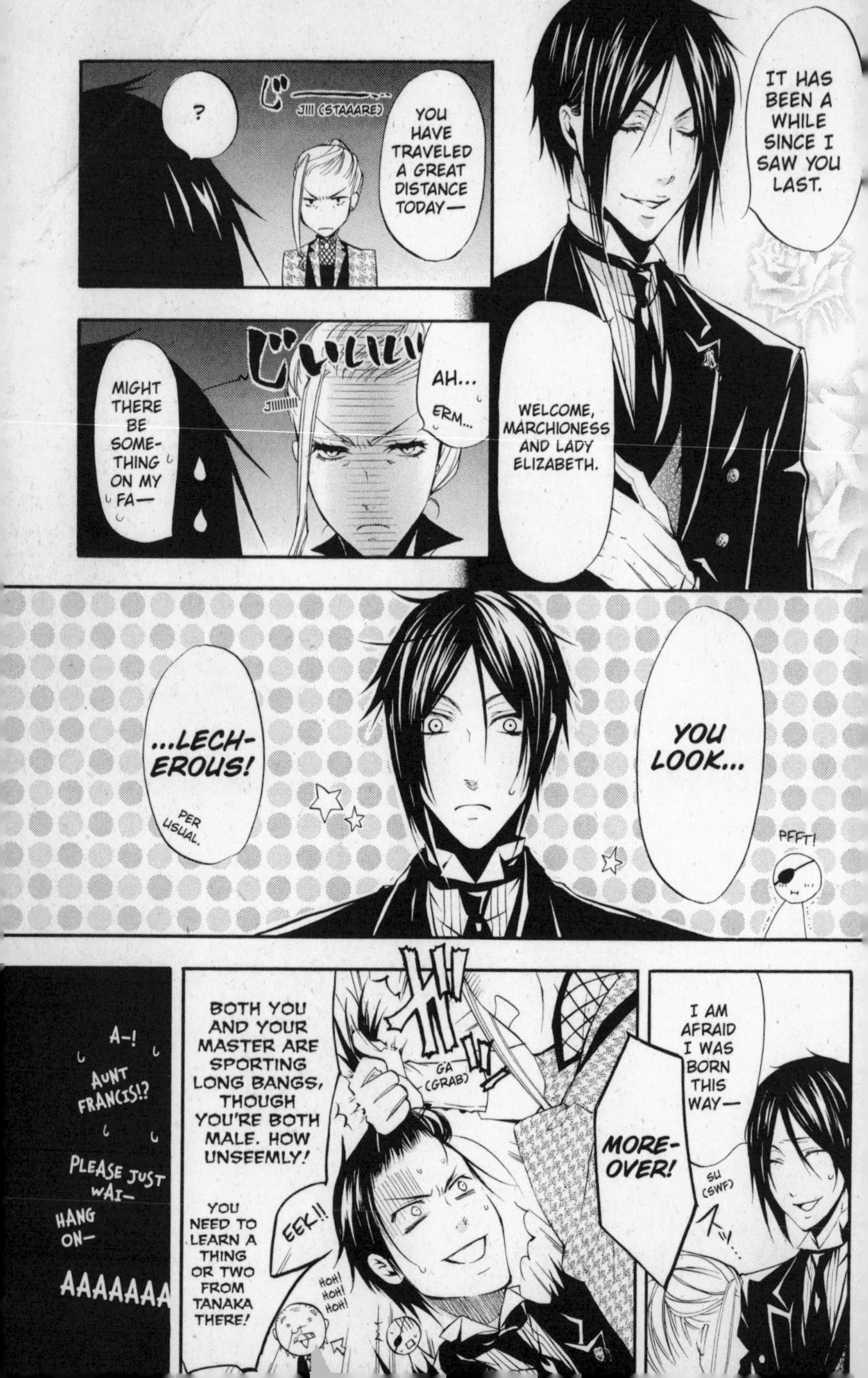
IT HAS BEEN A WHILE SINCE I SAW YOU LAST.
WELCOME, MARCHIONESS AND LADY ELIZABETH.
YOU HAVE TRAVELED A GREAT DISTANCE TODAY—
JIII (STAAARE)
?
AH... ERM...
JIIIIIIII
MIGHT THERE BE SOMETHING ON MY FA—
YOU LOOK...
PFFT!
...LECHEROUS!
PER USUAL.
I AM AFRAID I WAS BORN THIS WAY—
SU (SWF)
MOREOVER!
BOTH YOU AND YOUR MASTER ARE SPORTING LONG BANGS, THOUGH YOU'RE BOTH MALE. HOW UNSEEMLY!
GA (GRAB)
EEK!!
YOU NEED TO LEARN A THING OR TWO FROM TANAKA THERE!
HOH! HOH! HOH!
A—!
AUNT FRANCIS!?
PLEASE JUST WAI—
HANG ON—
AAAAAAA

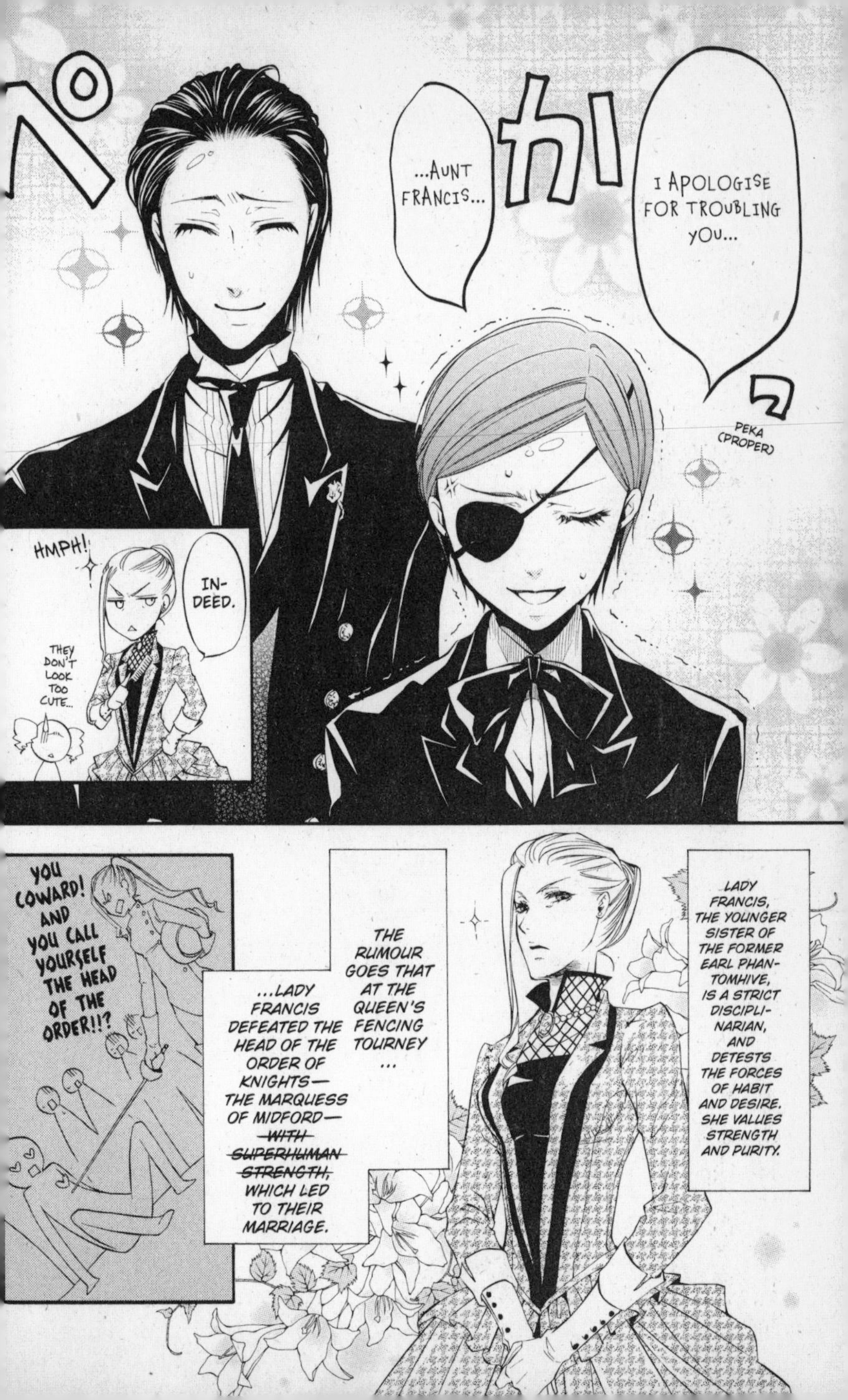

ペかっ
I APOLOGISE FOR TROUBLING YOU...
...AUNT FRANCIS...
PEKA (PROPER)
HMPH!
IN-DEED.
THEY DON'T LOOK TOO CUTE...
LADY FRANCIS, THE YOUNGER SISTER OF THE FORMER EARL PHAN-TOMHIVE, IS A STRICT DISCIPLI-NARIAN, AND DETESTS THE FORCES OF HABIT AND DESIRE. SHE VALUES STRENGTH AND PURITY.
THE RUMOUR GOES THAT AT THE QUEEN'S FENCING TOURNEY ...
...LADY FRANCIS DEFEATED THE HEAD OF THE ORDER OF KNIGHTS—THE MARQUESS OF MIDFORD—~~WITH SUPERHUMAN STRENGTH,~~ WHICH LED TO THEIR MARRIAGE.
YOU COWARD! AND YOU CALL YOURSELF THE HEAD OF THE ORDER!!?

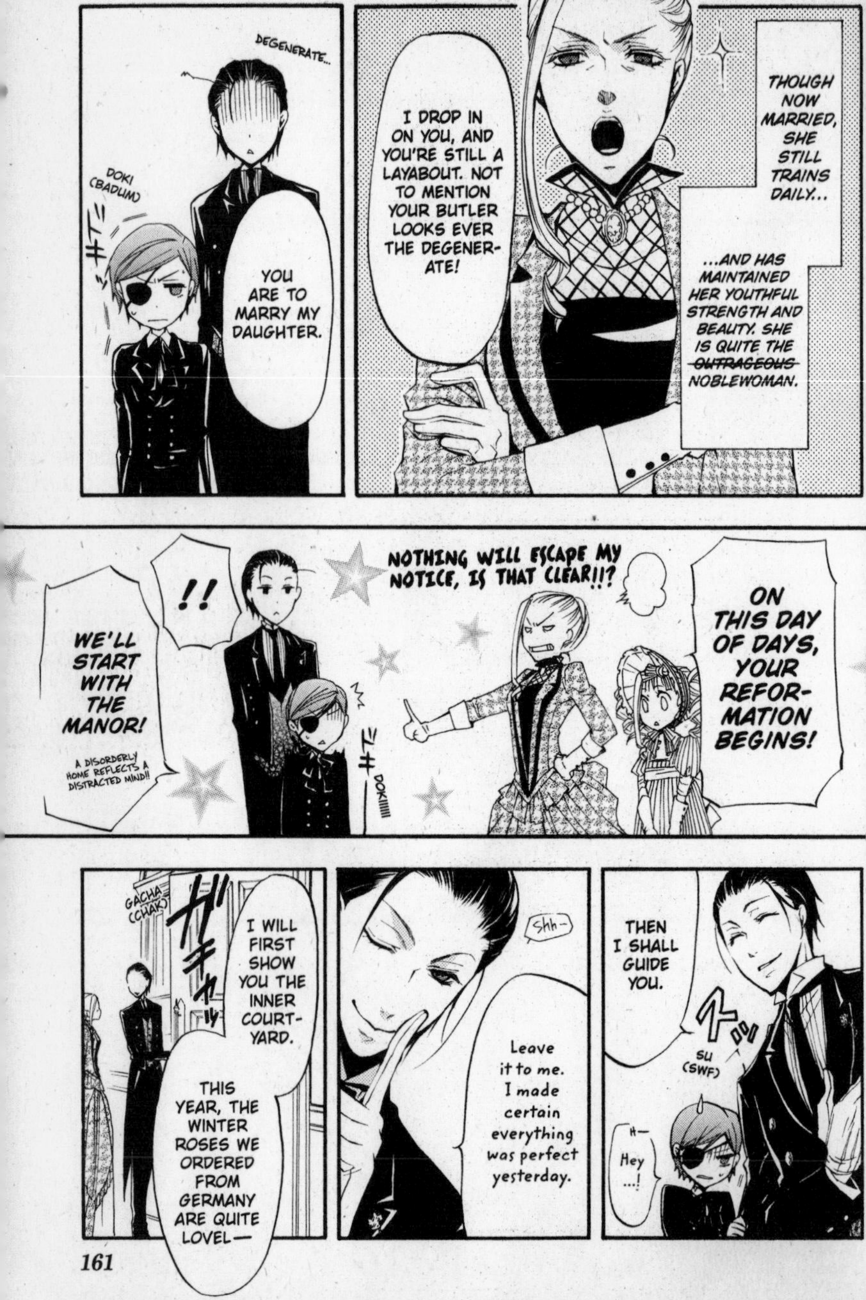
THOUGH NOW MARRIED, SHE STILL TRAINS DAILY...
...AND HAS MAINTAINED HER YOUTHFUL STRENGTH AND BEAUTY. SHE IS QUITE THE ~~OUTRAGEOUS~~ NOBLEWOMAN.
I DROP IN ON YOU, AND YOU'RE STILL A LAYABOUT. NOT TO MENTION YOUR BUTLER LOOKS EVER THE DEGENER-ATE!
DEGENERATE...
DOKI (BADUM)
YOU ARE TO MARRY MY DAUGHTER.
ON THIS DAY OF DAYS, YOUR REFOR-MATION BEGINS!
NOTHING WILL ESCAPE MY NOTICE, IS THAT CLEAR!!?
DOKI!!!!!
!!
WE'LL START WITH THE MANOR!
A DISORDERLY HOME REFLECTS A DISTRACTED MIND!!
THEN I SHALL GUIDE YOU.
SU (SWF)
H— Hey ...!
Shh—
Leave it to me. I made certain everything was perfect yesterday.
GACHA (CHAK)
I WILL FIRST SHOW YOU THE INNER COURT-YARD.
THIS YEAR, THE WINTER ROSES WE ORDERED FROM GERMANY ARE QUITE LOVEL—

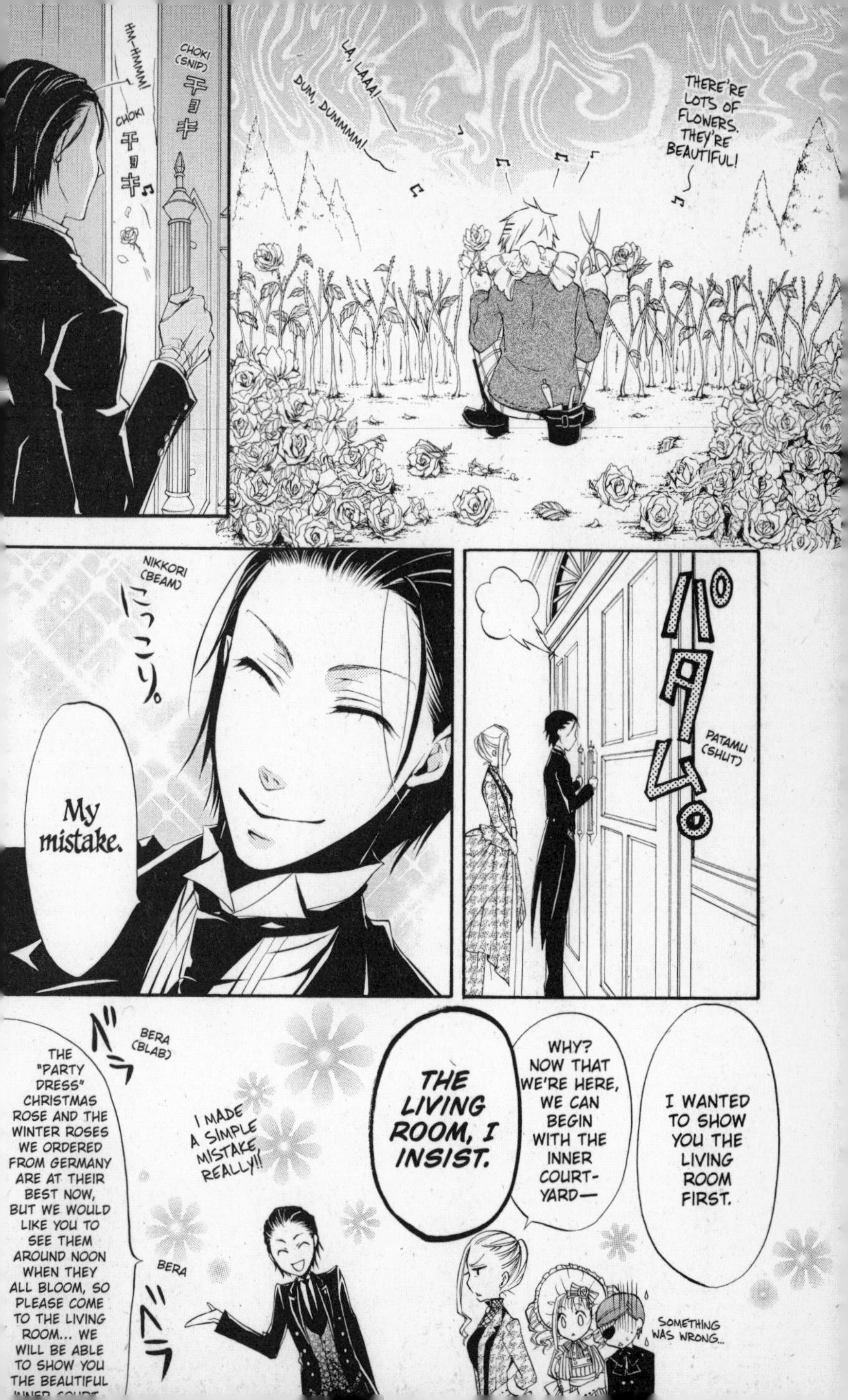
THERE'RE LOTS OF FLOWERS. THEY'RE BEAUTIFUL!
LA, LAAA!
DUM, DUMMMM!
CHOKI (SNIP)
チョキ
HM-HMMM!
CHOKI
チョキ
パタム。
PATAMU (SHUT)
NIKKORI (BEAM)
にっこり。
My mistake.
I WANTED TO SHOW YOU THE LIVING ROOM FIRST.
WHY? NOW THAT WE'RE HERE, WE CAN BEGIN WITH THE INNER COURT-YARD—
THE LIVING ROOM, I INSIST.
I MADE A SIMPLE MISTAKE REALLY!!
ベラ
BERA (BLAB)
THE "PARTY DRESS" CHRISTMAS ROSE AND THE WINTER ROSES WE ORDERED FROM GERMANY ARE AT THEIR BEST NOW, BUT WE WOULD LIKE YOU TO SEE THEM AROUND NOON WHEN THEY ALL BLOOM, SO PLEASE COME TO THE LIVING ROOM... WE WILL BE ABLE TO SHOW YOU THE BEAUTIFUL
BERA
ベラ
SOMETHING WAS WRONG...

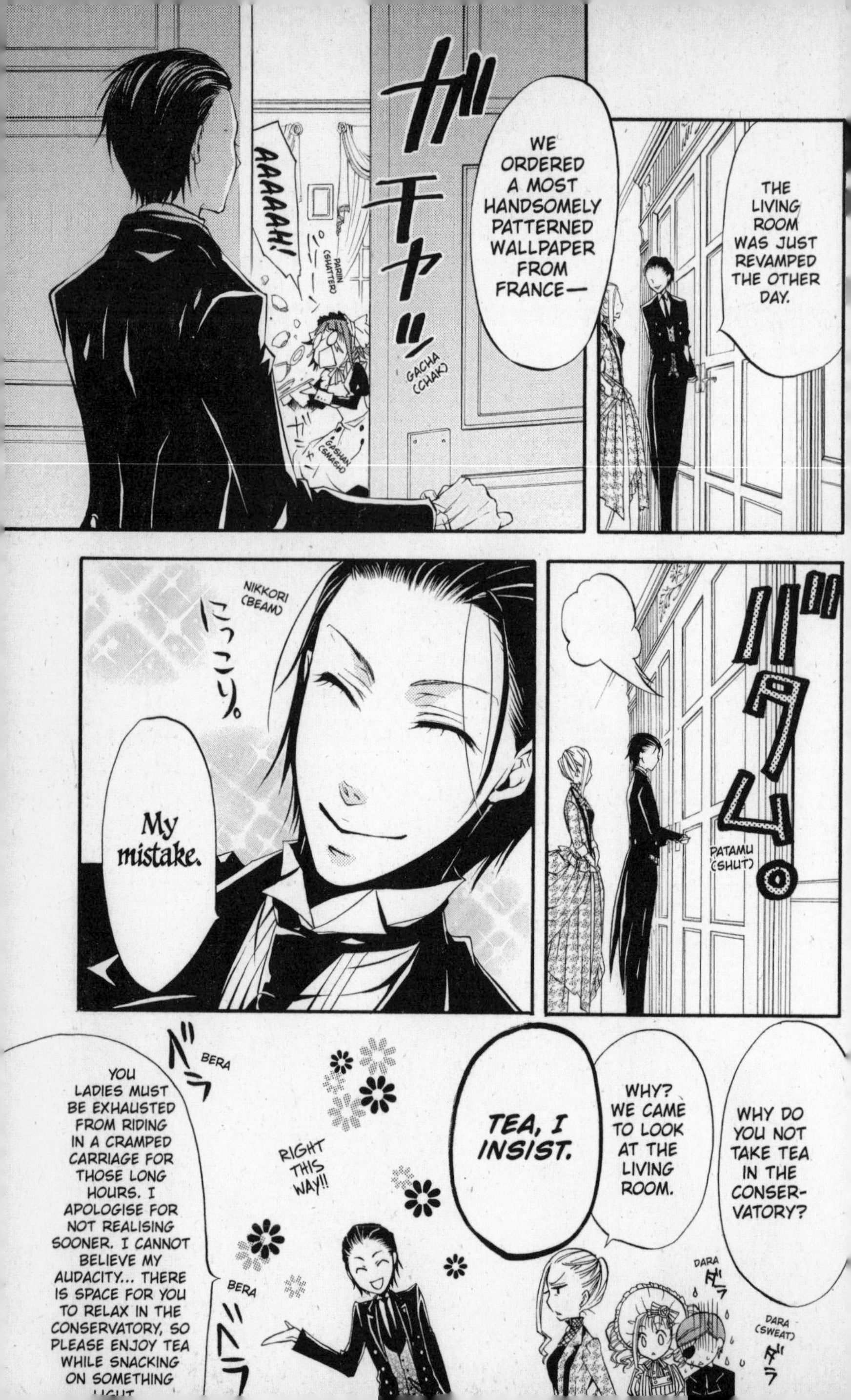
THE LIVING ROOM WAS JUST REVAMPED THE OTHER DAY.
WE ORDERED A MOST HANDSOMELY PATTERNED WALLPAPER FROM FRANCE—
ガチャッ
GACHA (CHAK)
AAAAAH!
PARIN (SHATTER)
GASHAN (SMASH)
バタム。
PATAMU (SHUT)
にっこり。
NIKKORI (BEAM)
My mistake.
WHY DO YOU NOT TAKE TEA IN THE CONSERVATORY?
DARA
DARA (SWEAT)
WHY? WE CAME TO LOOK AT THE LIVING ROOM.
TEA, I INSIST.
RIGHT THIS WAY!!
BERA
BERA
YOU LADIES MUST BE EXHAUSTED FROM RIDING IN A CRAMPED CARRIAGE FOR THOSE LONG HOURS. I APOLOGISE FOR NOT REALISING SOONER. I CANNOT BELIEVE MY AUDACITY... THERE IS SPACE FOR YOU TO RELAX IN THE CONSERVATORY, SO PLEASE ENJOY TEA WHILE SNACKING ON SOMETHING

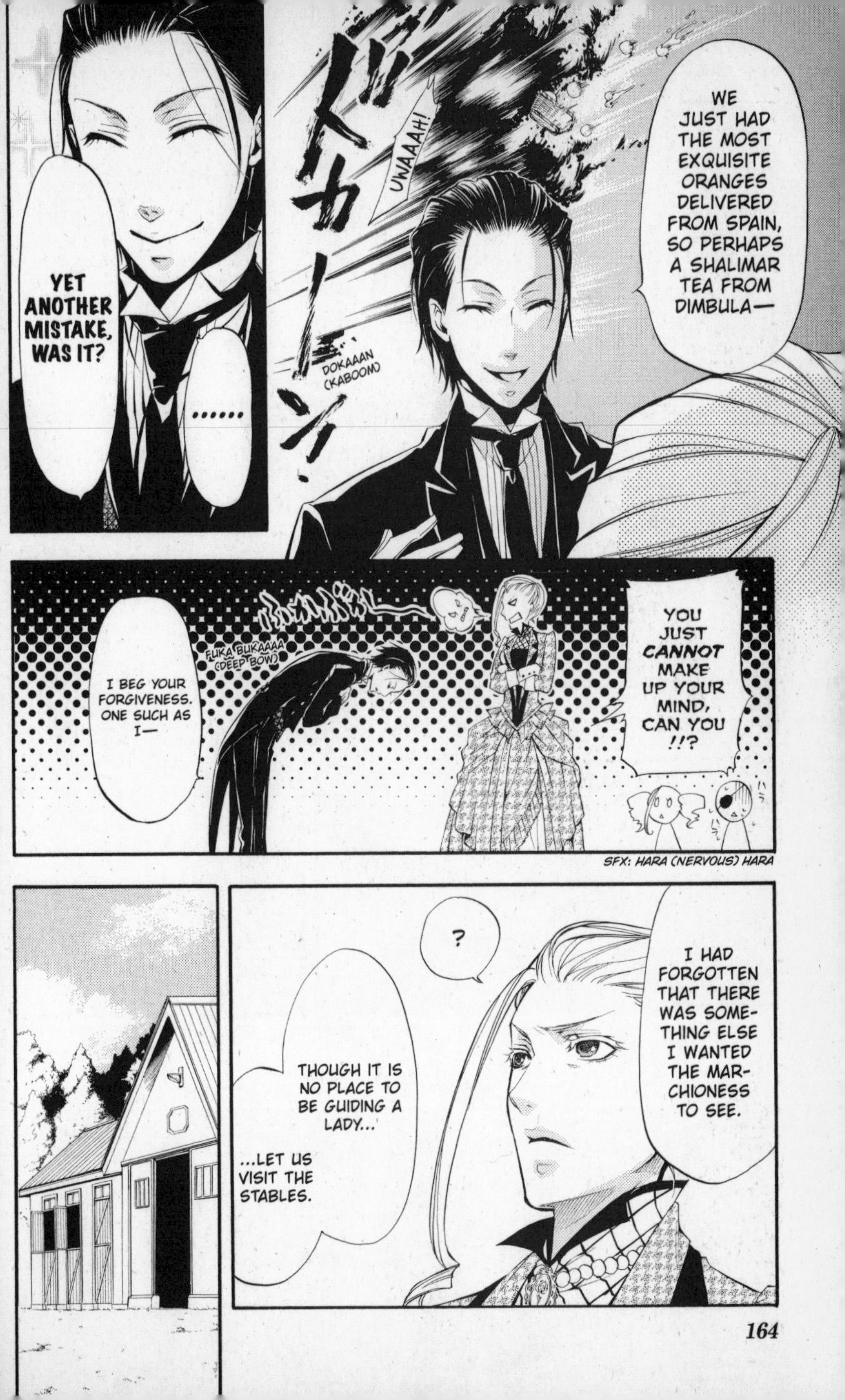
WE JUST HAD THE MOST EXQUISITE ORANGES DELIVERED FROM SPAIN, SO PERHAPS A SHALIMAR TEA FROM DIMBULA—
UWAAAH!
DOKAAAN (KABOOM)
......
YET ANOTHER MISTAKE, WAS IT?
YOU JUST CANNOT MAKE UP YOUR MIND, CAN YOU!!?
FUKA BUKAAAA (DEEP BOW)
I BEG YOUR FORGIVENESS. ONE SUCH AS I—
SFX: HARA (NERVOUS) HARA
I HAD FORGOTTEN THAT THERE WAS SOMETHING ELSE I WANTED THE MARCHIONESS TO SEE.
?
THOUGH IT IS NO PLACE TO BE GUIDING A LADY...
...LET US VISIT THE STABLES.

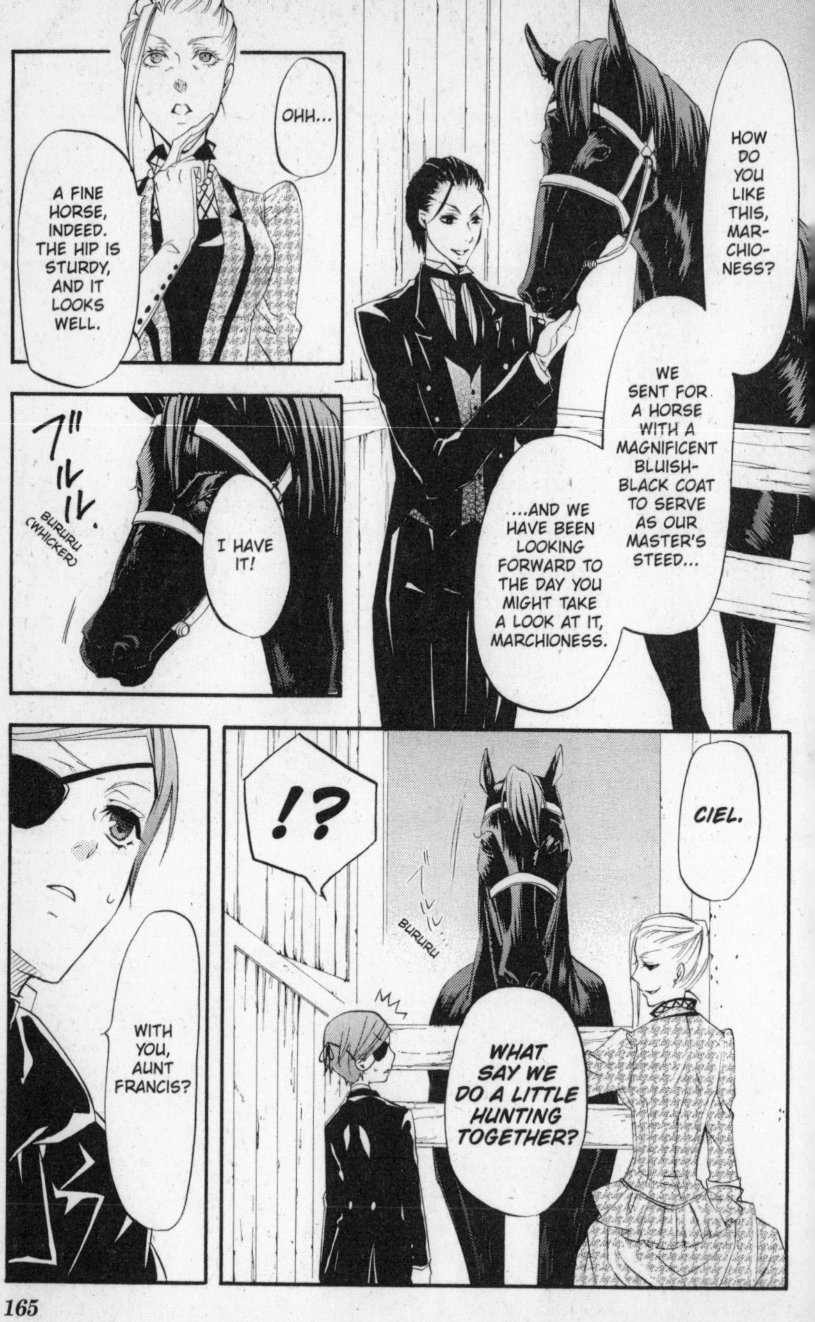
HOW DO YOU LIKE THIS, MARCHIONESS?
WE SENT FOR A HORSE WITH A MAGNIFICENT BLUISH-BLACK COAT TO SERVE AS OUR MASTER'S STEED...
...AND WE HAVE BEEN LOOKING FORWARD TO THE DAY YOU MIGHT TAKE A LOOK AT IT, MARCHIONESS.
OHH...
A FINE HORSE, INDEED. THE HIP IS STURDY, AND IT LOOKS WELL.
ブルル.
BURURU (WHICKER)
I HAVE IT!
CIEL.
!?
ブルル
BURURU
WHAT SAY WE DO A LITTLE HUNTING TOGETHER?
WITH YOU, AUNT FRANCIS?

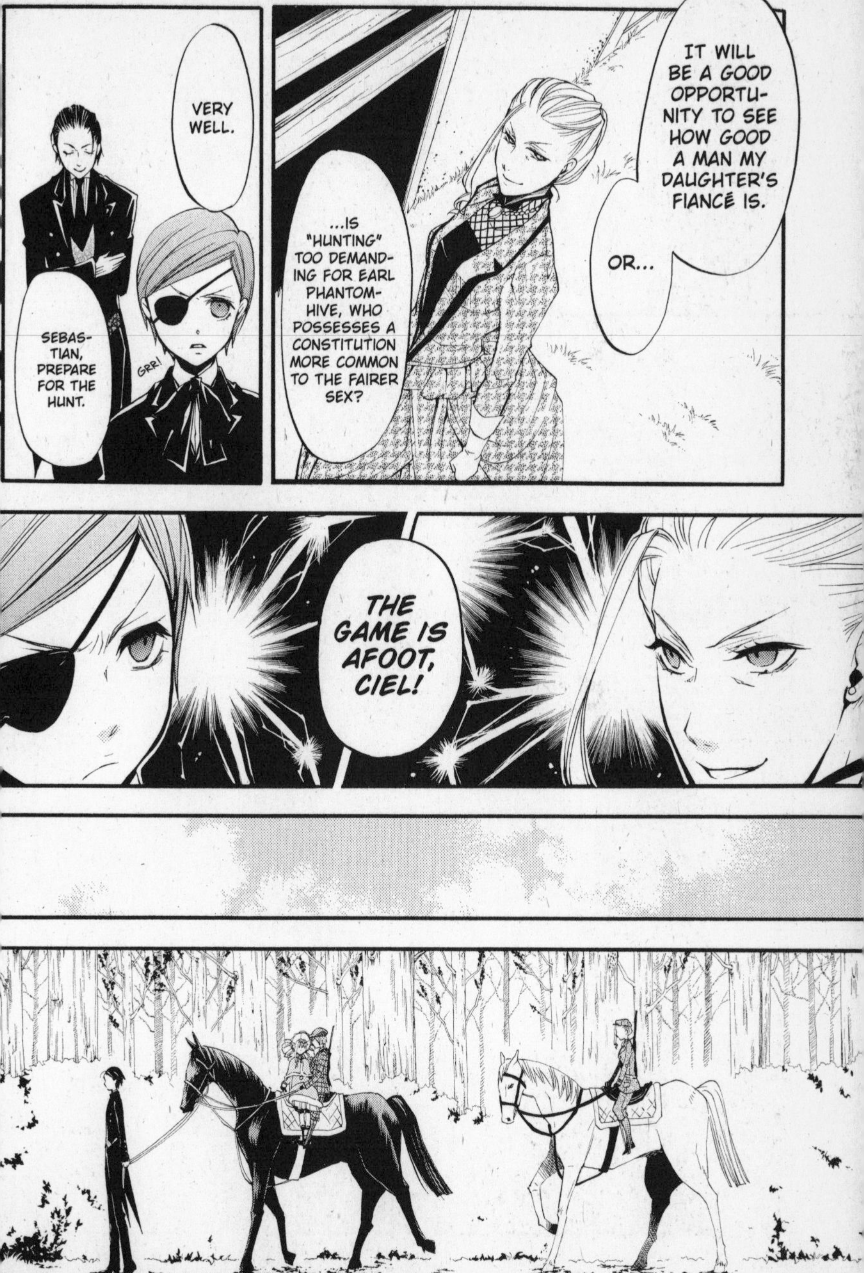
IT WILL BE A GOOD OPPORTUNITY TO SEE HOW GOOD A MAN MY DAUGHTER'S FIANCÉ IS.
OR...
...IS "HUNTING" TOO DEMANDING FOR EARL PHANTOMHIVE, WHO POSSESSES A CONSTITUTION MORE COMMON TO THE FAIRER SEX?
VERY WELL.
GRR!
SEBASTIAN, PREPARE FOR THE HUNT.
THE GAME IS AFOOT, CIEL!

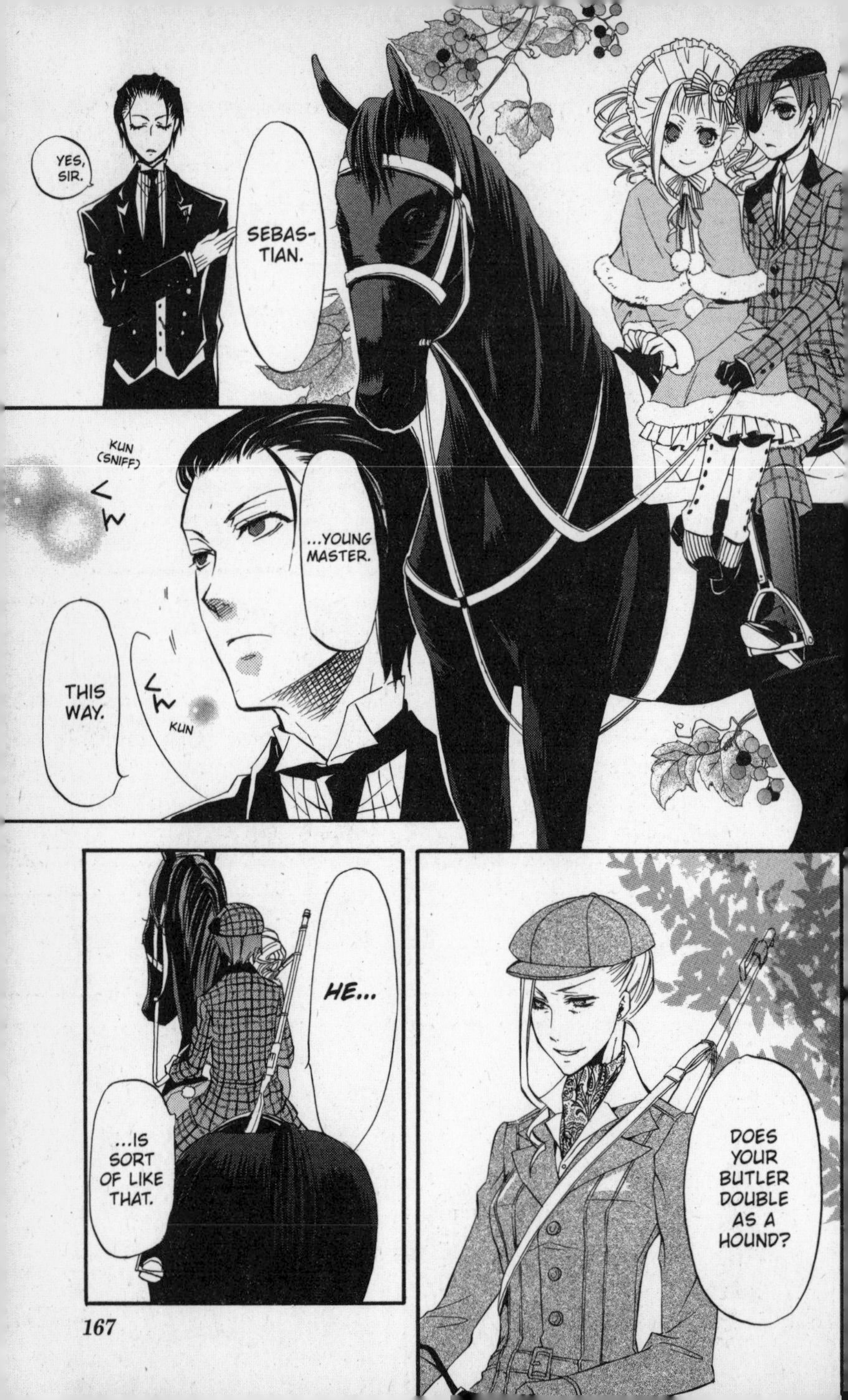
SEBAS-TIAN.
YES, SIR.
...YOUNG MASTER.
KUN (SNIFF)
THIS WAY.
KUN
DOES YOUR BUTLER DOUBLE AS A HOUND?
HE...
...IS SORT OF LIKE THAT.

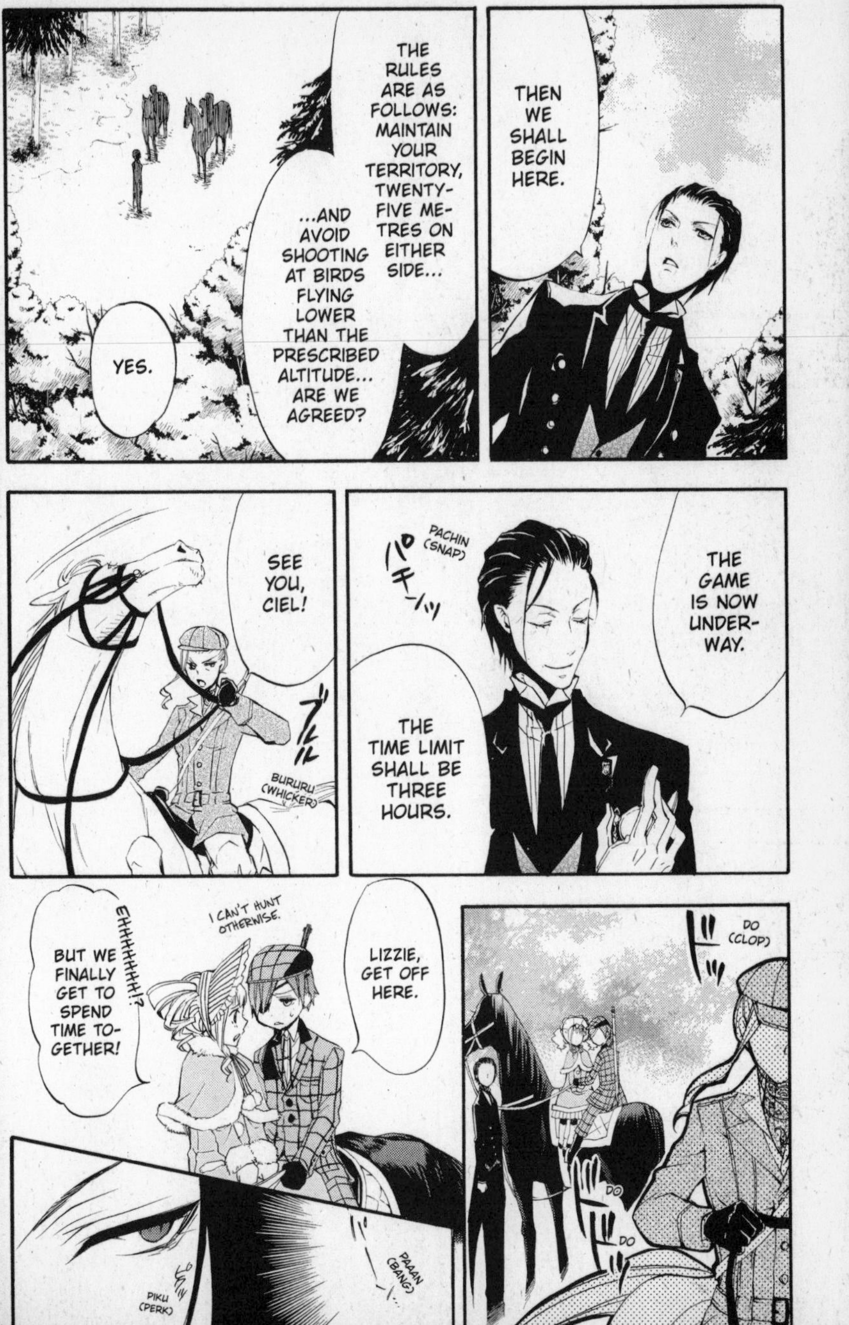
THEN WE SHALL BEGIN HERE.
THE RULES ARE AS FOLLOWS: MAINTAIN YOUR TERRITORY, TWENTY-FIVE METRES ON EITHER SIDE...
...AND AVOID SHOOTING AT BIRDS FLYING LOWER THAN THE PRESCRIBED ALTITUDE... ARE WE AGREED?
YES.
THE GAME IS NOW UNDERWAY.
PACHIN (SNAP)
THE TIME LIMIT SHALL BE THREE HOURS.
SEE YOU, CIEL!
BURURU (WHICKER)
DO (CLOP)
DO
DO
LIZZIE, GET OFF HERE.
I CAN'T HUNT OTHERWISE.
EHHHHHHH!?
BUT WE FINALLY GET TO SPEND TIME TOGETHER!
PAAAN (BANG)
PIKU (PERK)

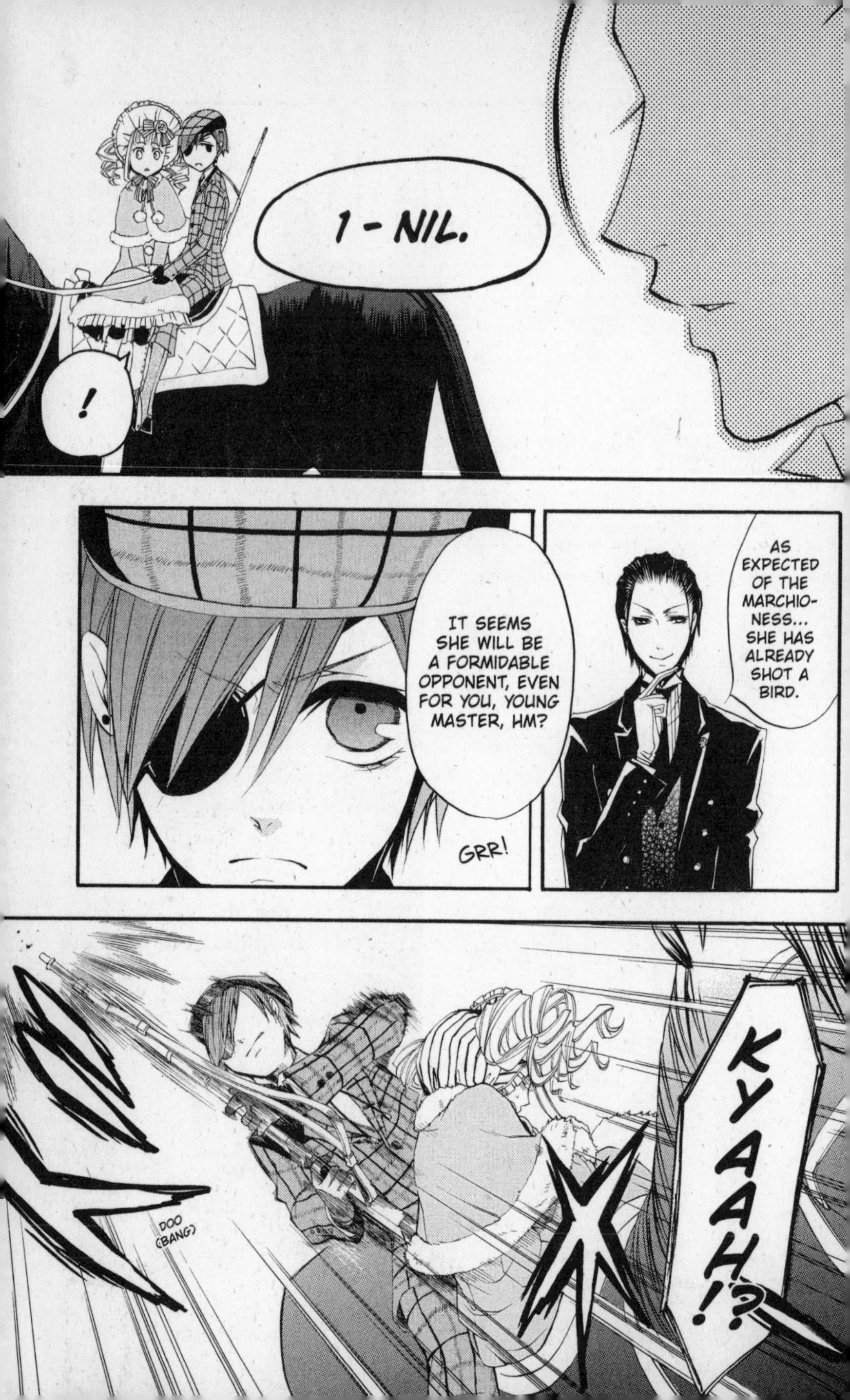
1 - NIL.
!
AS EXPECTED OF THE MARCHIONESS... SHE HAS ALREADY SHOT A BIRD.
IT SEEMS SHE WILL BE A FORMIDABLE OPPONENT, EVEN FOR YOU, YOUNG MASTER, HM?
GRR!
KYAAH!?
DOO (BANG)

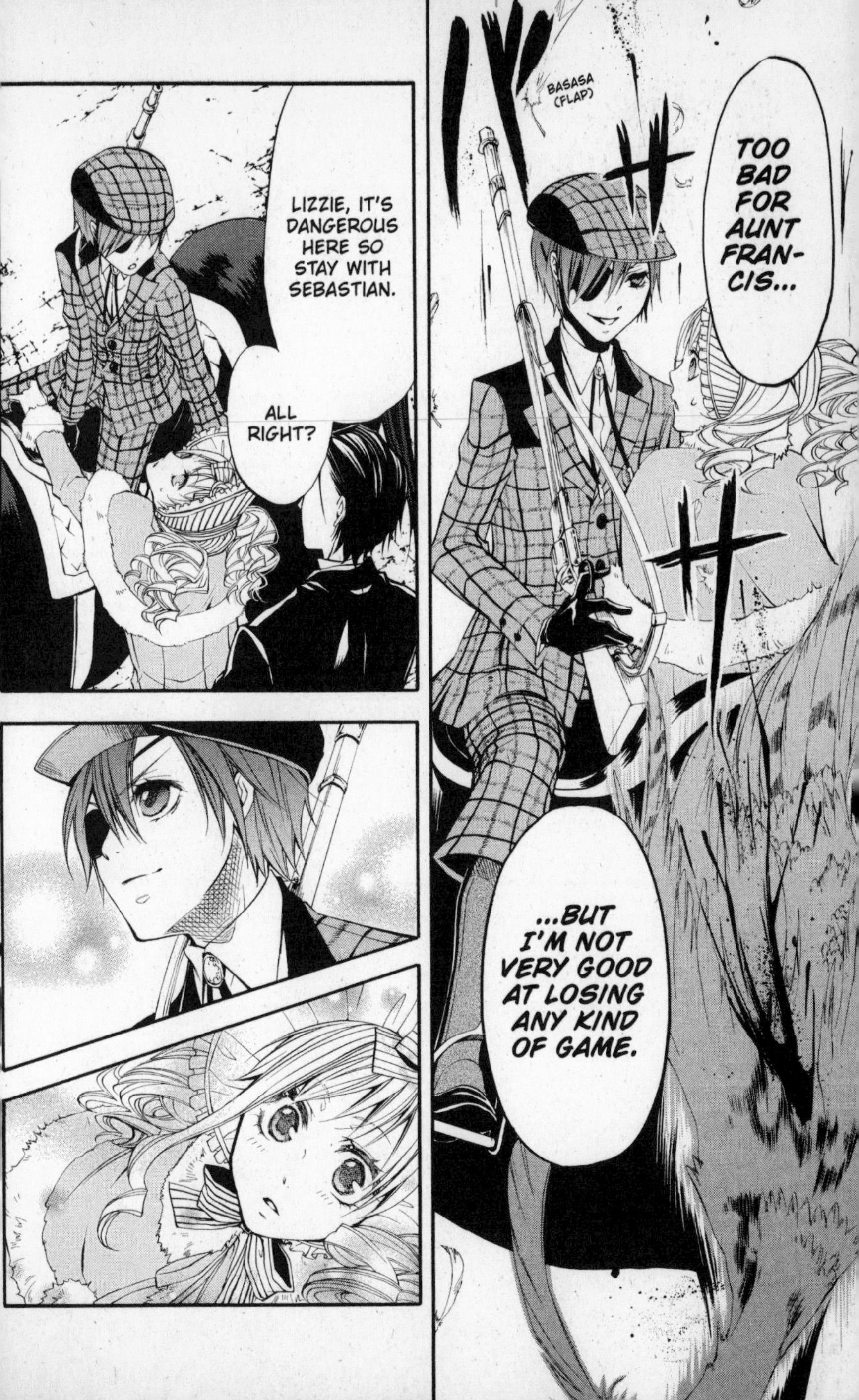
BASASA (FLAP)
TOO BAD FOR AUNT FRAN-CIS...
...BUT I'M NOT VERY GOOD AT LOSING ANY KIND OF GAME.
LIZZIE, IT'S DANGEROUS HERE SO STAY WITH SEBASTIAN.
ALL RIGHT?

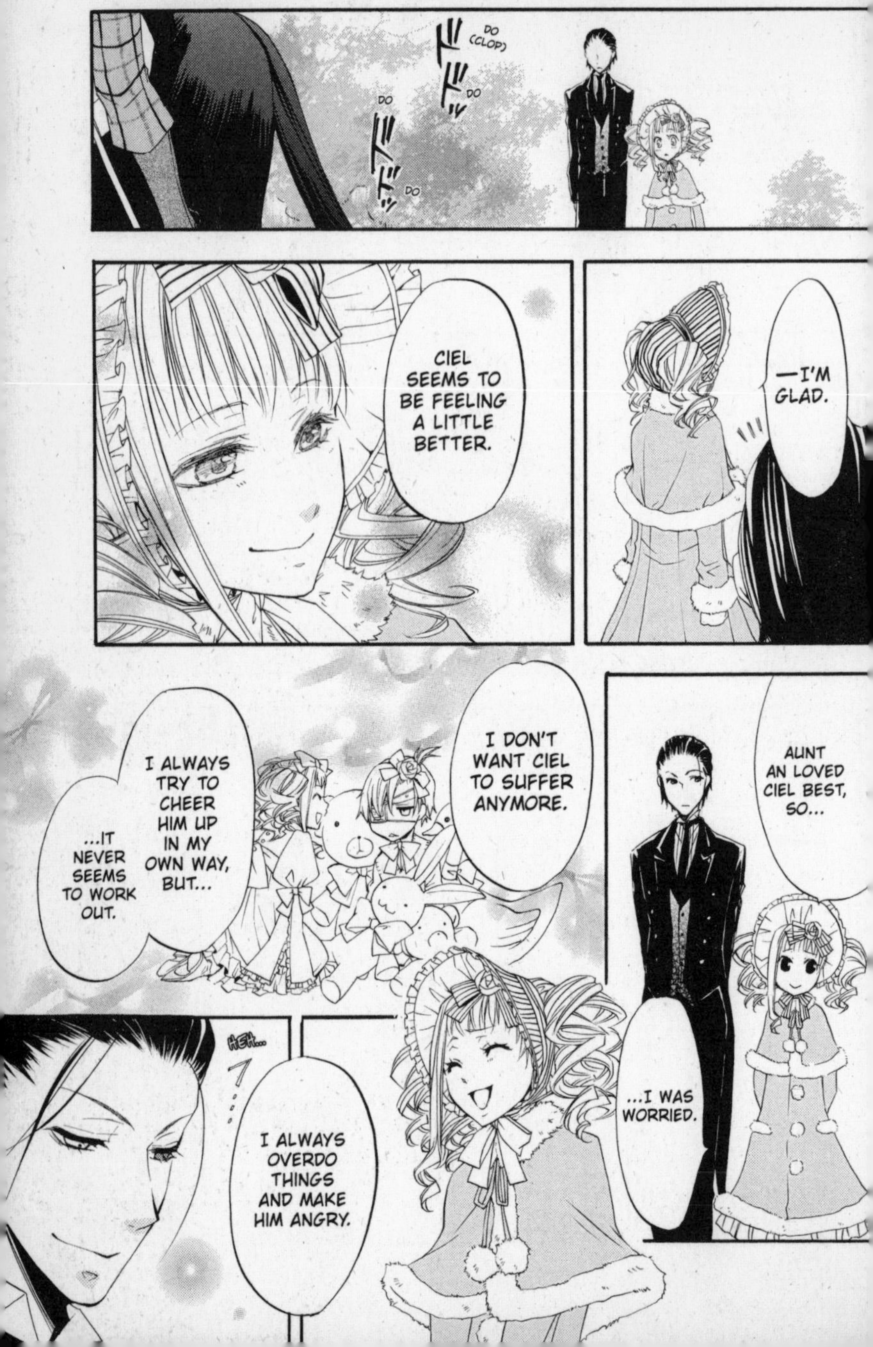
DO (CLOP)
DO
DO
DO
—I'M GLAD.
CIEL SEEMS TO BE FEELING A LITTLE BETTER.
AUNT AN LOVED CIEL BEST, SO...
...I WAS WORRIED.
I DON'T WANT CIEL TO SUFFER ANYMORE.
I ALWAYS TRY TO CHEER HIM UP IN MY OWN WAY, BUT...
...IT NEVER SEEMS TO WORK OUT.
I ALWAYS OVERDO THINGS AND MAKE HIM ANGRY.
HEH...

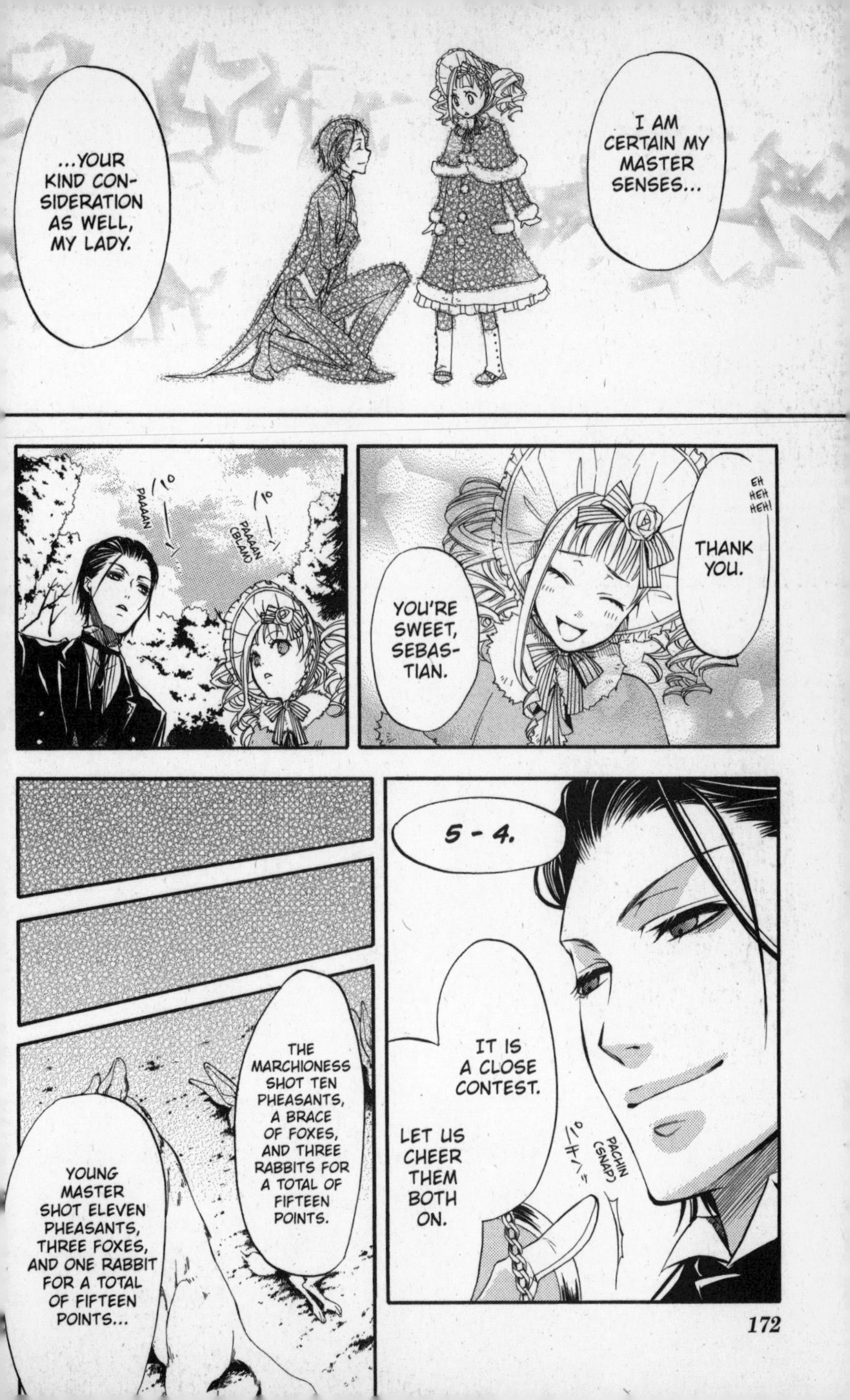
I AM CERTAIN MY MASTER SENSES...
...YOUR KIND CONSIDERATION AS WELL, MY LADY.
EH HEH HEH!
THANK YOU.
YOU'RE SWEET, SEBASTIAN.
PAAAAN (BLAM)
PAAAAN
5 - 4.
IT IS A CLOSE CONTEST.
LET US CHEER THEM BOTH ON.
PACHIN (SNAP)
THE MARCHIONESS SHOT TEN PHEASANTS, A BRACE OF FOXES, AND THREE RABBITS FOR A TOTAL OF FIFTEEN POINTS.
YOUNG MASTER SHOT ELEVEN PHEASANTS, THREE FOXES, AND ONE RABBIT FOR A TOTAL OF FIFTEEN POINTS...

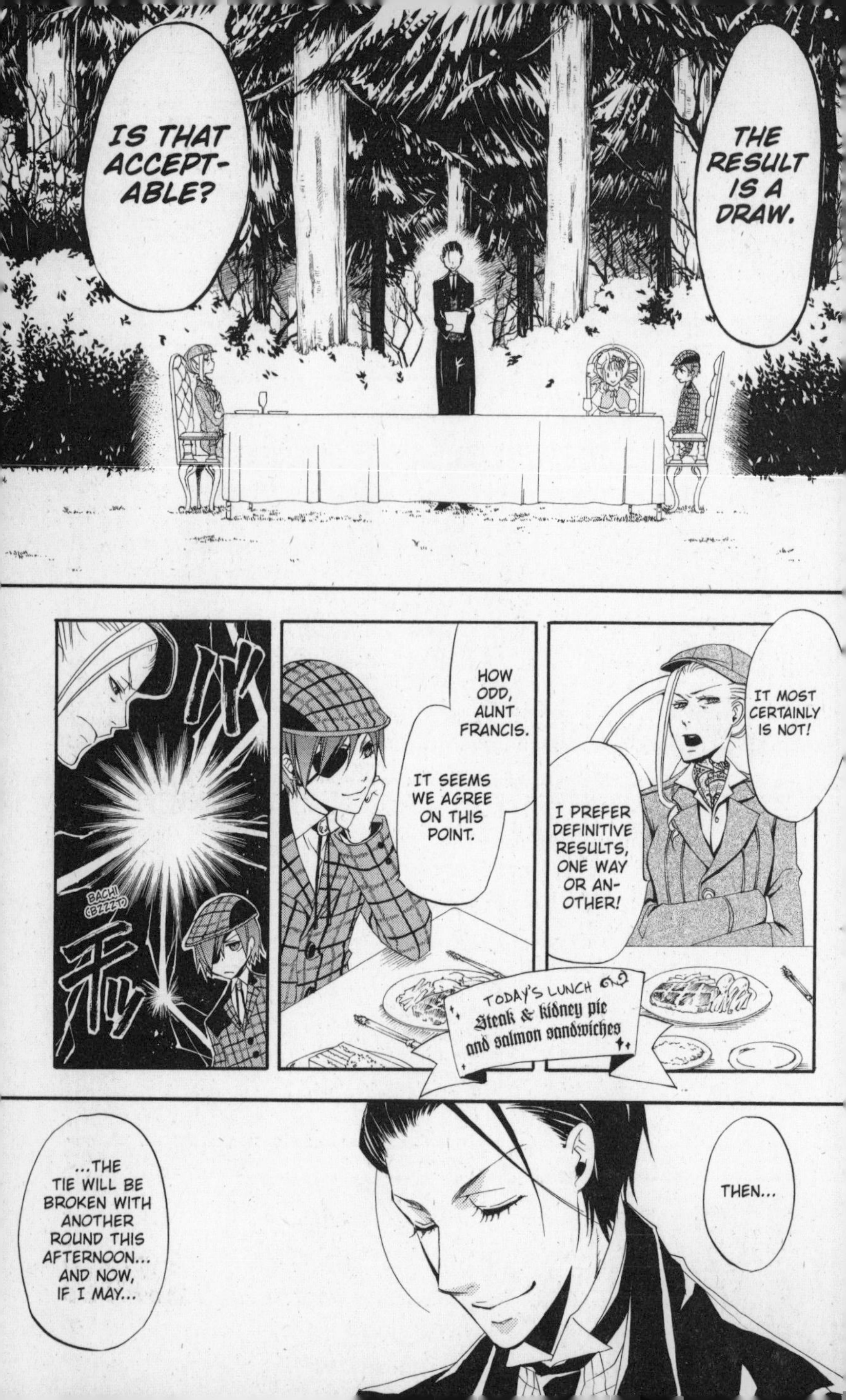
THE RESULT IS A DRAW.
IS THAT ACCEPT-ABLE?
IT MOST CERTAINLY IS NOT!
I PREFER DEFINITIVE RESULTS, ONE WAY OR AN-OTHER!
HOW ODD, AUNT FRANCIS.
IT SEEMS WE AGREE ON THIS POINT.
TODAY'S LUNCH
Steak & kidney pie and salmon sandwiches
BACHI (BZZZT)
THEN...
...THE TIE WILL BE BROKEN WITH ANOTHER ROUND THIS AFTERNOON... AND NOW, IF I MAY...

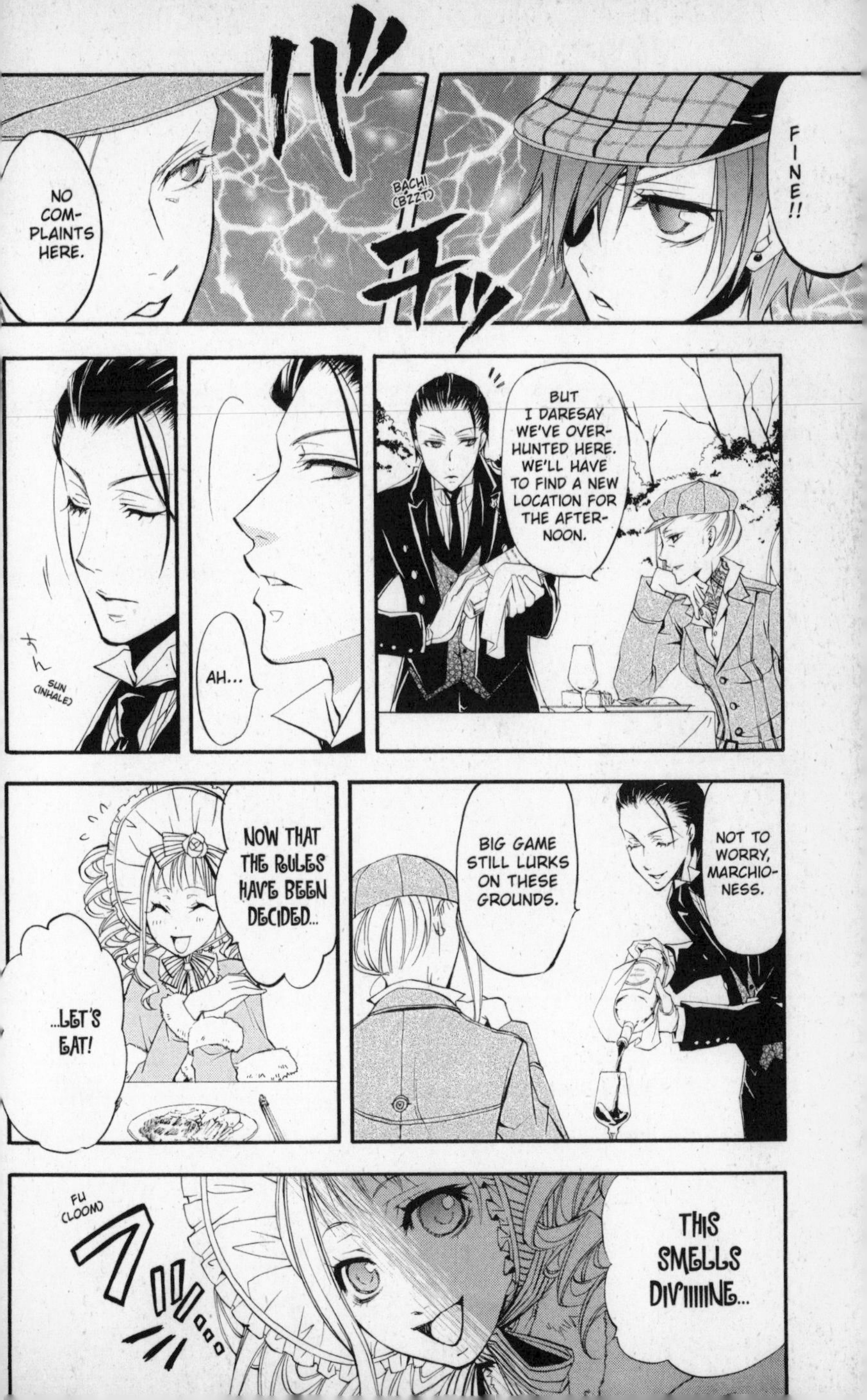
BACHI (BZZT)
FINE!!
NO COM-PLAINTS HERE.
BUT I DARESAY WE'VE OVER-HUNTED HERE. WE'LL HAVE TO FIND A NEW LOCATION FOR THE AFTER-NOON.
AH...
SUN (INHALE)
NOT TO WORRY, MARCHIO-NESS.
BIG GAME STILL LURKS ON THESE GROUNDS.
NOW THAT THE RULES HAVE BEEN DECIDED...
...LET'S EAT!
THIS SMELLS DIVIIIIINE...
FU (LOOM)

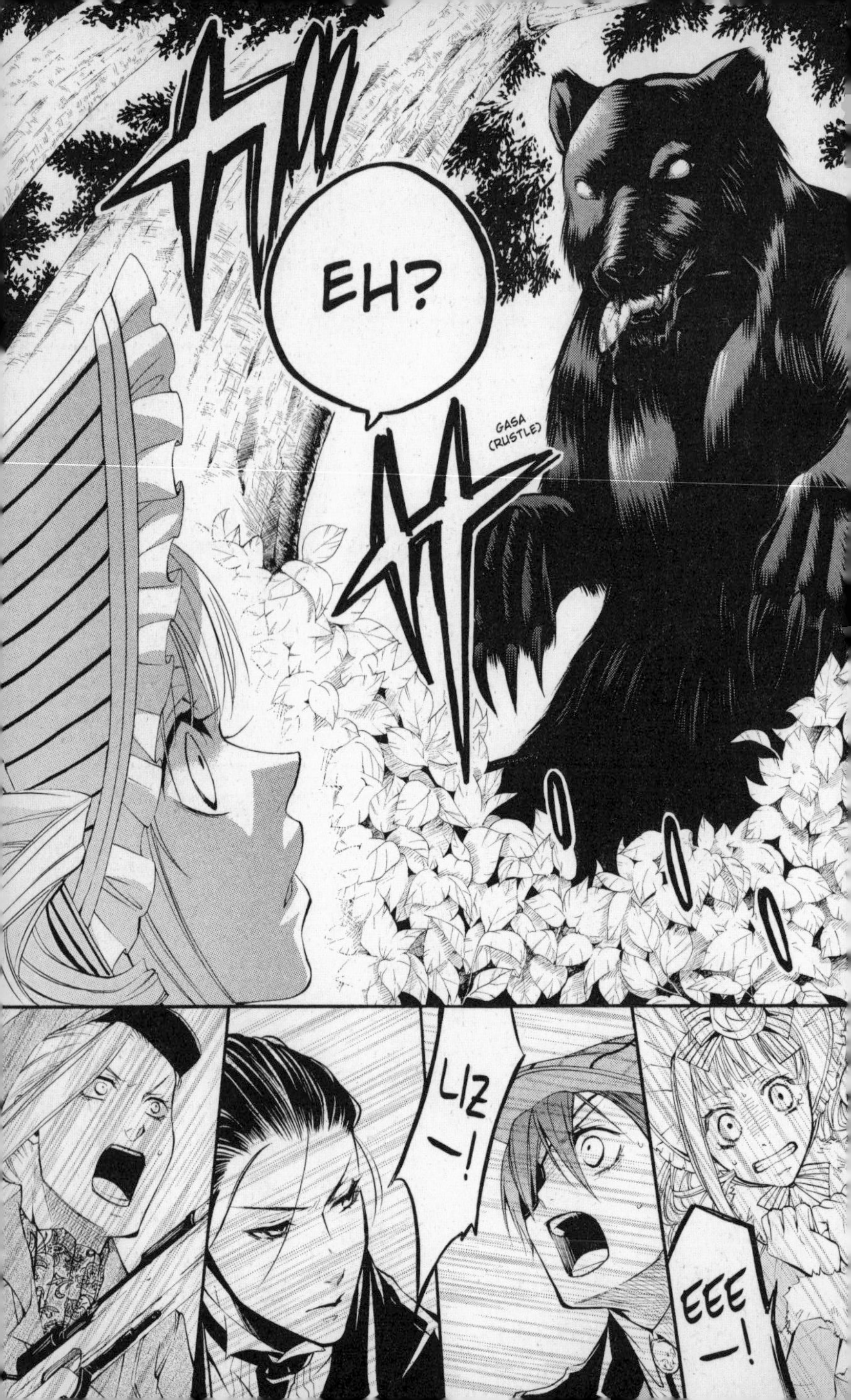
EH?
GASA (RUSTLE)
EEE—!
LIZ—!

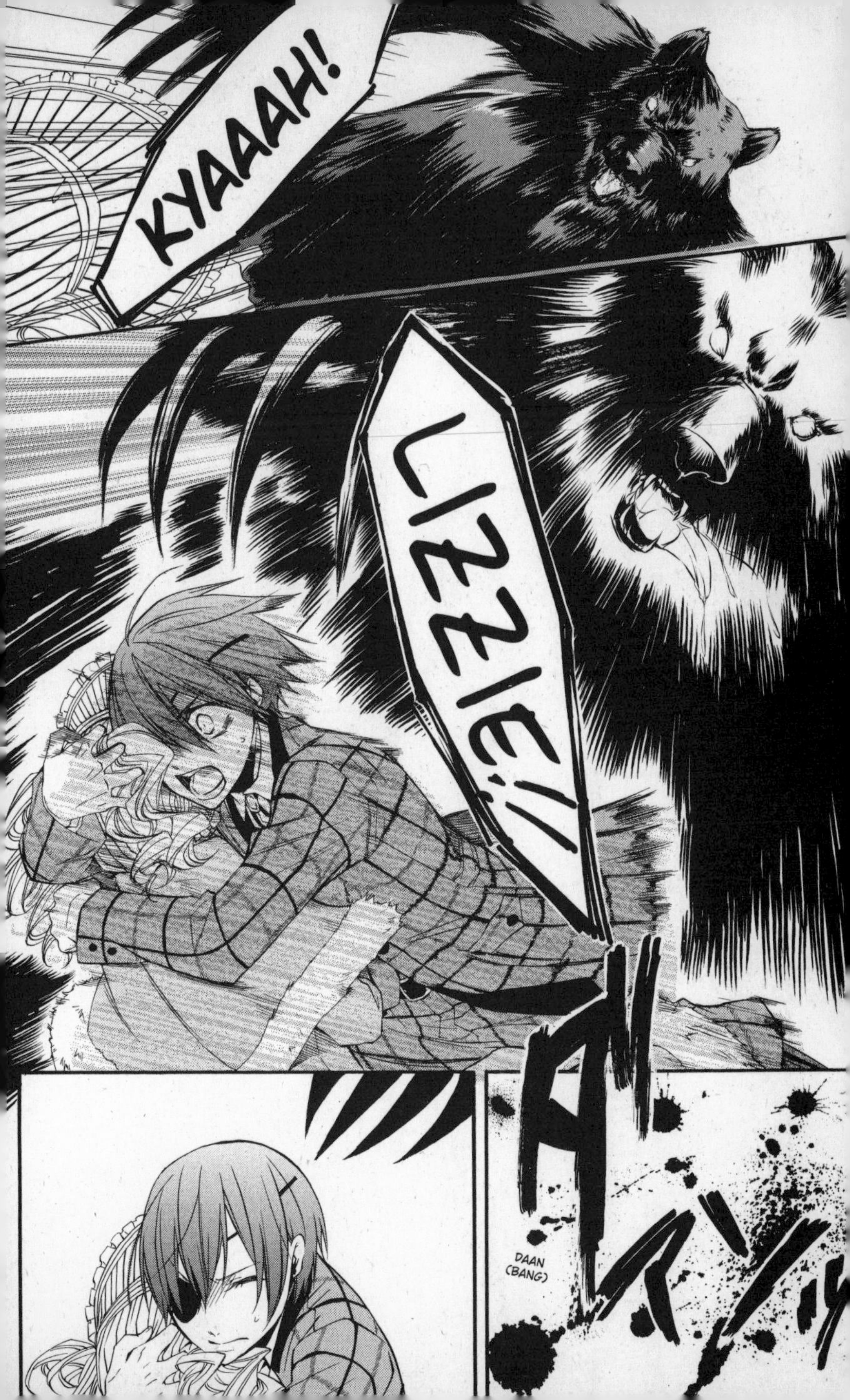
KYAAAH!
LIZZIE!!
DAAN (BANG)

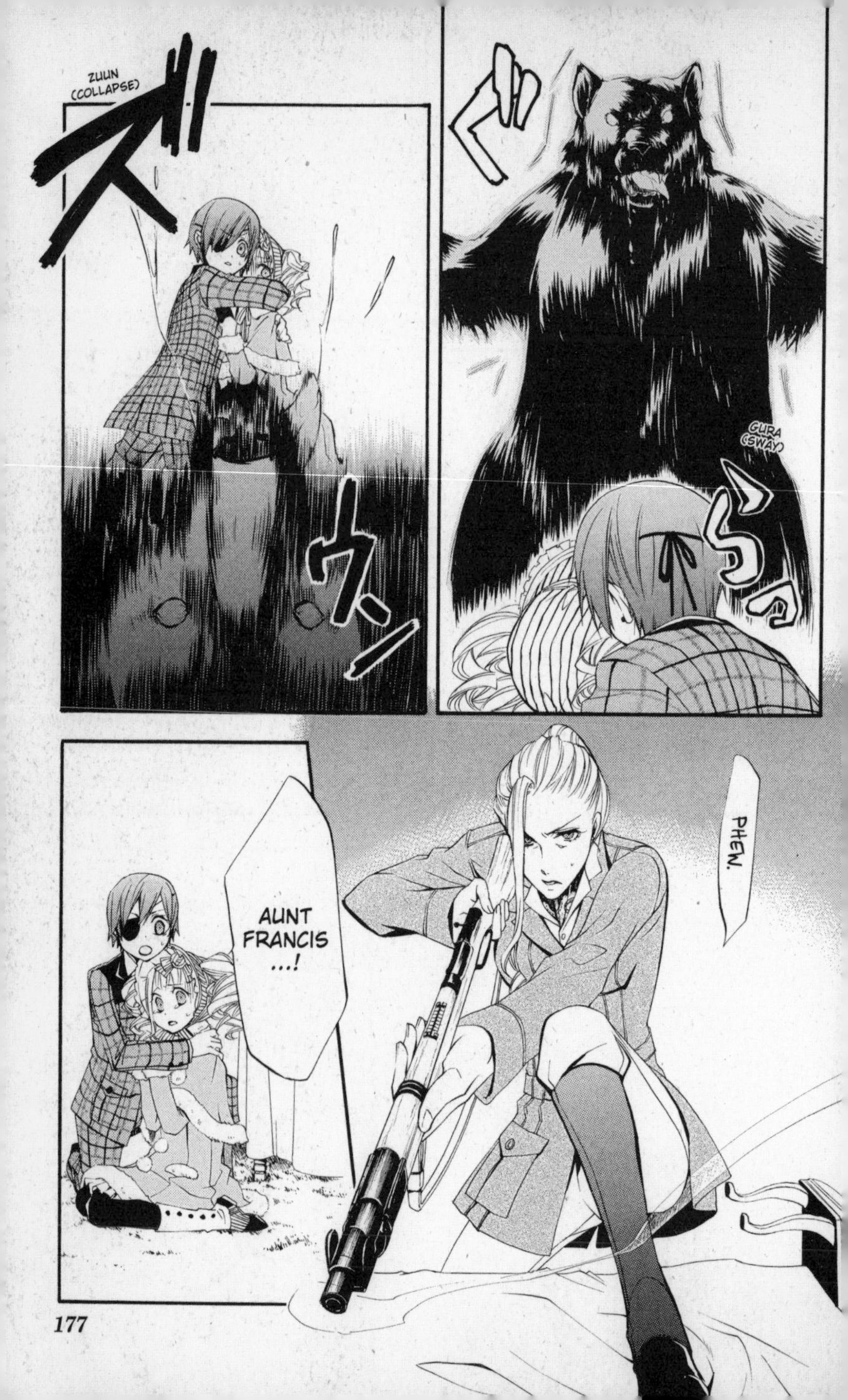
GURA (SWAY)
ZUUN (COLLAPSE)
PHEW.
AUNT FRANCIS ...!

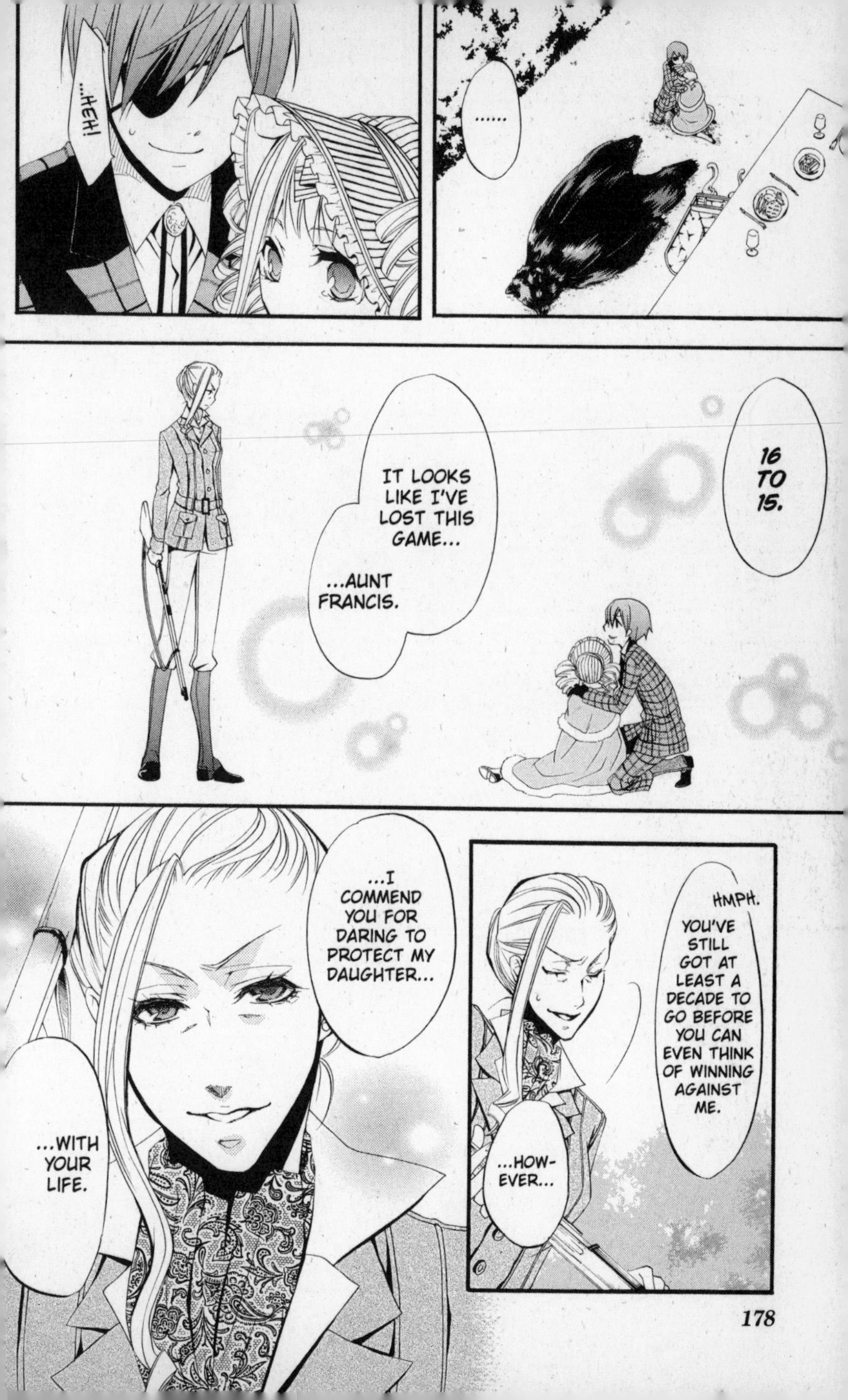
......
...HEH!
16 TO 15.
IT LOOKS LIKE I'VE LOST THIS GAME...
...AUNT FRANCIS.
HMPH.
YOU'VE STILL GOT AT LEAST A DECADE TO GO BEFORE YOU CAN EVEN THINK OF WINNING AGAINST ME.
...HOW-EVER...
...I COMMEND YOU FOR DARING TO PROTECT MY DAUGHTER...
...WITH YOUR LIFE.

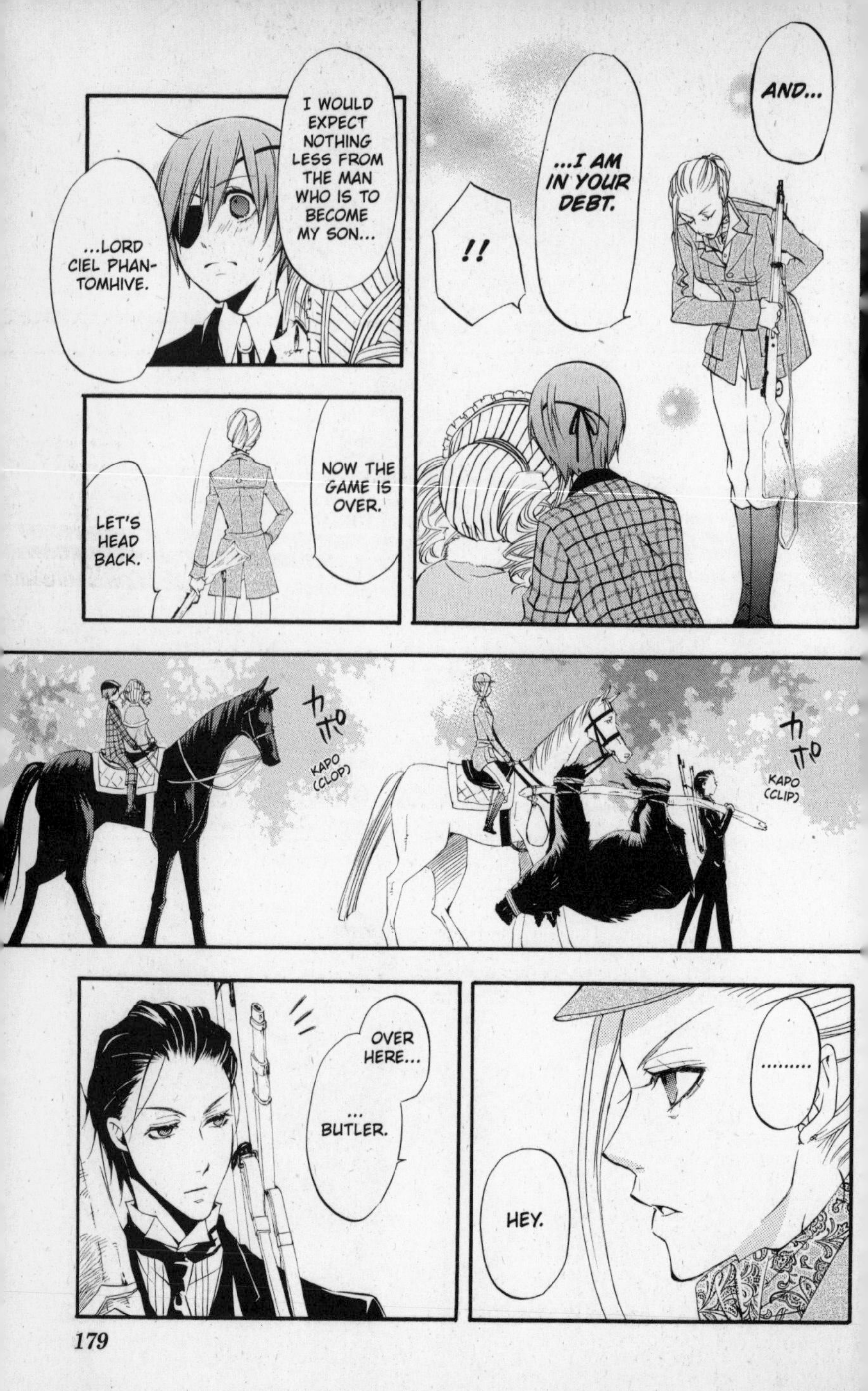
AND...
...I AM IN YOUR DEBT.
!!
I WOULD EXPECT NOTHING LESS FROM THE MAN WHO IS TO BECOME MY SON...
...LORD CIEL PHANTOMHIVE.
NOW THE GAME IS OVER.
LET'S HEAD BACK.
カポ
KAPO (CLIP)
カポ
KAPO (CLOP)
....
HEY.
OVER HERE...
...BUTLER.

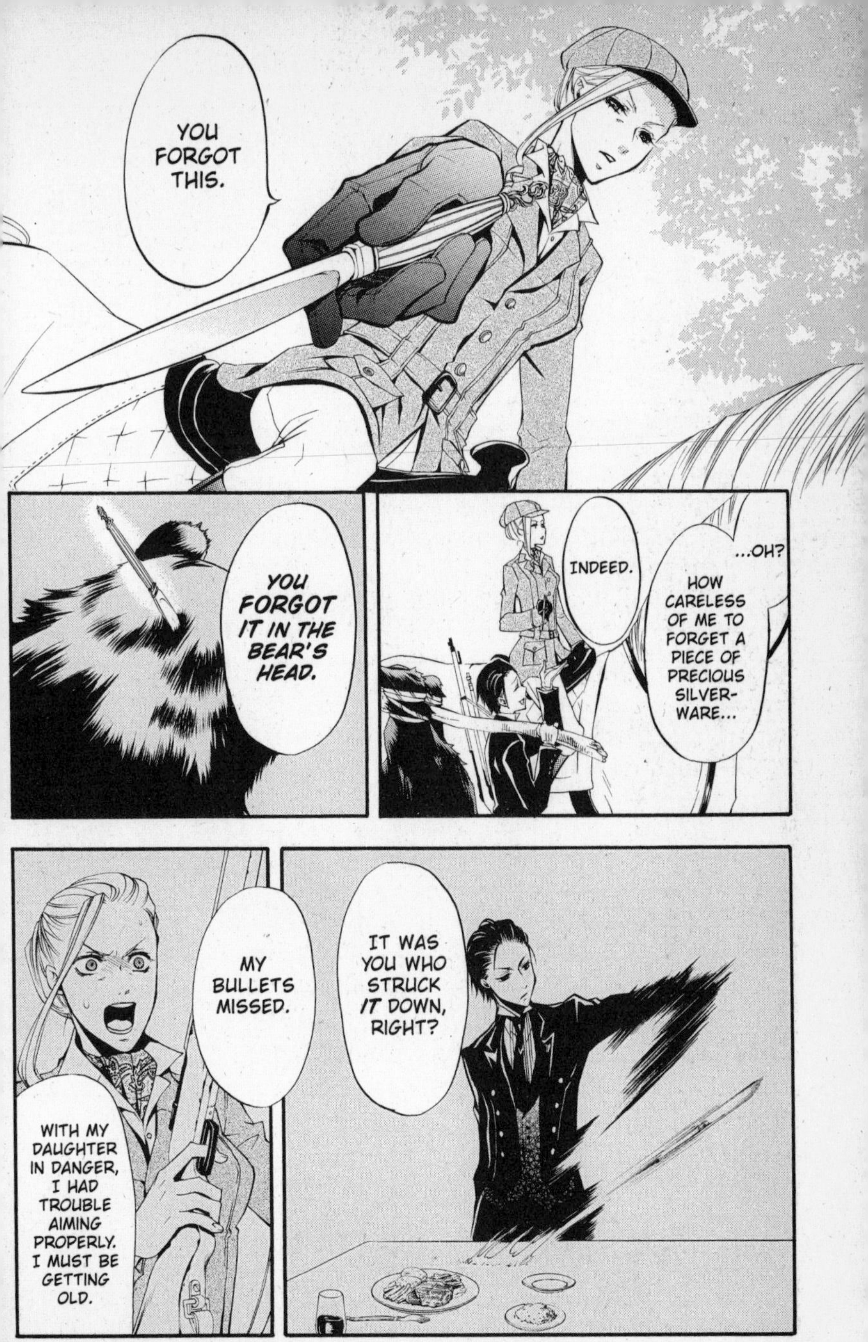
YOU FORGOT THIS.
...OH? HOW CARELESS OF ME TO FORGET A PIECE OF PRECIOUS SILVER-WARE...
INDEED.
YOU FORGOT IT IN THE BEAR'S HEAD.
IT WAS YOU WHO STRUCK *IT* DOWN, RIGHT?
MY BULLETS MISSED.
WITH MY DAUGHTER IN DANGER, I HAD TROUBLE AIMING PROPERLY. I MUST BE GETTING OLD.

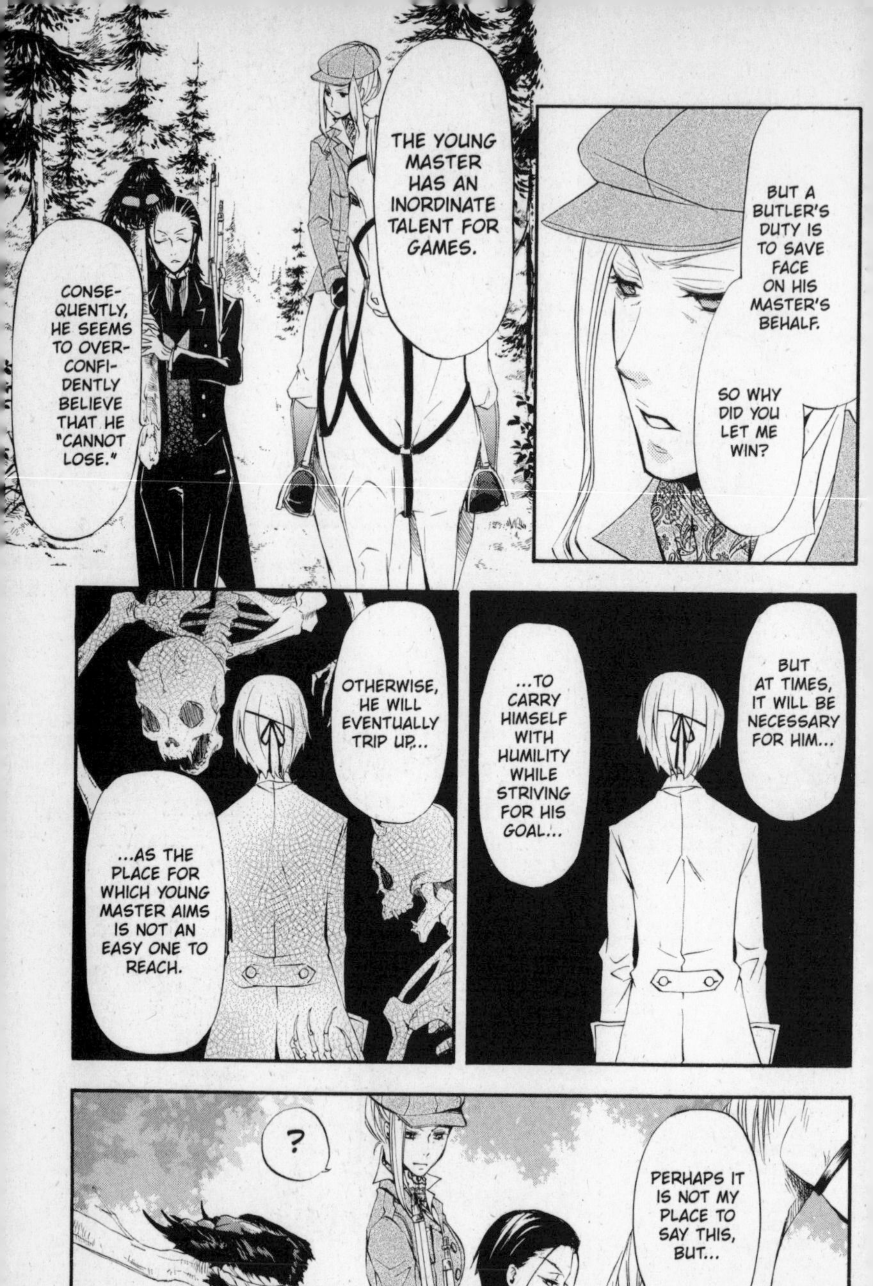
BUT A BUTLER'S DUTY IS TO SAVE FACE ON HIS MASTER'S BEHALF.
SO WHY DID YOU LET ME WIN?
THE YOUNG MASTER HAS AN INORDINATE TALENT FOR GAMES.
CONSE-QUENTLY, HE SEEMS TO OVER-CONFI-DENTLY BELIEVE THAT HE "CANNOT LOSE."
BUT AT TIMES, IT WILL BE NECESSARY FOR HIM...
...TO CARRY HIMSELF WITH HUMILITY WHILE STRIVING FOR HIS GOAL...
OTHERWISE, HE WILL EVENTUALLY TRIP UP...
...AS THE PLACE FOR WHICH YOUNG MASTER AIMS IS NOT AN EASY ONE TO REACH.
PERHAPS IT IS NOT MY PLACE TO SAY THIS, BUT...
?

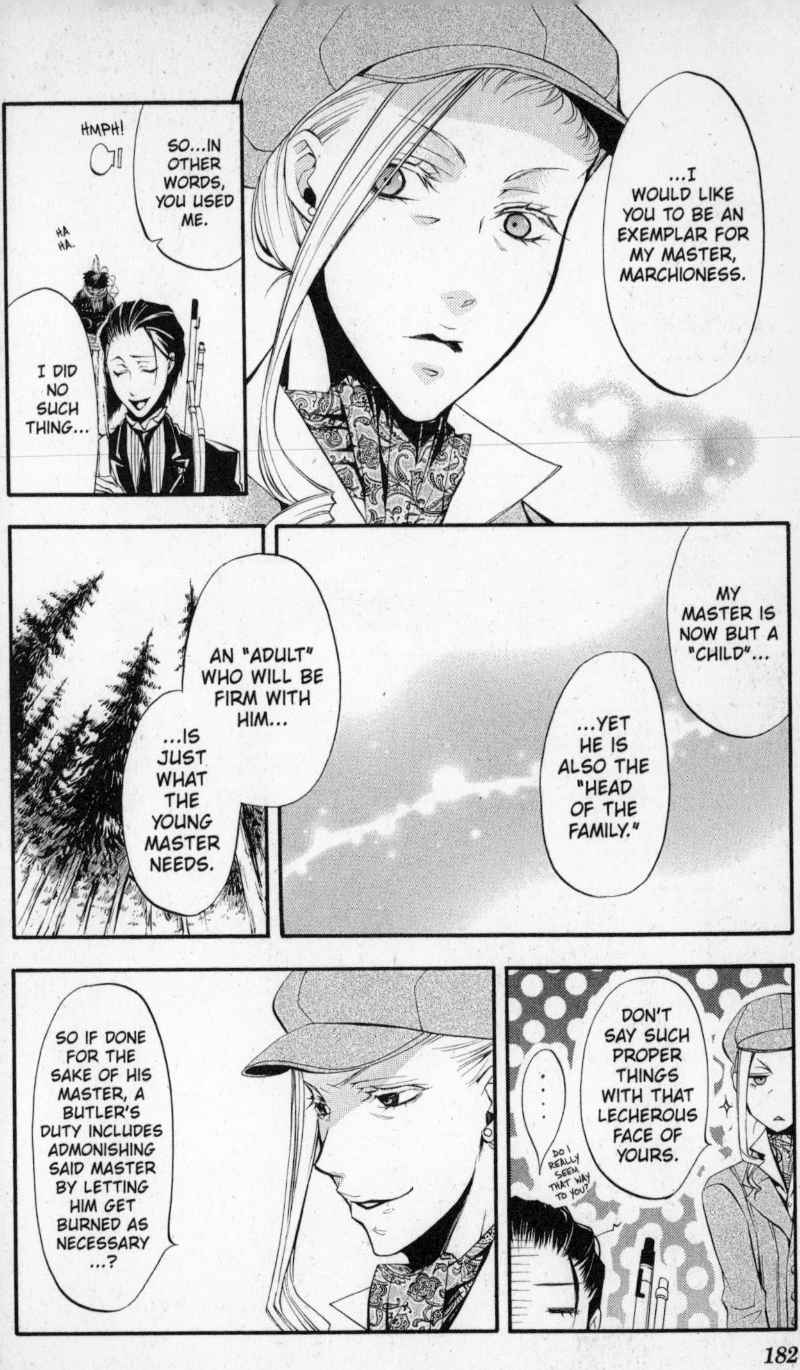
...I WOULD LIKE YOU TO BE AN EXEMPLAR FOR MY MASTER, MARCHIONESS.
HMPH!
SO...IN OTHER WORDS, YOU USED ME.
HA HA.
I DID NO SUCH THING...
MY MASTER IS NOW BUT A "CHILD"...
...YET HE IS ALSO THE "HEAD OF THE FAMILY."
AN "ADULT" WHO WILL BE FIRM WITH HIM...
...IS JUST WHAT THE YOUNG MASTER NEEDS.
DON'T SAY SUCH PROPER THINGS WITH THAT LECHEROUS FACE OF YOURS.
...
DO I REALLY SEEM THAT WAY TO YOU?
SO IF DONE FOR THE SAKE OF HIS MASTER, A BUTLER'S DUTY INCLUDES ADMONISHING SAID MASTER BY LETTING HIM GET BURNED AS NECESSARY ...?

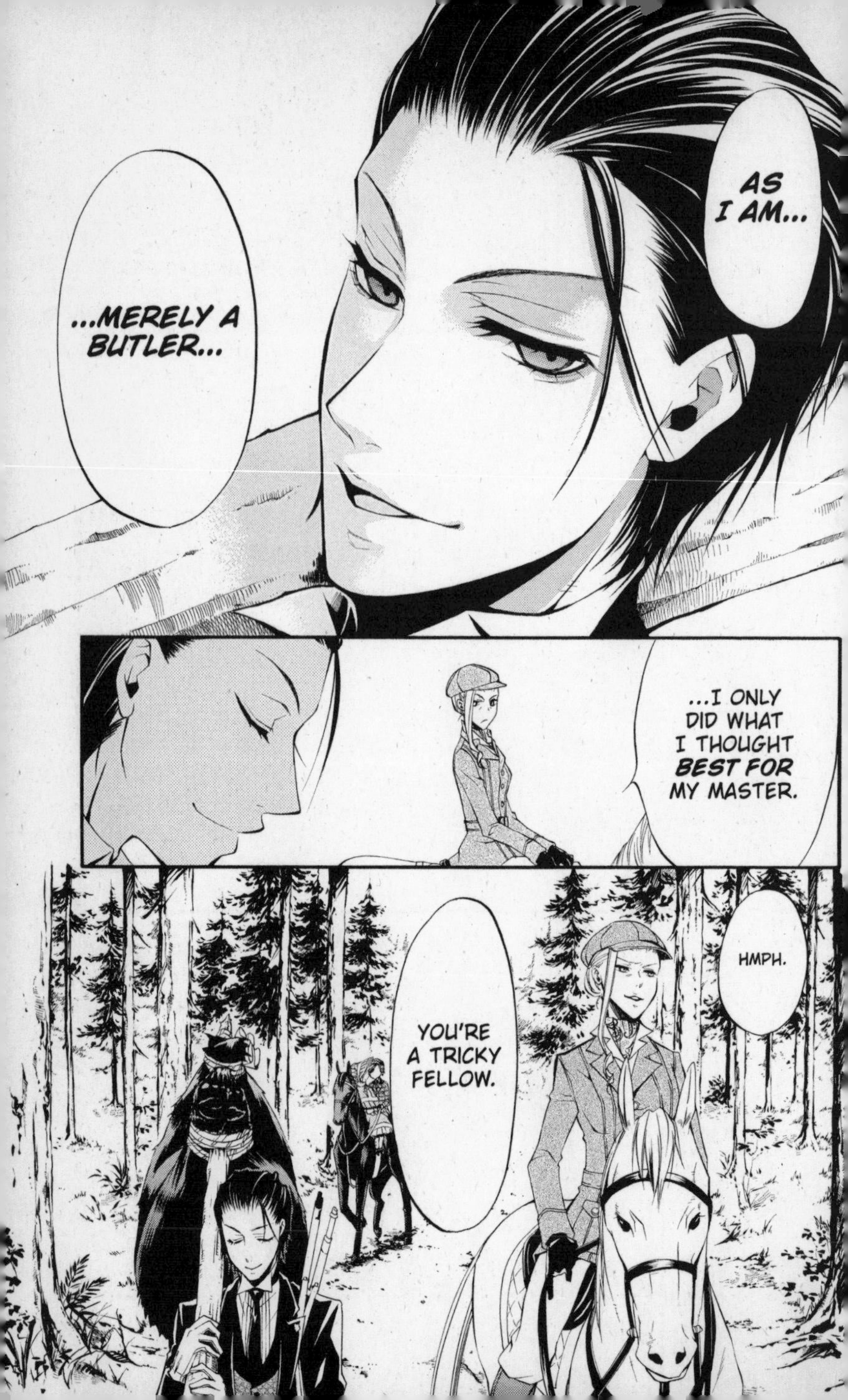
AS I AM...
...MERELY A BUTLER...
...I ONLY DID WHAT I THOUGHT BEST FOR MY MASTER.
HMPH.
YOU'RE A TRICKY FELLOW.

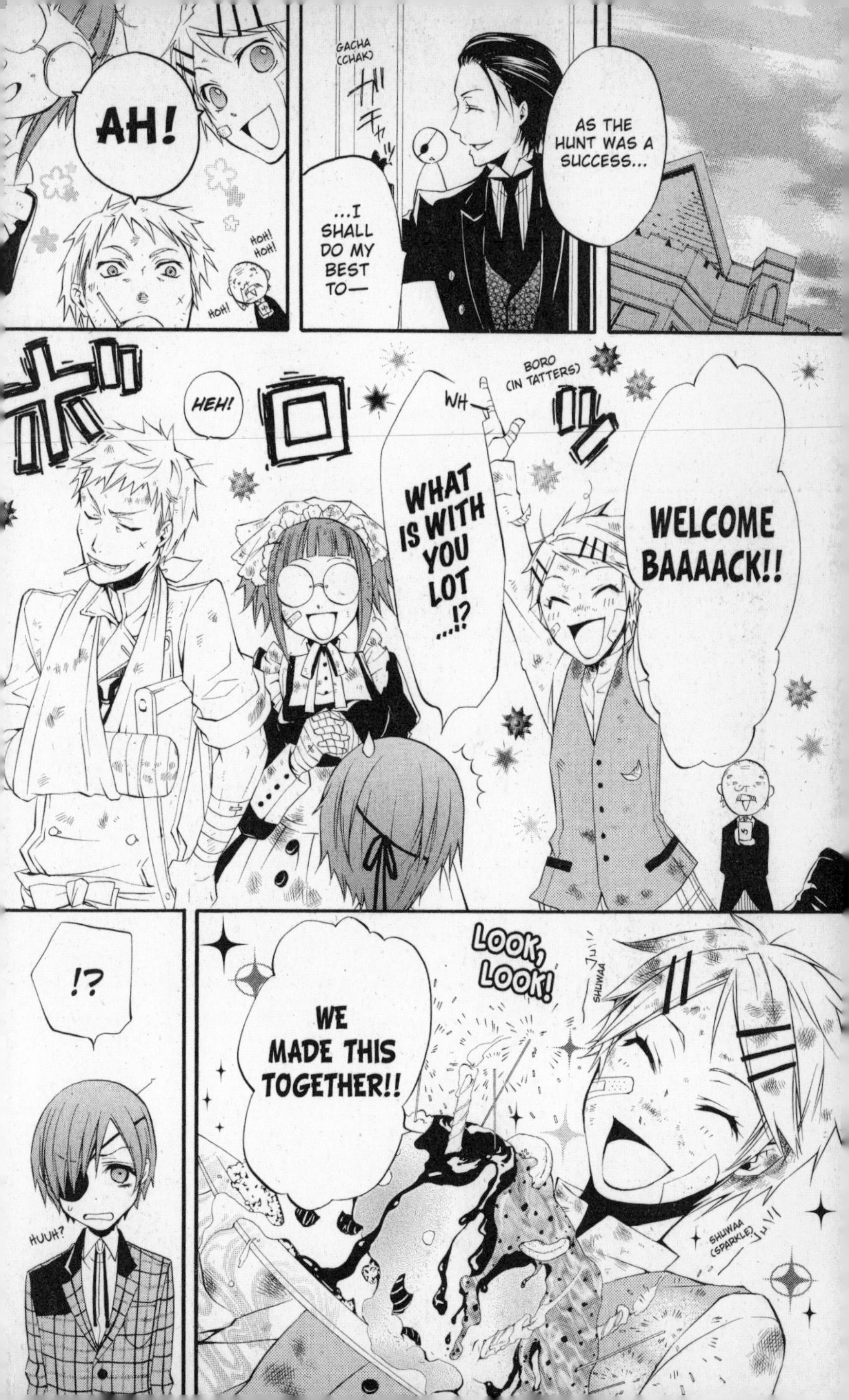
AS THE HUNT WAS A SUCCESS...
GACHA (CHAK)
...I SHALL DO MY BEST TO—
AH!
HOH! HOH!
HOH!
BORO (IN TATTERS)
WELCOME BAAAACK!!
WH—
WHAT IS WITH YOU LOT ...!?
HEH!
LOOK, LOOK!
SHUWAA
WE MADE THIS TOGETHER!!
SHUWAA (SPARKLE)
!?
HUUH?

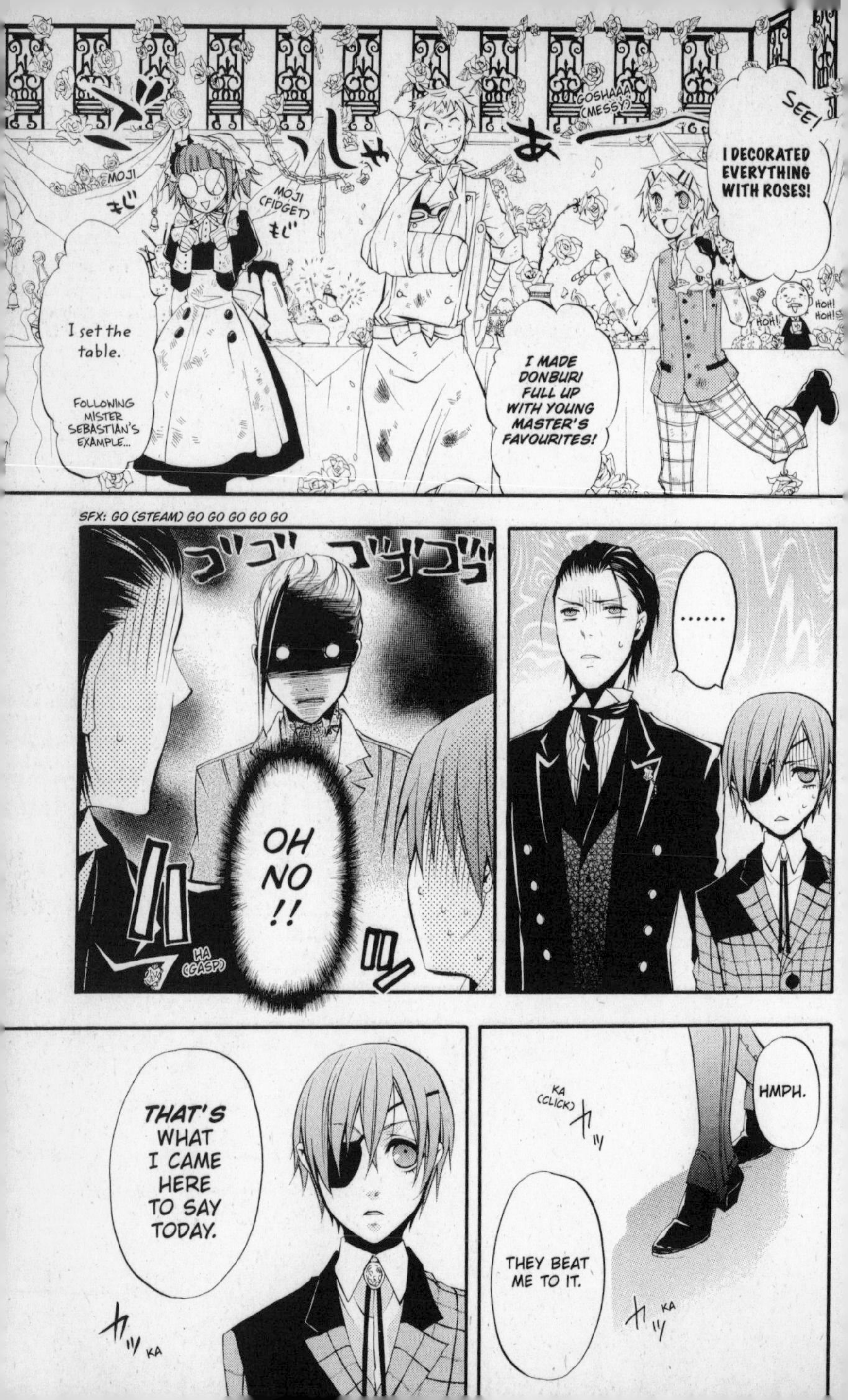
GOSHAAA (MESSY)
SEE!
I DECORATED EVERYTHING WITH ROSES!
HOH! HOH!
HOH!
I MADE DONBURI FULL UP WITH YOUNG MASTER'S FAVOURITES!
MOJI (FIDGET)
もじ
MOJI
もじ
I set the table.
FOLLOWING MISTER SEBASTIAN'S EXAMPLE...
SFX: GO (STEAM) GO GO GO GO GO
....
OH NO !!
HA (GASP)
HMPH.
KA (CLICK)
THEY BEAT ME TO IT.
KA
THAT'S WHAT I CAME HERE TO SAY TODAY.
KA

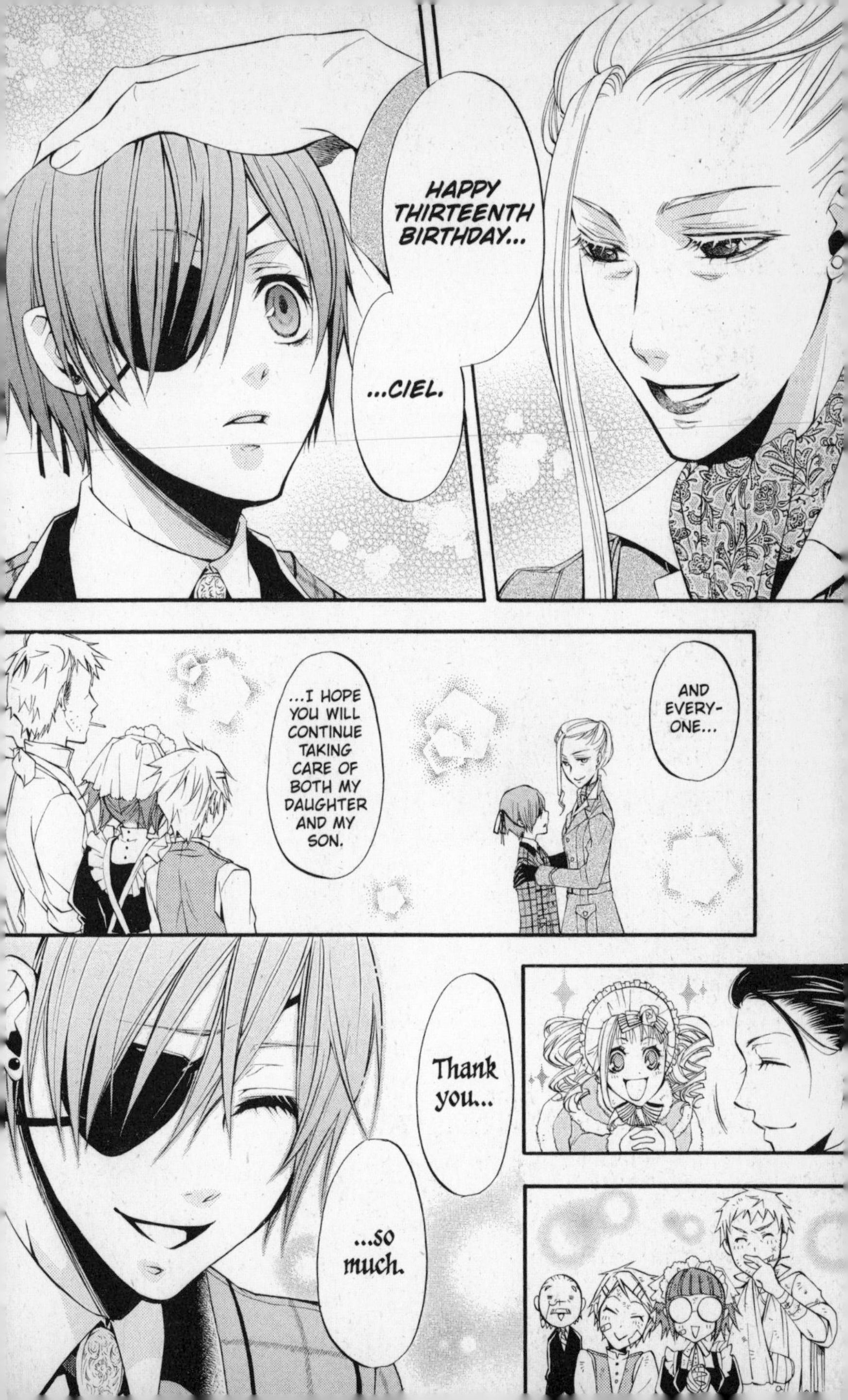
HAPPY THIRTEENTH BIRTHDAY...
...CIEL.
AND EVERY-ONE...
...I HOPE YOU WILL CONTINUE TAKING CARE OF BOTH MY DAUGHTER AND MY SON.
Thank you...
...so much.

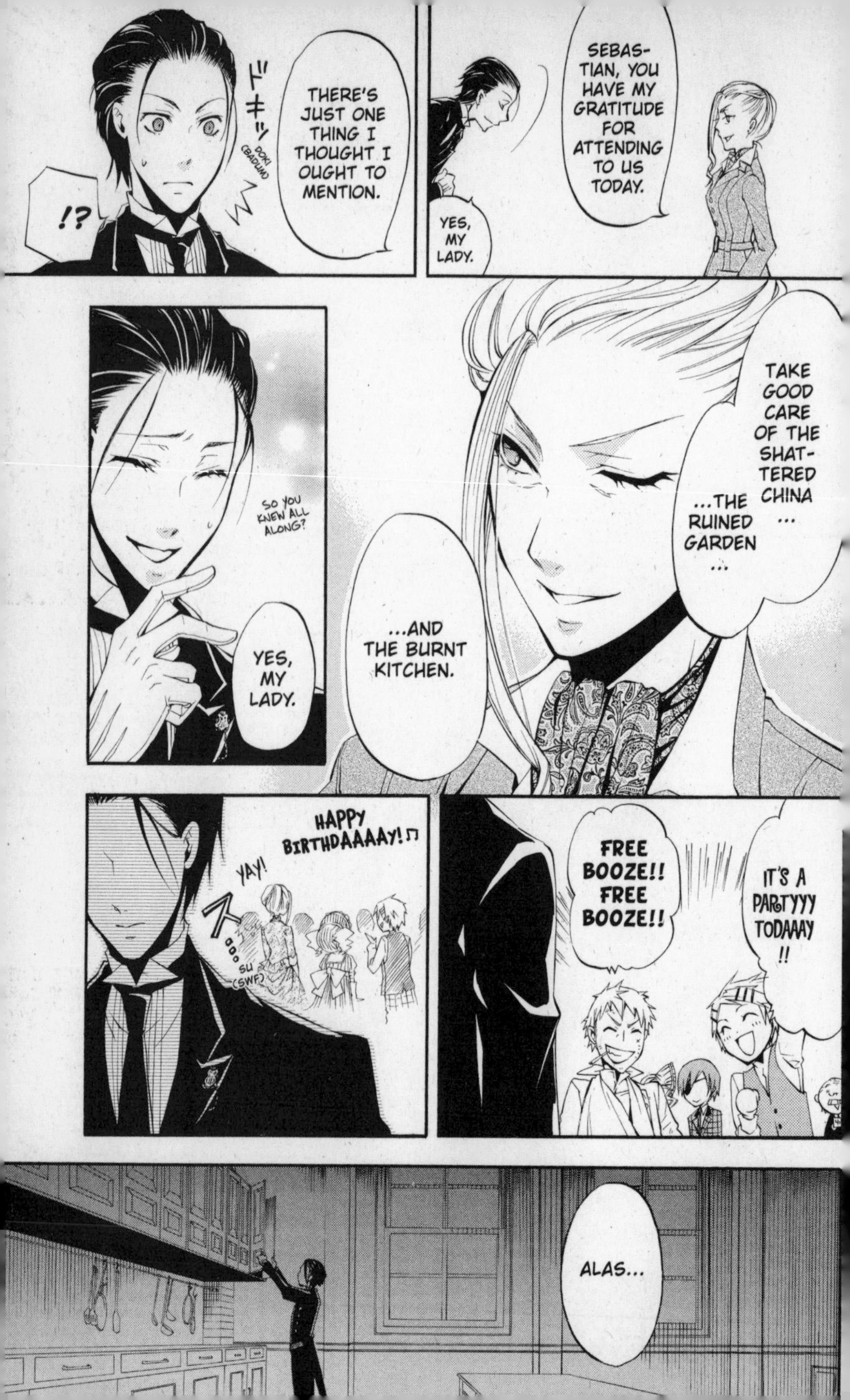
SEBASTIAN, YOU HAVE MY GRATITUDE FOR ATTENDING TO US TODAY.
YES, MY LADY.
THERE'S JUST ONE THING I THOUGHT I OUGHT TO MENTION.
ドキッ
DOKI (BADUM)
!?
TAKE GOOD CARE OF THE SHATTERED CHINA...
...THE RUINED GARDEN...
...AND THE BURNT KITCHEN.
So you knew all along?
YES, MY LADY.
IT'S A PARTYYY TODAAAY!!
FREE BOOZE!! FREE BOOZE!!
HAPPY BIRTHDAAAAY!♫
YAY!
SU (SWF)
ALAS...

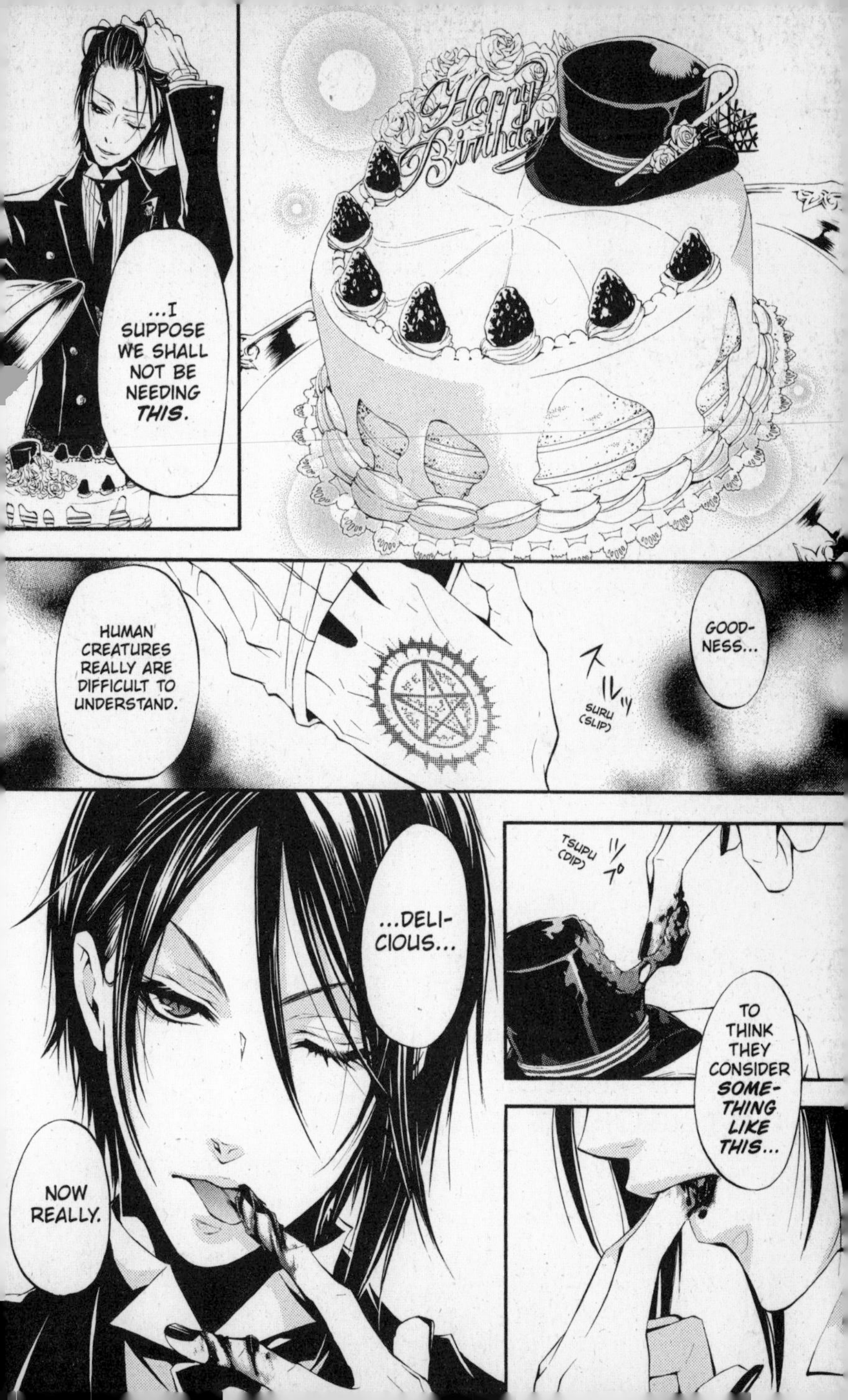

Happy Birthday
...I SUPPOSE WE SHALL NOT BE NEEDING *THIS*.
GOOD-NESS...
ズルッ
SURU (SLIP)
HUMAN CREATURES REALLY ARE DIFFICULT TO UNDERSTAND.
ツプ
TSUPU (DIP)
TO THINK THEY CONSIDER *SOME-THING LIKE THIS*...
...DELI-CIOUS...
NOW REALLY.

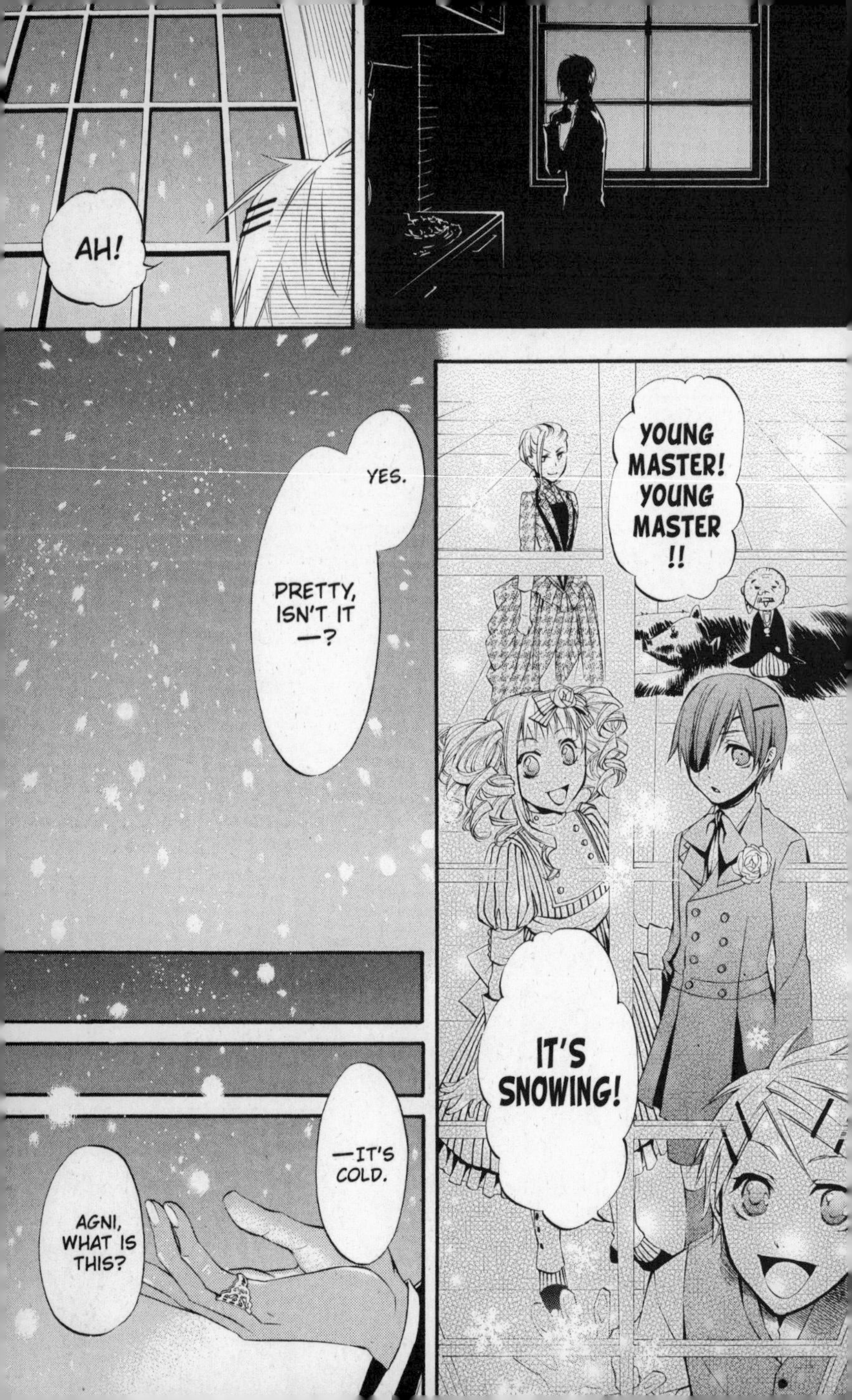
AH!
YOUNG MASTER! YOUNG MASTER!!
IT'S SNOWING!
YES.
PRETTY, ISN'T IT—?
—IT'S COLD.
AGNI, WHAT IS THIS?

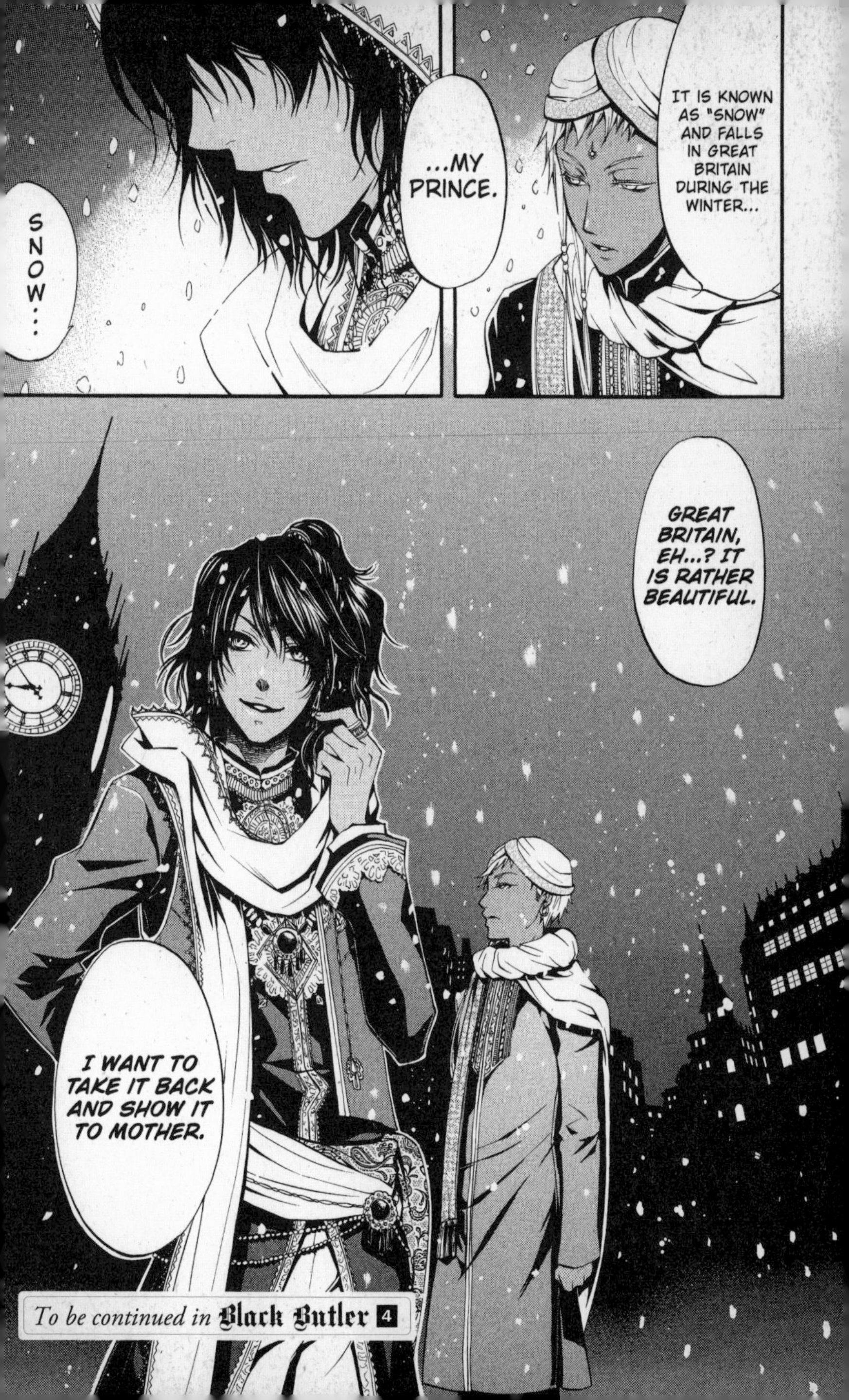
IT IS KNOWN AS "SNOW" AND FALLS IN GREAT BRITAIN DURING THE WINTER...
...MY PRINCE.
SNOW...
GREAT BRITAIN, EH...? IT IS RATHER BEAUTIFUL.
I WANT TO TAKE IT BACK AND SHOW IT TO MOTHER.
To be continued in Black Butler 4

黒執事

Black Butler

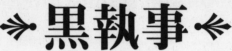

Downstairs

Wakana Haduki

Akiyo Satorigi

Yana's Mother

SuKe

KiYo

MiNe

*

Takeshi Kuma

*

Yana Toboso

SpecialThanks

for You!

Translation Notes

PAGE 4
Lycoris

Most likely a reference to *lycoris radiata*, the red spider lily. Due to the flower's unique appearance and characteristics, many legends exist around it. The highly poisonous flowers have been known to be planted around rice fields to discourage animals from eating the yield. For similar reasons, the flowers were planted in cemetaries to discourage predators in olden days. Despite its bright scarlet colour, the flower is commonly associated with darker concepts like longing, separation, death, and the afterlife.

PAGE 126
Mary Jane Kelly

Though a point of contention, Mary Jane Kelly is regarded as Jack the Ripper's final victim. Her background is largely unknown, but it is said she hailed from Ireland.

PAGE 162
"Party Dress" Christmas roses

Christmas roses are also known as hellebore, an extremely poisonous flowering plant that blooms in the winter and early spring. The "Party Dress" is a variety of Christmas rose.

PAGE 164
Dimbula

A tea-growing region of Ceylon, now modern-day Sri Lanka, known for its full-bodied, aromatic teas.

INSIDE BACK COVER
Bathing scene at 8:20

The popular Japanese period drama *Mito Koumon* always features a female ninja bathing. The show airs at 8 p.m.

Finny's lantern

In the Edo era, officials held lanterns painted with the word *goyou* ("official business") when they went to make an arrest, similar to the one Finny is holding here.

Oniwaban

A post set up by the eighth shogun, Yoshimune Tokugawa. Specialising in spying and intelligence, an Oniwaban ninja received orders directly from the shogun himself.

Nin

The *nin* on Sebastian's head band is fron the first character used to write "ninja" and can mean "conceal" or "spy."

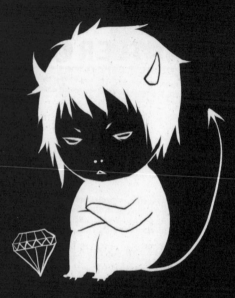

Yana Toboso

AUTHOR'S NOTE

People say that a ruby shines red no matter what colour light you shine on it.

It absorbs any kind of light, changes it to red, and sparkles.

A "red" that asserts itself, no matter how its environment changes. A colour that is different from black, completely dissimilar.

I'll be happy if you can feel that intense "red" in the black-and-white world of manga.

And so . . . *Black Butler* Volume 3.

BLACK BUTL P9-BTN-572

YANA TOBOSO

Translation: Tomo Kimura • Lettering: Tania Biswas

BLACK BUTLER Vol. 3 © 2008 Yana Toboso / SQUARE ENIX CO., LTD. All
rights reserved. First published in Japan in 2008 by SQUARE ENIX CO.,
LTD. English translation rights arranged with SQUARE ENIX CO., LTD.
and Hachette Book Group through Tuttle-Mori Agency, Inc.

Translation © 2010 by SQUARE ENIX CO., LTD.

Yen Press
Hachette Book Group
237 Park Avenue, New York, NY 10017

www.HachetteBookGroup.com
www.YenPress.com

Yen Press is an imprint of Hachette Book Group, Inc. The Yen Press name
and logo are trademarks of Hachette Book Group, Inc.

First Yen Press Edition: October 2010

ISBN: 978-0-316-08426-0

10 9 8 7 6 5 4 3 2 1

BVG

Printed in the United States of America